# FRENCH FIRST YEAR

## WORKBOOK

## ( New Edition )

**ELI BLUME**
Former Chairman of the Foreign Language Department
Forest Hills High School
New York City

**GAIL STEIN**
Foreign Language Department
Martin Van Buren High School
New York City

When ordering this book, please specify *either* **R 523 W** *or*
BLUME/STEIN FRENCH FIRST YEAR WORKBOOK

AMSCO

**AMSCO SCHOOL PUBLICATIONS, INC.**
315 Hudson Street/New York, N.Y. 10013

Cover photograph: Pont Valentré, Cahors, by Richard Turpin
Illustrations by Steven Duquette
Maps by Susan Detrich

ISBN 1-56765-305-7
NYC Item 56765-305-6

Printed in the United States of America

5 6 7 8 9 10          02 01 00

# Preface

The BLUME / STEIN FRENCH FIRST YEAR is designed to give students a comprehensive review and thorough introductory understanding of the elements of the French language and the highlights of French culture. Abundant and varied exercises help students master each phase of the work.

## ORGANIZATION

For ease of study and reference, the book is divided into six parts. In Parts One through Four, the chapters are organized around related grammatical topics, except the last two chapters which are devoted to vocabulary: synonyms, antonyms and topical vocabulary. Part Five covers the culture of France, dealing with language, geography, history, life-style, literature, art, music, architecture, and science. Part Six provides material for comprehensive practice and testing of the speaking, listening, reading, and writing skills.

## GRAMMAR

Each grammatical chapter deals fully with one major grammatical topic or several closely related ones. Explanations of structure are brief and clear. All points of grammar are illustrated by many examples, in which the key elements are typographically highlighted.

This first year review of French covers a basic grammatical sequence. Care has been taken, especially in the critical *Part One: Verb Structures,* to avoid the use of complex, structural elements. To enable students to concentrate on the structural practice, the vocabulary has been carefully controlled and systematically "recycled" throughout the grammatical chapters.

## EXERCISES

For maximum efficiency in learning, the exercises directly follow the points of grammar to which they apply. Carefully graded, the exercises proceed from simple assimilation to more challenging manipulation of elements and communication. To provide functional continuity of a grammatical topic, the exercises are set in communicative contexts. Many are also personalized to stimulate student response.

While the contents of the exercises afford extensive oral practice, the book's format also encourages reinforcement through written student responses, including English to French exercises intended to sharpen composition skills. The grammatical chapters conclude with Mastery Exercises, in which all grammatical aspects in the chapter are again practiced in recombinations of previously covered elements. English is used in directions to exercises to describe communicative situations, while simple specific directions are in French.

## FLEXIBILITY

The topical organization and the integrated completeness of each chapter permit the teacher to follow any sequence suitable to the objectives of the course and the needs of the students. This flexibility is facilitated by the detailed table of contents at the front of the book and the comprehensive grammatical index at the back. Teachers as well as students will also find the book useful as a reference source.

## CULTURE

The cultural chapters in Part Five are in English. Every effort has been made to keep the narratives clear and readable and to provide a wealth of cultural information. Each cultural chapter includes varied exercises designed to test comprehension. For the more advanced student, exercises in French are included.

## OTHER FEATURES

The Appendix features model verb tables and the principal parts of common irregular verbs, common reflexive verbs, prepositions, and basic rules of French punctuation and syllabication. French-English and English-French vocabularies and a comprehensive Index complete the book.

The BLUME / STEIN FRENCH FIRST YEAR is a thoroughly revised and updated edition. With its comprehensive coverage of the elements of level-one French, clear and concise explanations, extensive practice materials, and functional vocabulary, the book will help students strengthen their skills in the French language. As students pursue proficiency, they will also gain valuable insights into the culture of France in the narrative overview of French civilization.

# Contents

## Part One
## Verb Structures

# Part Two
# Noun Structures; Pronoun Structures; Prepositions

# Part Three
# Adjective / Adverb and Related Structures

# Part Four
# Word Study

# Part Five
# French Civilization

# Part Six
# Comprehensive Testing
### Speaking, Listening, Reading, Writing

# Appendix     *464*

# Part one
## Verb Structures

QUÉBEC

SAINT-PIERRE-
ET-MIQUELON

LOUISIANE

HAÏTI

GUADELOUPE
MARTINIQUE

GUYANE

BELGIQUE

LUXEMBOURG

FRANCE

SUISSE

MONACO

CORSE

MAROC

ALGÉRIE

TUNISIE

MAURITANIE

MALI

NIGER

TCHAD

SÉNÉGAL

GUINÉE

BURKINA FASO

CÔTE-D'IVOIRE

TOGO

BÉNIN

CAMEROUN

RÉPUBLIQUE
CENTRAFRICAINE

ZAÏRE

GABON

CONGO

# Chapter 1
## Present Tense of *-er* Verbs

## [ 1 ] AFFIRMATIVE CONSTRUCTIONS

The present tense of regular *-er* verbs is formed by dropping the infinitive ending (*-er*) and adding the personal endings *(e, es, e, ons, ez, ent)*.

| chanter *to sing* | | |
|---|---|---|
| **SINGULAR** | je chant**e** | *I sing, I am singing* |
| | tu chant**es** | *you sing, you are singing* |
| | il chant**e** | *he sings, he is singing* |
| | elle chant**e** | *she sings, she is singing* |
| **PLURAL** | nous chant**ons** | *we sing, we are singing* |
| | vous chant**ez** | *you sing, you are singing* |
| | ils chant**ent** | *they sing, they are singing* |
| | elles chant**ent** | *they sing, they are singing* |

NOTE:

1. *Tu* is generally used to address someone with whom the speaker is on familiar terms: a relative, a friend, a child. *Vous* is a more formal and respectful way to address an individual. To address two or more persons, *vous* is always used.

2. The *e* of *je* is dropped when the next word begins with a vowel or silent *h*.

| j'arrive | *I come, I am coming* |
|---|---|
| j'habite | *I live, I am living* |

3. The third-person pronouns *il, elle, ils, elles,* refer to both persons and things. To refer to nouns of different genders, *ils* is used.

| Le garçon et la fille chantent une chanson. | *The boy and the girl sing a song.* |
|---|---|
| Ils chantent une chanson. | *They sing a song.* |

Common *-er* verbs:

| | | |
|---|---|---|
| accompagner *to accompany* | chauffer *to heat, warm* | cuisiner *to cook* |
| aider *to help* | chercher *to look for* | danser *to dance* |
| aimer *to like, love* | collectionner *to collect* | décorer *to decorate* |
| ajouter *to add* | commander *to order* | déjeuner *to eat lunch* |
| allumer *to light, turn on* | comparer *to compare* | demander *to ask (for)* |
| apporter *to bring* | composer *to compose* | dépenser *to spend* (money) |
| arriver *to arrive* | compter *to count* | désirer *to desire* |
| bavarder *to chat* | continuer *to continue* | dîner *to dine* |
| camper *to camp* | coûter *to cost* | donner *to give* |
| chanter *to sing* | crier *to shout* | écouter *to listen (to)* |

emprunter  *to borrow*        montrer  *to show*          prêter  *to lend*
entrer  *to enter*            noter  *to note*            raconter  *to tell*
étudier  *to study*          organiser  *to organize*    regarder  *to look at, watch*
expliquer  *to explain*      oublier  *to forget*        rentrer  *to return*
fermer  *to close*           parler  *to speak*          réparer  *to repair*
gagner  *to win*             participer  *to participate*  respecter  *to respect*
garder  *to keep; to take care of*  passer  *to pass; to spend* (time)  rester  *to stay, remain*
habiter  *to live (in)*      patiner  *to skate*         retourner  *to return*
indiquer  *to indicate*      pêcher  *to fish*           téléphoner  *to phone*
inviter  *to invite*         penser  *to think*          toucher  *to touch*
jouer  *to play*             porter  *to carry; to wear*  travailler  *to work*
laver  *to wash*             pousser  *to push; to grow*  trouver  *to find*
marcher  *to walk*           préparer  *to prepare*      utiliser  *to use*
monter  *to go up*           présenter  *to introduce*   vider  *to empty*

## EXERCICE A

**Henri is telling his cousin what he and his friends do after school.** *Exprimez ce qu'il dit* **(says).**

EXEMPLE:    Grégoire / parler avec des amis
            Grégoire **parle** avec des amis.

*1.* Lise / téléphoner à des copines

_____

*2.* je / jouer au basket

_____

*3.* Robert et Lucien / réparer les voitures

_____

*4.* tu / collectionner les bandes dessinées *(comic books)*

_____

*5.* nous / regarder la télévision

_____ *regardons* _____

*6.* vous / écouter des cassettes

_____ *écoutez* _____

*7.* Jean et moi / travailler dans une pharmacie

_____ *travaillons* _____

*8.* Paul et Georgette / bavarder au café

_____ *ent* _____

## EXERCICE B

**Mme Lamont is describing the weekly chores assigned to each family member.** *Exprimez ce qu'elle dit.*

EXEMPLE:  laver la voiture (Pierre)
Pierre **lave** la voiture.

*1.* vider les ordures (tu)

_____

*2.* passer l'aspirateur (Papa)

_____

*3.* ranger le salon (André et Odette)

_____

*4.* travailler dans le jardin (vous)

_____

*5.* préparer les repas (je)

_____

*6.* garder le bébé (Janine et moi)

_____

## EXERCICE C

**Catherine and Isabelle live near Paris; they are fourteen years old and are in the same class. They and some friends are planning a party. Describe what each one is doing.** *Utilisez les suggestions.*

aider avec tous les détails
apporter les boissons
chercher des disques compacts
cuisiner

décorer le salon
inviter des amis
préparer des sandwiches

EXEMPLE:  Chantal **aide** avec tous les détails.

*1.* Lise _____ .

*2.* Tu _____ .

*3.* Pierre _____ .

*4.* Vous _____ .

*5.* Nous _____ .

*6.* Je _____ .

## EXERCICE D

**You received this postcard from a friend who is traveling in France.** *Complétez le texte avec les mots qui manquent* (the missing words).

|          |          |          |          |          |
|----------|----------|----------|----------|----------|
| adorer   | bavarder | désirer  | penser   | trouver  |
| apporter | coûter   | parler   | rester   | visiter  |

Chère Patricia,

Salut de Paris! J' _____ cette ville. Ma famille et moi, nous _____
               *1.*                                                                        *2.*

tous les monuments importants. Mes parents _____ que la vie ici
                                                                     *3.*

_____ assez cher. Nous _____ dans un hôtel luxueux et notre
         *4.*                                     *5.*

concierge _____ français avec un drôle d'accent. Je _____ cet
               *6.*                                            *7.*

homme très intéressant. Je _____ un peu avec lui tous les jours en français.
                                        *8.*

Qu'est-ce que tu _____ comme souvenir? Je t' _____ un cadeau
                     *9.*                                        *10.*

typique, d'accord?

                                       Grosses bises,
                                         Anaïs

## [ 2 ] NEGATIVE CONSTRUCTIONS

In a negative construction, *ne* precedes the verb and *pas* follows it.

| | |
|---|---|
| Je **ne** parle **pas** italien. | *I don't speak Italian.* |
| Luc **ne** joue **pas** au football. | *Luc isn't playing soccer.* |

*Ne* becomes *n'* before a vowel or a silent *h*.

| | |
|---|---|
| Vous **n'**écoutez **pas**. | *You aren't listening.* |
| Ils **n'**habitent **pas** loin. | *They don't live far.* |

## EXERCICE E

**The bad weather is ruining everybody's vacation.** *Exprimez ce que ces personnes ne font pas* (are not doing).

EXEMPLE:    Je joue au volley-ball.
                Je **ne** joue **pas** au volley-ball.

1. Nous jouons au tennis.

   _____

2. Claude nage dans la mer.

   _____

3. Tu campes en plein air.

   _____

4. Annick et Christine marchent sur la plage.

   _____

5. Je participe à un match de basket.

   _____

6. Lucie pêche dans l'océan.

   _____

7. Vous patinez dans le parc.

   _____

8. Jean et Michel déjeunent sur l'herbe.

   _____

## EXERCICE F

**Look at what the people in the pictures are doing. Say that they are _not_ doing it.**

EXEMPLE:

Pierre **ne joue pas** au football.

**1.**

Les amies _____.

**2.**

Il _____.

**3.**

Vous _____.

**4.**

Nous _____.

**5.**

Tu _____.

**6.**

Je _____.

## EXERCICE G

**Make a list of six things that you do not do in class.**

*1.* _____

*2.* _____

*3.* _____

*4.* _____

*5.* _____

*6.* _____

# [ 3 ] INTERROGATIVE CONSTRUCTIONS USING INTONATION ONLY

In spoken French nowadays, an interrogative intonation (shown in writing by a question mark) is often all that is needed to change a statement into a question. This is especially the case for questions that can be answered by yes or no.

Tu joues au tennis?        *Do you play tennis?*

Oui, bien sûr!             *Yes, of course!*

## EXERCICE H

Your French friends, Catherine and Isabelle, and their classmate Pierre are curious about you and life in the United States. *Répondez* (answer) *à leurs questions avec des phrases complètes.*

EXEMPLE:   Tu joues au tennis?
            **Oui, je joue** au tennis.
     *OR:*   **Non, je ne joue pas** au tennis.

1. Tu travailles beaucoup?

   _____

2. Tu déjeunes à l'école tous les jours?

   _____

3. Tu dînes avec la famille le soir?

   _____

4. En Amérique vous aimez les sports?

   _____

5. Vous organisez de bonnes fêtes souvent?

   _____

6. Vous aimez la France?

   _____

7. Les élèves parlent français avec le professeur?

   _____

8. Les parents américains donnent beaucoup de liberté aux enfants?

   _____

9. Vous désirez voyager en France?

   _____

10. Nous bavardons trop?

    _____

## [ 4 ]   INTERROGATIVE CONSTRUCTIONS USING *EST-CE QUE*

A question may also be formed by beginning a statement with *est-ce que,* which becomes *est-ce qu'* before a vowel or silent *h.*

| | |
|---|---|
| Tu parles français. | **Est-ce que** tu parles français? |
| Elles dansent bien. | **Est-ce qu'**elles dansent bien? |
| Henri invite Michelle. | **Est-ce qu'**Henri invite Michelle? |

## EXERCICE I

**A Canadian family has moved into your neighborhood. Ask Babette questions about herself and her family.** *Utilisez* **est-ce que.**

EXEMPLE:    tu / aimer notre ville
**Est-ce que tu aimes** notre ville?

*1.* vous / habiter la maison bleue

_____

*2.* je / parler bien le français

_____

*3.* ton père / travailler en ville

_____

*4.* tes sœurs / étudier l'anglais

_____

*5.* tu / préparer des plats typiques

_____

*6.* nous / jouer aux mêmes sports

_____

## EXERCICE J

**You are president of the French club, which is planning a French festival. Write the questions your fellow students asked, based on the answers you received.** *Utilisez* **est-ce que.**

EXEMPLE:    Oui, Pierre pense aider les autres.
**Est-ce que Pierre pense** aider les autres?

*1.* Oui, le club prépare un repas.

_____

*2.* Oui, Jules et Luc empruntent des disques aux membres du club.

_____

*3.* Oui, Marie chauffe tous les plats.

_____

*4.* Oui, la cuisinière aide les étudiants.

_____

*5.* Oui, les filles décorent la salle de classe.

_____

6. Oui, Charles et Jeanne dépensent beaucoup d'argent.

## [ 5 ] INTERROGATIVE CONSTRUCTIONS USING INVERSION

A question may also be formed by reversing the order of the subject pronoun and the conjugated verb and joining them with a hyphen.

| | |
|---|---|
| Tu travailles beaucoup. | **Travailles-tu** beaucoup? |
| Vous patinez bien. | **Patinez-vous** bien? |

NOTE:

1. This construction is less frequent in spoken French and almost never occurs in the first person singular *(je)*.

2. With *il, elle,* or *on* and an *-er* verb form, *-t-* is added between the verb and the pronoun to separate the vowels.

| | |
|---|---|
| Elle étudie les sciences. | **Étudie-t-elle** les sciences? |
| Il cherche son ami. | **Cherche-t-il** son ami? |
| On aime nager. | **Aime-t-on** nager? |

## EXERCICE K

**Ask your friends what you are going to do today.** *Demandez à vos amis ce que vous allez faire aujourd'hui.*

EXEMPLE:   nous / déjeuner ensemble
**Déjeunons-nous** ensemble?

1. tu / inviter Laurent au cinéma

2. tu / accompagner Marie au magasin

3. nous / patiner à deux heures

4. vous / dîner au restaurant

5. elle / jouer au tennis

6. il / rentrer à pied

## [ *6* ]  NEGATIVE INTERROGATIVE CONSTRUCTIONS

**A negative question can be formed using only intonation.**

| | |
|---|---|
| Tu n'aimes pas la viande? | *Don't you like meat?* |
| Pierre ne vient pas? | *Isn't Pierre coming?* |

**A negative question can also be formed with *est-ce que*.**

| | |
|---|---|
| Est-ce que je travaille bien? | *Do I work well?* |
| Est-ce que je ne travaille pas bien? | *Don't I work well?* |

NOTE: **The word *si* is used to give an affirmative response to a negative question.**

| | |
|---|---|
| Est-ce qu'il ne travaille pas bien? | *Doesn't he work well?* |
| Si, il travaille bien. | *Yes, he works well.* |

### EXERCICE L

**You are surprised by some of the negative things you've heard about your friends. Ask for more information.** *Exprimez vos questions.*

EXEMPLE:    Patrick / étudier beaucoup
Patrick **n'étudie pas** beaucoup?

*1.* Janine / aider ses parents

_____

*2.* Berthe et Michelle / jouer avec leurs sœurs

_____

*3.* Henri / collectionner les cartes postales

_____

*4.* Paul et Lucien / voyager partout

_____

*5.* Alice et Charles / danser souvent

_____

*6.* Hervé / nager bien

_____

*7.* Hélène / aimer ses leçons de piano

_____

# MASTERY EXERCISES

### EXERCICE M

**You took pictures while vacationing in Martinique.** *Décrivez* (describe) *les photos à vos amis.*

EXEMPLE:

Christine **marche dans le parc.**

**1.**

Je _____ .

**2.**

Nous _____ .

**3.**

Jean, Arthur et Luc _____ .

**4.**

Odette _____ .

**5.**

Tu _____ .

**6.**

Vous _____ .

**7.**

Henri _____.

**8.**

Barbara et Éric _____.

## EXERCICE N

**Isabelle's parents are asking her questions about herself and her friends.** *Exprimez ses réponses comme dans l'exemple.*

EXEMPLE:    Tu arrives toujours à l'heure? (non)
            Non, **je n'arrive pas** toujours à l'heure.

*1.* Tu déjeunes avec des amis tous les jours? (oui)

_____

*2.* Vous aimez jouer au tennis avec Catherine? (non)

_____

*3.* Est-ce que vous bavardez continuellement? (oui)

_____

*4.* Est-ce que Nicole aide à étudier les leçons? (non)

_____

*5.* Est-ce que Catherine et Lise habitent près d'ici? (oui)

_____

*6.* Tu invites Pierre à danser? (non)

_____

*7.* Est-ce que Pierre travaille bien? (oui)

_____

*8.* Posons-nous trop de questions? (oui)

_____

## EXERCICE O

**You have just made a new friend. Write a note in which you ask five personal questions to help you get to know him/her better.** *Utilisez l'inversion.*

EXEMPLE:    **Parles-tu français?**

_____

_____

_____

_____

_____

## EXERCICE P

**Write in French the questions that you and your friends ask about your classmates.** *Utilisez* **est–ce que.**

1. Does Robert sing well?

   _____

2. Do the boys play basketball every day?

   _____

3. Do Anne and Alice live far from here?

   _____

4. Is Paul explaining the story?

   _____

5. Are the girls preparing the party?

   _____

6. Doesn't Luc skate after school?

   _____

7. Don't we always arrive on time?

   _____

8. Do you like to dance?

   _____

9. Do you and your friends speak French at home?

   _____

10. Does Patrick work?

    _____

# Chapter 2
## Present Tense of *-ir* Verbs

ANGLETERRE PAYS-BAS ALLEMAGNE BELGIQUE LUXEMBOURG AUTRICHE
Brest Paris Strasbourg
Nantes FRANCE SUISSE

## [ 1 ] AFFIRMATIVE CONSTRUCTIONS

The present tense of regular *-ir* verbs is formed by dropping the infinitive ending *(-ir)* and adding the personal endings *(is, is, it, issons, issez, issent)*.

| finir   to finish | | |
|---|---|---|
| SINGULAR | **je fin*is*** | *I finish, I am finishing* |
| | **tu fin*is*** | *you finish, you are finishing* |
| | **il fin*it*** | *he finishes, he is finishing* |
| | **elle fin*it*** | *she finishes, she is finishing* |
| PLURAL | **nous fin*issons*** | *we finish, we are finishing* |
| | **vous fin*issez*** | *you finish, you are finishing* |
| | **ils fin*issent*** | *they finish, they are finishing* |
| | **elles fin*issent*** | *they finish, they are finishing* |

Common *-ir* verbs:

| | | |
|---|---|---|
| bâtir  *to build* | grossir  *to become fat* | remplir  *to fill* |
| choisir  *to choose* | guérir  *to cure, heal* | réussir  *to succeed* |
| désobéir  *to disobey* | maigrir  *to become thin* | rôtir  *to roast* |
| finir  *to finish* | obéir  *to obey* | rougir  *to blush* |
| grandir  *to grow* | punir  *to punish* | saisir  *to seize, grab* |

## EXERCICE A

**Anne and a friend describe their first day at school.** *Exprimez ce qu'elles disent.*

*1.* je / rougir souvent

_____

*2.* vous / obéir au professeur

_____

*3.* deux élèves / désobéir

_____

*4.* le professeur / punir un mauvais élève

_____

*5.* Georges et moi / réussir à donner des réponses correctes

_____

**6.** tu / choisir une bonne place

_____

**7.** Marie / finir tous les exercices

_____

**8.** nous / remplir les cartes de renseignements

_____

## EXERCICE B

**Say what each person is doing in the pictures below.**

**1.**

Le docteur _____ le malade.

**2.**

Je _____ le verre d'eau.

**3.**

Tu _____ le dîner.

**4.**

Nous _____ .

**5.**

Vous _____ un chien.

**6.**

Les ingénieurs _____ un pont.

## EXERCICE C

**Tell what each person is doing.** *Utilisez un élément de chaque colonne.*

| | | |
|---|---|---|
| elles | bâtir | la balle |
| Henri | choisir | le livre |
| je | finir | le poulet |
| le chef | obéir | le verre |
| nous | remplir | un bon disque |
| tu | rôtir | une grande maison |
| vous | saisir | toujours |

EXEMPLE:   Henri **finit** le livre.

1. _____

2. _____

3. _____

4. _____

5. _____

6. _____

## [ 2 ]   NEGATIVE AND INTERROGATIVE CONSTRUCTIONS

Negative, interrogative, and negative interrogative constructions with *-ir* verbs follow the same rules as with *-er* verbs.

Il ne finit pas son travail.                    *He doesn't finish his work.*

Il finit son travail?
Est-ce qu'il finit son travail?        } *Does he finish his work?*
Finit-il son travail?

Il ne finit pas son travail?
Est-ce qu'il ne finit pas son travail?  } *Doesn't he finish his work?*

## EXERCICE D

**Tell what these people do not do.** *Donnez la forme négative correcte du verbe qui convient* (fits).

| | | | |
|---|---|---|---|
| choisir | grossir | obéir | rougir |
| finir | maigrir | réussir | |

EXEMPLE:   Une personne qui mange très peu **ne grossit pas.**

1. Un élève qui n'étudie pas _____ la réponse correcte.

2. Une personne qui mange beaucoup de bonbons _____.

**3.** Quand vous travaillez lentement, vous _____ vite le travail.

**4.** Si je _____ à mes parents, ils me punissent.

**5.** Si tu n'es pas embarrassé, tu _____.

**6.** Nous _____ si nous n'étudions pas.


## EXERCICE E

**Write questions based on the pictures below.**

EXEMPLE:

il / le voleur
**Punit-il** le voleur?

**1.**

vous

_____

**2.**

tu / le livre

_____

**3.**

nous / les verres

_____

**4.**

il / le chien

_____

**5.**

elles / un château de sable

**6.**

elle

_____

_____

## EXERCICE F

**Write questions that express your surprise, and supply your friend's affirmative or negative answers.**

EXEMPLE:

Paul / réussir en classe
Paul **ne réussit pas** en classe?        OR:        Paul **ne réussit pas** en classe?
**Si, il réussit** en classe.                              **Non, il ne réussit pas** en classe.

**1.**

Yvette / maigrir

_____

_____

**2.**

les garçons / obéir en classe

_____

_____

**3.**

vous / finir toujours les devoirs

_____

_____

**4.**

tu / grandir vite

_____

_____

**5.**

Antoine / choisir bien ses amis

_____

_____

**6.**

les filles / saisir l'occasion de réussir

_____

_____

## EXERCICE G

**Janine conducted a survey of students in her class. Unfortunately she has lost the paper with her questions.** *Exprimez ses questions d'après les réponses* **(based upon the answers)** *des élèves.*

EXEMPLES:   Mais oui, le docteur Blois guérit les malades.
              **Est-ce que** le docteur Blois **guérit** les malades?

              Mais si, le docteur Blois guérit les malades.
    OR:   **Est-ce que** le docteur Blois **ne guérit pas** les malades?

**1.** Mais si, les adolescents d'aujourd'hui obéissent à leurs parents.

_____

**2.** Mais oui, nous réussissons dans toutes nos classes.

_____

**3.** Mais oui, je grossis un peu.

_____

**4.** Mais si, Marc grandit rapidement.

_____

**5.** Mais si, Lucie finit toujours son travail.

_____

**6.** Mais oui, je saisis toujours une bonne occasion.

_____

## M A S T E R Y   E X E R C I S E S

## EXERCICE H

**Françoise likes to chat with everyone. Complete the conversations she has with people waiting for the bus.** *Donner la forme correcte du verbe.*

**1.** *(rougir)* _____-vous souvent? Moi, je _____ tout le temps. Mais

ma sœur Christine, elle ne _____ jamais!

**2.** *(grandir)* Mon frère et moi, nous _____ vite. Comment est-ce que votre petit fils

_____? Généralement, les garçons _____ plus vite que les filles.

**3.** *(finir)* À quelle heure _____-tu ton travail? D'habitude je_____

tout avant neuf heures. Malheureusement, le travail de ma mère ne _____ jamais.

**4.** *(choisir)* Quand_____-vous vos vêtements pour la journée? Mon frère et moi, nous

_____ toujours au dernier moment. Moi, je _____ la couleur

d'abord. Ma sœur _____ le soir, avant d'aller au lit.

## EXERCICE I

**You are explaining why your friends from Meudon act the way they do.** *Choisissez le verbe qui convient sur la liste ci-dessous et donnez la forme correcte.*

| | | | | |
|---|---|---|---|---|
| bâtir | désobéir | grossir | maigrir | rôtir |
| choisir | finir | guérir | réussir | rougir |

Catherine _____ parce qu'elle aime beaucoup les gâteaux. Isabelle ne
            1.

_____ jamais; au contraire, elle _____ parce qu'elle déteste les
            2.                                              3.

desserts et ne mange pas beaucoup. Nicole, la sœur d'Isabelle, _____ bien ses
                                                                          4.

vêtements parce qu'elle désire être admirée. Pierre et Claude _____ leur travail
                                                                        5.

rapidement parce qu'ils sont très sérieux. Le père de Catherine _____ les malades
                                                                          6.

parce qu'il est médecin. Sa mère _____ des maisons parce qu'elle est architecte.
                                        7.

La mère d'Isabelle _____ un poulet tous les dimanches parce que toute la famille
                          8.

aime le poulet. Michel et Jacques _____ souvent parce qu'ils ne sont pas sages.
                                          9.

Chantal _____ quand elle parle à son professeur parce qu'elle est timide. Nous
                10.

_____ très bien dans nos études, expliquent les grands, parce que nous sommes
      11.

intelligents et parce que nous travaillons bien.

## EXERCICE J

**A new exchange student at your school is asking questions about you, your friends, and the school.** *Donnez des réponses négatives.*

EXEMPLE:    Réussissez-vous toujours?
**Je ne réussis pas** toujours.

1. Est-ce que les étudiants choisissent leurs classes?

   _____

2. Obéissez-vous toujours au professeur?

   _____

3. Désobéissez-vous au règlement?

   _____

4. Est-ce que le directeur punit beaucoup d'élèves?

   _____

5. Est-ce que les élèves finissent toujours leurs devoirs?

   _____

6. Choisis-tu toujours les bonnes réponses aux questions?

   _____

## EXERCICE K

**You are talking about an ideal new classmate with your parents.** *Exprimez en français ce que vous dites.*

1. Everybody likes Jacques; he never disobeys.

   _____

2. He often blushes.

   _____

3. Does he succeed? Of course.

   _____

4. His parents cure the sick. They are doctors.

   _____

5. His grandfather builds many houses.

   _____

6. He obeys his parents.

   _____

7. The teachers don't punish Jacques.

   _____

8. In school he chooses the right answers.

   _____

9. He seizes every opportunity.

   _____

10. Each day he finishes his work.

    _____

# Chapter 3
## Present Tense of -re Verbs

## [ 1 ] AFFIRMATIVE CONSTRUCTIONS

The present tense of regular -re verbs is formed by dropping the infinitive ending (-re) and adding the personal endings (s, s, -, ons, ez, ent).

| vendre *to sell* | | |
|---|---|---|
| SINGULAR | **je vends** | *I sell, I am selling* |
| | **tu vends** | *you sell, you are selling* |
| | **il vend** | *he sells, he is selling* |
| | **elle vend** | *she sells, she is selling* |
| PLURAL | **nous vendons** | *we sell, we are selling* |
| | **vous vendez** | *you sell, you are selling* |
| | **ils vendent** | *they sell, they are selling* |
| | **elles vendent** | *they sell, they are selling* |

Common -re verbs:

attendre  *to wait (for)*

correspondre  *to correspond; to exchange letters*

défendre  *to defend*

descendre  *to go down; to take down*

entendre  *to hear*

perdre  *to lose*

rendre  *to give back, return*

répondre (à)  *to answer*

vendre  *to sell*

## EXERCICE A

**Berthe describes the people she knows.** *Exprimez ce qu'elle dit.*

*1.* M. Lamont / perdre patience facilement

_____

*2.* Anne / correspondre avec une amie française

_____

*3.* je / attendre toujours mes amis

_____

*4.* vous / défendre vos amis

_____

*5.* Jimmy et Paul / répondre à toutes les questions de leurs parents

_____

**6.** les Dupont / vendre des bijoux dans un magasin

_____

**7.** Jean et moi / rendre ce que nous empruntons

_____

**8.** tu / descendre souvent chez tes amis

_____

## EXERCICE B

**The French club is trying to increase its membership.** _Exprimez ce que chaque membre fait pour aider._

attendre les questions du public     descendre chercher des brochures
correspondre avec les élèves     répondre à toutes les questions
défendre la langue française     vendre des affiches sur la France

**1.** Pierre _____ .

**2.** Nous _____ .

**3.** Vous _____ .

**4.** Les jeunes filles _____ .

**5.** Je _____ .

**6.** Tu _____ .

## EXERCICE C

**Someone asks you questions.** _Répondez en français._

**1.** Qui attendez-vous après l'école?

_____

**2.** Quand descendez-vous en ville?

_____

**3.** Qui défendez-vous?

_____

**4.** Qui répond souvent au téléphone chez vous?

_____

**5.** Quand perdez-vous patience?

_____

## [ 2 ] NEGATIVE AND INTERROGATIVE CONSTRUCTIONS

Negative, interrogative, and negative interrogative constructions of -re verbs follow the same rules as -er and -ir verbs.

Il ne répond pas au téléphone.        *He doesn't answer the phone.*

Il répond au téléphone?
Est-ce qu'il répond au téléphone?     *Does he answer the phone?*
Répond-il au téléphone?

Il ne répond pas au téléphone?
Est-ce qu'il ne répond pas au téléphone?     *Doesn't he answer the phone?*

### EXERCICE D

**Look at what the people in the pictures are doing. Say that they are *not* doing it.**

EXEMPLE:

Luc **ne répond pas** au téléphone.

**1.**

Les filles _____ l'autobus.

**2.**

Nous _____ la musique.

**3.**

Je _____ l'escalier.

**4.**

Tu _____ la voiture.

**5.**

**6.**

Le professeur _____ les devoirs.

Vous _____ votre argent.

## EXERCICE E

**Ask your friends what they do after school.** *Utilisez* **est-ce que.**

EXEMPLE: (Paul) perdre son temps
**Est-ce que Paul perd** son temps?

**1.** (Marie et Alice) défendre leur position dans un débat

_____

**2.** (Cécile) descendre en ville

_____

**3.** (les garçons) rendre la voiture de M. Rousseau

_____

**4.** (Jean) vendre des glaces

_____

**5.** (vous) répondre aux questions de vos parents

_____

**6.** (tu) entendre le rapport du président du club

_____

## EXERCICE F

**A new student is asking questions about various people.** *Exprimez ce qu'il dit en suivant l'exemple.*

EXEMPLE: (tu) attendre tes amis après les classes
**Attends-tu** tes amis après les classes?

**1.** (elles) vendre des affiches françaises

_____

**2.** (tu) correspondre avec un copain

_____

**3.** (nous) répondre bien en français

_____

**4.** (vous) rendre ce que vous empruntez

_____

**5.** (ils) perdre souvent leurs matches de football

_____

**6.** (elle) descendre en ville de temps en temps

_____

## EXERCICE G

**Detective Marcel Boirot asks many leading questions in the course of his investigation.** *Exprimez ses questions selon l'exemple.*

EXEMPLE:    il / descendre souvent en ville
            **Il ne descend pas** souvent en ville?

**1.** la femme / perdre souvent ses clefs

_____

**2.** vous / attendre le train de Paris

_____

**3.** nous / répondre à toutes les questions

_____

**4.** tu / vendre ta voiture

_____

**5.** Charles / défendre bien ses idées

_____

**6.** Charles et Jacques / correspondre depuis longtemps

_____

## M A S T E R Y   E X E R C I S E S

## EXERCICE H

*Complétez les conversations ci–dessous avec les formes correctes des verbes.*

**1.** *(attendre)* — Qui _____-vous après l'école?

— Moi, j'_____ tous mes amis.  Et quand j'arrive en retard, ils

m'_____.

**2.** *(vendre)* — _____-vous des gâteaux au chocolat?

— Oui, nous _____ toutes sortes de gâteaux. Toutes nos pâtisseries

_____ des gâteaux de la meilleure qualité.

**3.** *(correspondre)* — Tu _____ avec ton ami africain?

— Oui, bien sûr.  Je _____ avec lui et il _____ avec

moi tout le temps.

## EXERCICE I

**Look at what the people in the pictures are doing. Say that they are *not* doing it.**

EXEMPLE:

Ils **ne rendent pas** les livres.

**1.**

Le bébé _____ l'escalier.

**2.**

L'avocat_____ l'accusé.

**3.**

Les filles _____ au téléphone.

**4.**

Vous _____ le bus.

**5.**

Nous _____ la musique.

**6.**

Tu _____ dans le magasin.

## EXERCICE J

**Complete this story of an incident in our French friends' lives.** *Écrivez la forme correcte d'un verbe choisi dans la liste suivante.*

| | | | |
|---|---|---|---|
| attendre | entendre | rendre | vendre |
| descendre | perdre | répondre | |

Après l'école, Isabelle _____ son amie Catherine. Les deux filles
<br>1.

_____ en ville en bus. Elles entrent à la bibliothèque et _____
<br>2.                                                                 3.

des livres. Catherine cherche un livre en anglais. Tout à coup elles _____
<br>4.

leurs camarades Claude et Pierre. «Vous _____ votre temps!» Pierre crie,
<br>5.

«Vous _____ ?» Catherine _____ à Pierre: «Tu parles trop vite!
<br>6.                                                  7.

Je n' _____ pas.» Les amis _____ ensemble dans la rue
<br>8.                                                 9.

et entrent dans une librairie. «_____-vous des livres en anglais?» demande
<br>10.

Catherine. Le vendeur _____ : «Mais non, Mademoiselle, nous habitons la France!
<br>11.

Alors nous ne _____ pas de livres anglais!»
<br>12.

## EXERCICE K

**The students in your class were asked to interview classmates.** *Exprimez les questions et les réponses.*

**1.** Don't you exchange letters with a French student?

_____

No, I exchange letters with a Canadian boy.

_____

*2.* Do you go (down) to the city often?

_____

Yes, usually I go (down) to the city every weekend.

_____

*3.* Do your parents sell cars?

_____

No, they sell clothing.

_____

*4.* Do you and your friends wait for the bus every day?

_____

Yes, we wait near the school.

_____

*5.* Do you always return the books to the library?

_____

Sometimes I wait a long time, but I don't lose the books.

_____

# Chapter 4
## Spelling Changes in Certain *-er* Verbs

### [ 1 ] *-CER* VERBS

Verbs ending in *-cer* change *c* to *ç* before *o* to retain the soft *c* sound. Thus, the first person plural form of the present tense ends in *-çons*.

| commencer *to begin* | |
|---|---|
| je commence | nous commen**ç**ons |
| tu commences | vous commencez |
| il commence | ils commencent |
| elle commence | elles commencent |

Other verbs ending in *-cer:*

annoncer *to announce*   lancer *to throw*   prononcer *to pronounce*

avancer *to advance*   menacer *to threaten*   remplacer *to replace*

effacer *to erase*   placer *to place, set*   renoncer (à) *to give up*

### EXERCICE A

**Describe how each person expresses anger.** *Employez un élément de chaque colonne.*

| | | |
|---|---|---|
| je | annoncer que | crier |
| Jean et moi | avancer | des boules de papier |
| le professeur | commencer à | des insultes |
| les garçons | effacer | la situation ne peut pas durer |
| Lise | lancer | le tableau avec colère |
| nous | menacer de | parler gentiment |
| tu | prononcer | partir |
| vous | renoncer à | vers la porte |

EXEMPLE:   Lise **renonce à** parler gentiment.

1. _____

2. _____

3. _____

4. _____

5. _____

6. _____

7. _____

## EXERCICE B

**Ask your friends what they do before school begins.** *Notez leurs réponses.*

EXEMPLE: menacer de faire l'école buissonnière *(to play hooky)* (non)
    VOUS:    **Menacez-vous** de faire l'école buissonnière?
    VOS AMIS: Non, **nous ne menaçons pas** de faire l'école buissonnière.

*1.* lancer des papiers par la fenêtre (non)

    VOUS: _____

    VOS AMIS: _____

*2.* placer vos livres sur le pupitre (oui)

    VOUS: _____

    VOS AMIS: _____

*3.* commencer à étudier (oui)

    VOUS: _____

    VOS AMIS: _____

*4.* menacer les autres élèves (non)

    VOUS: _____

    VOS AMIS: _____

*5.* prononcer les mots de vocabulaire (oui)

    VOUS: _____

    VOS AMIS: _____

*6.* effacer le tableau (oui)

    VOUS: _____

    VOS AMIS: _____

# [ 2 ] -*GER* VERBS

Verbs ending in *-ger* insert a silent *e* between *g* and *o* to keep the soft *g* sound. Thus, the present-tense form ending in *-ons* has a silent *e* inserted.

| man**ger** *to eat* | |
|---|---|
| je mange | nous mang**e**ons |
| tu manges | vous mangez |
| il mange | ils mangent |
| elle mange | elles mangent |

Other verbs ending in *-ger:*

| | | |
|---|---|---|
| arranger *to arrange* | changer *to change* | déménager *to move* (to another residence) |
| bouger *to move* | corriger *to correct* | déranger *to disturb* |

| | | |
|---|---|---|
| diriger *to direct* | obliger *to oblige, compel* | songer (à) *to think (of)* |
| mélanger *to mix* | partager *to share, divide* | voyager *to travel* |
| nager *to swim* | plonger *to plunge, dive* | |
| neiger *to snow* | ranger *to put away; to put in order* | |

## EXERCICE C

*Exprimez ce qui se passe* (**what is happening**) *dans chaque image.*

**1.**

Nous _____.

**2.**

Elles _____.

**3.**

Il _____.

**4.**

Vous _____.

**5.**

Je _____.

**6.**

Tu _____.

## EXERCICE D

**Your friends are bragging about things they do.** *Exprimez ce qu'ils disent.*

EXEMPLE:  plonger bien
**Nous plongeons bien.**

*1.* manger énormément

**2.** partager tout

_____

**3.** nager tous les jours

_____

**4.** corriger toutes nos fautes

_____

**5.** ranger la maison

_____

**6.** changer nos habitudes

_____

# [ 3 ]    -YER VERBS

Verbs ending in *-yer* change *y* to *i* before silent *e*. (Verbs of this type are often called "shoe" verbs because the *je, tu, il, elle, ils, elles* forms, which have the same stem, form the profile of a shoe.)

| employ*er*  *to use* | |
|---|---|
| j'empl*oie* | nous employons |
| tu empl*oies* | vous employez |
| il empl*oie* | ils empl*oient* |
| elle empl*oie* | elles empl*oient* |

Other verbs ending in *-yer:*

ennuyer  *to bore; to bother*      essuyer  *to wipe*      renvoyer  *to send back; to fire*

envoyer  *to send*      nettoyer  *to clean*

NOTE: This change of *y* to *i* is optional for verbs whose infinitive ends in *-ayer.*

| pay*er*  *to pay* | |
|---|---|
| je pa*ie*  (je pa*ye*) | nous payons |
| tu pa*ies*  (tu pa*yes*) | vous payez |
| il pa*ie*  (il pa*ye*) | ils pa*ient*  (ils pay*ent*) |
| elle pa*ie*  (elle pa*ye*) | elles pa*ient*  (elles pay*ent*) |

Another verb ending in *-ayer:*

essayer (de)  *to try*

## EXERCICE E

**Raoul is graduating and is receiving many gifts.** *Exprimez ce que chaque personne lui envoie.*

EXEMPLE:    tante Lise / de l'argent
                    Tante Lise **lui envoie** de l'argent.

**1.** ses grands-parents / une montre

_____

**2.** je / une carte

_____

**3.** vous / un livre

_____

**4.** oncle Jules / un portefeuille

_____

**5.** tu / une serviette

_____

**6.** nous / des vêtements

_____

## EXERCICE F

*Exprimez ce que ces personnes font aujourd'hui (today) en donnant la forme correcte du verbe qui convient.*

ennuyer    essayer    payer
envoyer    nettoyer   renvoyer

**1.** Je _____ la maison.

**2.** Elle _____ les services du jardinier.

**3.** Tu _____ ton petit frère.

**4.** Nous _____ de finir notre travail scolaire.

**5.** Pierre et Jacques _____ un paquet en France.

**6.** M. LeGrange _____ son secrétaire.

## [ 4 ]   *-E* + CONSONANT + *-ER* VERBS

Verbs like *acheter* change the silent *e* to *è* in the *je, tu, il / elle, ils / elles* forms in the present tense.

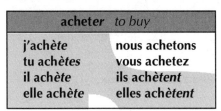

| **acheter** *to buy* | |
|---|---|
| j'ach**è**te | nous achetons |
| tu ach**è**tes | vous achetez |
| il ach**è**te | ils ach**è**tent |
| elle ach**è**te | elles ach**è**tent |

Other *e* + consonant + *er* verbs:

| | | |
|---|---|---|
| achever *to complete* | enlever *to remove, take off* | peser *to weigh* |
| amener *to bring, lead to* | geler *to freeze* | promener *to walk* |
| élever *to bring up, raise* | lever *to raise, lift* | ramener *to bring back* |
| emmener *to take away, lead away* | mener *to lead* | |

## EXERCICE G

**Your French class is planning a typical French picnic.** *Exprimez ce que chaque personne va acheter.*

EXEMPLE:   Lucien / du pâté
           Lucien **achète** du pâté.

*1.* nous / une baguette

_____

*2.* Paul et Georgette / du fromage

_____

*3.* je / des boissons

_____

*4.* vous / un gâteau

_____

*5.* tu / de la salade

_____

*6.* Jack / de la viande

_____

## EXERCICE H

**Complete the story about M. Constant and his dog.** *Écrivez la forme correcte du verbe qui manque* **(missing).**

| | | | |
|---|---|---|---|
| achever | emmener | lever | promener |
| élever | enlever | peser | ramener |

M. Constant _____ un très petit chien, Bobbi, qui _____ seulement
                    1.                                                          2.

trois kilos.  Chaque jour il _____ Bobbi au parc où il le _____
                                      3.                                          4.

pendant une demi-heure.  Après, quand ils _____ leur promenade, M. Constant
                                                      5.

_____ le chien à la maison.  Quand ils arrivent chez eux, M. Constant
       6.

_____ la laisse *(the leash)* attachée au cou de Bobbi. Il est très content et il

     7.

_____ une de ses pattes pour le remercier.

    8.

## [ 5 ] **APPELER** AND *JETER*

Two "shoe" verbs with silent *e, appeler* and *jeter,* double the consonant instead of changing *e* to *è.*

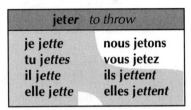

| appel**er**  *to call* | |
|---|---|
| j'app**elle** | nous appelons |
| tu app**elles** | vous appelez |
| il app**elle** | ils app**ellent** |
| elle app**elle** | elles app**ellent** |

| j**eter**  *to throw* | |
|---|---|
| je j**ette** | nous jetons |
| tu j**ettes** | vous jetez |
| il j**ette** | ils j**ettent** |
| elle j**ette** | elles j**ettent** |

## EXERCICE I

**The telephone is ringing everywhere.** *Dites qui appelle qui.*

EXEMPLE:    Luc / Régine
                Luc **appelle** Régine.

*1.* Nancy / Sophie

_____

*2.* nous / le docteur

_____

*3.* je / le professeur

_____

*4.* vous / vos parents

_____

*5.* les garçons / leurs amis

_____

*6.* tu / Éric

_____

## EXERCICE J

*Complétez chaque phrase avec la forme correcte du verb* **jeter.**

*1.* Le bébé _____ une balle.

*2.* Les secrétaires _____ les papiers inutiles.

**3.** Je _____ un coup d'œil *(a glance)* par là.

**4.** Nous _____ les mauvais fruits.

**5.** Tu _____ ton stylo.

**6.** Vous _____ la robe usée.

## [ 6 ]  É + CONSONANT + *-ER* VERBS

Verbs with *é* in the syllable before the infinitive ending change *é* to *è* before the silent endings *-e, -es, -ent* and thus are "shoe" verbs.

| **préférer**  *to prefer* | |
|---|---|
| je préfère | nous préférons |
| tu préfères | vous préférez |
| il préfère | ils préfèrent |
| elle préfère | elles préfèrent |

Other verbs ending in *é* + consonant + *-er*:

céder  *to yield*          espérer  *to hope*          protéger  *to protect*

célébrer  *to celebrate*   posséder  *to possess, own*  répéter  *to repeat*

## EXERCICE K

**What do you do to relax?** *Dites ce que vos amis et vous préférez faire.*

EXEMPLE:

Douglas **préfère jouer au golf.**

**1.**

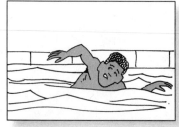

Michel _____.

**2.**

Vous _____.

**3.**

Tu _____ .

**4.**

Elles _____ .

**5.**

Nous _____ .

**6.**

Je _____ .

## EXERCICE L

**A classmate asks you and some of your friends to answer a few questions for a school survey.** *Exprimez vos réponses en employant le verbe indiqué.*

**1.** *(préférer)* — Quel genre d'émission de télévision _____-vous?

     —Je _____ les dessins animés.

     — Nous _____ les drames policiers.

**2.** *(espérer)* — Qu'est-ce que vous _____ devenir?

     —J'_____ devenir médecin.

     — Nous _____ devenir avocats.

**3.** *(célébrer)* — Quelle fête _____-vous en décembre?

     —Je _____ mon anniversaire.

     — Nous _____ Noël.

**4.** *(posséder)* — Combien de voitures _____-vous?

     —Je _____ une voiture.

     — Nous _____ aussi une voiture.

**5.** *(répéter)* — Qu'est-ce que vous _____ souvent en classe?

— Je _____ les mots de vocabulaire.

— Nous _____ des poèmes.

## M A S T E R Y  E X E R C I S E S

## EXERCICE M

**Who does what?** *Dites ce que font les personnes suivantes.*

| | |
|---|---|
| élever des animaux | peser la vérité |
| employer un ordinateur | promener les enfants |
| jeter la balle | protéger le public |
| nettoyer la maison | répéter la leçon |

**1.** Un joueur de base-ball _____ .

**2.** Un professeur _____ .

**3.** Une mère _____ .

**4.** Un agent de police _____ .

**5.** Un fermier _____ .

**6.** Un programmeur _____ .

**7.** Un juge _____ .

**8.** Une femme de ménage _____ .

## EXERCICE N

**A friend's mother would like to know you better.** *Répondez à ses questions.*

**1.** Vous et votre sœur, à quelle heure commencez-vous les devoirs?

Nous _____ .

**2.** Votre famille et vous, que mangez-vous au dîner?

Nous _____ .

**3.** Est-ce que vous rangez la maison le soir?

Nous _____ .

**4.** Quand célébrez-vous votre anniversaire?

Je _____ .

5. Qui amenez-vous au cinéma?

   J' _____ .

6. Quel genre de film préférez-vous?

   Je _____ .

## EXERCICE O

**A friend speaks about his vacation.** *Écrivez en français ce qu'il dit.*

1. In my family we travel together.

   _____

2. We always arrange our vacation in advance.

   _____

3. We prefer to visit Europe.

   _____

4. We always eat a lot.

   _____

5. I buy a lot of souvenirs.

   _____

6. My little brother bothers everybody.

   _____

7. I send postcards to all my friends.

   _____

8. I try to swim often.

   _____

9. My parents pay for everything.

   _____

10. We call our friends when we arrive home.

    _____

# Chapter 5
# Verbs Irregular in the Present Tense

The following verbs are irregular in the present tense and must be memorized.

| aller | faire | pouvoir | venir |
|-------|-------|---------|-------|
| avoir | lire | prendre | voir |
| dire | mettre | recevoir | vouloir |
| écrire | ouvrir | savoir | |
| être | partir | sortir | |

NOTE:

1. Negative, interrogative and negative interrogative constructions follow the same rules for irregular verbs as for regular ones.

| Pierre va en France cet été. | *Pierre is going to France this summer.* |
|---|---|
| Il ne voit pas bien. | *He does not see well.* |
| Claire vient ce soir? | *Claire is coming tonight?* |
| Est-ce que tu le connais? | *Do you know him?* |
| Est-elle intelligente? | *Is she intelligent?* |
| Tu ne vas pas chez Anne? | *Don't you go to Anne's?* |
| Est-ce que tu ne sors pas? | *Don't you go out?* |

2. Verbs that end in a vowel in the third person singular add *-t* before the pronouns *il, elle,* or *on* to separate the vowels in the inverted interrogative construction.

| Où va-t-il? | *Where is he going?* |
|---|---|
| A-t-elle le temps de venir? | *Does she have the time to come?* |
| Pourquoi ouvre-t-on la porte? | *Why do they open the door?* |

## [1] *ALLER:* TO GO

| je vais | nous allons |
|---------|-------------|
| tu vas | vous allez |
| il / elle va | ils / elles vont |

| Je vais en France cet été. | *I am going to France this summer.* |
|---|---|
| Allez-vous en France cet été? | *Are you going to France this summer?* |
| Nous n'allons pas en France. | *We are not going to France.* |

NOTE: The form *vais-je?* exists, but it is rarely used.

a. Common expressions with *aller:*

**aller** + adverb *to feel, to be* (describing a state of health or a situation)

| Comment allez-vous? | *How are you?* |
|---|---|
| Je vais bien. | *I'm fine.* |
| Les affaires vont mal. | *Business is bad.* |

aller à pied   *to walk, go on foot*
Je vais à l'école à pied.                    *I walk to school.*

aller à la pêche   *to go fishing*
Je vais à la pêche avec mon père.       *I go fishing with my father.*

aller en voiture   *to go by car*
Allez-vous au cinéma en voiture?        *Are you going to the movies by car?*

**b.** Forms of *aller* followed by an infinitive express a future action.

Je vais étudier.                             *I am going to study.*
Qu'est-ce que tu vas faire?               *What are you going to do?*

## EXERCICE A

**The Lenoirs are shopping for their party tomorrow.** *Dites dans quelles boutiques ils vont.*

EXEMPLE:     Alice / au supermarché
             Alice **va** au supermarché.

*1.* M. et Mme Lenoir / à la boucherie

_____

*2.* Geneviève / au marché

_____

*3.* je / à la fruiterie

_____

*4.* Maryse et moi, nous / à la boulangerie

_____

*5.* tu / à la pâtisserie

_____

*6.* vous / à la charcuterie

_____

## EXERCICE B

**What shall we do today?** *Utilisez les expressions données et dites ce que chacun va faire.*

aller au cinéma              jouer au basket              téléphoner à des copains
dîner au restaurant          regarder la télévision       travailler
écouter des cassettes

EXEMPLE:     Jean **va** jouer au basket.

*1.* M. Arnaud _____ .

*2.* Je _____ .

*3.* Tu _____ .

*4.* Nous _____ .

*5.* Les garçons _____ .

*6.* Vous _____ .

## [2] *AVOIR:* TO HAVE

| | |
|---|---|
| **j'ai** | **nous avons** |
| **tu as** | **vous avez** |
| **il/elle a** | **ils/elles ont** |

| | |
|---|---|
| J'ai un gros chien. | *I have a big dog.* |
| Nous n'avons pas sommeil. | *We are not sleepy.* |
| Est-ce qu'elle a un frère? | *Does she have a brother?* |

NOTE: **The form *ai-je?* exists, but it is rarely used.**

**a.** **Common expressions with *avoir:***

**avoir... ans**  *to be . . . years old*
| | |
|---|---|
| Quel âge as-tu? | *How old are you?* |
| J'ai vingt ans. | *I'm twenty years old.* |

**avoir besoin de**  *to need*
| | |
|---|---|
| Elle a besoin d'un stylo. | *She needs a pen.* |

**avoir chaud**  *to be hot* (of persons)
| | |
|---|---|
| Il a bien chaud. | *He is quite hot.* |

**avoir envie de**  *to desire, want; to feel like*
| | |
|---|---|
| J'ai envie de rire. | *I want to laugh.* |

**avoir faim**  *to be hungry*
| | |
|---|---|
| J'ai toujours faim. | *I'm always hungry.* |

**avoir froid**  *to be cold* (people)
| | |
|---|---|
| Ce bébé a très froid. | *This baby is very cold.* |

**avoir honte (de)**  *to be ashamed of*
| | |
|---|---|
| Ils n'ont pas honte de leur faute. | *They aren't ashamed of their mistake.* |

**avoir mal à**  *to have an ache in*
| | |
|---|---|
| J'ai mal à la tête. | *I have a headache.* |

**avoir peur (de)**  *to be afraid (of)*
| | |
|---|---|
| Avez-vous peur des chiens? | *Are you afraid of dogs?* |

**avoir raison**  *to be right*
| | |
|---|---|
| Vous savez que j'ai raison. | *You know I'm right.* |

**avoir soif**  *to be thirsty*
| | |
|---|---|
| Donne-lui de l'eau. Il a soif. | *Give him some water. He's thirsty.* |

**avoir sommeil**  *to be sleepy*
| | |
|---|---|
| Éric n'a jamais sommeil. | *Eric is never sleepy.* |

**avoir tort**  *to be wrong*
Il dit que nous avons tort.  *He says that we're wrong.*

**b.** Impersonal use of *avoir:*

**il y a**  *there is, there are*

**y a–t–il?**  *is there? are there?*

**il n'y a pas**  *there is not, there are not*

**n'y a–t–il pas?**  *isn't there? aren't there?*

## EXERCICE C

**Your new French pen pal, Lise, has written her first letter to you.** *Complétez la lettre avec la forme correcte du verbe* avoir.

Chère Jane,

J'_____ treize ans et j'_____ envie d'avoir une amie américaine.
⠀⠀⠀⠀⠀⠀1.⠀⠀⠀⠀⠀⠀⠀⠀⠀⠀⠀⠀⠀⠀⠀⠀⠀⠀⠀⠀2.

Quel âge _____-tu? Ma sœur _____ dix ans et mon frère
⠀⠀⠀⠀⠀⠀⠀⠀⠀3.⠀⠀⠀⠀⠀⠀⠀⠀⠀⠀⠀⠀⠀⠀⠀⠀4.

_____ huit ans. Ma famille et moi, nous _____ une grande maison
⠀⠀⠀⠀5.⠀⠀⠀⠀⠀⠀⠀⠀⠀⠀⠀⠀⠀⠀⠀⠀⠀⠀⠀⠀⠀⠀⠀⠀⠀6.

à la campagne. Est-ce que vous _____ un appartement ou une maison?
⠀⠀⠀⠀⠀⠀⠀⠀⠀⠀⠀⠀⠀⠀⠀⠀⠀⠀⠀7.

_____-vous un jardin? Mes amies Nicole et Isabelle _____ des
⠀⠀⠀⠀8.⠀⠀⠀⠀⠀⠀⠀⠀⠀⠀⠀⠀⠀⠀⠀⠀⠀⠀⠀⠀⠀⠀⠀⠀⠀⠀9.

cousins à New York. Elles désirent aller aux États-Unis, mais elles _____ peur
⠀⠀⠀⠀⠀⠀⠀⠀⠀⠀⠀⠀⠀⠀⠀⠀⠀⠀⠀⠀⠀⠀⠀⠀⠀⠀⠀⠀⠀⠀10.

d'aller en avion; moi, je n'_____ pas peur et j'espère te rencontrer. À bientôt.
⠀⠀⠀⠀⠀⠀⠀⠀⠀⠀⠀⠀⠀⠀⠀11.

⠀⠀⠀⠀⠀⠀⠀⠀⠀⠀⠀⠀⠀⠀⠀⠀⠀⠀⠀⠀⠀⠀⠀⠀⠀⠀⠀⠀⠀⠀⠀⠀⠀⠀⠀⠀⠀⠀Lise

## EXERCICE D

*Décrivez les personnes suivantes.*

**1.**

**2.**

Il _____ .⠀⠀⠀⠀⠀Nous _____ .

**3.**

Elles _____ .

**4.**

Vous _____ .

**5.**

Il _____ .

**6.**

Tu _____ .

## EXERCICE E

**Janine just arrived at her friend's home. Replace each picture with the correct word and fill in the appropriate form of *il y a* to describe what she sees.**

**1.** _____ un  _____ sur la table.

**2.** _____ des  _____ dans le vase.

**3.** _____ n' _____ pas de  _____ dans la cuisine.

**4.** _____ un  _____ dans le four?

**5.** N'_____ pas de _____ sur le bureau?

# [3] *ÊTRE:* TO BE

| je suis | nous sommes |
|---------|-------------|
| tu es | vous êtes |
| il/elle est | ils/elles sont |

Nous sommes prêts.                    *We are ready.*

Ils ne sont pas contents.             *They are not pleased.*

Au moins es-tu heureux?               *Are you happy at least?*

NOTE: The form *suis-je?* exists, but it is rarely used.

**Common expressions with** *être:*

**être à**  *to belong to*
À qui est cette montre?               *Whose watch is this?*
Elle est à moi.                       *It belongs to me. (It's mine)*

**être en train de**  *to be (in the process of) doing something*
Je suis en train d'étudier.          *I'm studying.*

## EXERCICE F

*Décrivez les personnes suivantes en employant la forme correcte du verbe* **être.**

**1.** Je _____ heureuse.          **2.** Elle _____ élégante.

**3.** Nous _____ intelligents.     **4.** Ils _____ charmants.

**5.** Vous _____ amusant.          **6.** Danielle et Anne _____ sociables.

**7.** Joseph _____ sympathique.    **8.** Tu _____ sérieux.

## EXERCICE G

**Describe what these people are doing by using the correct form of the expression** *être en train de.*

EXEMPLE:

Paul et François **sont en train de** jouer au tennis.

**1.**

Anne et Nicole _____

_____ .

**2.**

Je _____

_____ .

**3.**

Vous _____

_____ .

**4.**

Ils _____

_____ .

**5.**

Tu _____

_____ .

**6.**

Grand-père _____

_____ .

## [ 4 ] *FAIRE:* TO MAKE, DO

| | |
|---|---|
| **je fais** | **nous faisons** |
| **tu fais** | **vous faites** |
| **il / elle fait** | **ils / elles font** |

Maman fait un gâteau.              *Mom is making a cake.*
Il ne fait pas bien son travail.   *He does not do his work well.*
Fait-il un dessin?                 *Is he making a drawing?*

**a.** Another verb conjugated like *faire:*

refaire  *to redo*

**b.** Common expressions with *faire:*

**faire attention (à)** *to pay attention (to)*
Elle fait attention à la leçon. *She pays attention to the lesson.*

**faire des courses** *to go shopping*
Il fait des courses avec sa mère. *He goes shopping with his mother.*

**faire une promenade** *to go for a walk*
Mes parents font une promenade tous les soirs. *My parents go for a walk every evening.*

**faire un voyage (en avion, en voiture)** *to take a trip (by plane, by car)*
Nous faisons un voyage en voiture. *We are taking a trip by car.*

*Faire* with weather expressions:
Quel temps fait-il? *How's the weather?*
Il fait beau (temps). *It's nice.*
Il fait mauvais (temps). *It's bad weather.*
Il fait froid. *It's cold.*
Il fait chaud. *It's warm/hot.*
Il fait frais. *It's cool.*
Il fait du vent. *It's windy.*
Il fait du soleil. *It's sunny.*

*Faire* with sports expressions:
Nous faisons du basket. *We play basketball.*
Nous allons faire du ski. *We are going skiing.*

## EXERCICE H

**What's happening today?** *Exprimez ce que fait chacune des personnes suivantes.*

*1.* Juan et José / faire un voyage en France

_____

*2.* je / faire des courses

_____

*3.* Lucy / faire un voyage en voiture

_____

*4.* nous / faire une promenade

_____

*5.* vous / faire du bowling

_____

*6.* tu / faire attention en classe

_____

*7.* Lucien / faire du football

_____

*8.* les jeunes filles / faire du volley-ball

_____

## EXERCICE I

**Complete each sentence with the appropriate weather expression.**

*1.* Quand il fait _____, je marche dans le parc.

*2.* Quand il fait très _____, je vais à la plage.

*3.* Quand il fait _____, je fais du feu dans la cheminée.

*4.* Quand il fait _____, je mets des lunettes de soleil.

# [5] *METTRE:* TO PUT (ON)

| je mets | nous mettons |
|---------|--------------|
| tu mets | vous mettez |
| il / elle met | ils / elles mettent |

Je mets une robe verte.                *I put on a green dress.*

Mettez-vous le couvert?            *Do you set the table?*

Je ne mets pas le pain sur l'assiette.    *I do not put the bread on the plate.*

**Other verbs conjugated like** *mettre:*

permettre  *to allow*                remettre  *to put back; to deliver*

## EXERCICE J

*Décrivez les vêtements (clothes) que les étudiants mettent pour aller danser à l'école.*

EXEMPLE:

Marie **met un survêtement.**

*1.*

Ils _____ .

*2.*

Janine _____ .

**3.**

Tu _____ .

**4.**

Nous _____ .

**5.**

Je _____ .

**6.**

Vous _____ .

## [6] *OUVRIR:* TO OPEN

| | |
|---|---|
| **j'ouvre** | **nous ouvrons** |
| **tu ouvres** | **vous ouvrez** |
| **il/elle ouvre** | **ils/elles ouvrent** |

Le magasin ouvre à dix heures.     *The store opens at ten o'clock.*
Elle ouvre une boîte de thon.     *She opens a can of tunafish.*
Est-ce que Pierre ouvre la porte?     *Does Pierre open the door?*

**Another verb conjugated like** *ouvrir:*

découvrir   *to discover*

### EXERCICE K

**Your French class is having a party. Each student has brought something.** *Exprimez ce que chaque élève ouvre pour offrir à ses camarades.*

un paquet de bonbons     une barre de chocolat     une bouteille de soda
un sac de chips     une boîte de pâté     une corbeille de fruits

**1.** Claude et moi _____ .

**2.** Tu _____ .

*3.* Vous _____ .

*4.* J' _____ .

*5.* André _____ .

*6.* Anne et Sylvie _____ .

## [ 7 ]   *PRENDRE:* **TO TAKE**

| | |
|---|---|
| **je prends** | **nous prenons** |
| **tu prends** | **vous prenez** |
| **il / elle prend** | **ils / elles prennent** |

Je prends du café le matin.          *I have coffee in the morning.*

Est-ce que tu prends le train?          *Do you take the train?*

Il ne prend pas la voiture ce matin.          *He's not taking the car this morning.*

**Other verbs conjugated like** *prendre:*

apprendre  *to learn*

comprendre  *to understand*

### EXERCICE L

*Dites comment chaque personne va à son travail.*

**EXEMPLE:**          Jean **prend la bicyclette.**

*1.*          Vous _____ .

**2.** Je _____ .

**3.** Jean-Luc _____ .

**4.** Nous _____ .

**5.** Tu _____ .

**6.** Alice et Berthe _____ .

## [ 8 ]  *RECEVOIR:* TO RECEIVE

| | |
|---|---|
| **je reçois** | **nous recevons** |
| **tu reçois** | **vous recevez** |
| **il / elle reçoit** | **ils / elles reçoivent** |

Nous recevons le paquet.                *We receive the package.*

Il ne reçoit pas la lettre.             *He does not receive the letter.*

Est-ce qu'elle reçoit une récompense?   *Does she receive a reward?*

## EXERCICE M

*C'est Noël! Dites ce que reçoit chaque membre de la famille Manet.*

**1.**

Marianne _____

_____ .

**2.**

M. et Mme Manet _____

_____ .

**3.**

Je _____

_____ .

**4.**

Ma sœur et moi _____

_____ .

**5.**

Vous _____

_____ .

**6.**

Tu _____

_____ .

# [9] SAVOIR: TO KNOW (HOW)

| | |
|---|---|
| **je sais** | **nous savons** |
| **tu sais** | **vous savez** |
| **il/elle sait** | **ils/elles savent** |

Claude sait la leçon.

*Claude knows the lesson.*

Colette ne sait pas nager.

*Colette does not know how to swim.*

Ne sais-tu pas la fin de l'histoire?

*Don't you know how the story ends?*

NOTE: The form *sais-je?* exists, but it is rarely used.

## EXERCICE N

**What can the following persons do?** *Utilisez les suggestions ci-dessous.*

| | | | |
|---|---|---|---|
| chanter | danser | parler français | préparer une mousse au chocolat |
| cuisiner | jouer au tennis | patiner | |

EXEMPLE:    Ma sœur **sait patiner.**

*1.* Mes parents _____ .

*2.* Je _____ .

*3.* Mon ami et moi _____ .

*4.* Ma mère _____ .

*5.* Mon ami et vous _____ .

*6.* Tu _____ .

# [10] VENIR: TO COME

| | |
|---|---|
| **je viens** | **nous venons** |
| **tu viens** | **vous venez** |
| **il/elle vient** | **ils/elles viennent** |

Stéphane vient ce soir.

*Stéphane is coming tonight.*

Est-ce que tes amis viennent?

*Are your friends coming?*

Vous ne venez pas avec nous.

*You are not coming with us.*

**Other verbs conjugated like *venir*:**

devenir  *to become*

revenir  *to come back*

## EXERCICE O

*Exprimez à quelle heure ces personnes viennent travailler.*

EXEMPLE:

M. Dupont **vient à dix heures.**

**1.**

Je _____ .

**2.**

Mme Leclerc _____ .

**3.**

Vous _____ .

**4.**

Tu _____ .

**5.**

Les Martin _____ .

**6.**

Nous _____ .

## [ 11 ] *VOIR:* TO SEE

| | |
|---|---|
| **je vois** | **nous voyons** |
| **tu vois** | **vous voyez** |
| **il/elle voit** | **ils/elles voient** |

Nous voyons des nuages noirs.          *We see black clouds.*

Le chat ne voit pas la souris.          *The cat does not see the mouse.*

Vois-tu le bateau sur le lac?          *Do you see the boat on the lake?*

## EXERCICE P

**What do the Chenets and the Renauds see on their trip to Paris?** *Utilisez les noms donnés.*

| | | | |
|---|---|---|---|
| l'Arc de Triomphe | le Louvre | le Sacré-Cœur | l'Opéra |
| la tour Eiffel | le Panthéon | les Invalides | Notre-Dame |

EXEMPLE:　Lucien **voit** le musée d'Orsay.

*1.* Nous _____ .

*2.* Tu _____ .

*3.* M. Renaud _____ .

*4.* Je _____ .

*5.* Vous _____ .

*6.* Les Chenet _____ .

*7.* Mme Renaud _____ .

*8.* Anne et Marie _____ .

## [ 12 ] *POUVOIR:* TO BE ABLE TO, CAN / *VOULOIR:* TO WANT

| | |
|---|---|
| **je peux** | **nous pouvons** |
| **tu peux** | **vous pouvez** |
| **il/elle peut** | **ils/elles peuvent** |

| | |
|---|---|
| **je veux** | **nous voulons** |
| **tu veux** | **vous voulez** |
| **il/elle veut** | **ils/elles veulent** |

Pouvez-vous venir me voir?

Je peux venir demain, si tu veux.

Ne peut-il pas comprendre?

Elle ne veut pas me parler.

*Can you come see me?*

*I can come tomorrow if you want.*

*Can't he understand?*

*She does not want to speak to me.*

## EXERCICE Q

*Dites ce que chaque personne veut, mais ne peut pas, faire.*

EXEMPLE:　je / jouer de la guitare
　　　　　Je **veux** jouer de la guitare, mais je ne **peux** pas.

*1.* nous / aller au cinéma

_____

*2.* tu / lire des bandes dessinées

_____

*3.* Lucien / sortir jusqu'à minuit

_____

*4.* je / aller à la plage

_____

*5.* vous / faire du camping

_____

*6.* les garçons / écouter la radio

_____

*7.* je / manger du chocolat

_____

*8.* Anne et Françoise / acheter des robes neuves

_____

# [13] *PARTIR:* TO LEAVE, GO AWAY / *SORTIR:* TO GO OUT

| je pars | nous partons |
|---------|--------------|
| tu pars | vous partez |
| il/elle part | ils/elles partent |

| je sors | nous sortons |
|---------|--------------|
| tu sors | vous sortez |
| il/elle sort | ils/elles sortent |

| | |
|---|---|
| Les Martin partent demain. | *The Martins are leaving tomorrow.* |
| Après tout je ne pars pas. | *After all, I am not leaving.* |
| Ils ne partent pas demain? | *Aren't they leaving tomorrow?* |
| Vous sortez trop souvent. | *You go out too often.* |
| Sortez-vous ce soir? | *Are you going out tonight?* |

## EXERCICE R

**Tell what each person is doing and when.** *Donnez les formes correctes des verbes* **partir** *et* **sortir.**

EXEMPLE:    je / danser / dans une heure
            Je **sors** danser. Je **pars** dans une heure.

*1.* Sylvie / samedi soir / à sept heures

_____

*2.* vous / dîner / dans vingt minutes

_____

*3.* nous / au cinéma / à six heures

_____

*4.* Pierre / avec ses copains / dans quelques minutes

_____

*5.* tu / en auto / dans dix minutes

_____

*6.* elles / voir des amies / dans une demi-heure

_____

# [ 14 ] *DIRE:* TO SAY / *ÉCRIRE:* TO WRITE / *LIRE:* TO READ

| je dis | nous disons |
|--------|-------------|
| tu dis | vous dites |
| il/elle dit | ils/elles disent |

| j'écris | nous écrivons |
|---------|---------------|
| tu écris | vous écrivez |
| il/elle écrit | ils/elles écrivent |

| je lis | nous lisons |
|--------|-------------|
| tu lis | vous lisez |
| il/elle lit | ils/elles lisent |

| Qu'est-ce que tu dis? | *What are you saying?* |
|-----------------------|------------------------|
| Il ne dit jamais bonjour. | *He never says good morning.* |
| M. Brun lit un livre dans le train. | *Mr. Brun reads a book on the train.* |
| Je ne lis pas le journal. | *I do not read the newspaper.* |
| L'écrivain écrit chaque jour. | *The writer writes every day.* |
| Écrivez-vous à vos amis? | *Do you write to your friends?* |

## EXERCICE S

*Complétez le texte suivant avec la forme correcte du verbe qui convient:* **dire, écrire,** *ou* **lire.**

*1.* Je quitte la maison et je _____ «au revoir» à mes parents. Je _____

un journal en attendant le bus. J'_____ ensuite une lettre à l'éditeur du journal.

*2.* Nous _____ un article. Nous _____ qu'il est injuste.

Nous _____ à l'auteur.

*3.* Ils _____ à leurs correspondants. Ils _____ ce qu'ils font à l'école.

Ils _____ leurs lettres au professeur.

4. Vous _____ le livre parce que vous _____ une composition pour la classe d'anglais. Vous _____ que le livre est intéressant.

5. Elle _____ des poèmes qu'elle _____ à ses amis.

Ils _____ qu'ils sont excellents.

6. Tu _____ à ton oncle; tu lui _____ que tu _____ un livre extraordinaire.

7. Vous _____ à votre professeur que vous _____ un roman et vous _____ le premier chapitre à toute la classe.

## M A S T E R Y  E X E R C I S E S

### EXERCICE T

**We want to get to know you.** *Répondez aux questions avec des phrases complètes.*

1. À quelle heure venez-vous à l'école?

_____

2. Que faites-vous le week-end?

_____

3. Où allez-vous passer les vacances?

_____

4. Combien de frères et de sœurs avez-vous?

_____

5. Quand êtes-vous content(e)?

_____

6. Savez-vous bien parler français?

_____

7. Quelle note recevez-vous dans la classe de français?

_____

8. À qui écrivez-vous des lettres?

_____

9. Quel moyen de transport prenez-vous pour aller à l'école?

_____

**10.** Qu'est-ce que vous voulez faire après les classes aujourd'hui?

_____

## EXERCICE U

*Complétez cette histoire avec les formes correctes des verbes indiqués.*

Nous _____ un examen dans la classe de maths aujourd'hui et
        *1.* (avoir)

je ne _____ pas très content(e). Je _____ que les examens
     *2.* (être)                           *3.* (savoir)

de maths sont toujours difficiles. Je _____ de ma maison à sept heures.
                                          *4.* (partir)

Je _____ le train et je _____ à l'école de très bonne heure.
    *5.* (prendre)                     *6.* (aller)

J'arrive à la salle de classe et j'_____ tranquillement la porte.
                             *7.* (ouvrir)

Je _____ mes livres sur mon pupitre. Je _____ étudier mais
    *8.* (mettre)                                 *9.* (vouloir)

je ne _____ pas parce que je _____ deux de mes amis en train de
    *10.* (pouvoir)                      *11.* (voir)

parler et de rire. Je leur _____ que je _____ de mon mieux
                 *12.* (dire)               *13.* (faire)

pour étudier. Je _____ toutes mes notes. Je _____ un stylo.
             *14.* (lire)                     *15.* (prendre)

J'_____ des exemples dans mon cahier. À huit heures et demie le professeur et tous
  *16.* (écrire)

les autres élèves _____ en classe et l'examen commence. Je _____
               *17.* (venir)                              *18.* (recevoir)

mon examen; je le regarde et je pousse un soupir de soulagement car il est très facile.

## EXERCICE V

**Chantal is planning a party.** *Exprimez en français ce qu'elle vous dit sur ses projets.*

**1.** I am happy because I am going to have a party.

_____


**2.** I am writing the invitations, and I'm telling all my friends to come.

_____

_____


**3.** I know that almost everyone is going to accept.

_____

*4.* My friend Marcel wants to come, but he can't because he is going out with his family.

_____

_____

*5.* Janine is taking the bus because she cannot have the car.

_____

_____

*6.* Joseph and Jacqueline are coming by train.

_____

7. I am reading a recipe now because I am making a chocolate cake for the party.

_____

_____

*8.* My parents are going out to the theater that evening.

_____

*9.* I'm going to put on a red dress for the party.

_____

*10.* When I have a party, I immediately open all the gifts that I receive.

_____

_____

# Chapter 6
## Imperative

The imperative is a verb form used to give commands or suggestions.

## [ 1 ] IMPERATIVE OF REGULAR VERBS

**a.** *Forms of the imperative.* Most are the same as the corresponding forms of the present tense, except for the omission of the subject pronouns *tu, vous,* and *nous.*

| FAMILIAR | | FORMAL / PLURAL | | FIRST PERSON PLURAL | |
|---|---|---|---|---|---|
| **Joue!** | *Play!* | **Jouez!** | *Play!* | **Jouons!** | *Let's play!* |
| **Finis!** | *Finish!* | **Finissez!** | *Finish!* | **Finissons!** | *Let's finish!* |
| **Descends!** | *Go down!* | **Descendez!** | *Go down!* | **Descendons!** | *Let's go down!* |

NOTE: The familiar imperative of *-er* verbs drops the final *-s* of the present tense form.

| Tu joues bien. | **Joue bien!** | *Play well!* |
|---|---|---|
| Tu écoutes la radio. | **Écoute la radio!** | *Listen to the radio!* |
| Tu travailles vite. | **Travaille vite!** | *Work quickly!* |

## EXERCICE A

**Your parents are leaving on vacation, and you are staying home alone.** *Exprimez leurs instructions.*

EXEMPLE:   cuisiner les repas tous les jours
**Cuisine** les repas tous les jours!

1. parler à tes grands-parents chaque jour

_____

2. donner à manger au chien

_____

3. dîner avec ta sœur et ton frère

_____

4. rentrer tout de suite après l'école

_____

5. vider les ordures tous les jours

_____

6. téléphoner à notre hôtel en cas de problème

_____

**7.** garder ta sœur et ton frère

_____

**8.** aider ton frère avec ses devoirs

_____

## EXERCICE B

**Your friends are going away to college.** *Quels conseils* (advice) *leur donnez-vous?*

EXEMPLE:    *(bâtir)* **Bâtissez** des amitiés solides.

**1.** *(obéir)* _____ à tous les règlements.

**2.** *(remplir)* _____ toujours tous les formulaires nécessaires.

**3.** *(réussir)* _____ en tout.

**4.** *(saisir)* _____ chaque occasion.

**5.** *(finir)* _____ tout ce que vous commencez.

**6.** *(choisir)* _____ des cours intéressants.

## EXERCICE C

**You are going away to France as an exchange student.** *Exprimez les conseils de vos parents.*

EXEMPLE:    perdre ton accent américain
            **Perds** ton accent américain!

**1.** répondre à toutes les questions de tes hôtes

_____

**2.** descendre souvent en ville

_____

**3.** défendre tes idées

_____

**4.** correspondre avec tes amis

_____

**5.** rendre tout ce que tu empruntes

_____

**6.** attendre le succès avec patience

_____

## EXERCICE D

**Nicole is baby-sitting for her little brother and sister.** *Dites ce qu'elle leur suggère de faire.*

EXEMPLE:

**Sautons** à la corde!

**1.**

_____ une ronde!

**2.**

_____ une chanson!

**3.**

_____ ce disque compact!

**4.**

_____ nos croissants!

**5.**

_____ notre verre de lait!

**6.**

_____ la télévision!

**b.** *Negative imperative constructions.* In the negative imperative, *ne* and *pas* surround the verb.

| | |
|---|---|
| Ne parle pas si fort! | *Don't speak so loudly!* |
| Ne désobéissez pas! | *Don't disobey!* |
| Ne marchons pas si vite! | *Let's not walk so fast!* |

## EXERCICE E

**You have been hired as a cashier in a department store.** *Exprimez ce que le directeur vous dit.*

EXEMPLE:     parler trop
             **Ne parlez pas** trop!

*1.* vendre la marchandise au rabais *(discounted)*

_____

*2.* désobéir au règlement du magasin

_____

*3.* arriver en retard

_____

*4.* oublier d'être poli avec tous les clients

_____

*5.* rougir quand vous parlez aux clients

_____

*6.* perdre patience avec les clients

_____

*7.* acheter tout ce que vous voulez

_____

*8.* menacer les clients

_____

## EXERCICE F

**You are working as a secretary and want to make sure that you are doing what you are supposed to.** *Écrivez la réponse de votre patron (boss) à chacune de vos questions.*

EXEMPLES:   Je travaille jusqu'à 5 heures? (oui)
            **Oui, travaillez** jusqu'à 5 heures!

            Je travaille jusqu'à 5 heures? (non)
            **Non, ne travaillez pas** jusqu'à 5 heures.

*1.* J'attends toujours des instructions? (oui)

_____

**2.** Je remplis ces formulaires? (non)

_____

**3.** Je garde ces papiers dans mon bureau? (non)

_____

**4.** Je saisis chaque occasion de réussir? (oui)

_____

**5.** Je copie ces documents? (non)

_____

**6.** Je finis le travail de M. Dumont? (oui)

_____

**7.** Je corresponds avec les clients? (non)

_____

**8.** Je rends ces livres à Mme Bertrand? (oui)

_____

**9.** J'emploie cette machine à écrire? (non)

_____

**10.** Je répète ces phrases? (oui)

_____

## EXERCICE G

**You and your friend are making plans for the French club's food festival. Your friend makes some suggestions that you don't like.** *Menez le dialogue suivant avec un(e) camarade.*

EXEMPLE:  donner les recettes aux participants
VOTRE AMI(E):  **Donnons** les recettes aux participants!
VOUS:  **Non, ne donnons pas** les recettes aux participants!

**1.** vendre trois sortes de boissons

VOTRE AMI(E): _____

VOUS: _____

**2.** finir tout le travail au dernier moment

VOTRE AMI(E): _____

VOUS: _____

**3.** acheter beaucoup de desserts

VOTRE AMI(E): _____

VOUS: _____

**4.** rôtir beaucoup de viandes différentes

VOTRE AMI(E): _____

VOUS: _____

**5.** amener nos parents à la fête

VOTRE AMI(E): _____

VOUS: _____

**6.** décorer la salle de fête

VOTRE AMI(E): _____

VOUS: _____

## [ 2 ] IMPERATIVE OF IRREGULAR VERBS

The imperative of irregular verbs generally follows the same pattern as regular verbs.

| | | |
|---|---|---|
| **lire** | *to read* | **lis, lisez, lisons** |
| **faire** | *to do* | **fais, faites, faisons** |
| **partir** | *to leave* | **pars, partez, partons** |
| **venir** | *to come* | **viens, venez, venons** |

NOTE:

1. Verbs conjugated like *-er* verbs in the present tense and the verb *aller* drop the final *-s* in the familiar command form.

| Tu ouvres le cadeau. | **Ouvre le cadeau!** | *Open the gift!* |
| Tu vas au magasin. | **Va au magasin!** | *Go to the store!* |

2. The verbs *avoir*, *être*, and *savoir* have irregular forms in the imperative.

| | | |
|---|---|---|
| **avoir** | *to have* | **aie, ayez, ayons** |
| **être** | *to be* | **sois, soyez, soyons** |
| **savoir** | *to know* | **sache, sachez, sachons** |

## EXERCICE H

**You are going to visit friends for the weekend, and your mother gives you some instructions.** *Exprimez ce qu'elle vous dit.*

EXEMPLE: *(nettoyer)* **Nettoie** ta chambre.

**1.** *(être)* _____ toujours poli(e)!

**2.** *(acheter)* _____ des fleurs pour l'hôtesse!

**3.** *(mettre)* _____ la table!

**4.** *(avoir)* _____ la gentillesse d'aider la famille!

**5.** *(faire)* _____ ton lit tous les jours!

**6.** *(prendre)* _____ soin de tes affaires!

## EXERCICE I

**You and your sister are helping in the kitchen while your mother hurries to finish preparing a special dinner.** *Exprimez ce que votre mère vous dit de faire.*

EXEMPLE:   lire la recette
**Lisez** la recette.

**1.** prendre un plat dans le placard *(cupboard)*

_____

**2.** faire le dessert

_____

**3.** aller au marché

_____

**4.** mettre les légumes dans le réfrigérateur

_____

**5.** ouvrir une boîte de conserves

_____

**6.** sortir de la cuisine

_____

**7.** dire bonjour aux invités

_____

## EXERCICE J

**You're going out on your first date, and your parents have some advice for you.** *Exprimez ce qu'ils disent.*

EXEMPLE:   parler trop
**Ne parle pas** trop!

**1.** être timide

_____

**2.** avoir peur

_____

**3.** faire le clown

_____

**4.** prétendre tout savoir

_____

**5.** revenir tard

_____

**6.** dire: «Je t'aime»

_____

## EXERCICE K

**You are on a tour with other students, and the counselor gives the group the following instructions before leaving the airport.** _Exprimez ce qu'il dit._

EXEMPLE:   venir ici
          **Venez** ici!

**1.** mettre les valises dans le car _(tour bus)_

_____

**2.** monter rapidement dans le car

_____

**3.** être responsables

_____

**4.** écouter le conducteur

_____

**5.** obéir à tous les règlements

_____

**6.** prendre soin de votre appareil-photo

_____

**7.** lire l'itinéraire avec attention

_____

**8.** dire «merci» au conducteur

_____

## EXERCICE L

**You and some friends are in Quebec for** _Carnaval_. **The hotel manager answers your questions.** _Exprimez ce qu'il dit._

EXEMPLE:   On apporte beaucoup d'argent? (non)
          Non, **n'apportez pas** beaucoup d'argent!

*1.* On emploie un guide? (oui)

_____

*2.* On achète des masques? (oui)

_____

*3.* On va à pied? (oui)

_____

*4.* On a peur? (non)

_____

*5.* On est prêt à quitter l'hôtel à huit heures? (oui)

_____

*6.* On prend le bus? (non)

_____

*7.* On fait le tour de la ville? (non)

_____

*8.* On voit tout? (oui)

_____

*9.* On met des costumes? (oui)

_____

*10.* On rentre à deux heures du matin? (non)

_____

## EXERCICE M

**You are trying to make vacation plans with a friend who disagrees with everything you suggest.** *Suggérez certaines activités et exprimez ses réponses.*

EXEMPLE:   camper dans les montagnes
        VOUS:          **Campons** dans les montagnes!
        VOTRE AMI(E):  **Ne campons pas** dans les montagnes!

*1.* aller au bord de la mer

     VOUS: _____

     VOTRE AMI(E): _____

*2.* nager dans un lac

     VOUS: _____

     VOTRE AMI(E): _____

**3.** faire le tour du monde

VOUS: _____

VOTRE AMI(E): _____

**4.** sortir tous les soirs

VOUS: _____

VOTRE AMI(E): _____

**5.** voir les îles Caraïbes

VOUS: _____

VOTRE AMI(E): _____

**6.** prendre l'avion à Nice

VOUS: _____

VOTRE AMI(E): _____

## M A S T E R Y   E X E R C I S E S

### EXERCICE N

**Your friends always ask you for advice.** *Exprimez ce que vous leur dites.*

EXEMPLE:    La voiture de Richard ne marche pas.
(emprunter la voiture de ton frère)

**Emprunte** la voiture de ton frère!

**1.** Georgette veut résoudre les problèmes de l'atmosphère.

(prendre ta bicyclette)

_____

**2.** La petite amie de Georges ne veut pas aller à la fête de Michel.

(aller tout seul)

_____

**3.** Robert perd toujours quelque chose.

(faire attention)

_____

**4.** Alice ne veut pas aller patiner parce que ses amies n'y vont pas.

(être plus indépendante)

_____

5. Suzanne travaille et vient de toucher son premier chèque.

   (mettre de l'argent à la banque)

   _____

6. Philippe veux aller en France mais il n'a pas assez d'argent.

   (avoir un peu de patience)

   _____

## EXERCICE O

**You are moving into a new house, and the moving van has arrived. The movers ask you questions.** *Exprimez vos réponses.*

EXEMPLE:    Je monte cette chaise? (non)
            Non, **ne montez pas** cette chaise!

1. Je descends ce carton? (oui)

   _____

2. Je ferme cette porte? (non)

   _____

3. Je mets le divan ici? (non)

   _____

4. Je sors cette lampe de la cuisine? (oui)

   _____

5. J'enlève cette couverture en plastique? (oui)

   _____

6. Je vais dans le garage? (non)

   _____

7. J'essuie ce miroir? (oui)

   _____

8. Je jette cette boîte? (oui)

   _____

9. Je fais le nettoyage? (non)

   _____

10. J'ouvre ce paquet? (non)

   _____

## EXERCICE P

**You are directing a school play and are giving instructions to the actors.** *Exprimez ces instructions en français.*

1. My friends, pay attention now.

   _____

2. Alice, come here!

   _____

3. Philippe, don't be shy!

   _____

4. Luz and Jean, take these papers!

   _____

5. Robert and Luc, don't be afraid!

   _____

6. Alfred, don't put the chairs over there!

   _____

7. François, repeat that sentence.

   _____

8. Serge, lead the children to the door!

   _____

9. Jean, try to speak louder.

   _____

10. My friends, for tomorrow, know the words of the song!

    _____

# Chapter 7
## *Passé composé* of Regular *avoir* Verbs

## [ 1 ] AFFIRMATIVE CONSTRUCTIONS

The *passé composé* is a past tense composed of two parts: the present tense of the auxiliary verb, or "helping" verb, and the past participle of the main verb. For most verbs, the auxiliary verb is *avoir* (to have).

| chanter *to sing* | finir *to finish* | vendre *to sell* |
|---|---|---|
| *I sang, I have sung* | *I finished, I have finished* | *I sold, I have sold* |
| j'*ai* chanté | j'*ai* fini | j'*ai* vendu |
| tu *as* chanté | tu *as* fini | tu *as* vendu |
| il / elle *a* chanté | il / elle *a* fini | il / elle *a* vendu |
| nous *avons* chanté | nous *avons* fini | nous *avons* vendu |
| vous *avez* chanté | vous *avez* fini | vous *avez* vendu |
| ils / elles *ont* chanté | ils / elles *ont* fini | ils / elles *ont* vendu |

NOTE:

1. The past participle of *-er* verbs is formed by dropping *-er* and adding *é*.

| | |
|---|---|
| Tu as parlé à Marie. | *You spoke to Marie.* |
| Il a écouté des disques. | *He listened to records.* |
| Vous avez ennuyé Luc. | *You bothered Luc.* |
| Elles ont acheté des robes. | *They bought dresses.* |

2. The past participle of *-ir* verbs is formed by dropping the *-r*.

| | |
|---|---|
| J'ai fini mes devoirs. | *I finished my work.* |
| Nous avons maigri. | *We have become thin.* |
| Vous avez rempli le verre. | *You have filled the glass.* |
| Elles ont désobéi. | *They disobeyed.* |

3. The past participle of *-re* verbs is formed by dropping *-re* and adding *-u*.

| | |
|---|---|
| J'ai vendu ma maison. | *I have sold my house.* |
| Tu as perdu ton livre. | *You have lost your book.* |
| Vous avez défendu vos amis. | *You defended your friends.* |
| Ils ont rendu mon argent. | *They gave back my money.* |

## EXERCICE A

*Exprimez ce que Pierre et sa famille ont fait* (did) *hier soir.*

EXEMPLE: Lucien / jouer au tennis
Lucien **a joué** au tennis.

*1.* je / patiner

**2.** papa / travailler

_____

**3.** Jules et moi / regarder une émission à la télévision

_____

**4.** maman / préparer le dîner

_____

**5.** vous / téléphoner à des copains

_____

**6.** mes parents / écouter les informations

_____

**7.** tu / ranger ta chambre

_____

**8.** Louise et Gabrielle / dîner au restaurant

_____

## EXERCICE B

**M. Dumas had to go away on business.** _Racontez ce que ses amis ont fait_ (did) _pour l'aider pendant son absence._

**1.** _(laver)_ Jean et Paul _____ sa voiture.

**2.** _(vider)_ J'_____ les ordures.

**3.** _(promener)_ Lucienne _____ son chien.

**4.** _(passer)_ Nous _____ l'aspirateur.

**5.** _(nettoyer)_ Tu _____ la maison.

**6.** _(ranger)_ Lise et Cécile _____ le salon.

**7.** _(placer)_ Vous _____ le courrier sur la table.

**8.** _(donner)_ Henri _____ à manger à ses poissons.

## EXERCICE C

_Exprimez ce que ces personnes ont fait hier matin._

**1.** _(finir)_ J'_____ mon travail tôt.

**2.** _(obéir)_ Les enfants _____ à leurs parents.

**3.** _(choisir)_ Nous _____ d'aller en France.

**4.** *(punir)* Le professeur _____ le mauvais élève.

**5.** *(guérir)* Vous _____ le malade.

**6.** *(réussir)* Tu _____ à ton examen.

## EXERCICE D

*Exprimez ce que ces personnes ont fait avant-hier.*

EXEMPLE:  Michel / rendre de l'argent à Jacques
Michel **a rendu** de l'argent à Jacques.

**1.** Geraldo / perdre son portefeuille

_____

**2.** Anna et René / entendre de bonnes nouvelles

_____

**3.** je / attendre mon ami pendant une heure

_____

**4.** vous / défendre à Victor de sortir

_____

**5.** nous / répondre à une annonce publicitaire

_____

**6.** tu / vendre ta bicyclette

_____

## [2] USES OF THE *PASSÉ COMPOSÉ*

The *passé composé* is used to narrate an action or event completed in the past. Note the English equivalents of the *passé composé:*

| | |
|---|---|
| J'ai téléphoné à mes amis. | *I (have) called my friends.* |
| Nous avons écouté des disques. | *We listened to records.* |
| Elle a déjà parlé à Claude. | *She has already spoken to Claude.* |

NOTE: **Some expressions that are often used with the *passé composé* are:**

l'année passée, l'année dernière *last year*

avant-hier *the day before yesterday*

hier *yesterday*

hier soir *last night*

le mois passé, le mois dernier *last month*

la semaine passée, la semaine dernière *last week*

## EXERCICE E

**Complete this letter that Hélène wrote to a friend while in Canada.** *Écrivez la forme correcte des verbes au passé composé.*

Chère Gabrielle,

Hier soir j'_____ à une fête chez mon amie Lucienne. Tout le monde
　　　　　*1. (assister)*

_____ l'anniversaire de sa sœur cadette, Denise. Beaucoup de personnes
　　*2. (célébrer)*

_____ à la fête et Denise _____ de joie à voir tous les cadeaux
　　*3. (assister)*　　　　　　　　　　　　　*4. (crier)*

pour elle. La fête _____ le soir après le dîner. À neuf heures précises,
　　　　　　　*5. (commencer)*

j'_____ ses amis. Ils _____ «Bon anniversaire» à Denise et après,
　　*6. (entendre)*　　　　　　　*7. (chanter)*

tout le monde _____ à danser. Nous _____ des spécialités
　　　　　　　*8. (commencer)*　　　　　　　*9. (manger)*

canadiennes. Sa mère _____ tous les plats et elle _____ un grand
　　　　　　　　*10. (cuisiner)*　　　　　　　　*11. (préparer)*

gâteau au chocolat. Je suis sûre que j'_____ parce que j'_____
　　　　　　　　　　　　　　　*12. (grossir)*　　　　　　　*13. (finir)*

tout ce que j'_____ . J'_____ la fin de la fête avant de rentrer.
　　　　*14. (choisir)*　　　*15. (attendre)*

Quelle fête formidable! À très bientôt.

　　　　　　　　　　　　　Grosses bises,
　　　　　　　　　　　　　Hélène

## EXERCICE F

**Last year Catherine, Isabelle, Pierre, and Claude went with their classmates to the Alps to attend "une classe de neige" (snow class).** *Racontez leur voyage avec le passé composé des verbes indiqués.*

| | | | | |
|---|---|---|---|---|
| attendre | durer | finir | neiger | réussir |
| choisir | écouter | habiter | partager | voyager |
| commencer | entendre | montrer | passer | |

1. Tous les élèves _____ ce voyage avec joie.

2. Les élèves et les professeurs _____ en train.

3. Le voyage _____ à la gare de Lyon à Paris.

4. Le voyage _____ six heures.

5. Les élèves et les professeurs _____ un chalet sur la montagne.

6. Catherine et Isabelle _____ une chambre avec Lise.

7. Pierre et Claude _____ le dortoir des garçons.

8. Quand ils _____ le dîner, ils _____ à dormir malgré leur excitation.

9. Il _____ toute la nuit.

10. Un professeur _____ comment skier prudemment et les élèves _____ attentivement.

11. Plus tard, ils _____ un programme sur les montagnes.

12. Ils _____ deux semaines merveilleuses aux sports d'hiver. La classe de neige est une idée formidable.

## [ 3 ] NEGATIVE AND INTERROGATIVE CONSTRUCTIONS

**a.** In a negative sentence in the *passé composé,* *ne* precedes the helping verb and *pas* follows it.

| | |
|---|---|
| Il n'a **pas** expliqué le problème. | *He did not explain the problem.* |
| Vous n'avez **pas** réussi. | *You did not succeed.* |
| Nous n'avons **pas** vendu la maison. | *We have not sold the house.* |

## EXERCICE G

**You and your friends are comparing what you've accomplished so far.** *Exprimez ce que vous n'avez pas encore fait.*

camper dans les montagnes
choisir de profession
entendre mon chanteur favori
gagner de championnat de tennis
jouer du piano dans un concert

répondre à toutes les questions
réussir à tous les examens
visiter de pays étranger
voyager au Canada

EXEMPLE:  Nous **n'avons pas** encore **visité** de pays étranger.

1. Les garçons _____ .

2. Vous _____ .

3. Annick _____ .

4. Je _____ .

5. Louise et Janine _____ .

6. Tu _____ .

7. Pierre _____ .

8. Serge et moi _____ .

## EXERCICE H

**Your mother has invited some friends to celebrate Bastille Day. She worries that everything is not ready yet.** *Écrivez ce qu'elle dit.*

EXEMPLE:     je / finir / tous les préparatifs
            Je **n'ai pas fini** tous les préparatifs.

1. les filles / nettoyer / la salle de bain

_____

2. Pierre / cueillir / les fleurs

_____

3. Christine / tondre / la pelouse *(lawn)*

_____

4. vous / acheter / les boissons

_____

5. nous / descendre / les chaises dans le jardin

_____

6. tu / amener / les chiens chez les voisins

_____

7. la cuisinière / rôtir / les poulets

_____

8. Marie et toi / apporter / les pâtisseries

_____

> **b.** A question may be indicated with intonation alone, or it can be formed by beginning the sentence with *est-ce que.*
>
> | | |
> |---|---|
> | Tu as répondu à sa lettre? | *Have you answered her letter?* |
> | **Est-ce que** tu as lavé la vaisselle? | *Did you wash the dishes?* |
> | **Est-ce qu'**elle a fini ses devoirs? | *Has she finished her homework?* |
>
> Inversion may also be used in the *passé composé* by inverting the subject pronoun and the auxiliary verb.
>
> | | |
> |---|---|
> | **As-tu étudié** la grammaire? | *Did you study the grammar?* |
> | **As-tu fini** tes devoirs? | *Have you finished your homework?* |
> | **Ont-elles répondu** à la lettre? | *Have they answered the letter?* |

## EXERCICE I

*Demandez à vos amis ce qu'ils ont fait pendant leurs vacances.*

EXEMPLE:    Luc / pêcher dans le lac
            **Est-ce que** Luc **a pêché** dans le lac?

*1.* Aisha / patiner

_____

*2.* Gino et Carlo / réussir à courir le Marathon

_____

*3.* les Lelong / dîner dans un restaurant élégant

_____

*4.* Joséphine et Marie / choisir de voyager en avion

_____

*5.* Gamal / attendre ses amis pour partir

_____

*6.* M. et Mme Carré / camper au Canada

_____

## EXERCICE J

**You have just returned from a trip to France. Answer the questions your friend asks you.** *Utilisez les indications données.*

*1.* Quel pays as-tu visité? (la France)

_____

*2.* Avec qui as-tu voyagé? (ma famille)

_____

*3.* Combien de temps avez-vous passé en France? (quinze jours)

_____

*4.* Qui a choisi d'aller en France? (mes parents)

_____

*5.* Quel moyen de transport avez-vous employé en France? (le train)

_____

*6.* Quel endroit as-tu préféré? (la Provence)

_____

## EXERCICE K

**Your parents gave you a list of things to do while they were away.** *Exprimez leurs questions et vos réponses basées sur la liste suivante.*

| | |
|---|---|
| *ranger le salon* | *chauffer le dîner* |
| *laver la voiture* ✓ | *finir le jardinage* ✓ |
| *trouver les clefs* | *promener le chien* |
| *fermer toutes les fenêtres* | *descendre les bagages* ✓ |
| *téléphoner à l'électricien* ✓ | *nettoyer la cuisine* ✓ |

EXEMPLES:   **As-tu rangé** le salon?
Non, **je n'ai pas** encore rangé le salon.

**As-tu lavé** la voiture?
Oui, **j'ai déjà lavé** la voiture.

1. _____

_____

2. _____

_____

3. _____

_____

4. _____

_____

5. _____

_____

6. _____

_____

7. _____

_____

8. _____

_____

**c.** A negative interrogative sentence in the *passé composé* may be indicated with intonation alone, or it can be formed by beginning the sentence with *est-ce que*.

Jean **n'a pas** dansé?                              *Didn't Jean dance?*

**Est-ce que** Jean n'a pas dansé?            *Didn't Jean dance?*

## EXERCICE L

**You are looking through your brother's yearbook.** *Posez des questions* (ask questions) *sur certains étudiants.*

EXEMPLE:     Claude Delbart / étudier la médecine
**Est-ce que** Claude Delbart **n'a pas étudié** la médecine?

1. Bernard Besset / gagner à la loterie

_____

2. Ginette Fleurat / épouser le professeur de biologie

_____

3. Jean Legrand / participer aux Jeux Olympiques

_____

4. Nicolas Loiseau / dépenser une fortune en bandes dessinées *(comic books)*

_____

5. Aimée Savin / finir ses études

_____

6. Catherine Fleury / réussir de chanson populaire

_____


## M A S T E R Y   E X E R C I S E S

## EXERCICE M

**You and a friend spent a weekend in another city.** *Racontez ce que vous avez fait en employant les suggestions ci-dessous.*

| | |
|---|---|
| acheter des affiches | jouer au volley-ball |
| choisir de visiter des musées | oublier tous nos problèmes |
| dépenser beaucoup d'argent | perdre un peu d'argent |
| dîner dans un restaurant français | répondre à beaucoup de questions |
| envoyer des cartes postales à des amis | |

EXEMPLE:     Nous **avons joué** au volley-ball.

1. _____

2. _____

3. _____

4. _____

**5.** _____

**6.** _____

**7.** _____

**8.** _____

## EXERCICE N

**While visiting Montreal, you run into someone who spent a year at your school as an exchange student. You bring her up to date about yourself and other people she knew, and you ask her about herself.** *Utilisez le passé composé.*

EXEMPLES:   Édouard / réussir à son examen.
             Édouard **a réussi** à son examen.

             tu / choisir une université?
             tu **as choisi** une université?

**1.** M. Lecomte / changer de travail

   _____

**2.** je / commencer à conduire une voiture

   _____

**3.** Lucie et moi / voyager à l'étranger

   _____

**4.** tu / finir ton bac?

   _____

**5.** le directeur / renvoyer M. Lechat

   _____

**6.** Lola / gagner une bourse

   _____

**7.** Mlle Legrand / annoncer sa retraite

   _____

**8.** M. Pierrot / vendre sa vieille motocyclette

   _____

**9.** tu / décider où travailler?

   _____

**10.** Ralph et Charles / choisir de devenir avocats

   _____

## EXERCICE O

*Dites ce qui s'est passé* **(happened)** *hier.*

EXEMPLE:   écouter son disque préféré (non)
François **n'a pas écouté** son disque préféré hier.

*1.* envoyer une lettre à Georgette (oui)

Paul _____ .

*2.* réussir à l'examen de chimie (oui)

Lise et Rosa _____ .

*3.* achever un grand projet scientifique (oui)

Ralph et moi _____ .

*4.* perdre son sac (non)

Berthe _____ .

*5.* changer vos chaussettes (non)

Vous _____ .

*6.* célébrer mon anniversaire (oui)

J' _____ .

*7.* attendre l'autobus après l'école (non)

Jean et Ken _____ .

*8.* déjeuner sur l'herbe (non)

Tu _____ .

## EXERCICE P

**You have to give a short oral report in French about your trip abroad last summer.** *Exprimez ce que vous dites.*

*1.* Last summer I spent one month in France.

_____

*2.* Before leaving, I bought a French dictionary.

_____

*3.* Then I forgot to bring the dictionary with me.

_____

*4.* My friends and I visited three cities.

_____

*5.* We traveled by bus and bicycle in each city.

_____

*6.* We spoke French all the time.

_____

**7.** In Paris, Pierre lost his passport.

_____

*8.* The police found the passport two days later.

_____

*9.* They returned the passport to Pierre.

_____

*10.* I gained weight because I ate a lot of delicious meals.

_____

# Chapter 8
## Verbs Irregular in the *passé composé*

All irregular verbs follow the same rules as regular verbs for negative, interrogative, and negative interrogative constructions in the *passé composé*.

The following verbs have irregular past participles:

| | | | | | |
|---|---|---|---|---|---|
| apprendre | dire | faire | ouvrir | recevoir | vouloir |
| avoir | écrire | lire | pouvoir | savoir | |
| comprendre | être | mettre | prendre | voir | |

## [ 1 ] PAST PARTICIPLES ENDING IN -U

| | | | | | |
|---|---|---|---|---|---|
| **avoir** | *to have* | *eu* | **savoir** | *to know* | *su* |
| **lire** | *to read* | *lu* | **voir** | *to see* | *vu* |
| **pouvoir** | *to be able to* | *pu* | **vouloir** | *to want* | *voulu* |
| **recevoir** | *to receive* | *reçu* | | | |

Paul a reçu deux lettres. *Paul received two letters.*

Je n'ai pas vu ce film. *I haven't seen this film.*

Avez-vous lu ce livre? *Did you read this book?*

## EXERCICE A

**Each of the following students was absent yesterday.** *Exprimez pourquoi en utilisant le passé composé du verbe* **avoir.**

EXEMPLE:   Jean / mal à l'estomac
Jean **a eu** mal à l'estomac.

*1.* je / mal à la gorge

_____

*2.* vous / la grippe

_____

*3.* ils / de la fièvre

_____

*4.* nous / mal au ventre

_____

## EXERCICE B

**Tell what each person read before going to bed last night.** *Employez les suggestions ci-dessous.*

| | | |
|---|---|---|
| des bandes dessinées | le journal | un roman policier |
| des poèmes | une histoire d'amour | |

EXEMPLE:    J'ai lu des poèmes.

**1.** Najeda _____ .

**2.** Vous _____ .

**3.** Tu _____ .

**4.** Les jeunes filles _____ .

## EXERCICE C

**These students had to study for a test yesterday.** *Dites ce qu'ils n'ont pas pu faire.*

EXEMPLE:    Marc **n'a pas pu** aller dans une discothèque.

**1.** Vous _____ jouer au tennis.

**2.** Nous _____ descendre en ville.

**3.** Tu _____ dîner au restaurant.

**4.** Michael et Éric _____ finir leurs devoirs.

## EXERCICE D

**Each person received a gift for his / her birthday this year.** *Dites ce que chacun a reçu.*

EXEMPLE:

Jimmy **a reçu une bicyclette.**

**1.**

Grand-père _____

_____ .

**2.**

Émile et Henri _____

_____ .

**3.**

Tu _____

_____ .

**4.**

J' _____

_____ .

## EXERCICE E

**The following students were finalists in a contest.** *Dites ce qu'ils ont su.*

EXEMPLE:  Marie / le nom de la capitale du Zaïre
Marie **a su** le nom de la capitale du Zaïre.

**1.** je / épeler «théâtre»

_____

**2.** Paul / répondre à toutes les questions

_____

**3.** vous / jouer du violon

_____

**4.** Nous / la table de multiplication par 9

_____

## EXERCICE F

**Each person saw something in René's backyard.** *Dites ce que chacun a vu.*

EXEMPLE:

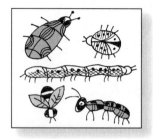

Vous **avez vu des insectes.**

**1.**

Nous _____

_____ .

**2.**

Tu _____

_____ .

**3.**

J'_____

_____ .

**4.**

Kim et Tisha _____

_____ .

## EXERCICE G

**Tell what each person wanted to do last Saturday.** *Employez les suggestions ci-dessous.*

marcher dans le parc     rester à la maison          voir un film
partir à la campagne     sortir avec des copains

EXEMPLE:    nous / partir à la campagne
            Nous **avons voulu** partir à la campagne.

**1.**  Simon et Luc _____ .

**2.** Sylvie et moi _____ .

**3.** Tu _____ .

**4.** Vous _____ .

## [ 2 ] PAST PARTICIPLES ENDING IN *-IS*

| | | | | | |
|---|---|---|---|---|---|
| **apprendre** | *to learn* | ***appris*** | **mettre** | *to put* | ***mis*** |
| **comprendre** | *to understand* | ***compris*** | **prendre** | *to take* | ***pris*** |

L'élève a bien appris la leçon.          *The pupil has learned the lesson well.*

Les enfants n'ont pas compris.          *The children did not understand.*

Avez-vous pris le livre?                      *Did you take the book?*

### EXERCICE H

*Exprimez ce que ces élèves ont mis dans leur cartable* (**school bag**).

**EXEMPLE:**          Sylvie **a mis des papiers.**

**1.**          J' _____ .

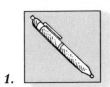

**2.**          Vous _____ .

**3.**          Josette et Colette _____ .

**4.**          Tu _____ .

## EXERCICE I

**The following travelers forgot to pack certain things.** *Dites ce qu'ils ont oublié.*

EXEMPLE:    tu / tes chèques de voyage
            Tu **n'as pas pris** tes chèques de voyage.

*1.* Yvonne / sa brosse à dents

_____

*2.* je / mon permis de conduire

_____

*3.* vous / votre appareil-photo

_____

*4.* Solange et moi / nos cartes de crédit

_____

## [ 3 ]  PAST PARTICIPLES ENDING IN *-IT*

| **dire** | *to say* | ***dit*** | **écrire** | *to write* | ***écrit*** |
|---|---|---|---|---|---|

Il a écrit une lettre à sa mère.        *He wrote a letter to his mother.*

Vous n'avez pas dit merci!              *You did not say thank you!*

A-t-il écrit un roman?                  *Did he write a novel?*

## EXERCICE J

**Paul has been accepted by a top university.** *Exprimez ce que ses amis lui ont dit en employant les suggestions données.*

bonne chance        c'est magnifique        félicitations
c'est formidable     c'est super

EXEMPLE:    Raymond **a dit:** «C'est magnifique!»

*1.* Vous _____ .

*2.* J' _____ .

*3.* Tu _____ .

*4.* Nadine et Colette _____ .

## EXERCICE K

**Ask questions about work that was submitted for publication in the school magazine.**

EXEMPLE:    Denis / un bon livre
**Est-ce que** Denis **a écrit** un bon livre?

*1.* Roger et moi / de bons poèmes

_____

*2.* vous / un article intéressant

_____

*3.* tu / une histoire romantique

_____

*4.* Bruno / un éditorial intelligent

_____

# [4] OTHER IRREGULAR PAST PARTICIPLES

| **être** | *to be* | *été* | **ouvrir** | *to open* | *ouvert* |
|----------|---------|-------|------------|-----------|----------|
| **faire** | *to do* | **fait** | | | |

Michel n'a pas été malade.       *Michel has not been sick.*
Vous avez fait une erreur.       *You made a mistake.*
A-t-il ouvert la fenêtre?        *Did he open the window?*

## EXERCICE L

*Exprimez quel sport les personnes suivantes ont pratiqué.*

EXEMPLE:                                          Vous **avez fait du patin.**

*1.*                                          Tu _____ .

2. Joseph et Maurice _____.

3. J'_____.

4. Christine _____.

## EXERCICE M

**Say where each person has not gone.** *Employez les suggestions ci-dessous.*

| | | |
|---|---|---|
| à la Martinique | en Afrique | en Grèce |
| au Canada | en Bretagne | |

EXEMPLE:     Tu **n'as pas été** en Grèce.

1. Guy _____.

2. Je _____.

3. Isabelle et moi _____.

4. Patricia et Brigitte _____.

## EXERCICE N

**The following persons are on a commuter train.** *Exprimez ce qu'elles ont ouvert.*

EXEMPLE:     Georges / une bouteille d'eau minérale
             Georges **a ouvert** une bouteille d'eau minérale.

**1.** Paulette / son sac

_____

**2.** vous / le journal

_____

**3.** tu / un livre

_____

**4.** Nicole et Jacqueline / un paquet de bonbons

_____

## MASTERY EXERCISES

## EXERCICE O

**You and your friends had some spare time.** *Exprimez ce que vous avez fait.*

EXEMPLE:     Suzette / préparer un gâteau
             Suzette **a préparé** un gâteau.

**1.** Rose / lire un roman

_____

**2.** je / écrire des lettres à des amis

_____

**3.** tu / être à un concert

_____

**4.** Éric et Émile / faire des courses

_____

**5.** vous / voir un film

_____

**6.** Henri et moi / avoir une boum

_____

## EXERCICE P

**Complete Catherine's entry in her diary.** *Employez les formes correctes du passé composé des verbes indiqués.*

Ce matin j'_____ chez mon amie Isabelle.  Son père _____ une
　　　　　　　*1. (être)*　　　　　　　　　　　　　　　　　　　　　　*2. (bâtir)*

maison de poupées pour sa petite sœur Chantal, qui _____ neuf ans hier.
　　　　　　　　　　　　　　　　　　　　　　　*3. (avoir)*

Elle _____ ce cadeau de ses grands-parents.  M. Dupont _____
　　　*4. (recevoir)*　　　　　　　　　　　　　　　　　　　　　　　　　　*5. (lire)*

avec soin toutes les instructions.  Mais il n'_____ pas _____ tout comprendre
　　　　　　　　　　　　　　　　　*6. (pouvoir)*

et il n'_____ pas _____ comment finir le projet.  J'_____ le regret
　　　*7. (savoir)*　　　　　　　　　　　　　　　　　　*8. (voir)*

dans les yeux de Chantal et j'_____ aider.  J'_____ tous les
　　　　　　　　　　　　*9. (vouloir)*　　　　　　　*10. (prendre)*

morceaux de bois et j'_____ tout en place.  Enfin j'_____ :
　　　　　　　　　　*11. (mettre)*　　　　　　　　　　　　　　*12. (dire)*

«Voilà.  J'_____ ».  Tout le monde _____ .
　　　　　*13. (finir)*　　　　　　　　　　　　　*14. (applaudir)*

## EXERCICE Q

**Continue reading Catherine's diary, but this time change the verbs from the present tense to the** *passé composé.*

1.  Je *(finis)* _____ donc de construire la maison de poupées et tout le

    monde *(applaudit)* _____ .

2.  J'*(ai)* _____ beaucoup de plaisir à aider M. Dupont et je *(suis)* _____

    très contente.

3.  Chantal *(prend)* _____ ma main et me *(dit)* _____: «Tu *(es)*

    _____ formidable et tu *(sais)* _____ tout faire!»

4.  Isabelle *(demande)* _____: «Où *(apprends-tu)* _____ à

    construire des maisons?»

5.  Je *(réponds)* _____: «Je *(réfléchis)* _____ et je *(comprends)*

    _____ comment faire.

6.  Ce *(n'est pas)* _____ très difficile et je *(veux)* _____ depuis

    longtemps devenir architecte!»

## EXERCICE R

*Dites si vous avez fait les choses suivantes la semaine dernière.*

|                         |                    |                       |
|-------------------------|--------------------|-----------------------|
| avoir une bonne semaine | faire des courses  | prendre l'avion       |
| écrire une lettre       | jouer au tennis    | recevoir une bonne note |
| être au théâtre         | lire un magazine   | voir un bon film      |

EXEMPLE:    J'**ai joué** au tennis.
     OR:    Je **n'ai pas joué** au tennis

1. _____

2. _____

3. _____

4. _____

5. _____

6. _____

7. _____

8. _____

## EXERCICE S

**Élise tells a friend about her date with Jean.** *Exprimez en français ce qu'elle dit en employant le passé composé.*

1. Jean and I decided to go out last night.

   _____

2. I answered: "Thank you, with pleasure!"

   _____

3. We wanted to go to the movies.

   _____

4. I read an article on a French film.

   _____

5. The article said that the film is excellent.

   _____

6. This film has had lots of success.

   _____

**7.** The weather was bad, and it was very cold all day.

_____

**8.** We took the bus to go to the movies.

_____

**9.** At the movies, many people waited a long time.

_____

**10.** We were very cold, and we were not able to see the film.

_____

# Chapter 9
## Passé composé of être Verbs

## [ 1 ] VERBS CONJUGATED WITH *ÊTRE*

Sixteen common verbs use the helping verb *être* instead of *avoir*. Their *passé composé* is formed by combining the present tense of *être* and the past participle of the verb. Most of these verbs express motion or change of place or state.

| INFINITIVE | PAST PARTICIPLE | INFINITIVE | PAST PARTICIPLE |
|---|---|---|---|
| **aller** *to go* | **allé** | **naître** *to be born* | **né** |
| **venir** *to come* | **venu** | **mourir** *to die* | **mort** |
| **arriver** *to arrive* | **arrivé** | **rentrer** *to go in again, return* | **rentré** |
| **partir** *to leave, go away* | **parti** | **retourner** *to go back, return* | **retourné** |
| **entrer** *to go in, enter* | **entré** | **revenir** *to come back* | **revenu** |
| **sortir** *to go out, leave* | **sorti** | **tomber** *to fall* | **tombé** |
| **monter** *to go up, come up* | **monté** | **rester** *to remain, stay* | **resté** |
| **descendre** *to go down* | **descendu** | **devenir** *to become* | **devenu** |

## [ 2 ] AGREEMENT

Past participles of verbs conjugated with *être* agree in gender (masculine or feminine) and number (singular or plural) with the subject.

| MASCULINE SUBJECTS | FEMININE SUBJECTS | |
|---|---|---|
| **je suis allé** | **je suis allée** | *I went* |
| **tu es allé** | **tu es allée** | *you went* |
| **il est allé** | **elle est allée** | *he / she went* |
| **nous sommes allés** | **nous sommes allées** | *we went* |
| **vous êtes allé(s)** | **vous êtes allée(s)** | *you went* |
| **ils sont allés** | **elles sont allées** | *they went* |

| | |
|---|---|
| Elles sont arrivées en retard. | *They arrived late.* |
| Où es-tu née, Marie? | *Where were you born, Marie?* |

NOTE:

1. When the subject is both masculine and feminine, the past participle is masculine plural.

   | | |
   |---|---|
   | Paul et Marie sont partis. | *Paul and Marie left.* |

2. Since the pronouns *je, tu, nous,* and *vous* may be masculine or feminine, and *vous* may be singular or plural, the past participles used with them vary in endings.

3. Negative, interrogative, and negative interrogative forms of the *passé composé* of verbs conjugated with *être* are:

   | | |
   |---|---|
   | Elle n'est pas partie. | *She didn't leave.* |

Elle est partie?

Est-elle partie?          } *Did she leave?*

Est-ce qu'elle est partie?

Elle n'est pas partie?

Est-ce qu'elle n'est pas partie?  } *Didn't she leave?*

## EXERCICE A

**Say where the following people went on Bastille Day** *(le 14 juillet).*

EXEMPLE:     je / en ville
Je **suis allé(e)** en ville.

nous (Hervé et Marie) / au cinéma
Nous **sommes allés** au cinéma.

*1.* je / à la tour Eiffel

_____

*2.* les Dupont / à Montmartre

_____

*3.* tu (Henri) / sur les quais de la Seine

_____

*4.* vous (Hector et Jacques) / à une fête

_____

*5.* nous (trois copines) / à la place de la Bastille

_____

*6.* Catherine et Isabelle / chez des amies.

_____

## EXERCICE B

*Dites quand les personnes suivantes sont sorties.*

EXEMPLE:     je / à midi
Je **suis sorti(e)** à midi.

vous (Lucy et sa tante) / de bonne heure
Vous **êtes sorties** de bonne heure.

*1.* François / à cinq heures

_____

*2.* tu (Rosa) / trop tard

_____

*3.* nous (les Martin) / très tôt le matin

_____

*4.* Joseph et Claude / dans l'après-midi

_____

*5.* vous (quatre cousines) / à minuit

_____

*6.* Catherine / à six heures du soir

_____

## EXERCICE C

**Say at what time the guests came to Liliane's party.** *Suivez l'exemple.*

EXEMPLE: Lise **est venue à neuf heures.**

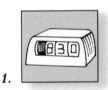

*1.* Jack _____ .

*2.* Nous, (Rosa et Michael) _____ .

*3.* Tu (Anne) _____ .

*4.* Vous (les Martin) _____ .

**5.** Je _____ .

**6** Gina et Claire _____ .

## EXERCICE D

**Yesterday was a holiday, and everyone had the day off. Explain what the following people did.** *Employez les suggestions données.*

aller au zoo
descendre en ville
partir pour la campagne
rentrer tard le soir

rester au lit
retourner à un musée favori
sortir avec des copains

EXEMPLES: Toute la famille **est descendue** en ville.
    OR: Clara et Liz **sont descendues** en ville.

**1.** Les filles Birot _____ .

**2.** Tu (Jim) _____ .

**3.** Colette _____ .

**4.** Je _____ .

**5.** Bernard et Richard _____ .

**6.** Andrew et moi _____ .

## EXERCICE E

**Your friend moved to a new neighborhood. When you meet again, he / she has many questions for you.** *Répondez négativement.*

EXEMPLE: Est-ce que Jean Legrand est resté dans le quartier?
    Non, **il n'est pas resté** dans le quartier.

**1.** Es-tu arrivé(e) à apprendre à patiner?

_____

**2.** Est-ce que les grands-parents de Sylvie sont venus en France?

_____

*3.* Est-ce que Mme Cassard et sa fille sont parties pour l'Angleterre?

_____

*4.* Chantal et toi, vous êtes sorti(e)s ensemble?

_____

*5.* Est-ce que Lise Martin est devenue professeur?

_____

*6.* M. Smith est rentré aux États-Unis?

_____

## EXERCICE F

**You just came back from vacation. Your friend wants to know all about your trip.** *Exprimez ses questions et vos réponses.*

EXEMPLE:     aller à la montagne (non)
             **Es-tu allé(e)** à la montagne?
             Non, **je ne suis pas allé(e)** à la montagne.

*1.* partir en bateau (non)

_____

_____

*2.* sortir avec tes parents (oui)

_____

_____

*3.* descendre en ville (non)

_____

_____

*4.* aller à la plage tous les jours (oui)

_____

_____

*5.* devenir expert(e) en ski nautique (non)

_____

_____

*6.* arriver à apprendre à faire du surf? (oui)

_____

_____

## EXERCICE G

**Your friend wants to confirm what happened at a party you both attended.** *Exprimez ses questions comme dans l'exemple.*

EXEMPLE:   Paul et moi / venir à l'heure
   **Est-ce que Paul et moi ne sommes pas venus** à l'heure?

*1.* Louise / rester avec Robert

_____

*2.* Pierre et moi / arriver à très bien danser ensemble

_____

*3.* tu / sortir prendre l'air

_____

*4.* Marc et Michel / devenir jaloux

_____

*5.* Lucie / tomber amoureuse de Claude

_____

*6.* Chantal et Christine / partir à minuit

_____

## MASTERY EXERCISES

## EXERCICE H

**Describe a trip you took.** *Répondez aux questions en employant le passé composé.*

*1.* Où es-tu allé(e)?

_____

*2.* Avec qui es-tu parti(e)?

_____

*3.* Quand êtes-vous arrivé(e)s?

_____

*4.* À quel hôtel êtes-vous descendu(e)s?

_____

*5.* Qu'est-ce que vous avez visité?

_____

*6.* Qu'est-ce que tu as acheté comme souvenir?

_____

*7.* De quoi as-tu pris des photos?

_____

*8.* Quand êtes-vous rentré(e)s?

_____

## EXERCICE I

**Complete the following sentences about what you did, using the verbs given in parentheses. Choose the appropriate helping verb.** *Suivez les exemples.*

EXEMPLES:  Pendant le week-end **je suis resté(e)** à la maison.
    *OR:*  Pendant le week-end **j'ai lu** trois romans policiers.

*1.* Pendant le week-end *(sortir)* _____ .

*2.* Samedi passé *(aller)* _____ .

*3.* Hier *(rester)* _____ .

*4.* La semaine dernière *(étudier)* _____ .

*5.* Ce matin *(déjeuner)* _____ .

*6.* L'année dernière *(travailler)* _____ .

## EXERCICE J

**Tell five things you did and five things you didn't do last week. Be careful to use the appropriate helping verb.** *Suivez l'exemple.*

        acheter un cadeau à une amie      jouer au tennis
        aller chez le dentiste             patiner
        arriver à l'école en retard        revenir tard le soir
        choisir d'aller voir un film       téléphoner à vos grands-parents
        descendre en ville             voir des amis
        faire des courses

EXEMPLE:  jouer au tennis
        **J'ai joué** au tennis.
    *OR:*  **Je n'ai pas joué** au tennis.

*1.* _____

*2.* _____

*3.* _____

*4.* _____

**5.** _____

**6.** _____

**7.** _____

**8.** _____

**9.** _____

**10.** _____

## EXERCICE K

**Exprimez en français ce que vous avez fait hier.** _Employez le passé composé._

**1.** Yesterday I went to buy a Walkman.

_____

**2.** I arrived at the store at 9:00.

_____

**3.** They opened the doors immediately, and I was able to enter.

_____

**4.** I saw an advertisement in the newspaper, and I chose the same Walkman.

_____

**5.** They told me the price and I paid.

_____

**6.** I went out of the store very happy.

_____

**7.** I went back home, I went upstairs, I entered my room, and I put a cassette in the Walkman.

_____

_____

**8.** The Walkman didn't work, so I left immediately.

_____

**9.** I returned to the store with the Walkman.

_____

**10.** They kept my money, but they gave me another Walkman.

_____

# Chapter 10
## Imperfect Tense

## [ 1 ]  REGULAR VERBS

The imperfect tense (*l'imparfait*) of regular verbs is formed by dropping the *-ons* ending of the *nous* form of the present tense and adding the imperfect tense endings (*ais, ais, ait, ions, iez, aient*).

| **danser** *to dance* | **rougir** *to blush* | **vendre** *to sell* |
|---|---|---|
| **nous dansons** | **nous rougissons** | **nous vendons** |
| *I danced, I was dancing I used to dance, etc.* | *I blushed, I was blushing I used to blush, etc.* | *I sold, I was selling I used to sell, etc.* |
| je dans*ais* <br> tu dans*ais* <br> il / elle dans*ait* <br> nous dans*ions* <br> vous dans*iez* <br> ils / elles dans*aient* | je rougiss*ais* <br> tu rougiss*ais* <br> il / elle rougiss*ait* <br> nous rougiss*ions* <br> vous rougiss*iez* <br> ils / elles rougiss*aient* | je vend*ais* <br> tu vend*ais* <br> il / elle vend*ait* <br> nous vend*ions* <br> vous vend*iez* <br> ils / elles vend*aient* |

NOTE:

1. Verbs ending in *-ions* and *-iez* in the present tense end in *-iions* and *-iiez* in the imperfect tense: *nous étudiions, vous étudiiez.*

2. Negative, interrogative, and negative interrogative constructions in the imperfect follow the same rules as in the present tense.

| Pierre ne chantait pas. | *Pierre was not singing.* |
|---|---|
| Elle rougissait? | *Was she blushing?* |
| Attendiez-vous le soleil? | *Were you waiting for the sun?* |
| Est-ce que Michel jouait? | *Did Michel play? (Was Michel playing?)* |
| Tu n'aimais pas jouer au basket? | *Didn't you like to play basketball?* |
| Est-ce qu'il ne chantait pas? | *Didn't he sing? (Wasn't he singing?)* |

## EXERCICE A

**At a high school reunion, some friends are remembering where they worked after school.** *Exprimez ce qu'ils disent.*

EXEMPLE:  ils / travailler à la fruiterie
Ils **travaillaient** à la fruiterie.

1. Louis et Georges / aider dans une pharmacie

_____

2. tu / nettoyer au supermarché

_____

*3.* Richard et moi / assister à l'hôpital

_____

*4.* je / cuisiner à la pâtisserie

_____

*5.* vous / travailler à la boucherie

_____

*6.* Jean / jouer de la guitare dans un café

_____


## EXERCICE B

**André and some of his friends have given up sweets.** *Dites ce qu'ils avaient l'habitude de choisir comme dessert.*

| | | |
|---|---|---|
| de la crème caramel | des bonbons | des tartes à la crème |
| de la glace | des profiteroles | du chocolat |
| de la mousse au chocolat | | |

EXEMPLE:   Pierre **choisissait** de la glace.

*1.* Thomas _____ .

*2.* Carole et moi _____ .

*3.* Arthur et Nicolas _____ .

*4.* Tu _____ .

*5.* Vous _____ .

*6.* Je _____ .


## EXERCICE C

**Some friends are discussing what they used to sell in the flea market.** *Exprimez ce qu'ils disent.*

EXEMPLE:              Jean **vendait des plantes vertes.**

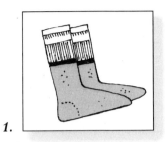

**1.** Suzanne et Laurent _____.

**2.** Je _____.

**3.** Tu _____.

**4.** Gilles _____.

**5.** Vous _____.

**6.**            Paul et moi _____.

## EXERCICE D

**Roger describes what his life was like when he was ten years old.** *Exprimez ce qu'il dit en employant l'imparfait.*

EXEMPLE:     je / habiter à Paris
                 **J'habitais** à Paris

**1.** mon père / parler beaucoup avec moi

_____

**2.** mes frères / jouer au football avec moi

_____

**3.** ma mère / travailler

_____

**4.** toute la famille / visiter mes grands-parents le samedi

_____

**5.** ma grand-mère / attendre nos visites avec impatience

_____

**6.** mes frères et moi / obéir toujours à nos parents

_____

**7.** je / correspondre avec un garçon au Canada

_____

**8.** mes sœurs / rougir tout le temps

_____

## EXERCICE E

**Your little brother asks your grandfather questions about his life. Write the answers to his questions.** *Employez l'imparfait et les indications données.*

EXEMPLE:     Où habitais-tu à mon âge? (un petit village)
                 **J'habitais** un petit village.

**1.** Quels jeux aimais-tu? (les jeux de cartes)

_____

**2.** Tes frères et toi, à quel sport jouiez-vous? (au base-ball)

_____

**3.** Quel sujet préférais-tu à l'école? (l'histoire)

_____

**4.** Avec qui correspondais-tu? (avec ta grand-mère)

_____

**5.** Qui aidais-tu? (tout le monde)

_____

**6.** Quel genre de livre choisissais-tu? (des livres d'aventures)

_____

## [ 2 ]  SPELLING CHANGES IN CERTAIN -*ER* VERBS

**a.** Verbs ending in -*cer* change *c* to *ç* before *a* to keep the soft *c* sound.

| **avancer**  *to advance, move forward* | |
|---|---|
| j'avan*çais* | **nous avancions** |
| **tu avan*çais*** | **vous avanciez** |
| **il/elle avan*çait*** | **ils/elles avan*çaient*** |

**b.** Verbs ending in -*ger* insert silent *e* between *g* and *a* to keep the soft *g* sound.

| **manger**  *to eat* | |
|---|---|
| **je man*geais*** | **nous mangions** |
| **tu man*geais*** | **vous mangiez** |
| **il / elle man*geait*** | **ils / elles man*geaient*** |

## EXERCICE F

**Say what used to happen in Mme Barrat's French class.** *Mettez le verbe approprié à l'imparfait.*

| | | |
|---|---|---|
| annoncer | lancer | placer |
| effacer | menacer | prononcer |

**1.** Tu _____ mal les mots.

**2.** Les garçons _____ des papiers dans la corbeille.

**3.** Je (J') _____ le tableau.

4. Clara et moi _____ nos bandes dessinées dans nos pupitres.

5. Le professeur _____ les examens au dernier moment.

6. Vous _____ de ne pas faire les devoirs.

## EXERCICE G

**Tell what these people did habitually in the past.** *Employez l'imparfait.*

1. Luc et moi / nager dans l'équipe de notre école

_____

2. tu / manger au même restaurant tous les jours

_____

3. je / songer à devenir astronaute

_____

4. vous / déménager chaque année

_____

5. Lily et Patricia / voyager à travers le monde

_____

6. M. Jouet / diriger les affaires d'une grande société

_____

## [ 3 ] IMPERFECT OF IRREGULAR VERBS

The imperfect of irregular verbs, with few exceptions, is formed in the same way as the imperfect of regular verbs.

| INFINITIVE | PRESENT *nous* FORM | IMPERFECT |
|---|---|---|
| **avoir** *to have* | avons | j'avais, tu avais, il / elle avait<br>nous avions, vous aviez, ils / elles avaient |
| **aller** *to go* | allons | j'allais, tu allais, il / elle allait<br>nous allions, vous alliez, ils / elles allaient |
| **faire** *to do* | faisons | je faisais, tu faisais, il / elle faisait<br>nous faisions, vous faisiez, ils / elles faisaient |
| **venir** *to come* | venons | je venais, tu venais, il / elle venait<br>nous venions, vous veniez, ils / elles venaient |
| **voir** *to see* | voyons | je voyais, tu voyais, il / elle voyait<br>nous voyions, vous voyiez, ils / elles voyaient |

NOTE: In the imperfect, *être* (to be) adds regular endings to an irregular stem.

| | |
|---|---|
| j'étais | nous étions |
| tu étais | vous étiez |
| il / elle était | ils / elles étaient |

## EXERCICE H

**Explain how these people felt in the following circumstances.** *Employez l'imparfait.*

EXEMPLE:   Pauline a gagné un prix. (contente)
  **Elle était** contente.

*1.* Jean allait passer un examen. (nerveux)

_____

*2.* J'avais peur de ne pas réussir. (anxieux)

_____

*3.* Janine et moi, nous allions être en retard. (pressés)

_____

*4.* Vous avez perdu votre portefeuille. (triste)

_____

*5.* Tu as trouvé un billet de cent francs. (heureux)

_____

*6.* Les garçons ont perdu le match. (fâchés)

_____

## EXERCICE I

**Who used to do this?** *Employez l'imparfait dans vos réponses.*

aller au cirque au printemps
dire la vérité à tout le monde
écrire des articles pour le journal de l'école
étudier jusqu'à trois heures du matin

faire du ski nautique chaque été
lire des poèmes d'amour à haute voix
prendre une limousine pour aller à une fête
regarder le coucher du soleil

*1.* Tu _____ .

*2.* Nous _____ .

*3.* Monique _____ .

*4.* Daniel et Denis _____ .

**5.** Vous _____ .

**6.** Je _____ .

**7.** Yvette et Maria _____ .

**8.** José _____ .

## [ 4 ] USES OF THE IMPERFECT

The imperfect tense expresses actions, circumstances, events, and situations that are continuous, repeated, or habitual in the past.

**a.** The imperfect describes what was happening, used to happen, or happened repeatedly in the past.

| | |
|---|---|
| Les enfants jouaient. | *The children were playing.* |
| J'habitais Paris. | *I lived (used to live) in Paris.* |
| Elle lisait un livre chaque jour. | *She read (would read, used to read) a book every day.* |

NOTE: The imperfect tense is usually equivalent to English *was / were* + *-ing* form of the verb and to English *used to,* and *would* (meaning *used to*).

**b.** The imperfect describes persons, things, or conditions in the past.

| | |
|---|---|
| Il était beau. | *He was handsome.* |
| La fenêtre était ouverte. | *The window was open.* |
| Il faisait froid. | *It was cold.* |

**c.** The imperfect is used to express the day, the month, and the time of day in the past.

| | |
|---|---|
| C'était samedi. | *It was Saturday.* |
| C'était le mois de juin. | *It was June.* |
| Il était neuf heures. | *It was nine o'clock.* |

**d.** The imperfect describes a situation or circumstance that was going on in the past when some single action or event occurred; this action or event is expressed in the *passé composé.*

| | |
|---|---|
| Je réparais le moteur quand le téléphone a sonné. | *I was fixing the motor when the telephone rang.* |
| Il pleuvait quand j'ai ouvert la porte. | *It was raining when I opened the door.* |

NOTE: Two actions going on simultaneously in the past are both expressed in the imperfect.

| | |
|---|---|
| Il jouait pendant que j'étudiais. | { *He played while I studied.* <br> *He was playing while I was studying.* |
| Pendant que je parlais, elle riait beaucoup. | *While I was talking, she was laughing a lot.* |

## EXERCICE J

**Describe what the Moreaus used to do.** *Employez l'imparfait.*

| | |
|---|---|
| aller au cinéma le samedi soir | voir les matches de football le samedi |
| partir à la campagne le week-end | faire un voyage à l'étranger pendant l'été |
| recevoir de bonnes notes à l'école | prendre la nouvelle voiture tout le temps |

*1.* Je _____ .

*2.* Cécile et Odette _____ .

*3.* Tu _____ .

*4.* Papa _____ .

*5.* Vous _____ .

*6.* Maman et moi _____ .

## EXERCICE K

**M. Chabrol just bought a new video camera. His daughter Catherine is describing what his first video showed.** *Employez l'imparfait.*

EXEMPLE:    les oiseaux / voler dans le ciel
            Les oiseaux **volaient** dans le ciel.

*1.* il / neiger

_____

*2.* le ciel / être gris

_____

*3.* Claudine / avoir froid

_____

*4.* je / bâtir un bonhomme de neige

_____

*5.* Pierre et Jacques / jeter des boules de neige

_____

*6.* François / faire du patin à glace

_____

*7.* tu / manger un cornet de neige

_____

*8.* Maman et moi / préparer du chocolat

_____

## EXERCICE L

**What was everybody doing during the following weather conditions?** *Employez l'imparfait dans vos réponses.*

EXEMPLE: Il **allait** au cinéma quand **il pleuvait.**

Nous _____

_____ .

1.

Elle _____

_____ .

2.

Vous _____

_____ .

3.

Je _____

_____ .

4.

5. Ils _____

_____ .

Tu _____

6. _____ .

## EXERCICE M

**How were the following people interrupted in what they were doing?** *Employez l'imparfait et le passé composé.*

EXEMPLE:   je / parler au téléphone / mon père / dire bonjour
Je **parlais** au téléphone quand mon père **a dit** bonjour.

1. Hélène / sortir / le téléphone / sonner

_____

2. ma mère / faire le dîner / elle / voir une souris

_____

3. je / regarder la télévision / je / entendre mes amis dehors

_____

_____

4. Vincent et moi / faire une promenade / il / commencer à pleuvoir

_____

_____

5. tu / avancer vers la maison / Janine / ouvrir la porte

_____

_____

6. ils / lire un livre / maman / téléphoner

_____

**7.** Jean et Georges / patiner sur le lac / la glace / craquer

_____

_____

**8.** les filles / rôtir un poulet / leurs invités / sonner à la porte

_____

_____

## EXERCICE N

**Who was your hero or heroine when you were younger?** _Décrivez-le (la) en employant l'imparfait._

EXEMPLE:    Mon héroïne **était** ma tante. **Elle était** grande et **elle avait** les cheveux noirs. **Elle cuisinait** très bien et **nous passions** de très bons moments ensemble.

_____

_____

_____

_____

_____

## MASTERY EXERCISES

## EXERCICE O

**Using the expressions given, describe what each person used to do.** _Employez l'imparfait._

| | | |
|---|---|---|
| chaque après-midi | le samedi matin | trois fois par jour |
| deux fois par semaine | le week-end | tous les jours |
| le mercredi | | |

EXEMPLE:

Les jeunes filles **jouaient au volley-ball le mercredi.**

**1.**

Je _____.

**2.**

Jacques et moi _____.

**3.**

Vous _____.

**4.**

Tu _____.

**5.**

M. Robert _____ .

**6.**

Les garçons _____ .

## EXERCICE P

**Rewrite the story in the imperfect tense.**

C'**est** la fin du semestre. Il **est** une heure du matin. J'**ai** une composition à écrire pour ma classe d'anglais. Je **songe** au sujet qui n'**est** pas du tout intéressant. Je **passe** beaucoup de temps à marcher de long en large dans ma chambre. De temps en temps je **mange** des chips et des biscuits. J'**espère** trouver de l'inspiration. Malheureusement, l'inspiration nécessaire ne **vient** pas à mon esprit. Je ne **sais** pas pourquoi. Je **réussis** toujours dans cette classe. D'habitude j'**écris** d'excellentes compositions. J'**ai** de très bonnes notes et je **fais** de grands progrès. Je **saisis** chaque occasion de parler anglais. Le professeur **dit** que je **suis** un excellent élève. Pourquoi est-ce qu'il **est** tellement impossible d'écrire quelque chose de brillant? Il **est** quatre heures, cinq heures, six heures du matin. Ma mère **entre** dans ma chambre pendant que mon réveil **sonne**. Elle **dit** que je **rêve** et que je **vais** être en retard pour le déjeuner chez grand-mère. C'**est** dimanche.

_____

_____

_____

_____

_____

_____

_____

_____

_____

_____

_____

_____

_____

_____

_____

_____

_____

_____

_____

## EXERCICE Q

**Daniel's father tells him about his youth.** *Exprimez ce qu'il dit en français.*

1. When I was your age, I was very responsible.

   _____

2. I used to study and work.

   _____

3. I wanted to buy a car.

   _____

4. I needed money because I had a girlfriend, Lisette.

   _____

5. She was very pretty, and she liked to dance.

   _____

6. Saturday nights, we went to a discotheque.

   _____

7. We used to go to a lot of parties and soccer games, too.

_____

8. Lisette's parents were very strict, and we couldn't go out alone.

_____

9. Lisette's younger sister, who cried a lot, used to go with us.

_____

10. I wasn't happy, but I liked Lisette a lot.

_____

11. We always obeyed our parents.

_____

12. Life was different when I was your age.

_____

# Chapter 11
## Future Tense

## [ 1 ] ALLER + INFINITIVE

In French as in English, the near future may be expressed with a form of the present tense of the verb *aller* (to be going to) plus the infinitive.

| | |
|---|---|
| Je vais danser. | *I'm going to dance.* |
| Je vais aller au cinéma. | *I'm going to go to the movies.* |

The negative construction is:

| | |
|---|---|
| Je ne vais pas aller au cinéma. | *I am not going to go to the movies.* |

The interrogative constructions are:

| | |
|---|---|
| Tu vas jouer au tennis? | *Are you going to play tennis?* |
| Qu'est-ce que tu vas faire? | *What are you going to do?* |
| Où vas-tu aller? | *Where are you going to go?* |

## EXERCICE A

Georges is curious about what his friends are going to do after school. *Écrivez ses questions et les réponses de ses amis.*

EXEMPLE:  tu / jouer au football
**Tu vas** jouer au football?

Oui, **je vais** jouer au football.
OR:    Non, **je ne vais pas** jouer au football.

*1.* Denis et Paul / écouter des disques

_____

_____

*2.* Luz / lire un livre

_____

_____

*3.* tu / rester à la maison

_____

_____

*4.* Miguel et vous / jouer du piano

_____

_____

5. Fatimah / participer au cercle français

_____

_____

6. vous et moi / aller au concert

_____

_____

7. tu / écrire à ton correspondant français

_____

_____

8. Marie et Suzanne / faire des courses

_____

_____


## EXERCICE B

**What jobs are the following people sure they are not going to do?** *Employez* **aller** *et l'infinitif.*

diriger les affaires d'une grande société      parler au téléphone toute la journée
garder les enfants                             travailler dans un supermarché
laver les voitures                             vendre dans un magasin
nettoyer les maisons des autres

EXEMPLE:    Paul **ne va pas vendre** dans un magasin.

1. Je _____ .

2. Vous _____ .

3. Les garçons _____ .

4. Claire et moi _____ .

5. Tu _____ .

6. Marianne _____ .


## EXERCICE C

**It's the end of the day. Tell what you, your family, and your friends are going to do now.** *Écrivez six phrases selon l'exemple.*

EXEMPLE:    **Paul va dormir.**

1. _____

*2.* _____

*3.* _____

*4.* _____

*5.* _____

*6.* _____

## EXERCICE D

**The weather often affects what we are going to do.** *Dites ce que vous allez faire dans les circonstances suivantes.*

EXEMPLE:   S'il fait frais, **je vais jouer au football.**

*1.*   S'il fait du soleil, _____ .

*2.*   S'il fait froid, _____ .

*3.*   S'il pleut, _____ .

4. S'il fait chaud, _____.

5. S'il neige, _____.

6. S'il fait beau, _____.

## [ 2 ] FUTURE TENSE OF REGULAR VERBS

The future tense is formed by adding the following endings to the infinitive: *-ai, -as, -a, -ons, -ez, -ont.*

| **parler** *to speak* | **choisir** *to choose* | **vendre** *to sell* |
|---|---|---|
| *I will / shall speak* | *I will / shall choose* | *I will / shall sell* |
| je **parlerai** | je **choisirai** | je **vendrai** |
| tu **parleras** | tu **choisiras** | tu **vendras** |
| il / elle **parlera** | il / elle **choisira** | il / elle **vendra** |
| nous **parlerons** | nous **choisirons** | nous **vendrons** |
| vous **parlerez** | vous **choisirez** | vous **vendrez** |
| ils / elles **parleront** | ils / elles **choisiront** | ils / elles **vendront** |

NOTE:

1. Verbs ending in *-re* drop the final *e* before the future ending.

   vendre    je vendrai                    prendre    je prendrai

2. Negative, interrogative, and negative interrogative constructions in the future follow the same rules as in the present tense.

   Je ne parlerai pas avec Nicole.        *I will not speak with Nicole.*

Tu parleras avec Nicole?

Est-ce que tu parleras avec Nicole? } *Will you speak with Nicole?*

Parleras-tu avec Nicole?

Vous ne vendrez pas la maison? *You won't sell the house?*

Est-ce que vous ne vendrez *Won't you sell the house?*
pas la maison?

## EXERCICE E

**What do the following people promise to do as part of their New Year's resolutions?** *Employez le futur.*

**1.** *(donner)* Larry et moi _____ nos vieux vêtements aux pauvres.

**2.** *(maigrir)* Suzanne _____ .

**3.** *(répondre)* Guy _____ poliment à tout le monde.

**4.** *(obéir)* Vous _____ toujours à vos parents.

**5.** *(perdre)* Catherine et Gina _____ leurs mauvaises habitudes.

**6.** *(prendre)* Tu _____ soin de ton petit frère.

**7.** *(ranger)* Je _____ régulièrement ma chambre.

**8.** *(mettre)* Carlos et Joseph _____ leurs affaires en ordre.

## EXERCICE F

**Un ami curieux vous pose des questions.** *Répondez-lui.*

**1.** Qu'est-ce que tu donneras à ton/ta meilleur(e) ami(e) comme cadeau d'anniversaire?

_____

**2.** Avec qui correspondras-tu plus tard?

_____

**3.** En quelle année finiras-tu tes études universitaires?

_____

**4.** À qui téléphoneras-tu ce soir?

_____

**5.** Où choisiras-tu de vivre?

_____

**6.** Où aimeras-tu voyager?

_____

# [ 3 ] SPELLING CHANGES IN THE FUTURE TENSE

**a.** Most verbs with infinitives ending in *-yer* change *y* to *i* in the future.

| ennuyer   *to annoy; to bore* | |
|---|---|
| j'ennuierai | nous ennuierons |
| tu ennuieras | vous ennuierez |
| il / elle ennuiera | ils / elles ennuieront |

| nettoyer   *to clean* | |
|---|---|
| je nettoierai | nous nettoierons |
| tu nettoieras | vous nettoierez |
| il / elle nettoiera | ils / elles nettoieront |

NOTE:

1. Verbs with infinitives ending in *-ayer* may or may not change the *y* to *i* in all future-tense forms.

   **payer**   *to pay*

   je paierai (payerai), tu paieras (payeras), il / elle paiera (payera),

   nous paierons (payerons), vous paierez (payerez), ils / elles paieront (payeront)

2. The verb *envoyer* is irregular in the future.

   **envoyer**   *to send*

   j'enverrai, tu enverras, il / elle enverra,

   nous enverrons, vous enverrez, ils / elles enverront

## EXERCICE G

**What will each student use to complete an art project?** *Employez le futur du verbe* employer.

*1.* Paul et moi _____ une gomme.

*2.* Vous _____ un stylo.

*3.* J'_____ une règle.

*4.* Tu _____ du papier.

*5.* Gilles _____ de l'encre.

*6.* Marie et Louise _____ un bâton de craie.

*7.* Daniel et toi, vous _____ des crayons de couleur.

**b.** Verbs with silent *e* in the syllable before the infinitive ending change silent *e* to *è* in the future.

| amener *to bring* | |
|---|---|
| j'amènerai | nous amènerons |
| tu amèneras | vous amènerez |
| il / elle amènera | ils / elles amèneront |

## EXERCICE H

What will you and your friends buy Henri as a going-away present? *Employez le futur.*

EXEMPLE: Les filles **lui achèteront une affiche.**

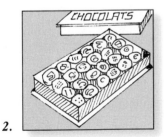

*1.* Lucie _____.

*2.* Nous _____.

*3.* Vous _____.

**4.** Les garçons _____.

**5.** Tu _____.

**6.** Je _____.

**c.** In the future, verbs like *appeler* and *jeter* double the consonant before the infinitive ending.

| appeler | *to call* |
|---|---|
| j'appellerai | nous appellerons |
| tu appelleras | vous appellerez |
| il / elle appellera | ils / elles appelleront |

| jeter | *to throw* |
|---|---|
| je jetterai | nous jetterons |
| tu jetteras | vous jetterez |
| il / elle jettera | ils / elles jetteront |

## EXERCICE I

**Describe what will happen at the class picnic.** *Employez le futur.*

| | |
|---|---|
| acheter des sandwiches | ennuyer Marc |
| amener un copain | essayer le pâté |
| appeler des amis à haute voix | jeter une balle |
| commencer à jouer de la guitare | manger beaucoup |

1. Je _____ .

2. Kadisha et Kim _____ .

3. Nous _____ .

4. Juliette _____ .

5. Vous _____ .

6. Pierre et Jules _____ .

7. Tu _____ .

8. Gilbert _____ .

## [ 4 ] VERBS IRREGULAR IN THE FUTURE

The following verbs have irregular stems in the future.

| INFINITIVE | FUTURE | INFINITIVE | FUTURE |
|---|---|---|---|
| **aller** *to go* | **j'irai** | **pouvoir** *to be able to* | **je pourrai** |
| **avoir** *to have* | **j'aurai** | **recevoir** *to receive* | **je recevrai** |
| **envoyer** *to send* | **j'enverrai** | **savoir** *to know* | **je saurai** |
| **être** *to be* | **je serai** | **venir** *to come* | **je viendrai** |
| **faire** *to do* | **je ferai** | **voir** *to see* | **je verrai** |
| **mourir** *to die* | **je mourrai** | **vouloir** *to want* | **je voudrai** |

## EXERCICE J

**What does Aunt Zoé predict for herself and the following people?** *Employez le futur.*

EXEMPLE:  tu / travailler dans une station-service
Tu **travailleras** dans une station-service.

1. je / faire le tour du monde

_____

2. Henri / être avocat

_____

3. vous / envoyer des fusées dans l'espace

_____

4. Chantal et Marie / vouloir quitter la France

_____

5. M. Legros / voir le président des États-Unis

_____

**6.** tu / savoir tout réussir

_____

**7.** le fils Vautrin / venir à Paris

_____

**8.** nous / recevoir une grosse somme d'argent

_____

**9.** Lise / avoir trois enfants

_____

**10.** Pierre et Lucien / aller en Afrique

_____

**11.** Mme Beaujour / mourir à l'âge de cent ans

_____

**12.** Claude et moi / pouvoir voyager beaucoup

_____

## EXERCICE K

**Catherine and Isabelle are talking about their summer plans.** _Exprimez ce qu'elles disent en mettant les verbes au futur._

— Cet été je _____ un grand voyage avec mes parents. Nous _____
            _1._ (faire)                                                   _2._ (aller)

  en Grèce. Mon frère François ne _____ pas.
                                          _3._ (venir)

— Où _____ François?
         _4._ (aller)

— Il _____ avec des copains camper à la montagne. Je _____ un
      _5._ (partir)                                          _6._ (être)

  peu triste sans lui, mais j'_____ beaucoup de plaisir avec mes parents.
                                 _7._ (avoir)

— Comment _____-vous?
               _8._ (voyager)

— Nous _____ l'avion, puis papa _____ une voiture. Nous
       _9._ (prendre)                                   _10._ (louer)

  _____ tous les endroits célèbres. Ensuite nous _____ sur un
     _11._ (visiter)                                      _12._ (monter)

  bateau et nous _____ par une croisière _(cruise)_ pour visiter les îles. Et toi,
               _13._ (finir)

Isabelle?  Que _____ -tu?
14. (faire)

—Je _____ visite à des amis de mes parents en Angleterre et puis je
15. (rendre)

_____ trois semaines dans une école internationale pour parler anglais.  Ma sœur
16. (passer)

Nicole _____ dans un magasin à Paris et maman _____ les
17. (travailler)                                                        18. (envoyer)

gosses, Chantal et Michel, en colonie de vacances.  Mes parents _____ ici.
19. (rester)

## M A S T E R Y   E X E R C I S E S

### EXERCICE L

**Where are the following people going to go, and what are they not going to do?** *Employez le futur comme l'exemple.*

| | |
|---|---|
| à la bibliothèque | lire longtemps |
| à la discothèque | danser |
| à la plage | nager |
| au cinéma | aimer le film |
| au concert | écouter la musique |
| au gymnase | jouer au basket-ball |
| au restaurant | dîner |
| au stade | participer à un match de football |
| au zoo | observer les animaux |

EXEMPLE:    Michel **va aller** à la bibliothèque, mais **il ne va pas lire** longtemps.

1. Joseph _____ .

2. Hervé et moi _____ .

3. Tu _____ .

4. Liliane et Marie _____ .

5. Vous _____ .

6. Je _____ .

7. Georges et Guy _____ .

8. Marthe _____ .

## EXERCICE M

**Consider the following developments and tell whether in the future they are likely or not. What is your opinion?** *Répondez affirmativement ou négativement en suivant les exemples.*

EXEMPLES:  les femmes / gagner plus d'argent
Oui, les femmes **gagneront** plus d'argent.
OR:  Non, les femmes **ne gagneront pas** plus d'argent.

le monde / avoir moins de problèmes
Oui, le monde **aura** moins de problèmes.
OR:  Non, le monde **n'aura pas** moins de problèmes.

*1.* les astronautes / faire plus d'explorations dans l'espace

_____

*2.* je / essayer plus de nouveaux produits alimentaires

_____

*3.* nous / envoyer moins d'aide aux pays pauvres

_____

*4.* les Américains / acheter moins de produits étrangers

_____

*5.* vous / manger plus de viande

_____

*6.* les gens / avoir moins de maladies contagieuses

_____

7. les hommes / protéger mieux l'environnement

_____

*8.* la société / employer moins d'énergie

_____

*9.* le monde / avoir plus de paix

_____

## EXERCICE N

**Your parents have found a house they like. Your father tells you about their plans.** *Exprimez ce qu'il dit.*

*1.* Your mother and I will buy the house with the large garden.

_____

*2.* We will pay a lot of money, but the house will be comfortable.

_____

3. We will move on August 7.

_____

4. You and your brother will see the house on Tuesday.

_____

5. You two will be very happy.

_____

6. We will have a swimming pool, and you will be able to swim every day.

_____

_____

7. We will send cards to all our friends.

_____

8. We will have a party for the whole family.

_____

9. It will be a big celebration.

_____

10. All our friends will come to see our house.

_____

# Chapter 12
## Reflexive Verbs

## [ 1 ] REFLEXIVE VERBS IN SIMPLE TENSES

**a.** In a reflexive construction, the action is performed by the subject on itself. The reflexive verb has a reflexive pronoun as its object. Thus, the subject and the pronoun object refer to the same person(s) or thing(s). The reflexive pronouns (*me, te, se, nous, vous*) generally precede the verb.

| PRESENT TENSE | | | |
|---|---|---|---|
| je | *me* | **lave** | *I wash (am washing) myself* |
| tu | *te* | **laves** | *you wash (are washing) yourself* |
| il / elle | *se* | **lave** | *he/she washes (is washing) himself/herself* |
| nous | *nous* | **lavons** | *we wash (are washing) ourselves* |
| vous | *vous* | **lavez** | *you wash (are washing) yourself/yourselves* |
| ils / elles | *se* | **lavent** | *they wash (are washing) themselves* |

| IMPERFECT TENSE | | | |
|---|---|---|---|
| je | *me* | **lavais** | *I washed (was washing) myself* |
| tu | *te* | **lavais** | *you washed (were washing) yourself* |
| il / elle | *se* | **lavait** | *he/she washed (was washing) himself/herself* |
| nous | *nous* | **lavions** | *we washed (were washing) ourselves* |
| vous | *vous* | **laviez** | *you washed (were washing) yourself/yourselves* |
| ils / elles | *se* | **lavaient** | *they washed (were washing) themselves* |

| FUTURE TENSE | | | |
|---|---|---|---|
| je | *me* | **laverai** | *I will wash myself* |
| tu | *te* | **laveras** | *you will wash yourself* |
| il / elle | *se* | **lavera** | *he/she will wash himself/herself* |
| nous | *nous* | **laverons** | *we will wash ourselves* |
| vous | *vous* | **laverez** | *you will wash yourself/yourselves* |
| ils / elles | *se* | **laveront** | *they will wash themselves* |

**b.** Negative, interrogative, and negative interrogative constructions follow the same rules as regular verbs. The reflexive pronouns remain before the verb.

| | |
|---|---|
| Ils ne se lèvent pas. | *They aren't getting up.* |
| Jeanne se lève? | *Is Jeanne getting up?* |
| Est-ce qu'il se lève tôt? | *Does he get up early?* |
| Se lèvent-ils? | *Are they getting up?* |
| Ils ne se lèvent pas? <br> Est-ce qu'ils ne se lèvent pas? } | *Aren't they getting up?* |
| Est-ce que tu t'amuses? | *Are you having a good time?* |
| T'amuses-tu toujours? | *Do you always have a good time?* |

| | |
|---|---|
| Tu ne t'amuses pas toujours. | *You don't always have a good time.* |
| Est-ce que les enfants s'amusent? | *Do the children have a good time?* |

### c. Common reflexive verbs

| | |
|---|---|
| s'amuser  *to have a good time, enjoy oneself* | se lever  *to get up; to rise* |
| s'appeler  *to be called* | se maquiller  *to put on make-up* |
| se brosser  *to brush oneself* | se mettre en route  *to start out* |
| se coucher  *to lie down; to go to bed* | se peigner  *to comb one's hair* |
| se dépêcher  *to hurry* | se préparer  *to prepare oneself* |
| se déshabiller  *to get undressed* | se promener  *to take a walk* |
| s'ennuyer  *to get bored* | se rappeler  *to remember* |
| s'habiller  *to get dressed* | se raser  *to shave oneself* |
| se laver  *to wash (oneself), get washed* | se réveiller  *to wake up* |

NOTE:

1. *Me, te,* and *se* become *m', t',* and *s'* before a verb beginning with a vowel or a silent *h: elle s'amuse* (she has fun); *je m'habille* (I dress myself).

2. Remember the spelling changes in the following reflexive verbs: *s'appeler (ll), s'ennuyer (uie), se lever (è), se promener (è).*

3. A verb that is reflexive in French is not necessarily reflexive in English.

| | |
|---|---|
| Nous nous habillons. | *We are getting dressed.* |
| Il se couche de bonne heure. | *He goes to bed early.* |
| Elle se lève. | *She gets up.* |

4. Some reflexive verbs may be used with a direct object in addition to the reflexive pronoun. This direct object often denotes a part of the body.

| | |
|---|---|
| Jeanne se lave. | *Jeanne washes herself.* |
| Jeanne se lave les mains. | *Jeanne washes her hands.* |

5. Most transitive verbs can become reflexive verbs when used with the reflexive pronoun.

| | |
|---|---|
| se donner  *to give oneself* | s'acheter  *to buy oneself (something)* |

## EXERCICE A

**Each person has a daily routine.** *Exprimez ce que chacun fait.*

EXEMPLE:  Nous / se brosser trois fois les dents
Nous **nous brossons** trois fois les dents.

*1.* je / s'habiller avec soin

**2.** Fabien / se laver avec de l'eau froide

_____

**3.** Marie et Louise / se brosser cent fois les cheveux

_____

**4.** tu / se lever à six heures

_____

**5.** nous / se coucher tard

_____

**6.** vous / se déshabiller vite

_____

**7.** Paco et Shaquille / se raser avant de manger

_____

**8.** Karin / se maquiller bien

_____

## EXERCICE B

**What will the following people not do while on vacation?** _Employez le futur._

EXEMPLE:     Jacques quittera l'hôtel à 11h du matin. (se mettre en route de bonne heure)
             **Il ne se mettra pas** en route de bonne heure.

**1.** Janine oubliera son rouge à lèvres. (se maquiller)

_____

**2.** Peter et Luc ne rencontreront pas de copains. (s'amuser)

_____

**3.** Je n'entendrai pas mon réveil. (se lever tôt)

_____

**4.** Nous serons toujours en retard. (se dépêcher)

_____

**5.** Tu danseras jusqu'à 2h du matin. (se coucher avant minuit)

_____

**6.** Karisma et vous sortirez tous les soirs. (s'ennuyer)

_____

## EXERCICE C

**You are trying to remember what you and your friends used to do at camp.** *Employez l'imparfait pour exprimer vos questions.*

| | |
|---|---|
| Albert | s'amuser tous les jours |
| Andrew | s'ennuyer tout le temps |
| Annick | s'habiller sans faire attention |
| Janine et Anne | se brosser rarement les dents |
| Robert et moi | se coucher très tôt |
| tu | se maquiller jour et nuit |
| vous | se promener tard le soir |

EXEMPLE: Est-ce qu'Albert **se couchait** très tôt?

1. _____

2. _____

3. _____

4. _____

5. _____

6. _____

## EXERCICE D

**Some of your friends are always late.** *Demandez-leur pourquoi.*

EXEMPLE: tu / se coucher trop tard
Tu **ne te couches pas** trop tard?

1. Berthe / se préparer à l'avance

   _____

2. tu / se réveiller tôt

   _____

3. Jean et Fabien / se lever tout de suite

   _____

4. vous / se mettre en route à l'heure

   _____

5. Nicolas / s'habiller rapidement

   _____

6. vous / se laver en cinq minutes

   _____

## [ 2 ] REFLEXIVE CONSTRUCTIONS WITH INFINITIVES

When used with an infinitive, the reflexive pronoun precedes the infinitive and agrees with the subject of the sentence.

Paul veut toujours **s'amuser.**          *Paul always wants to have fun.*

Je ne peux pas **me lever.**              *I cannot get up.*

Elle va **s'acheter** une robe.           *She is going to buy herself a dress.*

### EXERCICE E

You and your friends just came back from a picnic. *Dites ce que chacun veut faire maintenant.*

EXEMPLE:

Nous **voulons nous laver.**

**1.**

Louise _____ .

**2.**

Je _____ .

**3.**

Serge et Joseph _____ .

**4.**

Vous _____ .

**5.**

Tu _____ .

**6.**

Pedro et moi _____ .

## EXERCICE F

**You are on a camping trip with some friends.** *Exprimez ce que vous ne pouvez pas faire pendant ce voyage.*

EXEMPLE:    Lucie n'a pas de peigne. (se peigner)
Elle **ne peut pas se peigner.**

**1.** Jean est trop fatigué. (se réveiller)

_____

**2.** Je n'ai pas de brosse à dents. (se brosser les dents)

_____

**3.** Paul et moi n'avons pas de rasoir. (se raser)

_____

**4.** Vous avez peur du noir. (se coucher)

_____

**5.** Tu n'as pas de savon. (se laver)

_____

**6.** Les filles ont oublié leur rouge à lèvres. (se maquiller)

_____

## [ 3 ]  REFLEXIVE COMMANDS

In affirmative commands, reflexive pronouns follow the verb. After the imperative, *toi* is used instead of *te*. In negative commands, reflexive pronouns precede the imperative.

| AFFIRMATIVE IMPERATIVE | |
| --- | --- |
| **Lève-toi!** | *Get up!* |
| **Levez-vous!** | *Get up!* |
| **Levons-nous!** | *Let's get up!* |

| NEGATIVE IMPERATIVE | |
| --- | --- |
| **Ne te lève pas!** | *Don't get up!* |
| **Ne vous levez pas!** | *Don't get up!* |
| **Ne nous levons pas!** | *Let's not get up!* |

## EXERCICE G

You promised to wake up very early and help your father do some work around the house. You're tired, and you'd really like to stay in bed a little longer. *Exprimez le débat que vous avez avec votre conscience.*

EXEMPLE:  se réveiller
**Réveille-toi!** **Ne te réveille pas!**

*1.* se lever

_____

*2.* se dépêcher

_____

*3.* se laver

_____

*4.* se préparer

_____

*5.* s'habiller

_____

*6.* se peigner

_____

## EXERCICE H

Pierre has become very bossy, and he is ordering everybody around. What does he say to his friends? *Utilisez les suggestions ci-dessous.*

s'amuser se coucher se laver se raser
s'habiller se dépêcher se peigner

EXEMPLE:  Vous êtes décoiffé.
**Peignez-vous!**

*1.* Vous avez les mains sales.

_____

*2.* Vous êtes fatigué.

_____

*3.* Vous vous ennuyez.

_____

**4.** Vous êtes en pyjama à midi.

_____

**5.** Vous êtes en retard.

_____

**6.** Votre moustache est trop longue.

_____

## EXERCICE I

*Exprimez ce que Mme Dupont dit à ses filles de ne pas faire.*

EXEMPLE:     se maquiller dans la cuisine
             **Ne vous maquillez pas** dans la cuisine!

**1.** s'amuser dans le salon

_____

**2.** se brosser les dents dans la salle à manger

_____

**3.** se peigner dans la chambre

_____

**4.** se laver dans la cuisine

_____

**5.** se coucher dans la salle de séjour *(living room)*

_____

**6.** s'habiller dans la salle de bains

_____

## EXERCICE J

*Quelles suggestions faites-vous à votre ami(e) pour bien commencer la journée?*

EXEMPLES:     se réveiller à 6h (oui)
              **Réveillons-nous** à 6h!

              se réveiller à 6h (non)
              **Ne nous réveillons pas** à 6h!

**1.** se lever tout de suite (oui)

_____

**2.** se laver vite (oui)

_____

**3.** s'habiller lentement (non)

_____

**4.** se préparer un grand déjeuner (non)

_____

**5.** se brosser bien les dents (oui)

_____

**6.** se peigner pendant une demi-heure (non)

_____

**7.** se maquiller vite (oui)

_____

**8.** se mettre en route après deux heures (non)

_____

## MASTERY EXERCISES

### EXERCICE K

_Répondez à ces questions très personnelles._

**1.** Comment t'appelles-tu?

_____

**2.** À quelle heure te mets-tu en route pour l'école?

_____

**3.** Qu'est-ce que tu t'amuses à faire?

_____

**4.** À quelle heure te réveilles-tu le samedi matin?

_____

**5.** Quand te dépêches-tu?

_____

**6.** Combien de fois par jour te brosses-tu les dents?

_____

## EXERCICE L

**Catherine, Isabelle, and Lise are at a slumber party at Lise's house. It's morning.** *Complétez leur conversation avec les formes correctes des verbes indiqués.*

LISE: _____ , mes amies. Il est déjà neuf heures.
      *1. (se réveiller)*

ISABELLE: Je ne veux pas _____ tout de suite. _____ si tu
                        *2. (se lever)*                          *3. (se lever)*

veux. Moi, je reste au lit.

CATHERINE: Tant pis pour toi. Puisque je _____ la première, je peux
                                         *4. (se lever)*

_____ vite.
*5. (se laver)*

LISE: Pendant que tu _____ , je _____ . Isabelle,
                     *6. (se laver)*        *7. (se peigner)*

_____ . Vite, debout! Nous pouvons _____ ensemble.
*8. (se réveiller)*                                     *9. (se maquiller)*

ISABELLE: Vous pouvez _____ vous deux; moi, je _____ .
                      *10. (se préparer)*                          *11. (se coucher)*

CATHERINE: Ne _____ pas de nouveau. _____ et tu vas
              *12. (se coucher)*                        *13. (se laver)*

_____ . Tu vas voir.
*14. (se réveiller)*

LISE: Catherine, s'il te plaît, ne _____ pas ici dans la chambre.
                                   *15. (se maquiller)*

_____ dans la salle de bains.
*16. (se maquiller)*

CATHERINE: D'accord. Lise, tu _____ dans la salle de bains maintenant?
                              *17. (s'habiller)*

LISE: Non. Entre, si tu veux. Est-ce qu'Isabelle _____ de sortir du lit?
                                                 *18. (se dépêcher)*

CATHERINE: Je ne sais pas! Tu _____ ? Tu _____ ? Mais non!
                             *19. (se lever)*          *20. (se préparer)*

Regarde! Elle ne _____ pas! Cette fille est impossible. Qu'est-ce
                 *21. (se réveiller)*

qu'on va faire d'elle?

## EXERCICE M

**Janine describes a new friend.** *Exprimez en français ce qu'elle dit.*

**1.** Her name is Yvonne.

_____

**2.** She wakes up at seven o'clock.

_____

**3.** She washes, she gets dressed, and she brushes her hair and her teeth before breakfast.

_____

_____

**4.** She doesn't put on make-up.

_____

**5.** We don't like to start out for school before eight o'clock.

_____

**6.** Sometimes, she and I get bored in history class.

_____

**7.** The teacher says: "Yvonne and Janine, wake up!"

_____

**8.** We like to hurry to arrive home quickly.

_____

**9.** My parents always say: "Have a good time with Yvonne."

_____

_____

**10.** I will go to her house next week, we will have a good time, and we will go to bed very late.

_____

_____

_____

# Chapter 13
# Negation

## [ 1 ] NEGATIVE FORMS

**a.** The most common negatives are:

| | | | |
|---|---|---|---|
| ne… jamais | *never* | ne… plus | *no longer, no more* |
| ne… pas | *not* | ne… rien | *nothing, not . . . anything* |
| ne… personne | *no one, nobody* | | |

**b.** Position of negatives

In simple tenses and in the *passé composé, ne* comes before the conjugated verb and object pronouns, if there are any; the second part of the negative generally comes after the conjugated verb.

| | |
|---|---|
| Elle n'est **pas** contente. | *She isn't happy.* |
| Tu **ne** connais **pas** Lisa. | *You don't know Lisa.* |
| Nous n'avons **jamais** lu ce livre. | *We have never read that book.* |
| Ils **ne** veulent **rien** manger. | *They don't want to eat anything.* |
| Je **ne** connaissais **personne.** | *I didn't know anyone.* |
| Vous n'aurez **plus** de problèmes. | *You won't have any more problems.* |
| Tu n'as **rien** mangé? | *Didn't you eat anything?* |

NOTE: *Personne* follows the infinitive and the past participle.

| | |
|---|---|
| Je ne veux **voir personne.** | *I don't want to see anyone.* |
| Il n'a **vu personne.** | *He didn't see anyone.* |

## EXERCICE A

**Using *ne… pas,* say what these people are not doing.**

EXEMPLE:  Patricia / obéir à son frère tout le temps
Patricia **n'obéit pas** à son frère tout le temps.

*1.* vous / aller d'habitude au cinéma le week-end

_____

*2.* tu / sortir souvent avec tes amis

_____

*3.* Odette / préférer la musique rock

_____

*4.* Douglas et moi / manger beaucoup le matin

_____

149

**5.** je / faire le ménage tous les jours

_____

**6.** Charline et Grégoire / venir toujours en retard

_____

## EXERCICE B

**M. Richard is retiring, and his co-workers are throwing a farewell party for him.** *Employez l'imparfait et expliquez pourquoi.*

EXEMPLE:   ennuyer
        **Il n'ennuyait personne.**

**1.** irriter

_____

**2.** menacer

_____

**3.** trahir

_____

**4.** renvoyer

_____

**5.** punir

_____

**6.** déranger

_____

## EXERCICE C

**Pierre is in a bad mood and is accusing everybody, including himself, of various crimes and misdemeanors.** *Employez le passé composé et exprimez comment ses amis lui répondent.*

EXEMPLE:   Tu as pris mon argent.
        **Je n'ai jamais pris ton** argent.

**1.** Tu as lu mon journal intime.

_____

**2.** Claude est sorti avec ma petite amie!

_____

**3.** Claude et toi, vous êtes allés au cinéma sans moi!

_____

**4.** Nicole et François ont utilisé mon ordinateur.

_____

**5.** J'ai trahi mes amis.

_____

**6.** Papa et maman sont entrés dans ma chambre.

_____

**7.** Mes sœurs ont pris ma voiture!

_____

## EXERCICE D

**You and your friends say you will no longer do certain things.** *Employez le futur et les suggestions ci-dessous.*

| | | |
|---|---|---|
| critiquer les amis | être paresseux | parler toute la journée |
| désobéir | grossir | perdre patience |
| ennuyer les gens | | |

EXEMPLE:    Marc **ne critiquera plus** les amis.

**1.** Nous _____ .

**2.** Tu _____ .

**3.** Guy et Gilles _____ .

**4.** Vous _____ .

**5.** Lise _____ .

**6.** Je _____ .

## EXERCICE E

*Les personnes suivantes sont malades. Exprimez ce qu'elles ne font pas.*

EXEMPLE:    papa / pouvoir / sortir
           Papa **ne peut pas** sortir.

**1.** Sylvie et Charline / pouvoir / parler

_____

**2.** Denise et moi / vouloir / aller à l'école

_____

**3.** je / aller / faire le ménage

_____

**4.** vous / compter / jouer au tennis

_____

**5.** tu / aimer / beaucoup manger

_____

**6.** Richard / désirer / rester dans sa chambre

_____

## EXERCICE F

**You and your friends are being punished.** *Dites ce que vous ne pouvez pas faire.*

EXEMPLE:    Lucien (pas parler au téléphone)
            Lucien **ne peut pas** parler au téléphone.

**1.** je (rien regarder à la télévision)

_____

**2.** vous (plus écouter la radio)

_____

**3.** les garçons (voir personne)

_____

**4.** Régine (pas aller au cinéma)

_____

**5.** tu (jamais sortir seul)

_____

**6.** Christine et moi (rien acheter au magasin)

_____

> **c.** *Rien* and *personne* may be used as subjects, preceding the verb; *ne* remains before the conjugated verb.
>
> **Rien ne** m'intéresse.      *Nothing interests me.*
> **Personne n'**écoutait.      *Nobody was listening.*

## EXERCICE G

**M. Benoît is a pessimist.** *Exprimez ce qu'il pense.*

EXEMPLE:    intéressant
            **Rien n'est** intéressant.

**1.** facile

_____

**2.** amusant

_____

**3.** comique

_____

**4.** magnifique

_____

**5.** parfait

_____

**6.** joli

_____


## EXERCICE H

**Mme Charlier wanted to organize a talent show at the school, but there was a lack of enthusiasm.** _Expliquez pourquoi en employant l'imparfait._

EXEMPLE:     vouloir chanter
            **Personne ne voulait** chanter.

**1.** aimer danser

_____

**2.** désirer rester après les classes

_____

**3.** savoir organiser le spectacle

_____

**4.** avoir le temps de préparer le programme

_____

**5.** pouvoir aider avec la publicité

_____

**6.** vouloir participer

_____


> **d.** _Jamais_ used in the construction _ne... jamais_ or by itself means _never._ But _jamais_ in a clause without _ne_ means _ever._
>
> Non, je **ne** suis **jamais** allé en France.     _No, I've never gone to France._
> **Jamais?**                                          _Never?_
>
> Es-tu **jamais** allé en France?                    _Have you ever gone to France?_

## EXERCICE I

**You are playing "truth or dare" with a friend.** *Exprimez vos questions et ses réponses négatives, en employant le passé composé.*

EXEMPLE:   dépenser trop d'argent
**As-tu jamais dépensé** trop d'argent?
Non, **je n'ai jamais dépensé** trop d'argent.

*1.* trahir les amis

_____

_____

*2.* faire l'école buissonnière

_____

_____

*3.* voir un film interdit aux moins de dix-huit ans

_____

_____

*4.* désobéir aux parents

_____

_____

*5.* dire de terribles mensonges

_____

_____

*6.* danser jusqu'à quatre heures du matin

_____

_____

**e.** The second part of a negative may be used alone. (*Pas* and *plus* need a modifier.)

| | |
|---|---|
| Qui va t'accompagner? | *Who will go with you?* |
| **Personne.** | *Nobody.* |
| Qu'est-ce que tu manges? | *What are you eating?* |
| **Rien.** | *Nothing.* |
| Est-il allé en Floride? | *Did he go to Florida?* |
| **Jamais.** | *Never.* |
| Tu fais du vélo? | *Do you ride a bicycle?* |
| **Pas souvent.** | *Not often.* |

## EXERCICE J

*Répondez aux questions suivantes en employant un seul mot négatif.*

EXEMPLE:     Qui t'aide?
             **Personne.**

1. Quand vas-tu ranger ta chambre?

   _____

2. Qui t'a téléphoné hier soir?

   _____

3. Qu'est-ce que tu as acheté?

   _____

4. Qui sonne à la porte?

   _____

5. Qu'est-ce que tu veux faire?

   _____

6. Quand changeras-tu tes habitudes?

   _____

**f.** *Si* (yes) is used to contradict a negative statement or question.

| | |
|---|---|
| Il n'est pas intelligent. | *He isn't smart.* |
| **Si, il est très intelligent.** | *Yes, he's very smart.* |
| Elle ne travaille pas bien? | *Doesn't she work well?* |
| **Mais si!** | *Yes, she does!* |

## EXERCICE K

**A friend tries to find similarities between the two of you.** *Répondez affirmativement à ses questions.*

EXEMPLE:     Tu n'aimes pas les concerts de rock?
             **Mais si, j'aime** les concerts de rock.

1. Tu n'adores pas la mousse au chocolat?

   _____

2. Tu n'aimes pas aller à la plage?

   _____

3. Tu ne travailles pas après l'école?

   _____

**4.** Tu ne joues pas avec l'ordinateur?

_____

**5.** Tu ne lis pas les romans de science-fiction?

_____

**6.** Tu ne préfères pas jouer au tennis?

_____

## [ 2 ] COMMON NEGATIVE EXPRESSIONS

**ça ne fait rien** _it doesn't matter_
Il est parti sans nous.              _He left without us._
Ça ne fait rien.                     _It doesn't matter._

**de rien / il n'y a pas de quoi** _you're welcome_
Merci de ton aide.                   _Thank you for your help._
De rien.                             _You're welcome._

Merci beaucoup.                      _Thanks a lot._
Il n'y a pas de quoi.                _You're welcome._

**jamais de la vie!** _never! out of the question! not on your life!_
Voulez-vous une cigarette?           _Do you want a cigarette?_
Jamais de la vie!                    _Never!_

**pas du tout** _not at all_
Aimes-tu cette robe?                 _Do you like this dress?_
Pas du tout.                         _Not at all._

**pas encore** _not yet_
Est-il prêt?                         _Is he ready?_
Pas encore.                          _Not yet._

**pas maintenant** _not now_
Veux-tu voir ce film?                _Do you want to see this film?_
Pas maintenant.                      _Not now._

**pas aujourd'hui** _not today_
Tu viens chez moi?                   _Are you coming over?_
Pas aujourd'hui.                     _Not today._

## EXERCICE L

_**Employez une des expressions négatives ci-dessus (above) pour répondre aux situations suivantes.**_

**1.** Votre mère demande si vous avez déjà rangé votre chambre.

Vous répondez: _____

**2.** Votre amie vous dit merci de toute votre aide.

Vous répondez: _____

**3.** Votre sœur vous demande si vous voulez aller au cinéma, mais vous êtes trop fatigué(e).

Vous répondez: _____

**4.** Votre ami vous demande si ça vous ennuie qu'il écoute des disques quand vous parlez au téléphone.

Vous répondez: _____

**5.** Votre amie vous explique qu'elle ne peut pas vous accompagner au théâtre ce soir.

Vous répondez: _____

**6.** Votre ami vous demande si vous voulez acheter sa vieille voiture.

Vous répondez: _____

## M A S T E R Y   E X E R C I S E S

### EXERCICE M

*Répondez négativement aux questions de votre ami.*

**1.** Es-tu jamais allé(e) en Europe?

_____

**2.** Préfères-tu les histoires d'amour?

_____

**3.** As-tu perdu quelque chose?

_____

**4.** Menaces-tu toujours ton frère?

_____

**5.** Amènes-tu quelqu'un au bal?

_____

**6.** Vas-tu manger quelque chose?

_____

**7.** Aimais-tu faire du ski?

_____

**8.** As-tu jamais ennuyé tes amis?

_____

**9.** Arriveras-tu toujours en retard?

_____

**10.** Regardes-tu quelqu'un?

_____

## EXERCICE N

_Complétez l'histoire en ajoutant le mot négatif approprié._

Mme Chabrol n'aime _____ faire le ménage, _____ du tout.
                          1.                                    2.

«C'est ennuyeux!», dit elle. _____ ne l'aide avec les travaux ménagers. Son fils
                                     3.

François ne fait absolument _____ parce qu'il est toujours occupé avec ses amis.
                                   4.

Est-ce que sa fille Catherine range quelquefois sa chambre? Non! _____!
                                                                         5.

Autrefois, M. Chabrol aidait un peu sa femme, mais aujourd'hui il ne fait _____
                                                                                 6.

ce qu'il faisait alors. Un soir, Mme Chabrol déclare qu'elle ne fera _____ tout le
                                                                            7.

travail si les autres ne veulent _____ l'aider. Et un jour, les Chabrol rentrent et
                                        8.

_____ n'est heureux. La maison est sale. Ils demandent: «Pourquoi?» à Mme
       9.

Chabrol, mais elle ne dit _____ . Le jour suivant, quand elle se lève, elle voit
                                 10.

tout le monde en train de ranger la maison. Elle n'avait _____ cru cela possible.
                                                                 11.

_____ n'est plus heureux que Mme Chabrol ce jour-là.
       12.

## EXERCICE O

_Racontez l'histoire de Nicole en français._

**1.** François no longer wants to go out with his girlfriend Nicole.

_____

**2.** Nobody can help Nicole.

_____

**3.** Yesterday she couldn't eat anything.

_____

**4.** Nicole says it doesn't matter, but she isn't telling the truth.

_____

**5.** Has Nicole ever gone out with another boy? Never!

_____

**6.** Doesn't she want to forget François? Not yet.

_____

**7.** Will François change his mind? Out of the question.

_____

**8.** Their friends criticized no one.

_____

**9.** One friend asked: "Don't you love François anymore?"

_____

**10.** Nicole answered: "Yes, but I can't live with François, and I can't live without François!"

_____

_____

# Part two
# Noun Structures; Pronoun Structures; Prepositions

QUÉBEC

BELGIQUE

LUXEMBOURG

FRANCE

SUISSE

MONACO

SAINT-PIERRE-
ET-MIQUELON

CORSE

LOUISIANE

MAROC

TUNISIE

ALGÉRIE

HAÏTI

MAURITANIE

MALI

NIGER

TCHAD

GUADELOUPE
MARTINIQUE

SÉNÉGAL

GUINÉE

RÉPUBLIQUE
CENTRAFRICAINE

BURKINA FASO

GUYANE

CÔTE-D'IVOIRE

TOGO

BÉNIN

ZAÏRE

CAMEROUN

GABON

CONGO

# Chapter 14
## Definite Article and Nouns

## [ 1 ] FORMS OF THE DEFINITE ARTICLE

**a.** In English, the definite article is always *the*. In French, the definite article has four forms: *le, la, l', les.*

|  | MASCULINE | FEMININE |
|---|---|---|
| SINGULAR | *le* livre | *la* règle |
|  | *l'*étudiant | *l'*étudiante |
| PLURAL | *les* livres | *les* règles |
|  | *les* étudiants | *les* étudiantes |

NOTE:

1. The form *l'* is used before a singular noun of either gender beginning with a vowel or silent *h*.

   l'homme             *the man*

2. In French, the article is expressed before each noun, even though it may be omitted in English.

   **les** garçons et **les** filles      *boys and girls*

**b.** Contractions with the definite article:

The prepositions *à* and *de* contract with *le* and *les*, becoming *au* and *aux, du* and *des.*

à + **le** cousin = **au** cousin      *to the cousin*
à + **les** dames = **aux** dames      *to the ladies*
de + **le** cousin = **du** cousin      *of the cousin*
de + **les** dames = **des** dames      *of the ladies*

NOTE: There is no contraction with *la* or *l'*.

à **la** mère   *to the mother*      de **la** mère   *of the mother*
à **l'**élève   *to the student*      de **l'**élève   *of the student*

## EXERCICE A

**You are looking around the classroom.** *Dites ce que vous voyez.*

EXEMPLE:    bureau *(m.)* **Je vois le bureau.**

*1.* examen *(m.)* _____

*2.* devoirs *(m. pl.)* _____

*3.* livre *(m.)* _____

*4.* règle *(f.)* _____

5. cahiers *(m. pl.)* _____

6. stylo *(m.)* _____

7. exercice *(m.)* _____

8. leçon *(f.)* _____

9. crayons *(m. pl.)* _____

10. étudiante *(f.)* _____

11. tableau *(m.)* _____

12. craie *(f.)* _____

13. sac *(m.)* _____

14. élèves *(m. / f. pl.)* _____

15. classe *(f.)* _____

## [ 2 ] USES OF THE DEFINITE ARTICLE

The definite article is used when one wants to indicate a specific being or thing *(le chat)*, as in English *(the cat)*. It is also used in the following constructions where English does not use the article.

**a.** With nouns used in a general or abstract sense.

| | |
|---|---|
| **La vie** continue. | *Life goes on.* |
| J'aime **les chiens.** | *I like dogs.* |

**b.** With names of languages and school subjects, except directly after *parler*, after *en*, and in an adjective phrase with *de*.

| | |
|---|---|
| Étudiez-vous **le français?** | *Are you studying French?* |
| **Le japonais** n'est pas facile. | *Japanese isn't easy.* |
| Tu parles bien **l'italien.** | *You speak Italian well.* |
| Pierre adore **le dessin.** | *Pierre loves drawing.* |

*BUT*

| | |
|---|---|
| Je **parle espagnol.** | *I speak Spanish.* |
| Le roman est écrit **en russe.** | *The novel is written in Russian.* |
| Regarde mon livre **de français.** | *Look at my French book.* |
| Pierre est très fort **en dessin.** | *Pierre is very good in drawing.* |

**c.** In place of the possessive adjective, with parts of the body when the possessor is clear.

| | |
|---|---|
| Tourne **la tête.** | *Turn your head.* |
| Il a mal **au pied.** | *His foot hurts.* |

**d.** With days of the week in a plural sense.

Le dimanche je m'amuse.                *On Sunday(s) I have fun.*

L'école est fermée le samedi.          *School is closed on Saturday(s).*

**e.** With names of seasons except after the preposition *en*.

J'adore l'été.                         *I love (the) summer.*

En été et au printemps il fait beau.   *In summer and spring the weather is nice.*

**f.** In certain common expressions.

| | | | |
|---|---|---|---|
| à l'école | *to (in) school* | le week-end | *on the weekend* |
| à l'église | *to (in) church* | le mois prochain | *next month* |
| à la maison | *at home, home* | la semaine dernière | *last week* |
| le matin | *in the morning* | l'année passée | *last year* |
| l'après-midi | *in the afternoon* | l'été prochain | *next summer* |
| le soir | *in the evening* | | |

**g.** With dates.

C'est aujourd'hui dimanche, le onze juillet.     *Today is Sunday, July 11.*

On est le trois mai.                             *It's May 3.*

**h.** With names of most countries, except after the preposition *en*.

La France et l'Italie sont en Europe.    *France and Italy are in Europe.*

Je vais en France cet été.               *I go to France this summer.*

## EXERCICE B

**Fill in the definite article where it is necessary. If it is not necessary, leave a blank.**

PIERRE: Que fais-tu _____ week-end?
           *1.*

CLAUDE: Généralement _____ samedi matin, à _____ dix heures, je vais à _____
                        *2.*                       *3.*                              *4.*

Maison des Jeunes faire du karaté et apprendre à parler _____ japonais.
                                                            *5.*

_____ après-midi je reste à _____ maison faire _____ devoirs. Que fais-tu?
    *6.*                            *7.*                      *8.*

PIERRE: _____ natation me passionne. Je vais à _____ piscine couverte en ville et je
           *9.*                                        *10.*

nage pendant toute _____ matinée. _____ samedi après-midi je vais travailler
                       *11.*              *12.*

à _____ bibliothèque. Que fais-tu _____ dimanche?
     *13.*                                 *14.*

CLAUDE: Je me lève tôt. Je vais à _____ église; je déjeune en famille et je lis
15.

des livres de _____ science-fiction.
16.

PIERRE: Je me réveille à sept heures mais je referme tout de suite _____ yeux et je ne
17.

me lève pas avant midi. En _____ été je passe _____ après-midi à _____
18. 19. 20.

plage. En _____ hiver, je vais faire du patin à glace. Si tu veux, tu peux venir avec
21.

moi _____ dimanche prochain. Nous passerons _____ journée ensemble.
22. 23.

CLAUDE: Quelle est _____ date?
24.

PIERRE: C'est _____ douze juin.
25.

CLAUDE: Quelle bonne idée. Ça me fera plaisir.

## EXERCICE C

*Répondez aux questions d'un ami.*

**1.** Quelle langue parles-tu?

_____

**2.** Quand vas-tu généralement au cinéma?

_____

**3.** Quelle est la date d'aujourd'hui?

_____

**4.** Quelle saison aimes-tu?

_____

**5.** Quel cours aimes-tu à l'école?

_____

**6.** Que fais-tu l'après-midi?

_____

**7.** Quelles fleurs aimes-tu?

_____

**8.** Quel animal aimes-tu?

_____

## [ 3 ] GENDER OF NOUNS

French nouns are either masculine or feminine. There are no general rules to determine the gender of all nouns, but the gender of many nouns can be determined by their meaning or their ending. The gender of other nouns must be learned individually.

**a.** Nouns that refer to male beings are masculine. Nouns that refer to female beings are feminine.

| MASCULINE | | FEMININE | |
|---|---|---|---|
| l'homme | *man* | la femme | *woman* |
| le fils | *son* | la fille | *daughter* |
| le prince | *prince* | la princesse | *princess* |
| le dentiste | *dentist* | la dentiste | *dentist* |

**b.** The gender of some nouns may be determined by their ending.

| MASCULINE | | FEMININE | |
|---|---|---|---|
| -acle | spectacle | -ade | limonade |
| -age* | garage | -ale | cathédrale |
| -al | animal | -ance | distance |
| -eau* | bateau | -ence | essence |
| -et | livret | -ette | cassette |
| -ier | collier | -ie | compagnie |
| -isme | journalisme | -ique | gymnastique |
| -ment | gouvernement | -oire | histoire |
| | | -sion | expression |
| | | -tion | natation |
| | | -ure | figure |

**c.** Some feminine nouns are formed by adding *e* to the masculine.

| MASCULINE | FEMININE | |
|---|---|---|
| l'ami | l'amie | *friend* |
| l'avocat | l'avocate | *lawyer* |
| le client | la cliente | *client* |
| le cousin | la cousine | *cousin* |
| l'employé | l'employée | *employee* |
| l'étudiant | l'étudiante | *student* |
| le voisin | la voisine | *neighbor* |

**d.** Some feminine nouns are formed by changing the masculine ending to a feminine ending.

| MASCULINE | | FEMININE | | |
|---|---|---|---|---|
| -an | paysan | -anne | paysanne | *peasant* |
| -ien | Parisien | -ienne | Parisienne | *Parisian* |
| -on | patron | -onne | patronne | *boss* |
| -er | boulanger | -ère | boulangère | *baker* |

*Note these exceptions, which are all feminine: **la page, la plage; l'eau, la peau.**

| MASCULINE | | FEMININE | | |
|---|---|---|---|---|
| -ier | épicier | -ière | épicière | *grocer* |
| -eur | programmeur | -euse | programmeuse | *programmer* |
| -teur | acteur | -trice | actrice | *actress* |

**e.** Other masculine nouns and their feminine counterparts are:

| MASCULINE | | FEMININE | |
|---|---|---|---|
| le chat | *cat* | la chatte | *cat* |
| le chien | *dog* | la chienne | *dog* |
| l'hôte | *host* | l'hôtesse | *hostess* |
| le neveu | *nephew* | la nièce | *niece* |
| l'oncle | *uncle* | la tante | *aunt* |
| le roi | *king* | la reine | *queen* |

**f.** Some nouns have the same form in the masculine and the feminine.

| l'artiste | *artist* | l'enfant | *child* |
|---|---|---|---|
| le (la) camarade | *friend* | le (la) secrétaire | *secretary* |
| l'élève | *student* | le (la) touriste | *tourist* |

**g.** Some nouns are always masculine or feminine regardless of the gender of the person referred to.

| ALWAYS MASCULINE | | ALWAYS FEMININE | |
|---|---|---|---|
| l'agent de police | *police officer* | la personne | *person* |
| le bébé | *baby* | la victime | *victim* |
| le chef | *chef, cook, chief, head* | | |
| le médecin | *doctor* | | |
| le professeur | *teacher, professor* | | |

# EXERCICE D

*Exprimez qui est l'autre personne dans chacun des couples suivants.*

EXEMPLE:    la mère: **c'est le père**

**1.** la femme: _____

**2.** l'oncle: _____

**3.** le neveu: _____

**4.** la fille: _____

**5.** le grand-père: _____

**6.** le cousin: _____

**7.** l'enfant: _____

**8.** la camarade: _____

## EXERCICE E

**Both parents in each family work together. What is the job of the other parent?** *Suivez l'exemple.*

EXEMPLE:   M. Dumas est l'épicier de la ville.
Mme Dumas est **l'épicière** de la ville.

*1.* Mme Billet est la secrétaire du patron.

_____

*2.* M. Cavin est l'avocat de l'accusé.

_____

*3.* Mme Paillot est la pâtissière du restaurant.

_____

*4.* M. Lignon est le patron de la société.

_____

*5.* Mme Silvain est la mécanicienne du garage.

_____

## EXERCICE F

**Janine has to match the following words to the definitions below.** *Exprimez les mots qu'elle trouve avec l'article défini approprié.*

bateau *(m.)*        cathédrale *(f.)*        livret *(m.)*        oncle *(m.)*
boucher *(m.)*        garage *(m.)*        mère *(f.)*        pâtisserie *(f.)*
cassette *(f.)*        gymnastique *(f.)*        natation *(f.)*

EXEMPLE:   le mari de la tante: **l'oncle**

*1.* le petit livre: _____

*2.* le sport où l'on nage: _____

*3.* ce qui permet de voyager sur l'eau: _____

*4.* la femme du père: _____

*5.* le magasin où l'on achète des gâteaux: _____

*6.* l'homme qui vend la viande: _____

*7.* le lieu où l'on garde la voiture: _____

*8.* le sport où l'on fait des exercices: _____

*9.* ce qu'on met dans un baladeur: _____

*10.* une grande église: _____

# [ 4 ] PLURAL OF NOUNS

**a.** The plural of most French nouns is formed by adding *s* to the singular.

| SINGULAR | | PLURAL | |
|---|---|---|---|
| le garçon | *boy* | les garçons | *boys* |
| l'arbre *(m.)* | *tree* | les arbres | *trees* |
| la voiture | *car* | les voitures | *cars* |

**b.** Nouns ending in -*s*, -*x*, or -*z* remain unchanged in the plural.

| SINGULAR | | PLURAL | |
|---|---|---|---|
| le fils | *on* | les fils | *sons* |
| le prix | *price, prize* | les prix | *prices, prizes* |
| le nez | *nose* | les nez | *noses* |

Other nouns ending in -*s*:

| | | | | | |
|---|---|---|---|---|---|
| l'autobus | *bus* | la fois | *time* | le pays | *country* |
| le bras | *arm* | le mois | *month* | le repas | *meal* |

Other nouns ending in -*x*:

la croix *cross*      la voix *voice*

**c.** Nouns ending in -*eau* and -*eu* add *x* in the plural.

| SINGULAR | | PLURAL | |
|---|---|---|---|
| le bateau | *boat* | les bateaux | *boats* |
| le neveu | *nephew* | les neveux | *nephews* |

Other nouns ending in -*eau*:

| | | | | | |
|---|---|---|---|---|---|
| le bureau | *desk* | le couteau | *knife* | l'oiseau *(m.)* | *bird* |
| le cadeau | *gift* | l'eau *(f.)* | *water* | le tableau | *painting; board* |
| le chapeau | *hat* | le gâteau | *cake* | | |
| le château | *castle* | le manteau | *coat* | | |

Other nouns ending in -*eu*:

le cheveu* *hair*      le feu *fire*

**d.** Nouns ending in -*al* change -*al* to -*aux* in the plural.

| SINGULAR | | PLURAL | |
|---|---|---|---|
| l'animal *(m.)* | *animal* | les animaux | *animals* |
| le cheval | *horse* | les chevaux | *horses* |
| le journal | *newspaper* | les journaux | *newspapers* |
| l'hôpital | *hospital* | les hôpitaux | *hospitals* |

**e.** Some nouns have irregular plurals.

| SINGULAR | | PLURAL | |
|---|---|---|---|
| l'œil *(m.)* | *eye* | les yeux | *eyes* |

---

*Since **cheveu** refers to a single hair, the plural, **les cheveux,** is more common.

| SINGULAR | | PLURAL | |
|---|---|---|---|
| madame | *Madam, Mrs.* | mesdames | *ladies* |
| mademoiselle | *Miss* | mesdemoiselles | *Misses* |
| monsieur | *gentleman, Mr.* | messieurs | *gentlemen* |

**f.** A few nouns are used mainly in the plural.

| | | | |
|---|---|---|---|
| les gens *(m. or f.)* | *people* | les mathématiques *(f.)* | *mathematics* |
| les lunettes *(f.)* | *eyeglasses* | les vacances *(f.)* | *vacation* |

**g.** Family names do not add *s* in the plural.

les Bertrand       les Dupont

## EXERCICE G

**The students in M. Chaumont's art class are drawing pictures of mirror images.** *Exprimez ce que vous voyez dans chaque illustration.*

**EXEMPLE:**

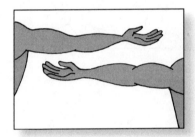

**Je vois deux bras.**

**1.**

_____

**2.**

_____

**3.**

_____

**4.**

_____

5.

_____

6.

_____

7.

_____

8.

_____

9.

_____

10.

_____

11.

_____

12.

_____

**13.**

**14.**

_____     _____

## EXERCICE H

**Fill in the words missing in this picture story.** *Complétez l'histoire.*

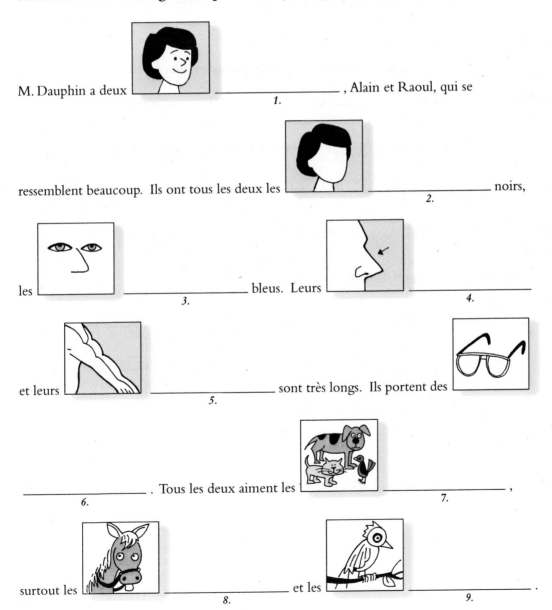

M. Dauphin a deux _____ 1. , Alain et Raoul, qui se

ressemblent beaucoup. Ils ont tous les deux les _____ 2. noirs,

les _____ 3. bleus. Leurs _____ 4.

et leurs _____ 5. sont très longs. Ils portent des

_____ 6. . Tous les deux aiment les _____ 7. ,

surtout les _____ 8. et les _____ 9. .

Alain et Raoul lisent les mêmes _____ et mangent les

10.

mêmes _____ . Pourquoi? Ils sont jumeaux.

11.

## MASTERY EXERCISES

## EXERCICE I

**Fill in the definite article where it is necessary. If it is not necessary, leave a blank.**

C'est aujourd'hui _____ mercredi _____ quatorze octobre. Nous sommes à

1.                          2.

_____ école. _____ mercredi nous avons beaucoup de cours: _____ anglais,

3.            4.                                                              5.

_____ français, _____ histoire, _____ biologie, _____ maths et _____

6.                7.                    8.                    9.                          10.

gymnastique sont _____ cours _____ mercredi. _____ français est mon cours

11.                12.                          13.

préféré. M. Lenoir est _____ prof de français. Il est français et formidable. _____

14.                                                                                   15.

classe de _____ français est toujours si amusante et intéressante que je lève _____

16.                                                                              17.

main mille fois par jour. Avant _____ vacances, en _____ été, M. Lenoir va donner

18.                          19.

une grande fête et nous inviter. Quelle chance pour nous!

## EXERCICE J

**Demandez à une amie de vous aider.** *Employez le pluriel des mots indiqués.*

EXEMPLE:    arranger / tableau
            **Arrange les tableaux, s'il te plaît.**

*1.* acheter / cadeau

2. chercher / couteau

_____

3. accepter / paquet

_____

4. fermer / rideau

_____

5. ramasser / journal

_____

6. allumer / feu

_____

7. contacter / hôpital

_____

8. couper / gâteau

_____

9. ranger / chambre

_____

10. préparer / repas

_____

## EXERCICE K

**A friend tells you about her French aunt.** *Exprimez en français ce qu'elle dit.*

1. My aunt Alice is the principal actress of the film *Garden in Winter.*

_____

2. She has blond hair and blue eyes.

_____

3. I am going to see her in the summer.

_____

4. She loves animals; she adores cats.

_____

5. Tennis is her favorite sport.

_____

**6.** She is also very good at swimming.

_____

**7.** She speaks French, and she does not speak English very well.

_____

**8.** In the evening, she performs in the theatre.

_____

**9.** In the morning, she stays home and sleeps till noon.

_____

**10.** She thinks that life is wonderful.

_____

# Chapter 15
## Indefinite and Partitive Articles

### [ 1 ]  FORMS

**a.** The indefinite singular article in French has two forms, *un* and *une,* corresponding to English *a (an).* It refers to beings and things not specifically identified (*a* cake, *any* cake, not *the* chocolate cake on the table).

| ARTICLE | USED BEFORE | EXAMPLE | MEANING |
|---|---|---|---|
| **un** | masculine singular nouns | **un livre** | *a book* |
| **une** | feminine singular nouns | **une règle** | *a ruler* |

Les Dupont ont **une** jolie maison dans **un** grand jardin.

*The Duponts have a pretty house in a large garden.*

### EXERCICE A

**M. Delatre is taking a walk in the country.** *Dites ce qu'il voit.*

EXEMPLE:   **Il voit un lac.**

1. _____

2. _____

3. _____

4. _____

5. _____

**6.** _____

**7.** _____

**8.** _____

**9.** _____

**10.** _____

**b.** The partitive article expresses an indefinite quantity or part of a whole *(some, any)*. It is expressed in French by *de* + definite article.

| ARTICLE | USED BEFORE | EXAMPLE | MEANING |
|---------|-------------|---------|---------|
| **du** | masculine singular nouns beginning with a consonant | **du pain** | *some (any) bread* |
| **de la** | feminine singular nouns beginning with a consonant | **de la viande** | *some (any) meat* |
| **de l'** | singular nouns beginning with a vowel | **de l'argent** **de l'eau** | *some (any) money* *some (any) water* |

| | |
|---|---|
| Je vais mettre **du** parfum. | *I'm going to put on some perfume.* |
| Il a envie de manger **de la** glace. | *He feels like eating some ice cream.* |
| As-tu **de l'**argent? | *Do you have any money?* |

NOTE: Unlike English, where *some* or *any* may be omitted, the partitive may not be omitted in French and is repeated before each noun.

| | |
|---|---|
| Veux-tu **du** poisson et **de la** salade? | *Do you want fish and salad?* |

## EXERCICE B

**Richard is packing a picnic basket.** *Exprimez ce qu'il met dedans.*

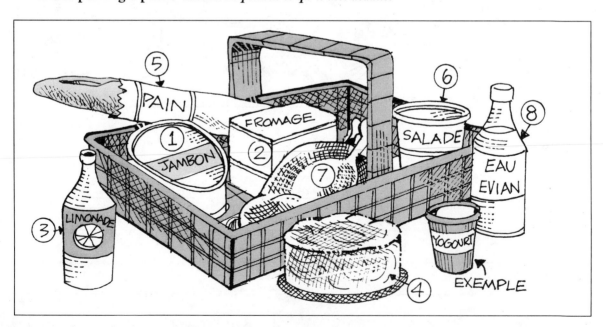

EXEMPLE:   Il met **du yogourt.**

1. _____

2. _____

3. _____

4. _____

5. _____

6. _____

7. _____

8. _____

## EXERCICE C

**What subjects are you taking in school?** *Dites-le en français.*

EXEMPLE:   physique *(f.)*
Je fais **de la physique.**

1. algèbre *(f.)*

_____

2. biologie *(f.)*

_____

3. français *(m.)*

_____

4. géométrie *(f.)*

_____

5. italien *(m.)*

_____

6. chimie *(f.)*

_____

7. histoire *(f.)*

_____

8. latin *(m.)*

_____

9. gymnastique *(f.)*

_____

**c.** The plural form is *des* (some, any) for both the indefinite and the partitive articles; it expresses more than one item or an unspecified amount or quantity. In English, *some* and *any* are often left unexpressed.

| ARTICLE | USED BEFORE | EXAMPLE | MEANING |
|---------|-------------|---------|---------|
| **des** | all plural nouns, masculine or feminine | **des légumes** **des confitures** **des hommes** **des idées** | *(some) vegetables* *(some) preserves* *(some) men* *(some) ideas* |

Elle a **des** problèmes.          *She has (some) problems.*

Les élèves ont **des** devoirs.     *The students have homework.*

Donnez-lui **des** crayons.         *Give him some pencils.*

Vois-tu **des** fautes?             *Do you see any mistakes?*

## EXERCICE D

**The Quentins are taking a tour of the new home their friends have just moved into.** *Exprimez ce qu'ils voient.*

EXEMPLES:   garage *(m.)*        Ils voient **un garage.**

　　　　　　balcons *(m. pl.)*   Ils voient **des balcons.**

**1.** jardin *(m.)* _____

**2.** cuisine *(f.)* _____

**3.** fenêtres *(f. pl.)* _____

**4.** terrasse *(f.)* _____

**5.** lampes *(f. pl.)* _____

**6.** escaliers *(m. pl.)* _____

**7.** piano *(m.)* _____

**8.** piscine *(f.)* _____

**9.** tableaux *(m. pl.)* _____

**10.** portes *(f. pl.)* _____

**11.** grenier *(m.)* _____

**12.** meubles *(m. pl.)* _____

**13.** chaises *(f. pl.)* _____

**14.** arbres *(m. pl.)* _____

## EXERCICE E

**What is sold in each of these stores in France?** *Suivez l'exemple.*

|  |  |  |  |  |
|---|---|---|---|---|
| crème | légumes | parfum | saucisson | viande |
| essence | médicaments | poisson | vêtements |  |

EXEMPLE:   Dans une charcuterie on vend **du saucisson.**

*1.* Dans une poissonnerie _____ .

*2.* Dans une pharmacie _____ .

*3.* Dans une station-service _____ .

*4.* Dans une épicerie _____ .

*5.* Dans une boutique _____ .

*6.* Dans une boucherie _____ .

*7.* Dans une parfumerie _____ .

*8.* Dans une crémerie _____ .

## EXERCICE F

**What does one need to buy in the following situations?** *Choisissez les mots appropriés.*

|  |  |  |  |  |  |
|---|---|---|---|---|---|
| bâton *(m.)* | chocolat *(m.)* | film *(m.)* | jambon *(m.)* | pain *(m.)* | skis *(pl.)* |
| beurre *(m.)* | crayon *(m.)* | fromage *(m.)* | laitue *(f.)* | papier *(m.)* | stylo *(m.)* |
| bottes *(pl.)* | crème *(f.)* | gomme *(f.)* | œuf *(m.)* | parfum *(m.)* | sucre *(m.)* |

EXEMPLE:   Lisette veut faire une omelette.
Elle achètera **des œufs et du jambon.**

*1.* Les Morin veulent faire du ski.

_____

*2.* Mme Laurin veut préparer une mousse au chocolat.

_____

*3.* Je veux faire un sandwich.

_____

*4.* Nous voulons prendre des photos.

_____

*5.* Vous voulez offrir un cadeau à une amie qui adore se parfumer.

_____

*6.* Tu veux te préparer pour la rentrée scolaire.

_____

NOTE:

1. When an adjective precedes a plural noun, *des* is usually replaced by *de* (*de* becomes *d'* before a vowel or silent *h*.)

| | |
|---|---|
| Je vois **de** jolies fleurs. | *I see pretty flowers.* |
| Elle met **de** vieux gants. | *She puts on old gloves.* |
| Il fait **de** bonnes crêpes. | *He makes good crepes.* |

2. When a plural adjective is part of a noun compound, the form *des* is used.

| | |
|---|---|
| des grands-mères | *grandmothers* |
| des petits pois | *peas* |
| des jeunes filles | *girls* |

## EXERCICE G

**Isabelle goes to the flea market with the Chabrols.** *Dites ce que chaque personne achète.*

EXEMPLE:    Mme Chabrol / bons chocolats
                    Mme Chabrol achète **de bons chocolats.**

*1.* Catherine / nouvelles cassettes

_____

*2.* François / bons livres

_____

*3.* M. Chabrol / vieux disques

_____

*4.* Isabelle / jolies affiches

_____

*5.* François / excellents articles de sport

_____

*6.* Mme Chabrol / belles assiettes

_____

**d.** In a negative sentence all forms of the indefinite article and of the partitive become *de* without the article.

| | |
|---|---|
| J'ai un chat et j'ai des chiens. | *I have a cat and I have dogs.* |
| *BUT* | |
| Je n'ai **pas de** chat et je n'ai **pas de** chiens. | *I don't have a cat and I don't have dogs.* |

Je n'ai **pas de** stylo.            *I don't have a pen.*
Il n'a **plus d'**argent.            *He doesn't have any money left.*
Je n'achète pas **de** vêtements.    *I am not buying clothes.*

NOTE: *de* becomes *d'* before a vowel or a silent *h*.

## EXERCICE H

**What's in the Duvals' refrigerator? What's not there?** *Employez la forme correcte du partitif.*

EXEMPLE:   glace / viande
           Il y a **de la glace** mais il n'y a **pas de viande.**

**1.** beurre / pain

_____

**2.** café / crème

_____

**3.** légumes / fruits

_____

**4.** soupe / biscuits

_____

**5.** poisson / fromage

_____

**6.** œufs / saucisses

_____

## EXERCICE I

**Mme Legros talks with her friends about ways to stay thin. Using the future tense and the negative word provided, write what they say they will not do while dieting.**

EXEMPLE:   Elles mangeront du beurre. (pas)
           Elles **ne mangeront pas** de beurre.

**1.** Elle mangera de la glace. (jamais)

_____

**2.** Vous éviterez des plats légers. (plus)

_____

**3.** Je préparerai des gâteaux. (pas)

_____

*4.* Ils mangeront du chocolat. (plus)

_____

*5.* Nous prendrons des desserts. (jamais)

_____

*6.* Tu boiras du soda. (pas)

_____

## EXERCICE J

**Say what these people do and don't do in the following situations.**

EXEMPLE:     Georges veut s'amuser.  lire: bandes dessinées, roman, livre d'école
             Il lit **des bandes dessinées.**
             Il lit **un roman.**
             Il **ne** lit **pas de livre d'école.**

*1.* Alain veut jouer au golf.  employer: raquette, balles, club

_____

_____

_____

*2.* Les filles veulent préparer un dessert.  acheter: glace, bœuf, fruits

_____

_____

_____

*3.* Je veux aller à la plage.  mettre: sandales, manteau, maillot de bain

_____

_____

_____

*4.* Nous avons mal à l'estomac.  prendre: médicaments, thé, bonbons

_____

_____

_____

*5.* Tu offres un cadeau à une amie.  donner: disque, livres, argent

_____

_____

_____

**6.** Vous voulez impressionner votre professeur.  apporter: bandes dessinées, gâteau, affiches

_____

_____

_____

## [ 2 ] OMISSION OF THE INDEFINITE ARTICLE

**a.** The indefinite article is omitted after *être* and *devenir* with unmodified names of nationalities, occupations, or professions.

Je suis Américain.          *I'm an American.*

Son père est médecin.          *His father is a doctor.*

NOTE: **The article is used if the noun is modified or when *c'est* is used.**

M. Legrand est un bon professeur.          *Mr. Legrand is a good teacher.*

C'est un ingénieur.          *He is an engineer.*

**b.** The indefinite article is omitted after the exclamatory adjectives *quel, quelle, quels, quelles.*

Quel bon film!          *What a good movie!*

**c.** The indefinite article is omitted before the numbers *cent* and *mille.*

cent hommes          *one hundred men*

mille dollars          *a thousand dollars*

## EXERCICE K

**A friend writes you a note about a friend of hers. Fill in any needed definite or indefinite articles. If none is needed, leave a blank.**

Chère Gisèle,

Je voudrais te présenter mon ami Pierre. C'est _____ professeur célèbre.  Il est _____
                                            *1.*                                         *2.*

Anglais. Il a publié _____ articles dans des revues pédagogiques.  Quel _____ homme
                              *3.*                                         *4.*

intéressant!  Il a beaucoup voyagé en Europe. _____ langues étrangères le passionnent.  Il parle
                                                     *5.*

bien _____ français, _____ anglais et _____ japonais.  Quand il a du temps libre
       *6.*                   *7.*                 *8.*

il est _____ entraîneur pour _____ équipe de football au lycée du quartier.  J'espère que tu
        *9.*                   *10.*

peux faire la connaissance de mon ami.

                         Ton amie Françoise

## EXERCICE L

**Both parents in each family have the same job.** *Décrivez en français la profession de l'autre parent.*

EXEMPLE:    Mme Bagot est artiste.
            **M. Bagot: C'est un artiste.**

*1.* M. Seguin est vendeur.

_____

*2.* Mme Guérin est un bon médecin.

_____

*3.* M. Hervé est infirmier.

_____

*4.* M. Ribet est professeur.

_____

*5.* Mme Joubert est programmeuse.

_____

*6.* M. Destombes est acteur.

_____

# [ 3 ]  NOUNS AND ADVERBS OF QUANTITY

Nouns and adverbs that express quantity or measure are followed by *de* alone before another noun. Some common nouns of quantity are:

| | |
|---|---|
| une boîte  *a box* | un paquet  *a package* |
| une bouteille  *a bottle* | un sac  *a bag* |
| une douzaine  *a dozen* | une tasse  *a cup* |
| une paire  *a pair* | un verre  *a glass* |

Donnez-moi **une douzaine d'œufs.**      *Give me a dozen eggs.*
Elle ouvre **un sac de** chips.          *She opens a bag of chips.*
Je voudrais **une bouteille d'**eau.     *I would like a bottle of water.*

Some common adverbs of quantity are:

| | |
|---|---|
| assez de  *enough* | peu de  *little, few* |
| beaucoup de  *much, many* | plus de  *more* |
| combien de  *how much, how many* | trop de  *too much, too many* |
| moins de  *less, fewer* | |

J'ai **beaucoup d'**amis.         *I have many friends.*
Avez-vous **assez de** pain?      *Do you have enough bread?*

NOTE: With some expressions constructed with *de, de* is used alone.

| | |
|---|---|
| avoir besoin de *to need* | avoir envie de *to desire* |
| J'ai besoin d'argent. | *I need money.* |
| J'ai envie de sortie | *I feel like going out.* |

## EXERCICE M

**What do you need to bake a cake?** *Exprimez la réponse en français.*

EXEMPLE:  **J'ai besoin d'un verre d'eau.**

**1.** _____

**2.** _____

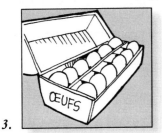

**3.** _____

**4.** _____

**5.** _____

**6.** _____

## EXERCICE N

_Décrivez votre personnalité en employant les suggestions données._

| | | |
|---|---|---|
| assez | ambition | imagination |
| beaucoup | charme | intelligence |
| besoin | courage | patience |
| peu | énergie | prudence |
| trop | enthousiasme | talent |
| | force | |

EXEMPLE:   **J'ai beaucoup de force.**

**1.** _____

**2.** _____

**3.** _____

**4.** _____

**5.** _____

**6.** _____

7. _____

8. _____

9. _____

10. _____

## [ 4 ] THE PARTITIVE AND THE DEFINITE ARTICLE

While the partitive is used to express *some* or *part* of something, the definite article is used with nouns in a general sense.

| | |
|---|---|
| Les Anglais aiment **le thé.** | *The British like tea* (in general). |
| Je bois **du thé** pendant les repas. | *I drink tea during meals.* |

## EXERCICE O

**You are in a restaurant with a friend who says what she likes to eat. Suggest that you order some.**

EXEMPLE:   jambon *(m.)*   **J'aime le jambon.**
Alors, **commandons du jambon.**

1. salade *(f.)*

_____

_____

2. eau minérale *(f.)*

_____

_____

3. poisson *(m.)*

_____

_____

4. fromage *(m.)*

_____

_____

5. frites *(f.)*

_____

_____

6. mousse au chocolat *(f.)*

_____

_____

## EXERCICE P

*Exprimez ce que vous aimez ou n'aimez pas manger.*

1. Mon plat préféré est _____.

2. Je déteste _____.

3. Quand j'ai soif je prends _____.

4. Le matin je mange _____.

5. Au déjeuner à la cantine à l'école je choisis _____

   _____.

6. Quand ma mère prépare de la soupe pour moi, j'aime _____

   _____.

7. Comme dessert je choisis _____.

8. Mon légume préféré est _____.

9. Mon fruit préféré est _____.

10. Quand je veux maigrir je ne prends pas _____.

11. Je mange toujours _____.

12. Je ne mange jamais _____.

## M A S T E R Y   E X E R C I S E S

## EXERCICE Q

**You and a friend are preparing a chocolate mousse. Complete what you say to each other.** *Employez les articles définis ou partitifs qui conviennent.*

EXEMPLE:   Ma spécialité est **la** mousse au chocolat.

1. J'ai acheté beaucoup _____ chocolat.

2. Tu dois allumer _____ four.

3. Est-ce qu'on utilise _____ crème et _____ beurre?

4. Oui, et il faut ajouter _____ œufs.

5. On met une douzaine _____ œufs.

6. Il est nécessaire de séparer _____ œufs, n'est-ce pas?

**7.** Oui, tu mets _____ jaunes dans le bol et tu fouettes *(whip)* _____ blancs.

**8.** Il faut que tu ajoutes _____ café.

**9.** Tu as acheté _____ sucre?

**10.** On ne met pas _____ sucre dans _____ recette.

## EXERCICE R

**Nicole is having a party. Complete the description of how she prepares for it.** *Ajoutez les articles définis, indéfinis ou partitifs qui conviennent.*

_____ semaine dernière Nicole a envoyé _____ invitations à beaucoup _____ amis.
<br>1.        2.        3.

Elle a indiqué _____ date et _____ heure de la boum. _____ boum est aujourd'hui.
<br>4.     5.     6.

Nicole et ses sœurs mettent _____ décorations partout. Puisqu'elle adore _____ ballons,
<br>7.     8.

elle met _____ ballons de toutes _____ couleurs sur _____ murs du salon. Elle a aussi
<br>9.     10.     11.

préparé _____ douzaines _____ sandwiches et _____ gâteaux au chocolat et à la vanille.
<br>12.     13.     14.

Sa mère a déjà acheté _____ bouteilles _____ soda, _____ sacs _____ chips
<br>15.     16.     17.     18.

et _____ paquets _____ bonbons et _____ glace. Elle n'a pas trouvé _____ biscuits.
<br>19.     20.     21.     22.

Tant pis. Elle trouve qu'elle a acheté assez _____ choses et puis, les jeunes d'aujourd'hui
<br>23.

n'aiment pas tellement _____ biscuits. Ils préfèrent _____ gâteau. Maintenant Nicole
<br>24.     25.

cherche _____ vieux disques et aussi _____ cassettes. Elle est très nerveuse parce que
<br>26.     27.

_____ boum va commencer dans une heure.
<br>28.

## EXERCICE S

**Friends are telling you about a new *hypermarché* — a very large supermarket — that opened near their house.** *Exprimez en français ce que vos amis disent.*

**1.** The store is very large.

_____

**2.** French people and tourists like to go there.

_____

*3.* Prices are very reasonable there.

_____

*4.* You need a lot of money because there are a lot of good things to buy.

_____

*5.* They sell food from many countries.

_____

*6.* They also have good cider from Calvados, excellent bouillabaisse from Marseilles, and delicious pastries from Paris.

_____

_____

*7.* Yesterday I bought a dozen eggs, butter, sugar, and a bag of nuts to prepare some cakes.

_____

_____

*8.* Do you like French wine?  They sell wine, too.

_____

*9.* Young people work in the store, and they are very friendly.

_____

*10.* There is never a problem when you go to this store.

_____

# Chapter 16
## Subject Pronouns

A pronoun is a word used in place of a noun. A subject pronoun is used in place of a subject noun.

## [ 1 ] FORMS

| SINGULAR | | PLURAL | |
|---|---|---|---|
| **je (j')** | *I* | **nous** | *we* |
| **tu** | *you* (familiar) | **vous** | *you* (also formal singular) |
| **il** | *he* | **ils** | *they* (masculine) |
| **elle** | *she* | **elles** | *they* (feminine) |
| **on** | *one, you, we, they* | | |

NOTE:

1. A subject pronoun normally precedes the verb.

   Tu travailles bien. — *You work well.*

2. In an inverted question, a subject pronoun follows the verb in simple tenses and follows the helping verb in compound tenses.

   Travailles-tu à la maison? — *Do you work at home?*

   Est-elle allée à la bibliothèque? — *Has she gone to the library?*

   When the question is formed with *est-ce que,* there is no inversion of the verb and pronoun.

   Est-ce que tu travailles à la maison? — *Do you work at home?*

   Est-ce qu'elle est allée à la bibliothèque? — *Has she gone to the library?*

   Inversion with *je* is generally avoided and occurs only with a few verbs: *avoir, être, pouvoir, savoir.*

   Puis-je venir? — *May I come?*

3. Subject pronouns are omitted in the imperative.

   Écoute les informations! — *Listen to the news!*

   Regardez cet article! — *Look at this article!*

   Allons au cinéma! — *Let's go to the movies!*

4. The familiar singular subject pronoun *tu* is used to address a friend, a relative, a child, or a pet, and the formal *vous* is used in the singular to show respect, or to address an older person or someone one does not know well.

5. The third-person pronoun *on* means *one* or *someone.* It may also refer to an indefinite *you, we, they,* or *people* in general.

   On a besoin d'amitié. — *One needs (People need / We need) friendship.*

On dit que le français est la langue
de l'amour.                                  *They say that French is the language of love.*

On a pris mon stylo.                         *Someone took my pen.*

**In spoken French, *on* is often used in place of *nous*.**

On va au parc?                               *Are we going to the park?*

## EXERCICE A

**Write who did what yesterday.** *Employez le pronom sujet approprié.*

EXEMPLE:    **Elle** est revenue tard.

*1.* _____ t'es amusé.

*2.* _____ avons joué avec l'ordinateur.

*3.* _____ est allée à une fête.

*4.* _____ ai joué au tennis.

*5.* _____ sont restés à la maison.

*6.* _____ avez travaillé dur.

*7.* _____ se sont promenées.

*8.* _____ est venu chez Roger.

## EXERCICE B

**Complete the description of the guests at Janine's party.** *Employez le pronom sujet approprié.*

*1.* Marie et Sylvie sont sœurs. _____ travaillent dans le même bureau.

*2.* Êtes-_____ professeur de biologie? _____ suis experte en physique.

*3.* Henri étudie les maths. _____ veut devenir ingénieur.

*4.* Claire et moi, _____ suivons un cours de latin.

*5.* Pierre et Jean réparent les voitures. _____ sont mécaniciens.

*6.* _____ es le meilleur élève de la classe.

*7.* La mère de Berthe va à l'université. _____ étudie l'histoire.

## EXERCICE C

**State the rules observed in the office of Laurent Enterprises.** *Employez* on.

EXEMPLES:    écouter le directeur              ne pas faire de bruit
             **On écoute** le directeur.        **On ne fait pas** de bruit.

*1.* arriver à l'heure

_____

*2.* ne pas téléphoner à ses amis

_____

*3.* travailler consciencieusement

_____

*4.* ne pas parler trop fort

_____

*5.* respecter les autres

_____

*6.* ne jamais oublier ses responsabilités

_____


# [2] *CE + ÊTRE*

The pronoun *ce (c')* (it, he, she, this, that, they, these, those) is used with the verb *être* to describe someone or something. *Ce* can replace *il, elle, ils,* and *elles* in the following constructions:

### a. Before a modified noun.

| | |
|---|---|
| C'est une erreur. | *It's a mistake.* |
| C'est un bon film. | *That's a good film.* |
| Ce sont de vieux amis. | *They're old friends.* |

*BUT*

| | |
|---|---|
| Il est docteur. | *He's a doctor.* |

### b. Before a proper noun.

| | |
|---|---|
| Qui est là? — C'est Marc. | *Who is it? — It's Marc.* |
| Quelle est la capitale de la France? | *What is the capital of France?* |
| — C'est Paris. | *— It's Paris.* |

### c. In dates.

| | |
|---|---|
| C'est aujourd'hui lundi. | *Today is Monday.* |
| Demain ce sera le 6 juin. | *Tomorrow will be June 6.* |

NOTE: Use *Il est* to express the hour of the day.

| | |
|---|---|
| Il est neuf heures. | *It is nine o'clock.* |

### d. Before a pronoun.

| | |
|---|---|
| Qui frappe à la porte? C'est vous? | *Who's knocking at the door? Is it you?* |

# EXERCICE D

**Explain what everyone thinks Joseph's abstract painting represents.** *Employez* c'est *ou* ce sont.

EXEMPLES:

C'est un arbre.

Ce sont des arbres.

1.

_____

2.

_____

3.

_____

4.

_____

5.

_____

6.

_____

## EXERCICE E

**Answer your Social Studies teacher's questions.** *Employez* **c'est** *ou* **ce sont.**

*1.* Qui est le premier président des États-Unis?

_____

*2.* Quelle est la capitale des États-Unis?

_____

*3.* Quels sont deux sites touristiques intéressants aux États-Unis?

_____

*4.* Qui est le maire *(mayor)* de votre ville?

_____

## EXERCICE F

**What are the dates of the following holidays?** *Utilisez* **c'est.**

*1.* Noël _____

*2.* Le Nouvel An _____

*3.* Independence Day _____

*4.* Bastille Day _____

*5.* La Saint Valentin _____

## EXERCICE G

**Richard is talking about people and things with his new friend Christophe.** *Complétez ce qu'il dit en employant* **ce (c'), il, elle, ils,** *ou* **elles.**

*1.* Regarde cette fille. _____ est Janine, ma sœur. _____ est très jolie.

*2.* Qui sonne à la porte? — _____ sont Paul et Luc. _____ sont en retard.

*3.* Quelle est la date? — _____ est le premier mai. Anne célèbre son anniversaire aujourd'hui.

_____ a quatorze ans.

*4.* Qui sont les filles là-bas? — _____ sont Odette et Danielle. _____ sont dans ma classe d'anglais.

*5.* Qu'est-ce que c'est? — _____ est mon scooter. Jean le répare. _____ est mécanicien.

# M A S T E R Y   E X E R C I S E S

## EXERCICE H

*Complétez l'histoire suivante en employant* ce/c' *ou le pronom sujet correct.*

_____ est mercredi après-midi. _____ est quatre heures précises. Quelqu'un sonne à la porte.
1.                                    2.

Qui est- _____ ? Je pense que _____ est Jacques, mon frère. _____ ai tort. Imagine
3.                          4.                                    5.

ma surprise. _____ est M. Mercier. _____ est bibliothécaire. Que fait- _____ ici?
6.                              7.                                        8.

Il dit: « _____ est une affaire sérieuse. Ma petite fille, _____ as beaucoup de problèmes. Ton
9.                                                      10.

frère et toi, _____ avez négligé de rendre vos livres à la bibliothèque.» _____ réponds que
11.                                                                      12.

c'est impossible puisque _____ allons à la bibliothèque chaque semaine. M. Mercier pense que
13.

_____ avons vingt livres à la maison! _____ veut parler à mes parents, mais _____ ne
14.                                        15.                                        16.

sont pas à la maison. Finalement Annick, ma sœur aînée, arrive. _____ est elle qui est responsable
17.

de tous ces livres. _____ est vraiment très embarrassée.
18.

## EXERCICE I

*Répondez aux questions des parents d'un ami. Employez* ce (c') *ou un pronom sujet.*

1. Quelle est la date de ton anniversaire?

   _____

2. Que fais-tu après l'école?

   _____

3. Où est-ce que ta famille habite?

   _____

4. À quelle heure est-ce que tu rentres de classe?

   _____

5. Qui est ta meilleure amie?

   _____

6. Est-ce que tes parents travaillent tous les deux?

   _____

# EXERCICE J

*Racontez en français comment vos amis français ont passé un samedi après-midi.*

1. It is Saturday afternoon. It is spring.

   _____

2. Catherine and Isabelle want to go to Paris.

   _____

3. They ask Pierre and Claude to come along.

   _____

4. They are all in the same class in school.

   _____

5. Catherine says: "We can't go by car. I think we'll take the train."

   _____

   _____

6. Pierre asks: "Where do you want to go?"

   _____

7. She answers: "To the Beaubourg museum. There's a big rock concert."

   _____

   _____

8. "It's today! It's a good concert."

   _____

9. "Great! We shall go to the concert!" says Claude.

   _____

10. He adds: "It's a very good idea!"

    _____

# Chapter 17
## Object Pronouns

## [ 1 ] DIRECT OBJECT PRONOUNS

### a. Forms

| SINGULAR | | PLURAL | |
|---|---|---|---|
| **me (m')** | *me* | **nous** | *we* |
| **te (t')** | *you* (familiar) | **vous** | *you* (also formal singular) |
| **le (l')** | *him, it* (masculine) | **les** | *them* |
| **la (l')** | *her, it* (feminine) | | |
| **se (s')** | *himself, herself, oneself* | **se (s')** | *themselves* |

### b. Uses of direct object pronouns

A direct object pronoun replaces a direct object noun and answers the question *whom?* or *what?*

| | |
|---|---|
| Je vois **Richard**. | *I see Richard.* |
| Je **le** vois. | *I see him.* |
| Nous regardons **la télévision**. | *We watch television.* |
| Nous **la** regardons. | *We watch it.* |
| Il cherche **ses amis**. | *He looks for his friends.* |
| Il **les** cherche. | *He looks for them.* |

NOTE: Verbs like *attendre* (to wait for), *écouter* (to listen to), *chercher* (to look for), *demander* (to ask for), *payer* (to pay for), and *regarder* (to look at) take a direct object in French.

| | |
|---|---|
| Je **l'**écoute. | *I am listening to him (her, it).* |
| Il **les** regarde. | *He looks at them.* |

### c. Position of direct object pronouns

(1) The direct object pronoun precedes the words *voici* (here is, here are) and *voilà* (there is, there are).

| | |
|---|---|
| **Me** voici. | *Here I am.* |
| **Le** voilà. | *There he (it) is.* |

(2) The direct object pronoun normally precedes the verb of which it is the object.

| | |
|---|---|
| Il **le** prend. | *He takes it.* |
| **Te** cherche-t-il? | *Is he looking for you?* |
| **S'**amusent-ils? | *Are they having fun?* |
| Il **l'**a fait. | *He did it.* |
| Je ne **vous** attendrai pas. | *I will not wait for you.* |

## EXERCICE A

**Danielle is packing a bag to go away for the weekend. She is late and her sister is helping her.**
*Exprimez ce qu'elle cherche et comment sa sœur répond à ses questions.*

EXEMPLE:

Où est mon **chapeau**?
**Le voilà.**

1.

Où sont mes _____ ?

_____

2.

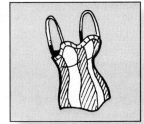

Où est mon _____ ?

_____

3.

Où est ma _____ ?

_____

4.

Où est mon _____ ?

_____

5.

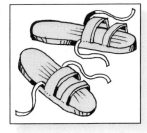

Où sont mes _____ ?

_____

6.

Où est ma _____ ?

_____

**7.**

Où est ma _____ ?

_____

**8.**

Où est mon _____ ?

_____

## EXERCICE B

**You and a friend are discussing your likes and dislikes.** *Exprimez votre conversation.*

EXEMPLE:    écouter la musique classique
            AMI:    **L'écoutes-tu?**
            VOUS:   Oui, **je l'écoute.**
            AMI:    Moi, **je ne l'écoute pas.**

**1.** collectionner les bandes dessinées

AMI:    _____

VOUS:   _____

AMI:    _____

**2.** aimer la natation

AMI:    _____

VOUS:   _____

AMI:    _____

**3.** préférer le rock

AMI:    _____

VOUS:   _____

AMI:    _____

**4.** adorer la poésie moderne

AMI:    _____

VOUS:   _____

AMI:    _____

**5.** lire le journal tous les jours

AMI: _____

VOUS: _____

AMI: _____

**6.** regarder souvent les films vidéo

AMI: _____

VOUS: _____

AMI: _____

## EXERCICE C

**What were these people doing in the** *Galeries Lafayette* **department store?** *Suivez l'exemple.*

EXEMPLE:   chercher ses amis
            Pierre **les** cherchait.

**1.** acheter les vêtements

Je _____ .

**2.** regarder les mannequins

Janine _____ .

**3.** chercher leur fille

Les Pompon _____ .

**4.** trouver la vendeuse

Nous _____ .

**5.** attendre ton amie

Tu _____ .

**6.** payer le caissier

Vous _____ .

(3) **When a pronoun is the direct object of an infinitive, the pronoun precedes the infinitive.**

| | |
|---|---|
| Il voulait voir **Pauline.** | *He wanted to see Pauline.* |
| Il voulait **la** voir. | *He wanted to see her.* |
| Sais-tu réparer **la radio?** | *Do you know how to repair the radio?* |
| Sais-tu **la** réparer? | *Do you know how to repair it?* |
| Je ne vais pas **le** faire. | *I'm not going to do it.* |

## EXERCICE D

**Your mother has asked you to help in the kitchen and would like to know what you want to do. For each of the following, write her question and your negative or affirmative answer.**

EXEMPLES:    goûter la soupe (non)        laver les fruits (oui)
**Veux-tu la goûter?**          **Veux-tu les laver?**
**Non, je ne veux pas la goûter.   Oui, je veux les laver.**

*1.* faire la vaisselle (non)

_____

_____

*2.* arranger les fruits (oui)

_____

_____

*3.* préparer la salade (oui)

_____

_____

*4.* mettre le couvert (non)

_____

_____

*5.* laver les légumes (non)

_____

_____

*6.* allumer le four (oui)

_____

_____

*7.* couper le pain (non)

_____

_____

(4) In an affirmative command, the object pronoun follows the verb and is attached to it by a hyphen. The pronouns *me* and *te* change to *moi* and *toi* after the verb. In a negative command, the object pronoun retains its usual position before the verb.

| AFFIRMATIVE COMMAND | | NEGATIVE COMMAND | |
|---|---|---|---|
| **Ouvre-le.** | *Open it.* | **Ne l'ouvre pas.** | *Don't open it.* |
| **Regardez-moi.** | *Look at me.* | **Ne me regardez pas.** | *Don't look at me.* |
| **Lève-toi.** | *Get up.* | **Ne te lève pas.** | *Don't get up.* |

## EXERCICE E

**Paul can never make a decision about anything. He sees things he wants to buy but he's not sure, and his two friends don't help.** *Exprimez ce qu'ils disent.*

EXEMPLE:    Quel bel imperméable!
**Achète-le!**
**Ne l'achète pas!**

**1.** Quel beau portefeuille!

_____

_____

**2.** Quelle belle montre!

_____

_____

**3.** Quels beaux vêtements!

_____

_____

**4.** Quelle belle chemise!

_____

_____

**5.** Quel beau pantalon!

_____

_____

**6.** Quelles belles chaussettes!

_____

_____

## EXERCICE F

**Nicole is driving her boyfriend crazy. One day she's wild about him, and the next day she's not.** *Exprimez ce qu'elle lui dit.*

EXEMPLE:    pardonner
**Pardonne-moi!**
**Ne me pardonne pas!**

**1.** regarder

_____

_____

*2.* embrasser

_____

_____

*3.* oublier

_____

_____

*4.* attendre

_____

_____

*5.* aimer

_____

_____

*6.* écouter

_____

_____

## EXERCICE G

**A friend gives you advice on getting ready for school in the morning.** *Exprimez ce que votre ami dit.*

EXEMPLE:    se lever à 7h, pas à 8h
              **Lève-toi** à 7h.
              **Ne te lève pas** à 8h.

*1.* se réveiller à 7h, pas à 7h15

_____

_____

*2.* se laver avant le petit déjeuner, pas après

_____

_____

*3.* s'habiller dans ta chambre, pas dans la salle de bains

_____

_____

*4.* choisir tes vêtements le soir, pas le matin

_____

_____

5. se préparer pour l'école le soir, pas le matin

_____

_____

6. se coucher à 11h, pas à minuit

_____

_____

## EXERCICE H

**Your parents ask you about your friends.** *Écrivez leurs questions et vos réponses.*

EXEMPLE:     aimer
               Tes amis **t'**aiment?
               Mes amis **m'**aiment.

1. écouter

_____

_____

2. respecter

_____

_____

3. aider

_____

_____

4. trouver sympathique

_____

_____

## EXERCICE I

**Now your friends ask you and your brother about your parents.** *Écrivez leurs questions et vos réponses.*

EXEMPLE:     menacer
               Vos parents **vous** menacent?
               Nos parents **ne nous** menacent **jamais**.

1. gâter

_____

_____

*2.* punir

_____

_____

*3.* ennuyer

_____

_____

*4.* gronder

_____

_____

# [ 2 ] INDIRECT OBJECT PRONOUNS

**a.** The forms of indirect object pronouns are the same as those of direct object pronouns, except for the third person singular *(lui)* and the third person plural *(leur)*.

| SINGULAR | | PLURAL | |
|---|---|---|---|
| **me (m')** | *(to) me* | **nous** | *(to) us* |
| **te (t')** | *(to) you* (familiar) | **vous** | *(to) you* (also formal singular) |
| **lui** | *(to) him, (to) her* | **leur** | *(to) them* |
| **se (s')** | *(to) himself, (to) herself, (to) itself* | **se (s')** | *(to) themselves* |

**b.** Uses of indirect object pronouns

An indirect object pronoun replaces an indirect object noun and answers the questions *to whom? for whom?*

| | |
|---|---|
| Je parle à **Georges**. | *I speak to Georges.* |
| Je **lui** parle. | *I speak to him.* |
| | |
| Elle donne des pommes **aux enfants**. | *She gives apples to the children.* |
| Elle **leur** donne des pommes. | *She gives them apples.* |

NOTE: The verbs *obéir* (to obey), *désobéir* (to disobey), *répondre* (to answer), *ressembler* (to resemble), and *téléphoner* (to telephone) take an indirect object in French.

| | |
|---|---|
| J'obéis à **mes parents**. | *I obey my parents.* |
| Je **leur** obéis. | *I obey them.* |
| | |
| Elle téléphone à **son ami**. | *She phones her friend.* |
| Elle **lui** téléphone. | *She calls him (her).* |

**c.** Position of indirect object pronouns

(1) Indirect object pronouns, including reflexives, normally precede the verb.

| | |
|---|---|
| Il **lui** parle. | *He speaks to him (her).* |
| **Leur** obéis-tu? | *Do you obey them?* |

|  |  |
|---|---|
| **Se** brossent-ils les dents? | *Do they brush their teeth?* |
| Les enfants **leur** ont écrit. | *The children wrote to them.* |
| Je ne **vous** parlerai pas. | *I will not speak to you.* |

## EXERCICE J

**You are talking with a teacher about yourself and your family.** *Racontez votre conversation en suivant l'exemple.*

EXEMPLES:  obéir à vos parents (oui)  désobéir à vos parents (non)
**Leur obéissez-vous?**  **Leur désobéissez-vous?**
**Oui, je leur obéis.**  **Non, je ne leur désobéis pas.**

*1.* parler à vos parents de vos problèmes (oui)

_____

_____

*2.* prêter de l'argent à vos frères (non)

_____

_____

*3.* écrire à vos grands-parents (oui)

_____

_____

*4.* dire la vérité à votre père (oui)

_____

_____

*5.* défendre à votre frère cadet de sortir (non)

_____

_____

*6.* répondre à vos parents avec respect (oui)

_____

_____

*7.* téléphoner à vos parents quand vous allez être en retard (oui)

_____

_____

*8.* raconter tout à votre mère (non)

_____

_____

(2) When a pronoun is the indirect object of an infinitive, the pronoun precedes the infinitive.

| | |
|---|---|
| Il voulait parler à **Pauline**. | *He wanted to speak to Pauline.* |
| Il voulait **lui** parler. | *He wanted to speak to her.* |
| Peux-tu téléphoner **aux filles**? | *Can you call the girls?* |
| Peux-tu **leur** téléphoner? | *Can you call them?* |
| Je ne vais pas **leur** écrire. | *I'm not going to write to them.* |

## EXERCICE K

**Your fellow employees in a store are asking you questions. For each of the following, write the question being asked and your negative or affirmative answer.**

EXEMPLE:   donner les commandes à Jacques (non)
**Peux-tu lui donner** les commandes?
**Non, je ne peux pas lui donner** les commandes.

**1.** prêter le stylo à Luz (non)

_____

_____

**2.** répondre aux clients (oui)

_____

_____

**3.** montrer la marchandise à M. Legrand (oui)

_____

_____

**4.** demander les renseignements au directeur (non)

_____

_____

**5.** lire le journal à Marcos et à Rita (non)

_____

_____

**6.** écrire aujourd'hui à Mme Bonnet (oui)

_____

_____

**7.** offrir le café au propriétaire (non)

_____

_____

**8.** apprendre le travail aux nouveaux employés (oui)

_____

_____

(3) In an affirmative command, the object pronoun follows the verb and is attached to it by a hyphen. The pronouns *me* and *te* change to *moi* and *toi*. In a negative command, the object pronoun retains its usual position before the verb.

| AFFIRMATIVE COMMAND | | NEGATIVE COMMAND | |
|---|---|---|---|
| **Téléphone-moi!** | *Call me.* | **Ne me téléphone pas!** | *Don't call me.* |
| **Dépêche-toi!** | *Hurry up.* | **Ne te dépêche pas!** | *Don't hurry!* |
| **Écrivez-leur!** | *Write to them.* | **Ne leur écrivez pas!** | *Don't write to them.* |

## EXERCICE L

**What would you tell a friend to do in the following situations?** *Exprimez vos conseils en employant les indications données.*

EXEMPLES:  Il a eu une dispute avec son meilleur ami. (téléphoner)
**Téléphone-lui.**

Son ami est parti en vacances. (ne pas téléphoner)
**Ne lui téléphone pas.**

**1.** Ses grands-parents sont allés en Floride. (écrire)

_____

**2.** Son frère a envie d'emprunter son nouveau pull. (ne pas prêter le pull)

_____

**3.** Sa petite amie est triste. (donner des fleurs)

_____

**4.** Il fait la connaissance d'un nouvel élève. (demander son numéro de téléphone)

_____

**5.** Des étudiants l'ennuient. (ne pas parler)

_____

**6.** Un homme veut acheter sa voiture. (ne pas vendre ta voiture)

_____

**7.** C'est l'anniversaire de ses parents. (acheter un cadeau)

_____

**8.** Des élèves essaient de copier ses réponses à un examen. (ne pas montrer les réponses)

_____

## EXERCICE M

**Your friend asks you what your boyfriend does for you.** *Exprimez ses questions et vos réponses.*

EXEMPLE:   prêter sa voiture
           **Il te prête** sa voiture?
           Oui, **il me prête** sa voiture.

**1.** écrire des lettres d'amour

_____

_____

**2.** dire: «Je t'aime»

_____

_____

**3.** donner des bonbons

_____

_____

**4.** acheter des fleurs

_____

_____

## EXERCICE N

**A friend asks what your parents tell you and your sister to do.** *Exprimez ses questions et vos réponses.*

EXEMPLE:   conseiller d'étudier tout le temps
           **Vous conseillent-ils** d'étudier tout le temps?
           **Ils ne nous conseillent pas** d'étudier tout le temps.

**1.** défendre de sortir

_____

_____

*2.* dire de rester toujours à la maison

_____

_____

*3.* ordonner de faire le ménage

_____

_____

*4.* demander souvent d'aller faire les courses

_____

_____

## [ 3 ] PRONOUN *Y*

The adverbial pronoun *y* always refers to previously mentioned things or places. It generally replaces *à* + noun but may also replace other prepositions of position or location such as *chez, dans, en, sous,* or *sur* + noun. The pronoun *y* most commonly means *to it / them, in it / them, on it / them,* and *there.*

| | |
|---|---|
| Je vais **à Paris.** | *I am going to Paris.* |
| J'**y** vais. | *I am going there.* |
| Elle répond **à la lettre.** | *She answers the letter.* |
| Elle **y** répond. | *She answers it.* |
| Ils sont **dans le bureau?** | *They are in the office?* |
| Ils **y** sont. | *They are there.* |

Sometimes the meaning of *y* is not expressed in English.

| | |
|---|---|
| Le chat est **sous la chaise?** | *Is the cat under the chair?* |
| Oui, il **y** est. | *Yes, he is.* |

NOTE:

1. The pronoun *y* follows the same rules of position in the sentence as direct and indirect object pronouns.

| | |
|---|---|
| Il voulait **y** aller. | *He wanted to go there.* |
| **Y** vas-tu? | *Are you going there?* |
| Je n'**y** vais pas. | *I am not going there.* |
| Je ne vais pas **y** rester. | *I'm not going to stay there.* |

2. Affirmative familiar commands (*tu* form) of *-er* verbs and *aller* retain the final *s* before *y*.

| | |
|---|---|
| Restes-**y**! | *Stay there!* |
| N'**y** reste pas! | *Don't stay there!* |
| Vas-**y**! | *Go there!* |
| N'**y** va pas! | *Don't go there!* |

## EXERCICE O

**Your younger sister wants to know about you and your friend's plans for your senior prom.** *Répondez à ses questions selon le modèle suivant.*

EXEMPLES:    Vous allez à un bal élégant? (oui) / (non)
**Oui, nous y allons.**
**Non, nous n'y allons pas.**

*1.* Le bal est dans les salons de l'hôtel Prince? (non)

_____

*2.* Vous dînez à l'hôtel? (oui)

_____

*3.* Vous pensez à la fête? (oui)

_____

*4.* La limousine arrive chez nous à sept heures? (non)

_____

*5.* Vous restez longtemps au bal? (oui)

_____

*6.* Vous dansez sur la terrasse? (oui)

_____

*7.* Vous allez au parc après? (non)

_____

*8.* Vous descendez en ville prendre le petit déjeuner? (non)

_____

## EXERCICE P

**Your friend suggests how you can spend your vacation. For each of the following, write your friend's suggestion and your negative or affirmative answer.**

EXEMPLE:    aller au Canada (non)
**Veux-tu y aller?**
**Non, je ne veux pas y aller.**

*1.* dormir à la belle étoile (non)

_____

_____

*2.* voyager en Italie (oui)

_____

_____

**3.** dîner dans des restaurants élégants (non)

_____

_____

**4.** rester chez ta grand-mère (non)

_____

_____

**5.** aller aux îles Caraïbes (oui)

_____

_____

**6.** jouer au golf (oui)

_____

_____

**7.** assister à un cours de dance (non)

_____

_____

**8.** travailler dans une disco (oui)

_____

_____

## EXERCICE Q

**You have schoolwork to do but you're feeling lazy. Your conscience is wavering as contradictory ideas pop into your head.** *Exprimez ces idées.*

EXEMPLE:   aller à la bibliothèque
           **Vas-y. / N'y va pas.**

**1.** penser au travail scolaire

_____

**2.** jouer au tennis

_____

**3.** dîner dans un restaurant

_____

**4.** aller chez des amis

_____

**5.** rester dans ta chambre

_____

## [ 4 ] PRONOUN *EN*

**a.** The adverbial pronoun *en* refers to previously mentioned nouns introduced by *de*. It means *about it/them, from it/them, of it/them,* or *from there* when it replaces a noun referring to places or things and introduced by the preposition *de*.

| | |
|---|---|
| Nous venons **de Paris.** | *We come from Paris.* |
| Nous **en** venons. | *We come from there.* |
| Je parle **de ma voiture.** | *I'm talking about my car.* |
| J'**en** parle. | *I'm talking about (of) it.* |

**b.** *En* means *some* or *any (of it/of them)* when it replaces a noun introduced by the partitive article. In this case it may refer to persons as well as things.

| | |
|---|---|
| Elle veut **de la glace?** | *Does she want some ice cream?* |
| Oui, elle **en** veut. | *Yes, she wants some.* |
| Il ne prend pas **de légumes.** | *He doesn't take any vegetables.* |
| Il n'**en** prend pas. | *He doesn't take any.* |
| As-tu **des amis?** | *Do you have friends?* |
| J'**en** ai. | *I have some.* |

**c.** *En* is also used when the noun is omitted after a number or an expression of quantity.

| | |
|---|---|
| J'ai vingt dollars. | *I have twenty dollars.* |
| J'**en** ai vingt. | *I have twenty (of them).* |
| As-tu de l'argent? | *Do you have any money?* |
| Oui, j'**en** ai beaucoup. | *Yes, I have a lot (of money).* |

**d.** *En* is always expressed in French even though it may have no English equivalent.

| | |
|---|---|
| Avez-vous **du sucre?** | *Do you have any sugar?* |
| Oui, j'**en** ai. | *Yes, I do (have some).* |
| Tu joues **du piano.** | *You play the piano.* |
| Tu **en** joues souvent. | *You play often.* |

NOTE:

**1.** *En* follows the same rules of position in the sentence as other object pronouns.

| | |
|---|---|
| Il voulait **en** acheter. | *He wanted to buy some.* |
| Je n'**en** veux pas. | *I don't want any.* |
| **En** veux-tu? | *Do you want some (any)?* |
| Peux-tu **en** trouver ? | *Can you find any?* |
| Je ne peux pas **en** trouver. | *I can't find any.* |

**2.** Affirmative familiar commands (*tu* form) of *-er* verbs retain the *s* before *en*.

| | |
|---|---|
| Manges-**en**! | *Eat some!* |
| N'**en** mange pas! | *Don't eat any!* |

**3.** *En* precedes *voici* and *voilà*.

| | |
|---|---|
| En voici deux. | *Here are two of them.* |
| En voilà. | *Here are some.* |

## EXERCICE R

*Exprimez ce qui arrive aux personnes suivantes après l'école.*

EXEMPLE:   Jean a des problèmes.
Jean **en a.**

*1.* Je sors du lycée.

_____

*2.* Tisha et moi mangeons de la glace.

_____

*3.* Vous parlez de vos classes.

_____

*4.* Tu achètes des bonbons.

_____

*5.* Janine et Valeria trouvent de l'argent.

_____

*6.* Antoine prépare des sandwiches.

_____

## EXERCICE S

**The Dubois have decided to lose weight.** *Exprimez ce qu'ils vont faire.*

EXEMPLE:   Maman va acheter du poisson.
Maman va **en** acheter.

*1.* Papa ne va pas manger de viande.

_____

*2.* Je vais faire des exercices.

_____

*3.* Julien va préparer une recette amaigrissante.

_____

*4.* Les filles ne vont pas choisir de dessert.

_____

*5.* Claude et moi, nous allons prendre des vitamines.

_____

*6.* Tu ne vas pas acheter de gâteau.

_____

**7.** Mariane ne va pas parler de son régime.

_____

**8.** Les garçons vont avoir de la salade.

_____

## EXERCICE T

**Say what your friends want you to do and not do on vacation.** *Utilisez* en *dans vos réponses.*

EXEMPLE:   chercher de l'amusement, pas d'ennuis
          **Cherches-en. N'en cherche pas.**

**1.** faire du sport, pas de travail

_____

**2.** acheter des souvenirs, pas de vêtements

_____

**3.** manger des spécialités, pas de plats ordinaires

_____

**4.** parler de tes aventures, pas de tes problèmes

_____

**5.** raconter des histoires drôles, pas d'histoires ennuyeuses

_____

**6.** porter des vêtements sport, pas de vêtements élégants

_____

## MASTERY EXERCISES

## EXERCICE U

**A friend asks you questions about an upcoming trip. In each of your answers, use a direct object pronoun, an indirect object pronoun, or an adverbial pronoun.**

EXEMPLE:   L'avion va partir de Chicago?
          Oui, il va **en** partir.

          Vas-tu téléphoner à tes parents tous les jours?
          Non, je ne vais pas **leur** téléphoner tous les jours.

*1.* Vas-tu voyager en Europe?

_____

*2.* Penses-tu visiter la France?

_____

*3.* Vas-tu écrire à tes amis?

_____

*4.* Vas-tu passer plusieurs jours à Paris?

_____

*5.* Descends-tu dans des hôtels de luxe?

_____

*6.* Aimes-tu visiter les musées importants?

_____

7. Achètes-tu souvent des souvenirs?

_____

*8.* Offres-tu un cadeau à ta mère?

_____

*9.* Vas-tu revenir d'Europe avant septembre?

_____

*10.* Vas-tu rentrer à Chicago tout de suite après le voyage?

_____

## EXERCICE V

**Express your feelings about the following people and things.** *Employez les pronoms appropriés.*

EXEMPLE:     ta tante (écrire de temps en temps, aimer beaucoup)
**Je lui écris** de temps en temps.
**Je l'aime** beaucoup.

*1.* ta meilleure amie (embrasser continuellement, téléphoner tous les jours)

_____

_____

*2.* le cinéma (aller le samedi soir, aimer beaucoup)

_____

_____

*3.* tes parents (parler souvent, respecter)

_____

_____

*4.* des bonbons (manger deux par jour, acheter pour une fête)

_____

_____

*5.* le tennis (jouer tous les jours, aimer beaucoup)

_____

_____

*6.* la France (vouloir visiter, compter rester deux semaines)

_____

_____

## EXERCICE W

**Catherine and her friend Tyron love desserts. They have a conversation with the organizer of a bake sale at their school.** *Exprimez leur conversation en français.*

*1.* Desserts? I like them a lot.

_____

*2.* You prepared chocolate mousse? Can I taste it? It's delicious. I want some.

_____

_____

*3.* You made pies! I want to buy one and take it home.

_____

*4.* Look at that chocolate cake. Give some to my friend Tyron, please.

_____

_____

*5.* Sell me some cookies. They are delicious.

_____

*6.* The apple pie. Put it in a box. Hurry!

_____

*7.* My parents? I want to bring them some eclairs.

_____

8. Go to the Gaumont pastry shop. The cakes there are delicious.

_____

_____

9 . I want to work there. Then I can eat some for breakfast, lunch, and dinner.

_____

_____

10. Catherine, you'll become fat and sick. You can't do it.

_____

_____

# Chapter 18
## Stress Pronouns

## [ 1 ]  FORMS

| SINGULAR | | | PLURAL | | |
|---|---|---|---|---|---|
| (je) | **moi** | *I, me* | (nous) | **nous** | *we* |
| (tu) | **toi** | *you* (familiar) | (vous) | **vous** | *you* (also formal singular) |
| (il) | **lui** | *he, him* | (ils) | **eux** | *they, them* |
| (elle) | **elle** | *she, her* | (elles) | **elles** | *they, them* |

## [ 2 ]  USES OF STRESS PRONOUNS

A stress pronoun can function either as subject or as object. It can either replace another word or reinforce it for added emphasis.

**a.** Stress pronouns are used in a compound subject or object.

**Lui et Marie** arrivent.   *He and Marie are arriving.*

J'ai invité **Jean et lui.**   *I invited Jean and him.*

NOTE:

1. If one of the stress pronouns is *moi*, the verb is put in the first person plural. The pronoun *nous* may or may not be expressed.

**Paul et moi sommes** contents.   } *Paul and I are happy.*
**Paul et moi, nous sommes** contents.

2. If *toi* is one of the stress pronouns, the verb is put in the second person plural.

**Luc et toi êtes** en retard.   } *Luc and you are late.*
**Luc et toi, vous êtes** en retard

## EXERCICE A

A friend of yours is sick, and you want to cheer him up. *Dites ce que les personnes suivantes ont décidé de faire.*

lui acheter un livre amusant
lui apporter quelque chose à manger
lui donner des bandes dessinées
lui écrire une lettre

lui envoyer des cartes
lui offrir un nouveau disque
lui parler au téléphone

EXEMPLE:   Claire et vous, **vous allez lui écrire une lettre.**

*1.* Toi et moi _____ .

*2.* Leticia et eux _____ .

*3.* Denise et toi _____ .

**4.** Shandelle et lui _____ .

**5.** Les filles Dupont et elle _____ .

**6.** Yoko et nous _____ .

**b.** Stress pronouns are used when there is no verb expressed.

| | |
|---|---|
| Qui est là? —**Moi.** | *Who's there? —Me. (I am.)* |
| J'aime le golf. **Lui aussi.** | *I like golf. He does too.* |
| Il est plus grand **que toi.** | *He is taller than you.* |

## EXERCICE B

**Your youth group had tryouts for a play it plans to present. Your friend asks who got picked.** *Exprimez vos réponses.*

EXEMPLE:    Claude et toi?
            Oui, **nous** aussi.

**1.** Toi?

_____

**2.** Lise?

_____

**3.** Lise et toi?

_____

**4.** Tara et Patrick?

_____

**5.** Catherine et Teresa?

_____

**6.** Miguel?

_____

**7.** Moi?

_____

**8.** Éric et moi?

_____

**c.** Stress pronouns are used to add emphasis to a noun or another pronoun.

| | |
|---|---|
| **Moi,** je vais étudier. | *I'm going to study.* |
| Paul, **lui,** est très intelligent. | *Paul is very intelligent.* |
| Je l'aime bien, **elle.** | *I do like her.* |

## EXERCICE C

*Dites de quel sport les personnes suivantes sont passionnées.*

EXEMPLE:    Marc / football
**Lui, il est passionné de** football.

1. vous / golf

_____

2. Aldo et Serge / base-ball

_____

3. Ginette / tennis

_____

4. tu / ski

_____

5. nous / rugby

_____

6. Brigitte et Noriko / volley-ball

_____

**d.** Stress pronouns are used after *ce + être.*

    Qui est-ce ? —**C'est moi.**     *Who is it? —It's I.*
    **C'est lui** qui est parti.     *He's the one who left.*

NOTE:    Before the stress pronouns *eux* and *elles,* the verb *être* may be used either in the singular (*c'est eux, c'est elles*) or in the plural (*ce sont elles, ce sont eux*) although the singular is more commonly used.

## EXERCICE D

**The principal wants to know who does what in your class.** *Exprimez vos réponses à ses questions selon l'exemple.*

EXEMPLE:    Qui est très gentille? (Suzanne)
**C'est elle.**

1. Qui efface le tableau tout le temps? (Amar)

_____

2. Qui aide les élèves après l'école? (je)

_____

**3.** Qui écrit les devoirs au tableau? (Nicole et moi)

_____

**4.** Qui fait attention? (les filles)

_____

**5.** Qui étudie la leçon? (tu)

_____

**6.** Qui travaille sérieusement? (les garçons)

_____

**7.** Qui corrige les fautes au tableau? (Vinnie et vous)

_____

> **e.** Stress pronouns are used after a preposition to refer to people.
>
> | | |
> |---|---|
> | Elle va **chez toi**. | *She is going to your house.* |
> | Je parle **d'eux**. | *I'm speaking about them.* |
> | Je pense souvent **à lui**. | *I often think of him.* |
> | Ce livre est **à moi**. | *This book belongs to me.* |

## EXERCICE E

**Your younger brother is curious about you and your friends.** *Répondez à ses questions en suivant l'exemple.*

EXEMPLE:     Tu danses avec Jacques?
             Oui, je danse **avec lui.**

**1.** Tu joues au tennis avec Monica et Patricia?

_____

**2.** Tu vas souvent chez Marvin?

_____

**3.** Nous habitons près de Lucie?

_____

**4.** Raoul est assis à côté de toi dans la classe de français?

_____

**5.** Tu travailles quelquefois pour les Moreau?

_____

**6.** Est-ce que tu parles de mes amis et de moi?

_____

**7.** Tu veux aller au parc sans moi?

_____

**8.** Anne et toi, vous parlez entre vous?

_____

**f.** Stress pronouns _moi_ and _toi_ are used in affirmative commands instead of the pronouns _me_ and _te_.

| | |
|---|---|
| Écoutez-**moi**. | _Listen to me._ |
| Donne-**moi** un journal. | _Give me a newspaper._ |
| Repose-**toi** demain. | _Take a rest tomorrow._ |

## M A S T E R Y   E X E R C I S E S

### EXERCICE F

**Complete Isabelle's story about life with her two sisters.** _Utilisez le pronom accentué approprié._

_____ , je m'appelle Isabelle. D'habitude, mes sœurs et _____ , nous sommes bonnes amies.
_1._ _2._

Ma sœur Nicole est plus grande que _____ . J'aime parler avec _____ . C'est avec
_3._ _4._

_____ que je discute de tous mes problèmes. Chantal a neuf ans et elle n'est pas toujours sage.
_5._

Hier elle a pris mon bracelet et elle a dit : «Il est à _____ .» «Il n'est pas à _____ !» j'ai
_6._ _7._

répondu. Elle a pleuré et a appelé maman. «Donne-_____ mon bracelet!» j'ai crié. Maman
_8._

nous a dit: « _____ , les filles, vous n'êtes pas sages. Qui a commencé cette querelle? Répondez
_9._

_____ .» J'ai dit: «Ce n'est pas _____ . C'est _____ !» Chantal a dit: «C'est _____
_10._ _11._ _12._ _13._

qui a commencé! » et elle a pleuré. Heureusement maman a emmené Chantal faire des courses avec

_____ , et Nicole et _____ avons fait une promenade ensemble. Je lui ai dit: « _____ ,
_14._ _15._ _16._

Nicole, tu es ma meilleure amie.» Nous avons rencontré nos amis Pierre et Claude et nous avons parlé

avec _____ un moment. Ensuite nous sommes rentrées chez _____ . La journée a bien fini.
_17._ _18._

## EXERCICE G

**Your father is a little angry and wants to know what is going on. Use stress pronouns in your answers.**

EXEMPLE:   Est-ce que Paul travaille avec Michel?
Paul travaille **avec lui.**

*1.* Est-ce que tu es allé chez tes amis?

Je suis allé _____.

*2.* Vous ne faites rien sans vos sœurs.

Nous ne faisons rien _____.

*3.* Est-ce vous qui faites tout ce bruit?

Ce n'est pas _____.

*4.* Sylvie a cassé le vase bleu?

Ce n'est pas _____.

*5.* Est-ce que ce livre est à ton frère?

Ce livre est _____.

*6.* Venez-vous au cinéma avec votre mère et moi?

Je vais au cinéma _____.

## EXERCICE H

**You are about to take a trip.** *Parlez de vos projets.*

*1.* Me, I love winter sports.

_____

*2.* During the winter, my friends and I always go to the mountains.

_____

_____

*3.* For us, it's the ideal time to go skiing and ice skating.

_____

_____

*4.* Antoine and Patrick? They are the ones who organize all the excursions.

_____

_____

*5.* Have you met Jean Dupont? It is he who is the ski instructor.

_____

**6.** His brother is more amusing than he.

_____

**7.** We ski with them after the lessons.

_____

**8.** They live near you.

_____

**9.** It's eight o'clock. We're leaving now. Come with us, you two.

_____

**10.** Who isn't here? Lise and Maria? We're not leaving without them.

_____

_____

# Chapter 19
## Relative Pronouns

A relative pronoun introduces a clause that describes someone or something mentioned in the main clause. The person or thing the pronoun refers to is called the antecedent because it precedes the relative pronoun. The most common relative pronouns are *qui* and *que*.

## [ 1 ] QUI

*Qui* (who, which, that) serves as the subject of the verb in the relative clause that it introduces. It is used for both persons and things.

[relative clause]
Où est *la fille* **qui parle** si bien?     *Where is the girl who speaks so well?*
*[antecedent]* [subject] [verb]

[relative clause]
Voilà *une voiture* **qui coûte** cher.     *There is a car that is expensive.*
*[antecedent]* [subject] [verb]

NOTE: The verb of a relative clause introduced by *qui* agrees with its antecedent noun or stress pronoun.

[relative clause]
C'est *toi* **qui** en **es** responsable.     *You are the one who is responsible for it.*
*[antecedent]* [subject] [verb]

[relative clause]
C'est *nous* **qui sommes restés.**     *We are the ones who stayed.*
*[antecedent]* [subject]     [verb]

## EXERCICE A

You are looking through binoculars from the top of the Eiffel Tower. Describe what you see below. *Employez le pronom relatif* **qui.**

EXEMPLE:    Je vois des voitures. Elles roulent vite.
           Je vois des voitures **qui** roulent vite.

*1.* Il y a un homme. Il consulte un plan de la ville.

_____

*2.* Regarde ces enfants. Ils jouent dans la rue.

_____

*3.* Voilà une église. Elle est magnifique.

_____

*4.* Une femme entre dans un musée. Il n'est pas loin.

_____

*5.* J'observe des dames. Elles prennent des photos.

_____

*6.* Une famille marche dans une rue. La rue est très animée.

_____

*7.* Un monsieur rencontre une femme. Elle a l'air très belle.

_____

*8.* Cette fille prend un bus. Il va sur les quais de la Seine.

_____

## EXERCICE B

**Use a stress pronoun and a relative clause in the** *passé composé.* *Exprimez ce que les personnes suivantes ont fait.*

EXEMPLE:    je / écrire cette lettre
           **C'est moi qui ai écrit** cette lettre.

*1.* nous / manger tout le gâteau

_____

*2.* tu / oublier de vider les ordures

_____

*3.* il / jeter le journal d'aujourd'hui

_____

*4.* elles / laver le chien

_____

*5.* je / déranger les autres

_____

*6.* vous / couper les fleurs

_____

7. elle / crier à haute voix

_____

*8.*   ils / téléphoner toute la soirée

_____

## EXERCICE C

*Donnez votre opinion en utilisant le pronom relatif* **qui.**

EXEMPLE:    Le président est un homme **qui travaille dur.**

*1.* Paris est une ville _____ .

*2.* La Porsche est une voiture _____ .

*3.* Mon professeur de français est une personne _____ .

*4.* Le base-ball est un sport _____ .

*5.* Eddie Murphy est un acteur _____ .

*6.* Le français est une langue _____ .

*7.* La glace est un dessert _____ .

*8.* Le cheval est un animal _____ .

# [ 2 ]  *QUE*

*Que* (whom, which, that) serves as the direct object of the verb in a relative clause and is usually followed by a subject noun or pronoun. It is used for both persons and things.

[relative clause]
C'est ***l'ami* que nous aimons.**
*[antecedent]* [object] [subject] [verb]

*It's the friend (that) we like.*

[relative clause]
Voilà ***le sac* que Lucie veut.**
[antecedent] [object] [subject] [verb]

*Here is the bag (that) Lucie wants.*

NOTE:

1.  The relative pronoun is always expressed in French although it is frequently omitted in English.

    C'est la chanson **que** j'adore.

    *That's the song (that) I love.*

2.  *Que* becomes *qu'* before a vowel.

    Je vais acheter le livre **qu'il recommande.**

    *I am going to buy the book (that) he recommends.*

## EXERCICE D

**Combine the sentences with the relative pronoun** *que. Exprimez ce que les personnes suivantes sont en train de faire* **(are doing).**

EXEMPLE:   Elle sort une cassette. Elle va écouter la cassette.
           Elle sort une cassette **qu'**elle va écouter.

*1.* Je cherche un disque. Je veux acheter le disque.

_____

*2.* Elles achètent des livres. Elles vont lire ces livres.

_____

*3.* Vous préparez un plat. Vous allez manger ce plat.

_____

*4.* Nous écoutons une chanson. Nous aimons cette chanson.

_____

*5.* Tu regardes un film. Tu trouves le film intéressant.

_____

*6.* Ils réparent une bicyclette. Ils vont utiliser cette bicyclette.

_____

*7.* Elle présente l'homme. Elle va épouser cet homme.

_____

*8.* Il écrit une lettre. Il va envoyer cette lettre à une amie.

_____

## EXERCICE E

**Using the relative pronoun** *que,* **explain how the following persons feel about these people.**
*Suivez l'exemple.*

EXEMPLE:   mon père est le parent / mon frère / trouver indulgent
            Mon père est le parent **que** mon frère trouve indulgent.

*1.* une amie est une personne / nous / respecter

_____

*2.* nos professeurs sont des gens / les étudiants / trouver sympathique

_____

*3.* le président est un homme / on / adorer

_____

*4.* ma mère est une femme / tu / estimer

_____

*5.* Kathleen Turner est une actrice / les gens / aimer

_____

*6.* Isaac Asimov est un auteur / tout le monde / trouver intéressant

_____

*7.* Mick Jagger est un musicien / je / admirer

_____

**8.** Michael Jordan est un athlète / vous / vouloir rencontrer

_____

## EXERCICE F

*Donnez votre opinion sur les personnes et les choses suivantes en employant* que.

EXEMPLE: Le président est un homme **que j'écoute.**

**1.** Paris est une ville _____ .

**2.** La Porsche est une voiture _____ .

**3.** Mon prof de français est une personne _____ .

**4.** Le base-ball est un sport _____ .

**5.** Tom Hanks est un acteur _____ .

**6.** Le français est une langue _____ .

**7.** La glace est un dessert _____ .

**8.** Le chien est un animal _____ .

## M A S T E R Y   E X E R C I S E S

## EXERCICE G

**Write a description of a person, place, or thing using** *qui* **and** *que.* **Then see if your classmates can guess what you've described.** *Suivez l'exemple.*

EXEMPLE: C'est un homme **que** tout le monde admire. C'est un homme **qui** travaille dans un restaurant. C'est l'homme **qui** prépare les repas. (Réponse: **C'est le chef.**)

_____

_____

_____

_____

## EXERCICE H

**What is your opinion?** *Complétez les phrases suivantes en employant* qui *ou* que.

**1.** Je respecte les gens _____ tout le monde admire.

Je respecte les gens _____ travaillent dur.

**2.** J'ai des professeurs _____ j'admire.

J'ai des professeurs _____ sont très sympathiques.

**3.** J'ai un ami _____ parle tout le temps au téléphone.

J'ai un ami _____ j'aime beaucoup.

**4.** J'ai vu un film _____ est trop violent.

J'ai vu un film _____ mes amies n'aiment pas.

**5.** Je vais acheter un disque compact _____ mon ami recommande.

Je vais acheter un disque laser _____ coûte trop cher.

**6.** Je veux une voiture _____ est très sport.

Je veux une voiture _____ mes amis trouvent chic.

**7.** J'ai un chien _____ est très fidèle.

J'ai un chien _____ tout le monde adore.

**8.** Je vais voir une pièce _____ les critiques trouvent excellente.

Je vais voir une pièce _____ se joue dans notre ville.

# EXERCICE I

**You are looking through a photo album with some friends.** *Décrivez les photos que vous voyez.*

**1.** These are the children (that) I take care of.

_____

**2.** Here are our friends who are very nice.

_____

**3.** This is the boy (that) I love.

_____

**4.** Look at the girls who work with me.

_____

**5.** This is the city that I want to visit again.

_____

**6.** You can see the restaurant that everyone loves.

_____

7. There are my friends who go out with me all the time.

   _____

8. I will show you the car (that) I hope to buy.

   _____

9. Here is my pen pal who lives in Canada.

   _____

10. This is my cousin who works in France.

   _____

# Chapter 20
## Prepositions

Prepositions relate two elements of a sentence (noun to noun; verb to noun, pronoun, or another verb).

| | |
|---|---|
| Regarde la maison **de** mon ami. | *Look at my friend's house (the house of my friend).* |
| Paul parle **à** ses parents. | *Paul speaks to his parents.* |
| Elle sort **avec** lui. | *She is going out with him.* |

The most frequently used prepositions in French are *à* and *de*.

## [ 1 ] PREPOSITION *À* (AT, IN, TO)

**a.** It often indicates a location or a moment in time.

| | |
|---|---|
| J'habite **à** la campagne. | *I live in the country.* |
| Elle viendra **à** midi. | *She will come at noon.* |
| Ils vont **au** cinéma. | *They are going to the movies.* |

**b.** A number of verbs require the preposition *à*.

| | |
|---|---|
| aller à *to go to* | penser à *to think of* |
| demander à *to ask* | répondre à *to answer* |
| donner à *to give* | |

NOTE: The preposition *à* contracts with the articles *le* and *les* to become *au* and *aux*. There is no contraction with *la* or *l'*.

| | |
|---|---|
| Allons **au** cinéma. | *Let's go to the movies.* |
| Elle va parler **aux** garçons. | *She is going to speak to the boys.* |
| Il donne des fleurs **à** la fille. | *He gives flowers to the girl.* |

### EXERCICE A

*Exprimez où vont les personnes suivantes.*

EXEMPLE:

Nous **allons à la bibliothèque.**

**1.**

Je _____.

**2.**

Les filles _____.

**3.**

Roger _____.

**4.**

Nous _____.

**5.**

Tu _____.

**6.**

Claire et moi _____.

## [ 2 ] PREPOSITION *DE* (ABOUT, FROM, OF)

**a.** *De* indicates possession, relationship, or a specific characteristic of a noun.

| | |
|---|---|
| C'est la maison **de** mon oncle. | *It is my uncle's house.* |
| Bruno est le frère **de** mon amie. | *Bruno is my friend's brother.* |
| Elle veut un collier **de** perles. | *She wants a pearl necklace.* |
| C'est la couleur **du** ciel. | *It is the color of the sky.* |

NOTE: The preposition *de* contracts with the articles *le* and *les* to become *du* and *des*. There is no contraction with *l'* or *la*.

| | |
|---|---|
| Ouvre la porte **du** jardin. | *Open the door of the garden.* |
| Voici les livres **des** étudiants. | *Here are the books of the students.* |
| Où est l'arrêt **de** l'autobus? | *Where is the bus stop?* |

**b.** A number of verbs are often followed by the preposition *de.*

parler de  *to speak of*                    venir de  *to come from*
partir de  *to leave from*

Nous **parlons du** docteur.              *We speak about the doctor.*
Nous **venons de** la plage.              *We come from the beach.*

## EXERCICE B

*De quoi parle-t-on?* **What are we talking about?**

EXEMPLE:    je / voyage *(m.)*
            Je **parle du** voyage.

**1.** Pedro et Henri / professeur *(m.)*

_____

**2.** tu / examens *(m. pl.)*

_____

**3.** nous / film *(m.)*

_____

**4.** M. Arnoux / classe *(f.)*

_____

**5.** les filles / garçons *(m. pl.)*

_____

**6.** je / école *(f.)*

_____

## [ 3 ]  OTHER COMMON PREPOSITIONS

**après** *after*
Il te verra après la classe.              *He'll see you after class.*

**autour de** *around*
Luc marche autour de la salle.            *Luc walks around the room.*

**avant (de)** *before*
Je partirai avant toi.                    *I shall leave before you.*
Avant de partir, je rangerai ma chambre.  *Before I leave, I'll tidy up my room.*

**avec** *with*
Viens avec moi.                           *Come with me.*

**chez** (+ person) *to, at* (the house / place of a person)
Vas-tu chez le docteur?                   *Are you going to the doctor's?*
Je vais chez moi.                         *I'm going home.*

**contre** *against*
C'est une course contre la montre.     *It's a race against time.*

**dans** *in, into, within*
Ne va pas dans la cuisine.     *Don't go into the kitchen.*
Je reviendrai dans dix minutes.     *I'll be back in ten minutes.*

**derrière** *behind*
Jean est derrière le garage.     *Jean is behind the garage.*

**devant** *in front of*
La voiture est devant la maison.     *The car is in front of the house.*

**en** *at; by; in*
Elle a fait le dîner en une heure.     *She made dinner in one hour.*
Je voudrais un sac en cuir.     *I would like a leather bag.*

**entre** *between, among*
Ils parlent entre eux.     *They speak among themselves.*

**loin de** *far from*
J'habite loin d'ici.     *I live far from here.*

**par** *by, through*
Ils sont entrés par la fenêtre.     *They entered through the window.*

**près de** *near*
Le théâtre est près d'ici.     *The theater is near here.*

**sans** *without*
Ne pars pas sans moi.     *Don't leave without me.*

**sous** *under*
Cherche sous le lit.     *Look under the bed.*

**sur** *on, upon*
Le livre est sur la table.     *The book is on the table.*

**vers** *towards*
Il marche vers le train.     *He's walking toward the train.*

## EXERCICE C

**Describe Marco's day by filling in each blank with a preposition from the list above.**

*1.* Marco est allé _____ son ami Paul.

*2.* Paul habite à cinq minutes de Marco. Ce n'est pas _____ sa maison.

*3.* Il a joué au basket _____ Paul.

*4.* _____ le match, ils avaient faim et soif.

*5.* Ils sont entrés _____ la cuisine.

*6.* Ils ont vu des biscuits et du soda _____ la table.

*7.* _____ leur goûter ils sont allés se laver les mains.

*8.* Ils ont mangé en silence _____ un mot.

## [ 4 ] PREPOSITIONS USED BEFORE AN INFINITIVE

In French, the infinitive is the verb form that normally follows a preposition.

| | |
|---|---|
| Il commence à **applaudir**. | *He begins to applaud.* |
| Elle a oublié **de** me **téléphoner**. | *She forgot to call me.* |
| Elle est partie **sans parler**. | *She left without speaking.* |

**a.** Some verbs require *à* before an infinitive.

| | |
|---|---|
| s'amuser à   *to have fun* | se mettre à   *to begin to* |
| commencer à   *to begin to* | penser à   *to think about* |
| continuer à   *to continue to* | se préparer à   *to prepare to* |
| demander à   *to ask to* | renoncer à   *to give up* |
| encourager à   *to encourage to* | réussir à   *to succeed in* |

| | |
|---|---|
| Jean **s'amuse** à jouer au football. | *John has fun playing soccer.* |
| Nous **demandons** à sortir. | *We ask to go out.* |

**b.** Some verbs require *de* before an infinitive.

| | |
|---|---|
| s'arrêter de   *to stop* | oublier de   *to forget to* |
| choisir de   *to choose to* | parler de   *to speak about* |
| décider de   *to decide to* | refuser de   *to refuse to* |
| se dépêcher de   *to hurry to* | regretter de   *to regret to* |
| essayer de   *to try to* | rêver de   *to dream about* |

| | |
|---|---|
| J'ai **décidé de** partir. | *I decided to leave.* |
| Tu **essaies de** patiner. | *You try to skate.* |

## EXERCICE D

**The following persons are trying to improve themselves.** *Exprimez comment.*

EXEMPLE:   Lise / commencer / travailler sérieusement
Lise **commence à** travailler sérieusement.

*1.* Luigi / essayer / trouver un bon emploi

_____

*2.* Régine et Clara / décider / étudier une autre langue étrangère

_____

*3.* Luc et moi / se préparer / passer le bac

_____

*4.* vous / parler / travailler davantage *(more)*

_____

**5.** je / se mettre / tout prendre au sérieux

_____

**6.** tu / encourager tes amis / respecter les autres

_____

## EXERCICE E

*Complétez l'histoire de Raoul avec les prépositions nécessaires.*

Mon ami Raoul rêve _____ devenir docteur.  Il commence _____ remplir les
　　　　　　　　　　　　　 **1.** 　　　　　　　　　　　　　 **2.**

papiers nécessaires pour aller à l'université.  Naturellement il parle _____ ses résultats scolaires.
　　　　　　　　　　　　　　　　　　　　　　　　　　　　　　　　　　　　　　　 **3.**

Ses professeurs l'encouragent _____ mentionner ses accomplissements sportifs. Il décide
　　　　　　　　　　　　　　　　 **4.**

_____ écrire un paragraphe sur son talent musical.  Aussi, il n'oublie pas _____ raconter
　 **5.** 　　　　　　　　　　　　　　　　　　　　　　　　　　　　　　　　　　 **6.**

une anecdote amusante.  Enfin, Raoul finit son essai et il s'arrête _____ écrire.  Je suis sûr qu'il
　　　　　　　　　　　　　　　　　　　　　　　　　　　　　　　　　　　 **7.**

réussira _____ devenir docteur.  C'est un garçon qui ne renonce jamais _____ ses ambitions.
　　　　　 **8.** 　　　　　　　　　　　　　　　　　　　　　　　　　　　　　　　 **9.**

Il choisit _____ envoyer sa demande d'inscription à toutes les universités renommées.
　　　　　 **10.**

## EXERCICE F

**Your friend is offering you tips on how to succeed. Use the command form of the verbs in parentheses and the appropriate preposition.** *Exprimez ce qu'il / elle dit.*

EXEMPLE:　　copier tes amis (renoncer)
　　　　　　　**Renonce à** copier tes amis.

**1.** saisir chaque occasion (choisir)

_____

**2.** étudier (continuer)

_____

**3.** gagner le respect des autres (penser)

_____

**4.** travailler plus dur (commencer)

_____

**5.** parler toujours correctement (essayer)

_____

**6.** trouver de bons amis (réussir)

_____

**7.** perdre ton temps (refuser)

_____

**8.** faire de ton mieux (décider)

_____

## EXERCICE G

**Complete these sentences about yourself.**

**1.** Je me prépare _____ .

**2.** Je choisis _____ .

**3.** Je commence _____ .

**4.** Je continue _____ .

**5.** J'oublie _____ .

**6.** Je regrette _____ .

**c.** Some other prepositions are commonly followed by an infinitive.

au lieu de _instead of_                     pour _in order to, for the purpose of_
avant de _before_                           sans _without_

Elle écoute des disques **au lieu d'étudier.**      _She listens to records instead of studying._
Il se peigne **avant de sortir.**                   _He combs his hair before going out._
Nous travaillons **pour gagner** de l'argent.       _We work to earn money._
Tu parles **sans penser.**                          _You speak without thinking._

## EXERCICE H

**Say what these people do.** _Combinez les phrases avec la préposition indiquée entre parenthèses._

EXEMPLE:    Jeanne quitte la maison. Elle ne fait pas ses devoirs. (sans)
            Jeanne quitte la maison **sans faire** ses devoirs.

**1.** Pierre regarde la télévision. Il ne lave pas la voiture de son père. (au lieu de)

_____

**2.** Roger se rase. Il sort avec Gisèle. (avant de)

_____

**3.** Lise garde les enfants. Elle gagne de l'argent. (pour)

_____

**4.** Marie prend la voiture. Elle ne demande pas la permission à ses parents. (sans)

_____

**5.** Paul met de l'argent de côté. Il se marie avec Georgette. (avant de)

_____

**6.** Janine va à un grand magasin. Elle ne prend pas son portefeuille. (sans)

_____

**7.** Joseph s'amuse. Il ne travaille pas. (au lieu de)

_____

**8.** Liliane dîne au restaurant. Elle célèbre son anniversaire. (pour)

_____

## EXERCICE I

*Complétez les phrases suivantes avec un verbe à l'infinitif.*

**1.** Je regarde ma montre avant de _____ .

**2.** Je vais en ville pour _____ .

**3.** Je quitte la maison sans _____ .

**4.** Je fais mes devoirs au lieu de _____ .

**d.** **Some verbs are followed by an infinitive without a preposition.**

| | |
|---|---|
| aimer *to like, love* | penser *to intend* |
| aller *to go* | pouvoir *to be able* |
| compter *to intend* | préférer *to prefer* |
| désirer *to wish, want* | savoir *to know how to* |
| espérer *to hope* | vouloir *to wish, want* |

| | |
|---|---|
| Il va sortir. | *He is going to go out.* |
| Nous ne savons pas cuisiner. | *We don't know how to cook.* |
| Peux-tu venir? | *Can you come?* |

## EXERCICE J

**Express the following people's hopes and dreams.** *Combinez un élément de chaque colonne.*

| | |
|---|---|
| aimer | acheter une villa en France |
| aller | changer le monde |
| compter | devenir un(e) athlète célèbre |
| désirer | écrire un livre |
| espérer | être bien connu(e)(s) |
| penser | explorer l'espace |
| pouvoir | faire fortune |
| préférer | gagner beaucoup d'argent |
| savoir | travailler en France |
| vouloir | voyager autour du monde |

*1.* Je _____ .

*2.* Carlos _____ .

*3.* Ces garçons _____ .

*4.* Danielle _____ .

*5.* Vous _____ .

*6.* Cette fille _____ .

*7.* Ma sœur et moi _____ .

*8.* Laura et Julie _____ .

*9.* Tu _____ .

*10.* Nous _____ .

## EXERCICE K

**Complete the sentences in French.** *Exprimez vos idées.*

*1.* Je sais _____ .

*2.* Je veux _____ .

*3.* Je préfère _____ .

*4.* Je compte _____ .

*5.* Je peux _____ .

*6.* J'espère _____ .

## [ 5 ] PREPOSITIONS WITH GEOGRAPHICAL EXPRESSIONS

**a.** To express *to* or *in* with names of places:

| en | feminine countries<br>continents<br>provinces<br>islands | **en France** *to (in) France*<br>**en Amérique du Sud** *to (in) South America*<br>**en Bretagne** *to (in) Brittany*<br>**en Corse** *to (in) Corsica* |
|---|---|---|
|  | masculine countries<br>beginning with vowel | **en Israël** *to (in) Israel* |
| au | masculine countries | **au Canada** *(to) in Canada* |
| aux | plural countries | **aux États-Unis** *(to) in the United States* |
| à | cities | **à Paris** *to (in) Paris* |

| Elle habite **en France**. | *She lives in France.* |
|---|---|
| Je vais aller **en Espagne** cet été. | *I'm going to Spain this summer.* |
| J'ai de la famille **au Canada**. | *I have relatives in Canada.* |
| As-tu jamais été **à New York**? | *Have you ever been to New York?* |

**b.** To express *from* with names of places:

| de | feminine countries<br>continents<br>provinces<br>islands | **de France** *from France*<br>**d'Amérique du Sud** *from South America*<br>**de Bretagne** *from Brittany*<br>**de Corse** *from Corsica* |
|---|---|---|
|  | masculine countries<br>beginning with vowel | **d'Israël** *from Israel* |
|  | cities | **de Paris** *from Paris* |
| du | masculine countries | **du Canada** *from Canada* |
| des | plural countries | **des États-Unis** *from the United States* |

| Il va venir **d'Italie**. | *He is going to come from Italy.* |
|---|---|
| Elle part **du Canada**. | *She is leaving from Canada.* |
| Le vol arrive **de Paris**. | *The flight is arriving from Paris.* |

NOTE:

1. Generally, geographical names are feminine if they end in *-e*, with the exception of *le Mexique, le Cambodge* (Cambodia), and *le Zaïre*.

2. The definite article is not used with *Israël* and *Haïti*.

**c.** Feminine countries, continents, provinces:

| | |
|---|---|
| l'Allemagne *Germany* | l'Égypte *Egypt* |
| l'Angleterre *England* | l'Espagne *Spain* |
| l'Autriche *Austria* | la France *France* |
| la Belgique *Belgium* | la Grèce *Greece* |
| la Chine *China* | Haïti *Haiti* |
| l'Écosse *Scotland* | la Hongrie *Hungary* |

l'Irlande *Ireland*  
l'Italie *Italy*  
la Norvège *Norway*  
la Pologne *Poland*  

la Roumanie *Romania*  
la Russie *Russia*  
la Suède *Sweden*  
la Suisse *Switzerland*  

l'Afrique *Africa*  
l'Amérique du Nord *North America*  
l'Amérique du Sud *South America*  

l'Asie *Asia*  
l'Australie *Australia*  
l'Europe *Europe*  

l'Alsace *Alsace*  
la Bourgogne *Burgundy*  
la Bretagne *Brittany*  
la Champagne *Champagne*  

la Flandre *Flanders*  
la Lorraine *Lorraine*  
la Normandie *Normandy*  
la Provence *Provence*  

**d.** Masculine countries:

le Brésil *Brazil*  
le Canada *Canada*  
le Cambodge *Cambodia*  
le Danemark *Denmark*  
les États-Unis *the United States*  
Israël *Israel*  

le Japon *Japan*  
le Maroc *Morocco*  
le Mexique *Mexico*  
les Pays-Bas *the Netherlands, Holland*  
le Portugal *Portugal*  
le Zaïre *Zaire*  

**e.** Mountains and waterways follow the rules for countries; they are usually feminine if they end in *-e.*

les Alpes *(f.)* *the Alps*  
le Jura *the Jura Mountains*  
les Pyrénées *(f.)* *the Pyrenees*  
les Vosges *(f.)* *the Vosges*  
la Manche *the English Channel*  
la mer Méditerranée *the Mediterranean Sea*  

la Loire *the Loire*  
le Rhin *the Rhine*  
la Seine *the Seine*  
le Rhône *the Rhone*  
la Garonne *the Garonne*  

## EXERCICE L

**You are taking a trip around the world, and you send postcards with pictures from the following countries.** *Dites dans quel pays vous êtes.*

EXEMPLE:

Je suis **en** France.

1.
_____

2.
_____

3.
_____

4.
_____

5.
_____

6.
_____

7.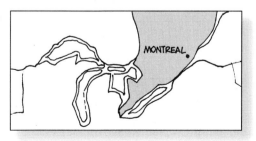
_____

8.
_____

**9.**

_____

**10.**

_____

## EXERCICE M

**People from far and wide attend your school.** *Dites d'où viennent les élèves suivants.*

EXEMPLE:   Luis / Mexique
Luis **vient du** Mexique.

**1.** Nathalie / Haïti

_____

**2.** Stavros / Grèce

_____

**3.** Juan / Espagne

_____

**4.** Hiro / Japon

_____

**5.** Maria / Italie

_____

**6.** Rabiat / Afrique

_____

**7.** Antonio / Portugal

_____

**8.** Jean-Paul / France

_____

**9.** Mark / Canada

_____

**10.** Ilya / Russie

_____

# [ 6 ] EXPRESSIONS INTRODUCED BY À

The preposition *à* is used in the following expressions:

**a.** Mode of travel *(on, by):*

à bicyclette *on a bicycle, by bicycle*    à pied *on foot*
à cheval *on horseback*

Il va à l'école **à pied.**    *He goes to school on foot. (He walks to school.)*

**b.** Time:

à bientôt *see you soon, so long*    à l'heure *on time; per hour*
à ce soir *see you tonight*    à tout à l'heure *see you later*
à demain *see you tomorrow*    au revoir *good-bye, see you again*
à samedi *see you Saturday*

Je pars. **À demain.**    *I'm leaving. See you tomorrow.*

**c.** Position and direction:

**à côté (de)** *next to, beside*
J'habite à côté de Marie.    *I live next door to Marie.*

**à droite (de)** *on (to) the right (of)*
La banque est à droite.    *The bank is on the right.*

**à gauche (de)** *on (to) the left (of)*
Tourne à gauche.    *Turn to the left.*

**au bas de** *at the bottom of*
Le livre est au bas de l'escalier.    *The book is at the bottom of the staircase.*

**au fond (de)** *in (at) the bottom (of)*
Il a trouvé de l'argent au fond du lac.    *He found some money at the bottom of the lake.*

**au haut (de)** *in (at) the top (of)*
Écris ton nom au haut de la page.    *Write your name at the top of the page.*

**au milieu (de)** *in the middle (of)*
Il danse au milieu de la rue.    *He is dancing in the middle of the street.*

**d.** Other expressions:

**à la campagne** *in (to) the country*
Nous sommes allés à la campagne.    *We went to the country.*

**à la maison** *at home, home*
Il est resté à la maison.    *He stayed home.*

**à l'école** *in (to) school*
J'aime aller à l'école.    *I like to go to school.*

**à peu près** *nearly, about, approximately*
J'ai à peu près vingt dollars.    *I have about $20.*

**à voix haute, à haute voix** *aloud, out loud, in a loud voice*
Il parle à voix haute.    *He speaks out loud.*

**à voix basse** *in a low voice*
Parle à voix basse.    *Speak in a low voice.*

**au contraire**  *on the contrary*
Ne sait-il pas jouer au football?          *Doesn't he know how to play soccer?*
—Au contraire, il joue bien.               *— On the contrary, he plays well.*

**au moins**  *at least*
Ça coûte au moins dix dollars.             *That costs at least $10.*

## EXERCICE N

**Your friend Nicolas wants to come to your house. Write to tell him how to get there.** *Employez les expressions appropriées.*

Si tu veux, tu peux venir _____ ou bien tu peux venir _____ .
                             *1.* (by bicycle)                               *2.* (on foot)

Va _____ . Tourne _____ . Continue tout droit pour trois rues.
      *3.* (to school)                *4.* (to the left)

Tu es à l'Avenue Vernon. Tourne _____ . Continue pour _____
                                 *5.* (to the right)                     *6.* (at least)

quatre rues encore.  Descends la petite colline.  Ma maison est juste là.  C'est la maison grise

_____ cette colline, _____ la pharmacie. Je t'attendrai
   *7.* (at the bottom of)                      *8.* (next to)

_____ . Viens _____ . Il te faut _____
      *9.* (at home)                 *10.* (on time)               *11.* (about)

une demi-heure pour venir chez moi. _____ .
                                   *12.* (See you later)

Daniel

## EXERCICE O

*Décrivez la soirée de Justine en complétant chaque phrase avec l'expression appropriée.*

| | | |
|---|---|---|
| à bicyclette | à la maison | au contraire |
| à bientôt | à l'heure | au milieu |
| à la campagne | à peu près | à voix haute |

**1.** Victor est arrivé en retard. Il n'est jamais _____ .

**2.** Rose n'est pas venue à pied. Elle est venue _____ .

**3.** La maison de Justine n'est pas petite, _____ elle est grande.

**4.** Il y a un grand arbre _____ du jardin.

**5.** Justine n'habite pas en ville. Elle habite _____ .

**6.** Ses parents sont sortis. Ils n'étaient pas _____ .

**7.** Claude crie toujours. Il parle _____ .

*8.* Il y avait _____ cinquante personnes à la fête.

*9.* Après la fête tout le monde a dit: «_____».

## [ 7 ]   EXPRESSIONS INTRODUCED BY *DE, EN,* AND *PAR*

**d'abord** *first, at first*
D'abord, écris ton nom.                    *First, write your name.*

**d'accord** *agreed, O.K.*
Tu veux aller au parc? —D'accord.          *Do you want to go to the park? —O.K.*

**de bonne heure** *early*
Lève-toi de bonne heure.                   *Get up early.*

**de l'autre côté (de)** *on the other side (of)*
Le magasin est de l'autre côté du parc.    *The store is on the other side of the park.*

**De quelle couleur...?** *What color . . . ?*
De quelle couleur est la robe?             *What color is the dress?*

**De rien.**
**Il n'y a pas de quoi.**
**Pas de quoi.**                            *You're welcome. Don't mention it.*
**Je vous en prie.**

Merci de ton aide. —De rien.               *Thanks for your help. —You're welcome.*

**de temps en temps** *from time to time*
Je vais au cinéma de temps en temps.       *I go to the movies from time to time.*

**en** (when one is inside the means of transportation) *by*

**en automobile (auto)** *by automobile*

**en avion** *by plane*

**en train** *by train*

**en voiture** *by car*
Je vais à Paris en voiture.                *I'm going to Paris by car.*

**en** (with the name of a language) *in*
Le livre est écrit en espagnol.            *The book is written in Spanish.*

**en bas** *downstairs,* (**en bas de** *at the bottom of*)
Cette famille habite en bas.               *That family lives downstairs.*

**en haut** *upstairs,* (**en haut de** *at the top of*)
Tes clefs sont en haut.                    *Your keys are upstairs.*

**en face (de)** *opposite*
Le café est en face du parc.               *The café is opposite the park.*

**en retard** *late, not on time*
Le train est arrivé en retard.             *The train arrived late.*

**en ville** *downtown, in (to, into) town*
Je suis allé(e) en ville avec papa.        *I went downtown with dad.*

> **par exemple** *for example*
> Je veux lire un bon livre, une histoire     *I want to read a good book, a love story,*
> d'amour, par exemple.     *for example.*
>
> **par jour (semaine, mois,** etc.**)** *a / per day (week, month, etc.)*
> Je gagne cinquante dollars par jour.     *I earn $50 per day.*
> Je vais au cinéma une fois par semaine.     *I go to the movies once a week.*

## EXERCICE P

*Répondez aux questions qu'un ami vous pose.*

**1.** Comment viens-tu à l'école?

_____

**2.** De quelle couleur est ton manteau?

_____

**3.** Tu vas au cinéma combien de fois par mois?

_____

**4.** Que fais-tu de bonne heure?

_____

**5.** Quand tu rentres après l'école, que fais-tu d'abord?

_____

**6.** Qu'est-ce que tu réponds quand une amie te dit merci?

_____

## MASTERY EXERCISES

## EXERCICE Q

*Complétez les phrases avec la préposition qui convient.*

**1.** Vladimir va passer ses vacances _____ la campagne.

**2.** Lucien a perdu son chapeau. Il l'a cherché pendant une heure _____ succès.

**3.** L'équipe des jaunes va jouer _____ l'équipe des rouges.

**4.** Mariam n'est pas très studieuse. Elle finit ses devoirs _____ cinq minutes.

**5.** Claire va sortir _____ Roger. Elle est allée _____ le coiffeur ce matin.

**6.** Le garçon met le plat de spaghetti _____ la table _____ moi.

**7.** Je veux gagner mille dollars _____ semaine.

**8.** Si tu ne trouves pas ton disque sur ton lit, cherche _____ ton lit.

## EXERCICE R

*Complétez les phrases suivantes avec l'expression opposée qui convient.*

**1.** Si ce n'est pas à droite, c'est _____ .

**2.** On dit bonjour quand on entre, on dit _____ quand on sort.

**3.** Si je me lève de bonne heure, je ne suis jamais _____ .

**4.** Si je parle à haute voix, je ne parle pas _____ .

**5.** Si je reste à la maison, je ne descends pas _____ .

**6.** Si je monte en haut, je ne descends pas _____ .

## EXERCICE S

*Complétez cette histoire en ajoutant une préposition si nécessaire.*

Jean a quitté sa maison _____ 8h ce matin. Il ne s'est pas levé _____ bonne heure parce qu'il
<br>1. <br>2.

a oublié _____ régler son réveil hier soir. Aujourd'hui il a peur d'arriver _____ sa première
<br>3. <br>4.

classe _____ retard. Le problème est que ça lui arrive _____ moins deux fois _____
<br>5. <br>6. <br>7.

semaine et naturellement le professeur encourage les élèves _____ arriver _____ l'heure.
<br>8. <br>9.

Malgré son retard, Jean s'amuse _____ jouer _____ son chien. Puis il choisit _____
<br>10. <br>11. <br>12.

parler _____ ses voisins. Il continue _____ parler pendant dix minutes. Il oublie _____
<br>13. <br>14. <br>15.

regarder sa montre. Finalement, il décide d'aller _____ l'école _____ bicyclette. Il ne peut
<br>16. <br>17.

pas aller _____ voiture parce que ses parents sont déjà partis. _____ il commence _____
<br>18. <br>19. <br>20.

pédaler lentement. Puis il se met _____ pédaler plus vite parce qu'il espère _____ arriver
<br>21. <br>22.

_____ l'heure. La classe va _____ commencer _____ cinq minutes. Jean se dépêche
<br>23. <br>24. <br>25.

_____ ne pas arriver en retard. Il compte _____ réussir _____ gagner cette course
<br>26. <br>27. <br>28.

_____ la montre.  Il peut _____ faire cela facilement.  Il va _____ doute être à sa place
         29.                          30.                                    31.

_____ commencement de la leçon, n'est-ce pas?
     32.

## EXERCICE T

*Exprimez en français ce que François va faire aujourd'hui.*

**1.** I am going to try to go to Nicole's house by car.

_____

**2.** My parents encourage me to take the car at least once a week.

_____

_____

**3.** Nicole lives in the same town, not very far from here, towards the park.

_____

**4.** Instead of going fast, I choose to be prudent.

_____

**5.** I prefer to go slowly and arrive on time without problems.

_____

**6.** Sometimes I go to her house by bicycle.

_____

**7.** Nicole and I, we like to walk in the streets downtown.

_____

_____

**8.** From time to time we go to a small restaurant near her house.

_____

_____

**9.** Once a month, we decide to go the movies in Paris.

_____

_____

**10.** We also like to go dancing with friends.

_____

# Part three
## Adjective/Adverb and Related Structures

# Chapter 21
## Adjectives

An adjective is a word that describes a noun or a pronoun.

| | |
|---|---|
| La fleur **rouge** est **jolie**. | *The red flower is pretty.* |
| Il est très **intelligent**. | *He's very intelligent.* |

## [ 1 ] AGREEMENT OF ADJECTIVES

French adjectives agree in gender (masculine or feminine) and in number (singular or plural) with the nouns or pronouns they modify. Adjectives are masculine or feminine, singular or plural, in the same way as the noun or pronoun they modify.

| | |
|---|---|
| le sable **blanc** *(masculine singular)* | *the white sand* |
| les sables **blancs** *(masculine plural)* | *the white sands* |
| la rose **blanche** *(feminine singular)* | *the white rose* |
| les roses **blanches** *(feminine plural)* | *the white roses* |

**a.** Gender of adjectives

**(1)** Most adjectives form the feminine by adding *e* to the masculine.

| MASCULINE | FEMININE | |
|---|---|---|
| allemand | allemande | *German* |
| américain | américaine | *American* |
| bleu | bleue | *blue* |
| brun | brune | *brown* |
| content | contente | *glad* |
| court | courte | *short* |
| espagnol | espagnole | *Spanish* |
| fort | forte | *strong* |
| français | française | *French* |
| grand | grande | *large, tall, big* |
| haut | haute | *high* |
| intelligent | intelligente | *intelligent* |
| intéressant | intéressante | *interesting* |
| joli | jolie | *pretty* |
| laid | laide | *ugly* |
| lourd | lourde | *heavy* |
| mauvais | mauvaise | *bad* |
| méchant | méchante | *naughty, wicked* |
| noir | noire | *black* |
| petit | petite | *small, little* |
| poli | polie | *polite* |
| prochain | prochaine | *next* |

| MASCULINE | FEMININE | |
|---|---|---|
| vert | verte | *green* |
| vrai | vraie | *true* |

NOTE: Adjectives ending in *-é* also form the feminine by adding *e*.

| MASCULINE | FEMININE | |
|---|---|---|
| âgé | âgée | *old* |
| fatigué | fatiguée | *tired* |
| passé | passée | *past* |

## EXERCICE A

**The two people named in each question share the characteristic mentioned.** *Décrivez ces personnes.*

EXEMPLE:    Jean est grand. Et Marisa?
            Marisa est **grande** aussi.

1. Béatrice est polie. Et Lucien?

   _____

2. Geraldo est fort. Et Berthe?

   _____

3. Grégoire est brun. Et Marianne?

   _____

4. Aisha est contente. Et Luc?

   _____

5. Riccardo est fatigué. Et Lisette?

   _____

6. Claudine est intelligente. Et Hubert?

   _____

7. Chun est amusant. Et Claire?

   _____

8. Mme Augier est âgée. Et M. Caron?

   _____

9. Richard est français. Et Marie-Claire?

   _____

10. Marcos est espagnol. Et Juanita?

    _____

**(2) Adjectives ending in silent -*e* do not change in the feminine.**

| MASCULINE | FEMININE | |
|---|---|---|
| aimable | aimable | *kind* |
| célèbre | célèbre | *famous* |
| confortable | confortable | *comfortable* |
| difficile | difficile | *difficult* |
| drôle | drôle | *funny, strange* |
| égoïste | égoïste | *selfish* |
| facile | facile | *easy* |
| faible | faible | *weak* |
| formidable | formidable | *great* |
| honnête | honnête | *honest* |
| jaune | jaune | *yellow* |
| jeune | jeune | *young* |
| magnifique | magnifique | *magnificent* |
| malade | malade | *sick* |
| moderne | moderne | *modern* |
| pauvre | pauvre | *poor* |
| populaire | populaire | *popular* |
| riche | riche | *rich* |
| rouge | rouge | *red* |
| splendide | splendide | *splendid* |
| sympathique | sympathique | *nice, likable* |
| triste | triste | *sad* |
| vide | vide | *empty* |

## EXERCICE B

**Describe the following people.** *Employez l'adjectif qui convient.*

*1.* M. Leroux a beaucoup d'argent. Il est _____ .

*2.* Odette n'aime pas prêter ses affaires. Elle est _____ .

*3.* Claude a mal à l'estomac. Il est _____ .

*4.* Mme Dupont n'est pas contente. Elle est _____ .

*5.* Jacques n'est pas fort. Il est _____ .

*6.* Josette dit toujours la vérité. Elle est _____ .

*7.* Claudine a seulement cinq ans. Elle est très _____ .

*8.* Robert fait rire tout le monde. Il est _____ .

**(3) Adjectives ending in *-x* form the feminine by changing *-x* to *-se*.**

| MASCULINE | FEMININE | |
|---|---|---|
| ambitieux | ambitie**use** | *ambitious* |
| conscientieux | conscientieuse | *conscientious* |
| courageux | courageuse | *courageous* |
| curieux | curieuse | *curious* |
| dangereux | dangereuse | *dangerous* |
| délicieux | délicieuse | *delicious* |
| furieux | furieuse | *furious* |
| généreux | généreuse | *generous* |
| heureux | heureuse | *happy* |
| malheureux | malheureuse | *unhappy* |
| paresseux | paresseuse | *lazy* |
| sérieux | sérieuse | *serious* |
| superstitieux | superstitieuse | *superstitious* |

## EXERCICE C

*Décrivez les personnes ou les choses* (things) *que vous voyez* (see) *dans les illustrations.*

EXEMPLE:

**Il est curieux.**

**1.**

**2.**

_____    _____

**3.**

_____

**4.**

_____

**5.**

_____

**6.**

_____

**7.**

_____

**8.**

_____

**(4) Adjectives ending in *-f* form the feminine by changing *-f* to *-ve*.**

| MASCULINE | FEMININE | |
|---|---|---|
| actif | active | *active* |
| attentif | attentive | *attentive* |
| imaginatif | imaginative | *imaginative* |
| impulsif | impulsive | *impulsive* |
| naïf | naïve | *naive* |
| neuf | neuve | *new* |
| sportif | sportive | *sporty* |
| vif | vive | *lively* |

## EXERCICE D

*Décrivez les personnes suivantes en employant les adjectifs indiqués.*

|         |            |         |
|---------|------------|---------|
| actif   | imaginatif | naïf    |
| attentif| impulsif   | sportif |

*1.* Ma mère est _____ .

*2.* Mon père est _____ .

*3.* Je suis _____ .

*4.* Ma sœur est _____ .

*5.* Mon frère est _____ .

*6.* Mon professeur de français est _____ .

**(5) Adjectives ending in *-er* form the feminine by changing *-er* to *-ère*.**

| MASCULINE | FEMININE |                |
|-----------|----------|----------------|
| cher      | chère    | *dear, expensive* |
| dernier   | dernière | *last*         |
| entier    | entière  | *entire, whole* |
| étranger  | étrangère| *foreign*      |
| fier      | fière    | *proud*        |
| léger     | légère   | *light (weight)* |
| premier   | première | *first*        |

**(6) Some adjectives double the final consonant before adding *-e* in the feminine.**

| MASCULINE | FEMININE  |                    |
|-----------|-----------|--------------------|
| ancien    | ancienne  | *old, ancient, former* |
| bas       | basse     | *low*              |
| bon       | bonne     | *good*             |
| cruel     | cruelle   | *cruel*            |
| européen  | européenne| *European*         |
| gentil    | gentille  | *nice, kind*       |
| gros      | grosse    | *fat*              |

**(7) Some adjectives have irregular feminine forms.**

| MASCULINE | FEMININE |                     |
|-----------|----------|---------------------|
| blanc     | blanche  | *white*             |
| complet   | complète | *complete*          |
| doux      | douce    | *sweet, mild, gentle* |

| | | |
|---|---|---|
| faux | fausse | *false* |
| favori | favorite | *favorite* |
| frais | fraîche | *fresh, cool* |
| franc | franche | *frank* |
| long | longue | *long* |
| secret | secrète | *secret* |
| beau (bel) | belle | *beautiful* |
| nouveau (nouvel) | nouvelle | *new* |
| vieux (vieil) | vieille | *old* |

NOTE: **The adjectives** *beau, nouveau,* **and** *vieux* **change to** *bel, nouvel,* **and** *vieil* **before a masculine singular noun beginning with a vowel or silent** *h.*

| | |
|---|---|
| Cet homme est beau. | *This man is handsome.* |
| Regarde ce **bel homme.** | *Look at this handsome man.* |
| | |
| Cet avion est nouveau. | *This plane is new.* |
| Regarde ce **nouvel avion.** | *Look at this new plane.* |
| | |
| Cet immeuble est vieux. | *This building is old.* |
| Regarde ce **vieil immeuble.** | *Look at this old building.* |

## EXERCICE E

*Complétez chaque paragraphe avec la forme correcte des adjectifs entre parenthèses.*

1. *(beau)* Nous sommes allés à un très _____ hôtel. Cet hôtel est _____

   à cause de sa _____ vue panoramique de la ville.

2. *(vieux)* Que cet appartement est _____! Un _____ homme en est

   le propriétaire et une _____ femme en est la concierge.

3. *(nouveau)* Une _____ pièce va être présentée dans un _____

   théâtre. Un _____ acteur joue le rôle principal.

## EXERCICE F

**Your sister always contradicts you.** *Écrivez ce qu'elle vous dit.*

EXEMPLE:   Le monument est grand.
            Mais non. **Il est petit.**

1. La pièce est mauvaise.

   _____

2. Elle est la première chanteuse de ce groupe.

   _____

**3.** Le livre est lourd.

_____

**4.** La montagne est haute.

_____

**5.** La dame est gentille.

_____

**6.** La blouse est jolie.

_____

**7.** Sa voix est dure.

_____

**8.** L'émission est courte.

_____

**9.** La réponse est vraie.

_____

**10.** La robe est noire.

_____

**b.** Plural of adjectives

**(1)** The plural of most adjectives is formed by adding -_s_ to the singular whether masculine or feminine.

| SINGULAR | PLURAL | |
|---|---|---|
| âgé _(m.)_ | âgé**s** | _old_ |
| blond _(m.)_ | blonds | _blond_ |
| bonne _(f.)_ | bonnes | _good_ |
| blanche _(f.)_ | blanches | _white_ |
| active _(f.)_ | actives | _active_ |

**(2)** Adjectives ending in -_s_ or -_x_ do not change in the masculine plural.

| MASCULINE SINGULAR | MASCULINE PLURAL | |
|---|---|---|
| anglais | anglais | _English_ |
| frais | frais | _fresh, cool_ |
| français | français | _French_ |
| gris | gris | _gray_ |
| heureux | heureux | _happy_ |
| mauvais | mauvais | _bad_ |

(3) Most adjectives ending in *-al* change *-al* to *-aux* in the masculine plural.

| MASCULINE SINGULAR | MASCULINE PLURAL | |
|---|---|---|
| égal | ég**aux** | *equal* |
| général | génér**aux** | *general* |
| loyal | loy**aux** | *loyal* |
| national | nation**aux** | *national* |
| principal | princip**aux** | *principal* |
| social | soci**aux** | *social* |
| spécial | spéci**aux** | *special* |

(4) The adjective *tout* is irregular in the masculine plural.

| tout | tous | *all* |
|---|---|---|

(5) Both masculine forms of *beau (bel)*, *nouveau (nouvel)*, and *vieux (vieil)* have the same plural forms.

| MASCULINE SINGULAR | MASCULINE PLURAL | |
|---|---|---|
| un **beau** garçon | de **beaux** garçons | *handsome guys* |
| un **bel** homme | de **beaux** hommes | *handsome men* |
| un **nouveau** disque | de **nouveaux** disques | *new records* |
| un **nouvel** immeuble | de **nouveaux** immeubles | *new buildings* |
| un **vieux** bateau | de **vieux** bateaux | *old boats* |
| un **vieil** appartement | de **vieux** appartements | *old apartments* |

NOTE:

1. When an adjective precedes a plural noun, *des* becomes *de*.

| de **nouveaux** magazines | *new magazines* |
|---|---|
| de **vieilles** robes | *old dresses* |

2. An adjective modifying two or more nouns of different genders is masculine plural.

| Le garçon et la fille sont **intelligents**. | *The boy and the girl are intelligent.* |
|---|---|

## EXERCICE G

*Décrivez les garçons et les filles de votre classe.* **Use the plural of the adjectives provided below.**

| actif | beau | fier | généreux | intelligent | sérieux |
|---|---|---|---|---|---|
| ambitieux | bon | fort | gentil | intéressant | sportif |
| américain | comique | franc | heureux | optimiste | sympathique |

*1.* Les garçons sont _____, _____,

_____, _____, _____,

_____, _____, _____,

**2.** Les filles sont _____, _____ .

_____ , _____ , _____ ,

_____ , _____ , _____ ,

**3.** Les garçons et les filles sont _____ , _____ .

_____ , _____ , _____ ,

_____ , _____ , _____ .

## EXERCICE H

_Décrivez vos amis et leurs familles._

EXEMPLE:     André est brun. Ses frères sont **bruns** aussi.

**1.** Tisha est sportive. Ses parents sont _____ aussi.

**2.** Louis est franc. Ses sœurs sont _____ aussi.

**3.** Fatimah est belle. Ses frères sont _____ aussi.

**4.** M. Chenet est vieux. Ses cousines sont _____ aussi.

**5.** Lucien est ambitieux. Ses sœurs sont _____ aussi.

**6.** Claudine est intellectuelle. Ses neveux sont _____ aussi.

**7.** Juan est loyal. Ses oncles sont _____ aussi.

**8.** Paolo est fier. Ses tantes sont _____ aussi.

**9.** Mme Legrand est gentille. Ses enfants sont _____ aussi.

**10.** M. Costeau est riche. Ses nièces sont _____ aussi.

## EXERCICE I

**The following people are getting rid of their old belongings and buying themselves some new things.** _Décrivez ce qu'ils achètent._

EXEMPLES:     M. Dupont / une radio
M. Dupont a **une vieille radio.**
Il s'achète **une nouvelle radio.**
**Quelle belle radio!**

Mlle Colin / des assiettes _(f.)_
Mlle Colin a **de vieilles assiettes.**
Elle s'achète **de nouvelles assiettes.**
**Quelles belles assiettes!**

*1.* Mlle Perrier / un appareil photo

_____

_____

_____

*2.* M. Richard / des meubles *(m.)*

_____

_____

_____

*3.* Mme Doucet / un ordinateur

_____

_____

_____

*4.* Mlle Charton / des casseroles *(f.)*

_____

_____

_____

*5.* Mme Ginet / une machine à laver

_____

_____

_____

*6.* M. Janic / des verres *(m.)*

_____

_____

_____

## [ 2 ] POSITION OF ADJECTIVES

**a.** Descriptive adjectives normally follow the noun they modify.

| | |
|---|---|
| une blouse blanche | *a white blouse* |
| un garçon actif | *an active boy* |

**b.** Some short descriptive adjectives usually precede the noun.

| | | |
|---|---|---|
| beau | gentil | joli |
| bon / mauvais | gros | nouveau |
| court / long | jeune / vieux | petit / grand |

une **courte** histoire     *a short story*
une **belle** femme     *a beautiful woman*

NOTE: *Des* becomes *de* when a plural adjective precedes a plural noun.
de **belles** femmes     *beautiful women*

**c.** Some other common adjectives that precede the noun.

| | | |
|---|---|---|
| autre *other* | plusieurs *(m./f. pl.) several* | quelques *(m./f. pl.) a few* |
| chaque *each* | premier *first* | tel *such* |
| dernier *last* | quelque *some* | |

un **autre** livre     *another book*
**d'autres** livres     *other books*
**plusieurs** robes     *several dresses*

**d.** The adjective *tout* (all, whole, every) precedes both the noun and the definite article.

tout le monde     *everybody*
toute la journée     *all day*
tous les jours     *every day*
toutes les filles     *every girl*

# EXERCICE J

**You are very hungry.** *Exprimez ce que vous mangez.*

EXEMPLE:      **Je mange tout le gâteau.**

**1.**  _____

**2.**  _____

**3.** 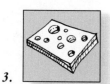 _____

**4.** _____

**5.** _____

**6.** _____

## EXERCICE K

**You recently went to your friends' new house.** *Décrivez la maison avec les adjectifs entre parenthèses.*

EXEMPLE:     une maison (grand)
             Ils ont une **grande** maison.

**1.** un balcon (magnifique)

_____

**2.** une chaîne stéréo (bon)

_____

**3.** deux salles de bains (bleu)

_____

**4.** une piscine (splendide)

_____

**5.** une table (long)

_____

**6.** un arbre (vieux)

_____

**7.** un grenier (charmant)

_____

**8.** deux garages (nouveau)

_____

**9.** trois chambres (joli)

---

**10.** un salon (énorme)

---

# [ 3 ]    COMPARISON OF ADJECTIVES

Things or people can be compared with each other by using the comparative or superlative of the adjectives that modify them. Comparisons are formed as follows.

> **plus** *(more)*
> **moins** *(less)*    } + adjective + **que**
> **aussi** *(as)*

| | |
|---|---|
| Le livre est **plus amusant que** le film. | *The book is more amusing than the movie.* |
| Anne est **moins gentille que** son frère. | *Anne is less nice than her brother.* |
| Les chats sont **aussi intelligents que** les chiens. | *Cats are as intelligent as dogs.* |

The superlative is formed as follows.

> **le, (la, les)    plus** *(the most)*
> **le, (la, les)    moins** *(the least)*    } + adjective + **de**

| | |
|---|---|
| Paul est **le plus beau** des garçons. | *Paul is the most handsome boy.* |
| Le printemps est la saison **la plus agréable.** | *Spring is the most pleasant season.* |
| Les pommes sont les fruits les **moins chers.** | *Apples are the least expensive fruit.* |

| POSITIVE | amusant (-e, -s, -es)  *amusing* |
|---|---|
| COMPARATIVE | **plus amusant** (-e, -s, -es) **que**  *more amusing than*<br>**moins amusant** (-e, -s, -es) **que**  *less amusing than*<br>**aussi amusant** (-e, -s, -es) **que**  *as amusing as* |
| SUPERLATIVE | **le, la, les plus amusant** (-e, -s, -es) **de**  *the most amusing in, of*<br>**le, la, les moins amusant** (-e, -s, -es) **de**  *the least amusing in, of* |

NOTE: The adjective *bon* (good) has an irregular comparative *meilleur* (better) and superlative *le meilleur* (the best). The comparative and superlative of the adjective *mauvais* (bad) are *pire* (worse) and *le pire* (the worst).

| | |
|---|---|
| Le pain est **bon,** mais le gâteau est **meilleur.** | *Bread is good, but cake is better.* |
| La pluie est **mauvaise,** mais la neige est **pire.** | *Rain is bad, but snow is worse.* |

## EXERCICE L

*Exprimez les opinions de vos amis en suivant l'exemple.*

EXEMPLES:  La physique / + / intéressant / la chimie
La physique est **plus intéressante que** la chimie.

les Américains / = / sportif / les Français
Les Américains sont **aussi sportifs que** les Français.

1. la viande / − / délicieux / le poisson

   _____

2. les joueurs de football / = / fort / les joueurs de volley-ball

   _____

3. un film comique / + / amusant / un film policier

   _____

4. les voitures de sport / + / rapide / les bicyclettes

   _____

5. la musique classique / − / agréable / le jazz

   _____

6. le français / = / utile / l'espagnol

   _____

## EXERCICE M

**What is written in the school yearbook about each of these students?** *Suivez l'exemple.*

EXEMPLES:  Delphine / − − − / optimiste
Delphine est **la moins optimiste de** la classe.

Jean et Henri / + + + / grand
Jean et Henri sont **les plus grands de** la classe.

1. Maria / + + + / intelligent

   _____

2. Carmen et Pablo / − − − / sympathiques

   _____

3. Monique et Sylvie / − − − / sérieux

   _____

4. Patrick / + + + / drôle

   _____

**5.** Teresa / + + + / franc

_____

**6.** Riccardo et Julie / − − − / sportif

_____

## M A S T E R Y   E X E R C I S E S

### EXERCICE N

**Describe the following people and things.** _Employez le plus d'adjectifs possible._

**1.** Mes parents sont _____ .

**2.** Ma mère est _____ .

**3.** Mon père est _____ .

**4.** Notre voiture est _____ .

**5.** Notre maison est _____ .

**6.** Mon école est _____ .

**7.** Mon professeur préféré est _____ .

**8.** Mes amis sont _____ .

**9.** Mes notes scolaires sont _____ .

**10.** Mes idées sont _____ .

### EXERCICE O

**You are writing a report about France. Describe the following people, places, and things that are typically French.** _Employez différents adjectifs._

EXEMPLE:    Paris (une ville)
            Paris est une **grande** ville.

**1.** la Normandie et la Bretagne (des provinces)

_____

**2.** l'Arc de Triomphe (un monument)

_____

**3.** le Louvre (un musée)

_____

**4.** le Sacré-Cœur (une église)

_____

**5.** Nice et Cannes (des villes)

_____

**6.** la bouillabaisse (une soupe)

_____

**7.** Euro Disney (un parc d'attractions)

_____

**8.** la Samaritaine et le Printemps (des magasins)

_____

**9.** la tour Eiffel (une tour)

_____

**10.** Gérard Depardieu (un acteur)

_____

## EXERCICE P

**Your friend Pierre went to a fortune teller.** *Exprimez en français ce qu'elle lui a dit.*

**1.** You are going to meet a rich woman.

_____

**2.** She lives in a beautiful castle near a famous lake.

_____

**3.** This woman is tall, beautiful, and young.

_____

**4.** She is generous, kind, and frank.

_____

**5.** The castle is old, but it is charming.

_____

**6.** It has six modern bathrooms, eight huge bedrooms, a magnificent kitchen, and a comfortable living room.

_____

_____

**7.** This woman and you are going to be very happy during your entire life.

_____

**8.** You will also buy a new apartment in an old neighborhood of Paris.

_____

**9.** You will be loyal, active, and happy.

_____

**10.** You will have two beautiful children, who will be ambitious, intelligent, imaginative, and kind.

_____

_____

# Chapter 22
## Adverbs

An adverb is a word that modifies a verb, an adjective, or another adverb.

| | |
|---|---|
| La fleur est **très** jolie. | *The flower is very pretty.* |
| Il court **lentement**. | *He runs slowly.* |
| Elle court **très vite**. | *She runs very fast.* |

## [ 1 ] FORMATION OF ADVERBS

Most French adverbs are formed by adding *-ment* to adjectives while most English adverbs are formed by adding *-ly* to adjectives.

**a.** When a masculine singular adjective ends in a vowel, *-ment* is added to the masculine singular form.

| ADJECTIVE | | ADVERB | |
|---|---|---|---|
| **facile** | *easy* | **facilement** | *easily* |
| **poli** | *polite* | **poliment** | *politely* |
| **possible** | *possible* | **possiblement** | *possibly* |
| **probable** | *probable* | **probablement** | *probably* |
| **rapide** | *quick* | **rapidement** | *quickly* |
| **triste** | *sad* | **tristement** | *sadly* |
| **vrai** | *true* | **vraiment** | *truly* |

## EXERCICE A

**Describe Joseph's behavior.** *Combinez les phrases ci–dessous* (below).

EXEMPLE:  Il parle. Il est sévère.
Il parle **sévèrement**.

1. Il joue. Il est timide.

_____

2. Il répond. Il est brave.

_____

3. Il demande. Il est poli.

_____

4. Il sort. Il est brusque.

_____

5. Il mange. Il est rapide.

_____

*6.* Il écrit. Il est sincère.

_____

*7.* Il travaille. Il est calme.

_____

*8.* Il nage. Il est remarquable.

_____

**b.** When a masculine singular adjective ends in a consonant, *-ment* is added to the feminine singular form.

| ADJECTIVE | | | ADVERB | |
|---|---|---|---|---|
| MASCULINE | FEMININE | | | |
| actif | active | *active* | activement | *actively* |
| certain | certaine | *certain* | certainement | *certainly* |
| correct | correcte | *correct* | correctement | *correctly* |
| cruel | cruelle | *cruel* | cruellement | *cruelly* |
| doux | douce | *soft, gentle* | doucement | *softly, gently* |
| fier | fière | *proud* | fièrement | *proudly* |
| franc | franche | *frank* | franchement | *frankly* |
| heureux | heureuse | *happy* | heureusement | *fortunately* |
| léger | légère | *light* | légèrement | *lightly* |
| secret | secrète | *secret* | secrètement | *secretly* |
| seul | seule | *only* | seulement | *only* |

# EXERCICE B

**Michel is learning how to swim. Describe his lesson.** *Remplacez l'adjectif par un adverbe.*

EXEMPLE:     Michel arrive. (immédiat)
Michel arrive **immédiatement.**

*1.* Le maître-nageur lui parle. (franc)

_____

*2.* Michel écoute. (attentif)

_____

*3.* Michel commence à nager. (nerveux)

_____

*4.* Le maître-nageur le rassure. (doux)

_____

**5.** D'abord il nage. (lent)

_____

**6.** Il s'applique. (sérieux)

_____

**7.** Enfin il nage. (fier)

_____

**8.** La maître-nageur applaudit. (vif)

_____

**c.** Some adverbs have forms distinct from the adjective forms.

| ADJECTIVE | | ADVERB | |
|---|---|---|---|
| **bon** | _good_ | **bien** | _well_ |
| **mauvais** | _bad_ | **mal** | _badly_ |
| **petit** | _little_ | **peu** | _little_ |

Jean est un **bon élève** parce qu'il écoute **bien**.

_Jean is a good student because he listens well._

Louise est une **petite fille** qui mange très **peu**.

_Louise is a little girl who eats very little._

## EXERCICE C

**Lucie does some babysitting. Describe the children she watches.** _Employez la forme correcte des mots entre parenthèses._

**1.** _(mauvais, mal)_ Janine joue _____ avec ce _____ garçon.

**2.** _(bon, bien)_ Carine est une _____ enfant qui m'écoute _____.

**3.** _(petit, peu)_ Le _____ Guy mange _____.

**4.** _(bon, bien)_ Je traite _____ ces _____ enfants.

**5.** _(petit, peu)_ Elle regarde très _____ la télévision, cette _____ fille.

**6.** _(mauvais, mal)_ Ces filles sont _____ parce qu'elles parlent _____.

**d.** Other common adverbs and adverbial expressions:

| | | |
|---|---|---|
| alors _then_ | aujourd'hui _today_ | bientôt _soon_ |
| après _afterward_ | aussi _also, too_ | déjà _already_ |
| assez _enough, quite_ | beaucoup _much_ | demain _tomorrow_ |

| | | |
|---|---|---|
| encore *still, yet, again* | même *even* | tôt *soon, early* |
| enfin *at last* | moins *less* | toujours *always, still* |
| ensemble *together* | partout *everywhere* | tout *quite, entirely* |
| ensuite *then* | peut-être *perhaps, maybe* | tout à coup *suddenly* |
| hier *yesterday* | plus *more* | tout à fait *entirely* |
| ici *here* | près *near* | tout de suite *immediately* |
| là *there* | quelquefois *sometimes* | très *very* |
| loin *far* | souvent *often* | trop *too much* |
| longtemps *a long time* | surtout *especially* | vite *quickly* |
| maintenant *now* | tard *late* | |

## EXERCICE D

**Read the following sentences about Guy. Rewrite each sentence, replacing the adverb in boldface with its opposite.**

*1.* Guy parle **beaucoup** au téléphone. _____

*2.* Il chante **bien**. _____

*3.* Voici ma maison. Il habite **près**. _____

*4.* Il va arriver **tard**, comme d'habitude. _____

*5.* Guy travaille **ici**. _____

*6.* Il va obtenir **certainement** son diplôme. _____

*7.* Il gagne **moins** d'argent que moi. _____

*8.* Il marche **lentement**. _____

*9.* Il prépare **rarement** ses repas. _____

*10.* Guy s'amuse **quelquefois**. _____

## [ 2 ] ADVERBS OF QUANTITY

Certain adverbs expressing quantity are followed by *de*, without an article, when they precede a noun.

| | |
|---|---|
| assez de *enough* | peu de *little, few* |
| beaucoup de *much, many* | plus de *more* |
| combien de *how much, how many* | trop de *too much, too many* |
| moins de *less, fewer* | |

| | |
|---|---|
| As-tu **assez d'argent**? | *Do you have enough money?* |
| J'ai **beaucoup de devoirs**. | *I have a lot of homework.* |

## EXERCICE E

**You are in a restaurant.** *Exprimez ce que le serveur vous apporte.*

beaucoup

EXEMPLE: **Il apporte beaucoup de soda.**

beaucoup

1. _____

beaucoup trop

2. _____

assez

3. _____

peu

4. _____

trop

**5.** _____

# [ 3 ] POSITION OF ADVERBS

**a.** When modifying a verb in a simple tense, an adverb is usually placed directly after the verb it modifies.

Il **mange rarement** des fruits.     _He rarely eats fruits._

Elle va **parler sérieusement.**     _She is going to speak seriously._

## EXERCICE F

**What happens in M. Moreau's French class?** _Mettez l'adverbe à la place qui convient._

EXEMPLE:     Les élèves arrivent en classe. (tôt)
                   Les élèves **arrivent tôt** en classe.

**1.** Les élèves écoutent le professeur. (attentivement)

_____

**2.** On écrit les devoirs sur le tableau. (généralement)

_____

**3.** M. Moreau parle aux élèves. (sérieusement)

_____

**4.** Les élèves parlent français. (beaucoup)

_____

**5.** On s'amuse en classe. (quelquefois)

_____

**6.** Les leçons sont intéressantes. (souvent)

_____

**7.** Les élèves participent à la leçon. (activement)

_____

**8.** M. Moreau explique la grammaire. (clairement)

_____

**b.** When modifying a verb in the *passé composé,* the adverb generally follows the past participle. However, a few common adverbs, such as *bien, mal, souvent, toujours, déjà,* and *encore,* as well as adverbs of quantity, usually precede the past participle.

Hier, Jean **est arrivé tard**.          *Yesterday, Jean arrived late.*

Tu **as beaucoup mangé** à la fête.          *You ate a lot at the party.*

## EXERCICE G

**Odette had an argument with her friend.** *Exprimez ce qu'elle a fait en mettant l'adverbe à la place qui convient.*

EXEMPLE:     Elle a présenté son point de vue. (bien)
Elle **a bien présenté** son point de vue.

*1.* Elle a crié à voix haute. (souvent)

_____

*2.* Elle a parlé. (impulsivement)

_____

*3.* Elle lui a répondu. (furieusement)

_____

*4.* Elle a blâmé son ami. (toujours)

_____

*5.* Elle a discuté la situation. (franchement)

_____

*6.* Elle a expliqué le problème. (mal)

_____

*7.* Elle a écouté son ami. (attentivement)

_____

*8.* Elle a quitté son ami. (brusquement)

_____

*9.* Ensuite, elle a regretté sa mauvaise humeur. (beaucoup)

_____

**c.** When modifying an adjective or another adverb, the adverb usually precedes the word it modifies.

une **très grande** maison          *a very large house*

lire **assez lentement**          *to read quite slowly*

## EXERCICE H

**Unscramble the words and form sentences to find out Paul's opinions of his classmates.** *Suivez l'exemple.*

EXEMPLE:     correct Pierre tout à fait est
            Pierre est **tout à fait correct.**

1. doucement Christophe trop parle

   _____

2. jolie bien est Madeleine

   _____

3. veut plus Carmela être optimiste

   _____

4. très Fabienne franche est

   _____

5. Miguel lentement assez lit

   _____

6. curieuses sont trop les filles

   _____

7. peut attentivement Jean écouter plus

   _____

8. répond sérieusement Annick très

   _____

9. assez les garçons intelligents sont

   _____

10. vraiment gentil Shaquille est

    _____

## MASTERY EXERCISES

## EXERCICE I

**Answer these questions.** *Employez un adverbe dans vos réponses.*

1. Avec qui parles-tu sincèrement?

   _____

**2.** Quand écoutes-tu attentivement?

_____

**3.** Pourquoi travailles-tu sérieusement?

_____

**4.** Comment traites-tu tes amis?

_____

**5.** Que fais-tu facilement?

_____

**6.** Où vas-tu souvent?

_____

**7.** Comment as-tu joué au tennis?

_____

**8.** Es-tu déjà allé(e) en France?

_____

## EXERCICE J

**Complete the descriptions of the following people.** *Employez un adverbe qui convient.*

EXEMPLE: Richard passe deux heures à parler au téléphone.
Il parle **longtemps** au téléphone.

**1.** Grégoire ne range jamais sa chambre. Il laisse ses vêtements, ses livres et ses disques

_____ .

**2.** Michelle dit toujours la vérité. Elle parle toujours _____ .

**3.** Suzanne a de bonnes manières. Elle dit toujours «merci», «s'il vous plaît» et «de rien». Elle parle

_____ .

**4.** Christophe va arriver dans dix minutes. Il va arriver _____ .

**5.** Clara joue au tennis avec beaucoup d'énergie et de force. Elle joue

_____ .

**6.** Abdel achète une motocyclette sans le dire à personne. Il l'achète _____ .

**7.** Janine ne sait pas si elle va aller au cinéma cet après-midi. À un moment elle dit «oui», puis elle dit

«non». Elle va _____ y aller.

8.  Claude va chez le docteur à cet instant. Il y va _____ .

9.  Leticia reçoit un coup de téléphone urgent. Elle part _____ .

10. Olivier va au match de football avec Roberto. Les deux garçons vont

_____ .

## EXERCICE  K

*Exprimez ce que Richard dit de son chien.*

1.  I have a dog, Spunky, that I love a lot.

    _____

2.  He plays very gently with all the children.

    _____

3.  He is only five years old.

    _____

4.  He walks slowly, but proudly.

    _____

5.  Spunky always listens to me attentively.

    _____

6.  We often take a walk together in the park.

    _____

7.  Afterwards, we generally watch television in my room.

    _____

8.  Fortunately, he eats well — a lot of good meat.

    _____

9.  Naturally, he guards our house courageously.

    _____

10. He truly protects all the people that he loves.

    _____

# Chapter 23
## Numbers

## [ 1 ] CARDINAL NUMBERS

| | | | | | |
|---|---|---|---|---|---|
| 0 | zéro | 20 | vingt | 88 | quatre-vingt-huit |
| 1 | un(e) | 21 | vingt et un | 90 | quatre-vingt-dix |
| 2 | deux | 22 | vingt-deux | 95 | quatre-vingt-quinze |
| 3 | trois | 30 | trente | 100 | cent |
| 4 | quatre | 31 | trente et un | 101 | cent un |
| 5 | cinq | 33 | trente-trois | 200 | deux cents |
| 6 | six | 40 | quarante | 316 | trois cent seize |
| 7 | sept | 45 | quarante-cinq | 500 | cinq cents |
| 8 | huit | 48 | quarante-huit | 527 | cinq cent vingt-sept |
| 9 | neuf | 50 | cinquante | 580 | cinq cent quatre-vingts |
| 10 | dix | 51 | cinquante et un | 1.000 | mille |
| 11 | onze | 57 | cinquante-sept | 1.001 | mille un |
| 12 | douze | 60 | soixante | 1.100 | mille cent / onze cents |
| 13 | treize | 61 | soixante et un | 1.200 | mille deux cents / douze cents |
| 14 | quatorze | 70 | soixante-dix | 3.000 | trois mille |
| 15 | quinze | 71 | soixante et onze | 3.210 | trois mille deux cent dix |
| 16 | seize | 75 | soixante-quinze | 10.000 | dix mille |
| 17 | dix-sept | 77 | soixante-dix-sept | 100.000 | cent mille |
| 18 | dix-huit | 80 | quatre-vingts | 1.000.000 | un million |
| 19 | dix-neuf | 81 | quatre-vingt-un | one billion | un milliard |

NOTE:

1.  The conjunction *et* is used with the numbers 21, 31, 41, 51, 61, and 71. In all other compound numbers through 99, the hyphen is used. *Un* becomes *une* before a feminine noun.

    | | |
    |---|---|
    | vingt et **un** étudiants | *twenty-one students* |
    | trente et **une** étudiantes | *thirty-one students* |

2.  *Quatre-vingts* and multiples of *cent* drop the *s* before another number.

    | | |
    |---|---|
    | quatre-vingts livres | *eighty books* |
    | quatre-vingt-deux livres | *eighty-two books* |
    | quatre cents livres | *four hundred books* |
    | quatre cent cinquante livres | *four hundred fifty books* |

3.  *Cent* and *mille* are not preceded by the indefinite article.

    | | |
    |---|---|
    | cent hommes | *a (one) hundred men* |
    | mille dollars | *a (one) thousand dollars* |

4.  *Mille* does not change in the plural.

    | | |
    |---|---|
    | sept mille personnes | *seven thousand people* |

5.  *Mille* often becomes *mil* in dates.

    | | |
    |---|---|
    | Il est né en mil neuf cent trente. | *He was born in 1930.* |

6. *Million* and *milliard* are nouns and must be followed by *de* if another noun follows.

| | |
|---|---|
| un million **d'**étoiles | *a (one) million stars* |
| deux milliards **de** dollars | *two billion dollars* |

7. In numerals and decimals, where English uses periods, French uses commas and vice versa. The period marking thousands is often replaced by a space.

| | |
|---|---|
| 4.000 / 4 000 quatre mille | *4,000 four thousand* |
| 0,05 zéro virgule zéro cinq | *.05 point zero five* |
| $4,60 quatre dollars soixante | *$4.60 four dollars and sixty cents* |

## EXERCICE A

*Exprimez le prix des articles suivants.*

EXEMPLE:

**un dollar**

1.

_____

2.

_____

3.

_____

4.

_____

**5.**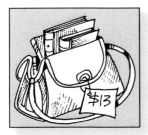

_____

**6.**

_____

**7.**

_____

**8.**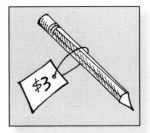

_____

## EXERCICE B

How much will the following items cost? *Additionnez les prix indiqués.*

EXEMPLE:

**quarante-six dollars**

**1.**

_____

**2.**

_____

**3.**

_____

**4.**

_____

**5.**

_____

**6.**

_____

**7.**

_____

**8.**

_____

**9.**

_____

**10.**

_____

## EXERCICE C

*Exprimez l'âge des cousins Delon.*

EXEMPLE:   Marc / 6
           **Marc a six ans.**

1. Lucie / 12

   _____

2. Raoul / 15

   _____

3. Jean / 20

   _____

4. Patrick / 14

   _____

5. Odette / 11

   _____

6. Robert / 3

   _____

7. Nathalie / 18

   _____

8. Jeanne / 13

   _____

9. Roger / 16

   _____

10. Berthe / 9

    _____

## EXERCICE D

**A new student in your class has asked for some of your friends' phone numbers.** *Exprimez ces numéros en français.*

EXEMPLE:   Suzanne Baillot  45.58.17.86
           **quarante-cinq, cinquante-huit, dix-sept, quatre-vingt-six**

1. Pierre Boyer  46.51.71.81

   _____

*2.* Victor Rivera   42.36.97.89

_____

*3.* Chun Wong   48.63.55.94

_____

*4.* Florence Belau   45.77.85.92

_____

*5.* Laura Rossini   43.73.16.68

_____

## EXERCICE E

**What number does each player wear on his / her jersey?** *Suivez l'exemple.*

EXEMPLE:

**Il porte le trente–deux.**

*1.*

_____

*2.*

_____

*3.*

_____

*4.*

_____

**5.**

**6.**

**7.**

**8.**

**9.**

**10.**

## EXERCICE F

**How many phone calls did each member of the Cordier family make last month?** *Suivez l'exemple.*

EXEMPLE:   Gisèle / 18
          Gisèle **a fait dix-huit coups de téléphone.**

*1.* maman / 24

_____

*2.* Oncle Henri / 32

_____

*3.* Jacques / 61

_____

**4.** Tante Lise / 58

---

**5.** Nadine / 87

---

**6.** papa / 75

---

**7.** Sylvie / 66

---

**8.** Ralph / 44

---

## EXERCICE G

**What are the license plate numbers of the following cars?** *Suivez l'exemple.*

EXEMPLE:    **937▴862**    **neuf cent trente-sept, huit cent soixante-deux**

**1.** _____

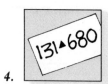

**2.** _____

**3.** _____

**4.** _____

5. `925▲134` _____

6. `411▲312` _____

## EXERCICE H

**On which page is your homework?** *Suivez l'exemple.*

EXEMPLE:    le latin / 138
            Le latin est **à la page cent trente-huit.**

1. le français / 315

_____

2. la biologie / 488

_____

3. l'anglais / 295

_____

4. l'histoire / 554

_____

5. les maths / 226

_____

6. l'algèbre / 165

_____

7. l'informatique / 211

_____

8. la géographie / 322

_____

## EXERCICE I

**You see an ad for a travel agency in the paper.** *Exprimez en français le prix d'un voyage aux destinations suivantes.*

**1.** Londres / $699 _____

**2.** Portugal / $1.019 _____

**3.** Grèce / $1.339 _____

**4.** Paris / $855 _____

**5.** Espagne / $1.229 _____

**6.** Irlande / $969 _____

**7.** Allemagne / $1.119 _____

**8.** Italie / $1.065 _____

## EXERCICE J

**You want to buy your first car. How expensive are the cars below?** *Exprimez le prix en français.*

EXEMPLE:

**cinq mille quatre cent vingt-six dollars**

**1.**

**2.**

_____ _____

3.

4.

5.

6.

7.

8.

## [ 2 ] ARITHMETIC EXPRESSIONS

The following expressions are used in arithmetic problems in French.

| | | | |
|---|---|---|---|
| **et** *plus* | | **moins** *minus* | |
| **fois** *multiplied by* | | **divisé par** *divided by* | |
| **font** *equals* | | | |

| | |
|---|---|
| huit et trois font onze | $8 + 3 = 11$ |
| deux fois sept font quatorze | $2 \times 7 = 14$ |
| dix moins quatre font six | $10 - 4 = 6$ |
| quinze divisé par cinq font trois | $15 \div 5 = 3$ |

## EXERCICE K

You are working in a French bank. Express the operations you must perform by doing the math in French. *Suivez l'exemple.*

EXEMPLE:   $80 \times 2 = 160$
**Quatre-vingts fois deux font cent soixante.**

*1.* $96 \times 13 = 1.248$

_____

*2.* $12.000 \div 100 = 120$

_____

*3.* $828 + 633 = 1.461$

_____

*4.* $1.947 - 179 = 1.768$

_____

*5.* $1.800 \div 9 = 200$

_____

*6.* $33 \times 49 = 1.617$

_____

*7.* $16.500 - 886 = 15.614$

_____

*8.* $496 + 384 = 880$

_____

## [ 3 ]  ORDINAL NUMBERS

| | | | | | |
|---|---|---|---|---|---|
| *1st* | **premier (première)** | *7th* | **septième** | *17th* | **dix-septième** |
| *2nd* | **deuxième, second(e)** | *8th* | **huitième** | *20th* | **vingtième** |
| *3rd* | **troisième** | *9th* | **neuvième** | *21st* | **vingt et unième** |
| *4th* | **quatrième** | *10th* | **dixième** | *34th* | **trente-quatrième** |
| *5th* | **cinquième** | *11th* | **onzième** | *100th* | **centième** |
| *6th* | **sixième** | *16th* | **seizième** | *103rd* | **cent-troisième** |

NOTE:

1.  Ordinal numbers are adjectives and agree in gender and number with the noun they modify. *Premier* and *second* are the only ordinal numbers to have a feminine form different from the masculine form.

    Elle est **la première** à gagner.    *She is the first one to win.*

Les **dix-huitièmes** anniversaires          *Eighteenth birthdays are very important.*
sont très importants.

2. Except for *premier* and *second,* ordinal numbers are formed by adding *-ième* to the cardinal numbers. Silent *e* is dropped before *-ième.*

3. Note the *u* in *cinquième* and the *v* in *neuvième.*

4. *Second(e)* generally replaces *deuxième* in a series which does not go beyond two.
   sa seconde fille                      *his / her second daughter*

5. The final *a* or *e* of the preceding article is not dropped before *huit, huitième, onze,* and *onzième.*

   le huit mai                           *the eighth of May*
   la onzième course                     *the eleventh race*

6. Ordinal numbers are abbreviated as follows in French:

   premier 1$^{er}$ (première 1$^{re}$)          seizième 16$^e$
   deuxième 2$^e$                         cinquantième 50$^e$
   dixième 10$^e$                         centième 100$^e$

## EXERCICE L

**Paris is divided into twenty *arrondissements* (boroughs).** *Exprimez les numéros et les arrondissements indiqués dans ces adresses parisiennes.*

EXEMPLE:     24, rue Niger, 12$^e$
             **vingt-quatre, rue Niger, douzième arrondissement.**

*1.* 92, boulevard Barbès, 18$^e$

_____

*2.* 12, rue Émile-Duclaux, 15$^e$

_____

*3.* 5, rue Delambre, 14$^e$

_____

*4.* 13, rue du Docteur-Lamaze, 19$^e$

_____

*5.* 224, rue de Belleville, 20$^e$

_____

*6.* 80, rue du Bac, 7$^e$

_____

*7.* 67, boulevard Suchet, 16$^e$

_____

## EXERCICE M

**Where are the following students seated in the classroom? Look at the seating plan below.** *Suivez l'exemple.*

| RANG 3 | Robert | Richard | André | Noriko | Suzanne | Marvin |
|--------|--------|---------|-------|--------|---------|--------|
| RANG 2 | Odette | Raoul | Gamal | Joseph | Annick | Maria |
| RANG 1 | Kelli | Paul | Georges | Rita | Luc | Tisha |

EXEMPLE: Joseph
Joseph **est au deuxième rang, à la quatrième place.**

1. Tisha

   _____

2. Gamal

   _____

3. Richard

   _____

4. Annick

   _____

5. Noriko

   _____

6. Kelli

   _____

## EXERCICE N

**Which birthday are the following people celebrating?** *Suivez l'exemple.*

EXEMPLE: Georgette / 46$^e$
Georgette **célèbre son quarante-sixième anniversaire.**

1. M. Duclos / 54$^e$

   _____

2. Mme Renard / 79$^e$

   _____

3. Kim / 28$^e$

   _____

4. Joseph / 11$^e$

   _____

**5.** Karisma / 36$^e$

_____

**6.** Mlle Ricciani / 102$^e$

_____

**7.** Le professeur Arnaud / 63$^e$

_____

## EXERCICE O

**You are applying for a job.** *Répondez aux questions ci-dessous.*

**1.** En quelle année êtes-vous né(e)?

_____

**2.** Quel âge avez-vous?

_____

**3.** Quelle est votre adresse?

_____

**4.** Quel est votre numéro de téléphone?

_____

**5.** Combien d'années d'expérience avez-vous?

_____

## MASTERY EXERCISES

## EXERCICE P

**You are refurnishing your room.** *Écrivez combien coûtent les objets suivants.*

EXEMPLE:  **Le tapis coûte cinq cent trente-cinq dollars.**

**1.**  _____

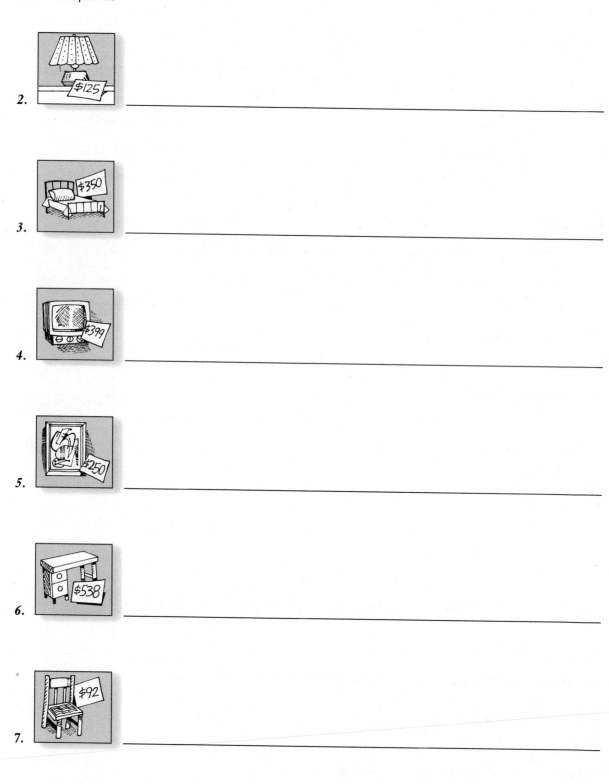

2. _____

3. _____

4. _____

5. _____

6. _____

7. _____

8. _____

## EXERCICE Q

Find all the numbers in the ads below. *Écrivez-les en toutes lettres.*

**1.**

### LES ACACIAS

*retraite privée – valides – semi-valides*
*28 chambres, 1 et 2 personnes*
*cadre agréable, jardin*
*19, rue des Acacias*
*94254 Sainte-Maure*
*400 m R.E.R. La Défense*
*Autobus 103*
*(1) 48 55 52 40*

**2.**

### LOCATION LARCOR

Chapiteaux 300 à 800 places
Gradins 5 à 17 rangs - Tentes 40 à 150 mètres
Chauffage air pulsé 50.000 à 1.000.000 calories

65229 Longueau
(1) 62 24 56 77

**1.** _____

_____

_____

_____

_____

**2.** _____

_____

_____

_____

_____

## EXERCICE R

**You are writing an article for the town paper about a wealthy resident in your area.** *Écrivez les nombres en toutes lettres.*

1.  Mr. Froment is going to take his ninth trip around the world with his wife.

    _____

    _____

2.  They are leaving in eleven days.

    _____

3.  The Froments are going to spend $265,000.

    _____

4.  They intend to visit twenty-one different countries, ten for the first time.

    _____

    _____

5.  They will take flight 697.

    _____

6.  This trip is going to be their twelfth to France in fifteen years.

    _____

7.  Their last trip was in April, 1993.

    _____

    _____

8.  In Paris they always go to the Hôtel de France, 51 avenue du Maine, 14ᵉ.

    _____

    _____

9.  The Froments will return after 176 days.

    _____

10. Call 555-1436 if you want to say good-bye.

    _____

# Chapter 24
## Time and Dates

## [ 1 ] TIME

| | |
|---|---|
| **Quelle heure est-il?** | *What time is it?* |
| **Il est une heure.** | *It is one o'clock.* |
| **Il est une heure cinq.** | *It is 1:05.* |
| **Il est une heure et quart.** | *It is 1:15.* |
| **Il est une heure vingt-cinq.** | *It is 1:25.* |
| **Il est une heure et demie.** | *It is 1:30.* |
| **Il est deux heures moins vingt-cinq.** | *It is 1:35.* |
| **Il est deux heures moins vingt.** | *It is 1:40.* |
| **Il est deux heures moins le quart.** | *It is 1:45.* |
| **Il est deux heures moins dix.** | *It is 1:50.* |
| **Il est deux heures moins cinq.** | *It is 1:55.* |
| **Il est midi.** | *It is twelve o'clock (noon).* |
| **Il est minuit.** | *It is twelve o'clock (midnight).* |
| **Il est midi (minuit) et demi.** | *It is half past twelve.* |

NOTE:

1. To express time after the hour, the number of minutes is placed directly after the hour; *et* is used only with *quart* and *demi(e)*. To express time before the hour, *moins* is used.

2. *Midi* and *minuit* are masculine.

## [ 2 ] TIME EXPRESSIONS

| | |
|---|---|
| **à quelle heure?** | *at what time?* |
| **à une heure** | *at one o'clock* |
| **à deux heures précises** | *at two o'clock sharp* |
| **deux heures du matin** | *2:00 a.m.* |
| **cinq heures de l'après-midi** | *5:00 p.m.* |
| **sept heures du soir** | *7:00 p.m.* |
| **vers onze heures** | *about eleven o'clock* |
| **un quart d'heure** | *a quarter of an hour* |
| **une demi-heure** | *a half hour* |
| **midi et quart** | *12:15 p.m.* |
| **minuit dix** | *12:10 a.m.* |

NOTE:

1. To express the time of day, *du matin* expresses *a.m.*, *de l'après-midi* expresses early *p.m.* and *du soir* expresses late *p.m.*

2. In public announcements such as timetables, the "official" twenty-four-hour system is commonly used, with midnight as the zero hour. The words *minuit, midi, quart,* and *demi* are not used and the number of minutes is expressed by a full number.

| | | |
|---|---|---|
| 0h20 | zéro heure vingt | *12:20 a.m.* |
| 11h10 | onze heures dix | *11:10 a.m.* |
| 15h30 | quinze heures trente | *3:30 p.m.* |
| 22h40 | vingt-deux heures quarante | *10:40 p.m.* |
| 21h15 | vingt et une heures quinze | *9:15 p.m.* |

## EXERCICE A

**You are learning how to tell time in French.** *Exprimez les heures indiquées.*

EXEMPLE:    2:30

**Il est deux heures et demie.**

1.  11:00

_____

2.  3:50

_____

3.  9:05

_____

4.  6:35

_____

5.  10:20

_____

6.  1:30

_____

7.  2:45

_____

8.  2:10

_____

9.  10:55

_____

10.  5:15

_____

**11.** 8:25

_____

**12.** 9:40

_____


## EXERCICE B

**At what time do you do the following?** *Suivez le modèle.*

EXEMPLE:                    **Je me réveille à sept heures du matin.**

**1.** _____

**2.** _____

**3.** _____

4. _____

5. _____

6. _____

7. _____

8. _____

## EXERCICE C

Each person in the Duval family has set his / her digital alarm clock for a different time. At what time does each wake up? *Dites-le en français.*

EXEMPLE: Jacques **se réveille à huit heures quatorze.**

1. Jean _____ .

2. Mme Duval _____ .

3. Claude et moi _____ .

4. Lise et Anne _____ .

5. M. Duval _____ .

6. La mère de Mme Duval _____ .

## EXERCICE D

**You are looking at the television section of a French newspaper. Tell your parents at what time the following shows can be seen.** *Suivez le modèle.*

| | | | |
|---|---|---|---|
| 6h58 | Météo | 15h45 | *Falcon Crest* |
| 8h25 | Télé-Shopping | 18h05 | *Hawaii, police d'état* |
| 10h30 | Disney Classique | 19h30 | *La roue de la fortune* |
| 11h35 | *Deux flics à Miami* | 23h45 | *Les défis de l'océan —* |
| 12h30 | *Le prix est juste* | | documentaire |
| 13h35 | *Feu d'artifice* — film allemand | 0h40 | Journal — Informations |

EXEMPLE:  *La roue de la fortune*
  *La roue de la fortune* **commence à dix-neuf heures trente.**

1. *Falcon Crest*

   _____

2. *Le prix est juste*

   _____

3. *Hawaii, police d'état*

   _____

4. le Journal — Informations

   _____

5. le Disney Classique

   _____

6. *Les défis de l'océan*

   _____

7. *Feu d'artifice*

   _____

8. le Télé-Shopping

   _____

9. la Météo

   _____

10. *Deux flics à Miami*

    _____

## EXERCICE E

**You want to go to the movies, and you call several theaters to learn at what time films start.**
*Dites à quelle heure les films suivants commencent.*

EXEMPLE:    Ciné Georges V — Batman: 14h15, 17h20, 20h25
*Batman* **commence à deux heures et quart, cinq heures vingt et huit heures vingt-cinq.**

*1.* Forum Orient Express — *L'Âge de l'innocence:* 14h10, 16h35, 19h, 21h25

_____

_____

_____

_____

*2.* Gaumont Opéra — *Quand Harry rencontre Sally:* 13h50, 15h35, 17h20, 19h05

_____

_____

_____

_____

*3.* Ciné Beaubourg — *Danse avec les loups:* 13h30, 16h05, 18h40, 21h15

_____

_____

_____

_____

## [ 3 ]  DAYS, MONTHS, SEASONS

| LES JOURS DE LA SEMAINE | LES MOIS DE L'ANNÉE | LES SAISONS DE L'ANNÉE |
|---|---|---|
| **lundi** *Monday* | **janvier** *January* | **le printemps** *spring* |
| **mardi** *Tuesday* | **février** *February* | **l'été** *summer* |
| **mercredi** *Wednesday* | **mars** *March* | **l'automne** *autumn* |
| **jeudi** *Thursday* | **avril** *April* | **l'hiver** *winter* |
| **vendredi** *Friday* | **mai** *May* | |
| **samedi** *Saturday* | **juin** *June* | |
| **dimanche** *Sunday* | **juillet** *July* | |
| | **août** *August* | |
| | **septembre** *September* | |
| | **octobre** *October* | |
| | **novembre** *November* | |
| | **décembre** *December* | |

NOTE:

**1.** Days, months, and seasons are all masculine and are not capitalized in French.

2.  To express *in* with months and seasons, *en* is used, except with *printemps*.

en janvier  *in January*          en été  *in (the) summer*

en août  *in August*             en automne  *in (the) autumn*

en novembre  *in November*        en hiver  *in (the) winter*

                                   *BUT*

                                   **au** printemps  *in (the) spring*

3.  The definite article is used with days of the week in a plural sense. If the day mentioned is a specific day, the article is omitted.

**Le dimanche** je me lève tard.      *On Sunday(s) I get up late.*

Appelez-moi **mardi**.                *Call me (on) Tuesday.*

## EXERCICE F

**Everybody's leaving for summer vacation.** *Regardez le calendrier* (calendar) *et dites quel jour chacun va partir.*

| L | M | M | J | V | S | D |
|---|---|---|---|---|---|---|
|   |   | 1 | 2 | 3 | 4 | 5 |
| 6 | 7 | 8 | 9 | 10 | 11 | 12 |
| 13 | 14 | 15 | 16 | 17 | 18 | 19 |
| 20 | 21 | 22 | 23 | 24 | 25 | 26 |
| 27 | 28 | 29 | 30 | 31 |   |   |

EXEMPLE:    Jean / le 6
            **Il va partir le lundi 6.**

*1.* Julie / le 9

_____

*2.* Odette et Clara / le 28

_____

*3.* Christophe / le 11

_____

*4.* Lucien et Georges / le 20

_____

*5.* Tiziana et moi / le 3

_____

**6.** Toi / le 12

_____

**7.** Paul et vous / le 22

_____

## EXERCICE G

**You have just received your new schedule for the term.** *Exprimez quels jours vous avez les classes suivantes.*

|          | lundi    | mardi    | mercredi | jeudi    | vendredi |
|----------|----------|----------|----------|----------|----------|
| **8–9**   | latin    | français | maths    | français | maths    |
| **9–10**  | biologie | anglais  | musique  | gym      | français |
| **10–11** | histoire | histoire | anglais  | anglais  | gym      |
| **11–12** | français | maths    | histoire | musique  | biologie |
| **12–1**  |          |          |          |          |          |
| **1–2**   | maths    | biologie | art      | maths    | histoire |
| **2–3**   | gym      | art      | latin    | biologie | anglais  |

EXEMPLE:   gym
**J'ai gym lundi, jeudi et vendredi.**

**1.** art

_____

**2.** maths

_____

**3.** musique

_____

**4.** français

_____

**5.** histoire

_____

**6.** biologie

_____

**7.** anglais

_____

**8.** gym

_____

## EXERCICE H

*En quel mois sommes-nous? Regardez l'illustration.*

EXEMPLE:

**Nous sommes en février.**

1.

2.

_____

_____

3.

4.

_____

_____

5.

6.

_____

_____

**7.**

_____

**8.**

_____

**9.**

_____

**10.**

_____

**11.**

_____

**12.**

_____

## EXERCICE 1

*Écrivez le nom des mois de chaque saison.*

| au printemps | en été | en automne | en hiver |
|---|---|---|---|
| _____ | _____ | _____ | _____ |
| _____ | _____ | _____ | _____ |
| _____ | _____ | _____ | _____ |

## [4] DATES

| Quelle est la date d'aujourd'hui? | What is today's date? |
|---|---|
| Quel jour (de la semaine) est-ce aujourd'hui?<br>Quel jour sommes-nous aujourd'hui? | What day of the week is today? |
| C'est aujourd'hui samedi.<br>Nous sommes samedi. | Today is Saturday. |
| C'est aujourd'hui le premier mai.<br>Aujourd'hui nous sommes le premier mai. | Today is May 1st (the first of May). |
| en dix-neuf cent quatre-vingt-quinze<br>en mil(le) neuf cent quatre-vingt-quinze | in 1995 |
| le trente juillet dix-neuf cent quatre-vingt-douze<br>le 30 juillet 1992 | July 30, 1992 |
| lundi 5 décembre 1993<br>le lundi 5 décembre 1993<br>lundi, le 5 décembre 1993 | Monday, December 5, 1993 |

NOTE:

1. In dates, *le premier* is used for the first day of the month. For all other days, cardinal numbers are used.

2. Years are commonly expressed in hundreds, as in English. The word for one thousand in dates, if used, is often written *mil*.

3. The date in numbers follows the sequence *day, month, year.*

   le 22 avril 1977 (22.4.77)      *April 22, 1977 (4/22/1977)*
   le 3 mai 1992 (3.5.92)      *May 3, 1992 (5/3/1992)*

## EXERCICE J

On which dates will you write the following information in your new calendar? *Suivez le modèle.*

EXEMPLE:   l'anniversaire de mon frère
          **le onze juillet**

*1.* mon anniversaire

_____

*2.* l'anniversaire de mon meilleur ami

_____

*3.* les classes finissent

_____

**4.** les examens commencent

_____

**5.** je vais en vacances

_____

**6.** je rentre à l'école

_____

**7.** je vais à une fête

_____

**8.** je vais à un concert

_____

## EXERCICE K

**You have recorded the birthdays of all the French exchange students who are visiting your school.** *Dites quand chaque étudiant célèbre son anniversaire.*

EXEMPLE:     Janine 5/8
             **Elle célèbre son anniversaire le huit mai.**

**1.** Hubert 9/12

_____

**2.** Lisette 7/11

_____

**3.** Roland 1/9

_____

**4.** Nadine 11/15

_____

**5.** Sylvie 6/1

_____

**6.** Michel 4/22

_____

**7.** Robert 2/16

_____

*8.* Denis 12/9

_____

*9.* Mireille 8/7

_____

*10.* Mathieu 5/4

_____

*11.* Christophe 10/26

_____

*12.* Anne 3/14

_____

## EXERCICE L

*Écrivez en français la date des anniversaires des membres de la famille Raspail.*

EXEMPLE:    Caroline, April 20, 1980
             Caroline, **le vingt avril dix-neuf cent quatre-vingts.**
   *OR:*    Caroline, **le vingt avril mil(le) neuf cent quatre-vingts.**

*1.* Mme Raspail, September 21, 1954

_____

*2.* M. Raspail, July 11, 1945

_____

*3.* Nicole, April 22, 1977

_____

*4.* Philippe, October 24, 1984

_____

*5.* la mère de Mme Raspail, April 15, 1922

_____

*6.* Cousin Jacques, February 1, 1992

_____

*7.* Oncle Paul, January 9, 1963

_____

*8.* le père de M. Raspail, June 30, 1918

_____

## MASTERY EXERCISES

### EXERCICE M

You are showing pictures of some past holidays to your pen pal who is visiting from France. *Pour chaque fête, donnez la date, le jour et l'heure. Suivez l'example*

EXEMPLE:

C'était le vingt-cinq décembre dix-neuf cent quatre-vingt-dix. Il était minuit dix.

1.

2.

3.

4.

## EXERCICE N

**You are studying French history.** *Écrivez la date des événements suivants en utilisant le mot mil(le).*

1. *(1412)* Jeanne d'Arc est née en _____

   _____ .

2. *(1598)* Henri IV a proclamé l'Édit de Nantes en_____

   _____ .

3. *(1634)* Le cardinal de Richelieu a fondé l'Académie française en_____

   _____ .

4. *(July 14, 1789)* Les habitants de Paris ont attaqué la Bastille le _____

   _____ .

5. *(1848)* Napoléon III a été élu président de la Seconde République en_____

   _____ .


## EXERCICE O

**A friend will be traveling to Paris soon and asks for your help.** *Exprimez en français ce que vous lui dites.*

1. The banks open at 9 a.m. and close at 4:30 p.m. Monday to Friday.

   _____

2. You can eat in restaurants from noon to 2 p.m. and from 7 p.m. to 10 p.m.

   _____

   _____

3. Go to the post office between 8 a.m. and 7 p.m. Monday to Friday and from 8 a.m. to noon on Saturday.

   _____

   _____

4. Take the metro between 5:30 a.m. and 1:15 a.m.

   _____

5. Visit the Louvre Monday and Wednesday from 9 a.m. to 7:45 p.m. and Thursday to Sunday from 9 a.m. to 6 p.m. The Louvre is closed on Tuesdays.

   _____

   _____

**6.** The musée d'Orsay is closed on Monday. Go there Tuesday to Sunday from 10 a.m. to 6 p.m. and Thursday from 10 a.m. to 9:45 p.m.

_____

_____

**7.** You can go to Notre-Dame every day from 8 a.m. to 7 p.m.

_____

**8.** Tourists go to the Eiffel Tower every day between 10 a.m. and 11 p.m.

_____

# Chapter 25
## Interrogatives and Exclamations

## [ 1 ] INTERROGATIVE ADVERBS

| | | | |
|---|---|---|---|
| **combien?** | *how much? how many?* | **d'où?** | *from where?* |
| **comment?** | *how?* | **pourquoi?** | *why?* |
| **où?** | *where (to)?* | **quand?** | *when?* |

**a.** Questions beginning with an interrogative adverb are frequently formed with *est-ce que* following the adverb.

Quand **est-ce que** tu sors?      *When do you go out?*

Comment **est-ce qu'il** va?      *How is he?*

Où **est-ce que** vous allez?      *Where are you going?*

Combien **est-ce que** ce livre coûte?      *How much does this book cost?*

**b.** A question beginning with an interrogative adverb can also be formed by inverting the verb and the subject pronoun.

Quand **sors-tu?**      *When do you go out?*

Comment **va-t-il?**      *How is he?*

Où **allez-vous?**      *Where are you going?*

NOTE:

1. With *combien, comment, où, d'où,* and *quand,* when the subject is a noun, and the verb has no object, a question may be formed by inverting the order of subject and verb.

Combien **coûte ce livre?**      *How much does this book cost?*

Comment **s'appelle ce café?**      *What's the name of this café?*

2. In colloquial spoken French, questions are often formed by placing an interrogative adverb after the verb.

Tu vas **où?**      *Where are you going?*

Il s'appelle **comment?**      *What's his name?*

Ce livre coûte **combien?**      *How much does this book cost?*

## EXERCICE A

Your French pen pal is coming to visit you. Use two ways to express each of the questions your friends are asking you about her. *Suivez l'exemple.*

EXEMPLE: Elle est jolie. (comment)
     **Comment est-elle?**
     **Comment est-ce qu'elle est?**

*1.* Elle est de Toulouse. (d'où)

_____

_____

**2.** Elle vient aux États-Unis en avion. (comment)

_____

_____

**3.** Elle paie son billet $250. (combien)

_____

_____

**4.** Elle habitera chez moi. (où)

_____

_____

**5.** Elle arrivera dans une semaine. (quand)

_____

_____

**6.** Elle vient aux États-Unis pour perfectionner son anglais. (pourquoi)

_____

_____

**7.** Elle retournera en France dans un mois. (quànd)

_____

_____

## EXERCICE B

**Write as many questions as you can about the following people.** *Suivez l'exemple.*

EXEMPLE:    Jeudi, à cinq heures, Lise, qui vient du Canada, marche
            lentement en ville parce qu'elle a mal aux pieds.
            **Quand est-ce que Lise marche en ville?**
            **D'où vient-elle?**
            **Lise marche comment?**
            **Où est-ce que Lise marche?**
            **Pourquoi marche-t-elle lentement?**

**1.** À trois heures de l'après-midi, Marie Legros danse parfaitement bien trois nouvelles danses modernes devant le miroir du studio parce qu'elle fait partie du club de danse.

_____

_____

_____

_____

**2.** Marc sort rapidement de sa chambre à quatre heures de l'après-midi parce qu'il voit deux jolies filles marcher devant sa maison.

_____

_____

_____

_____

_____

## [ 2 ] INTERROGATIVE ADJECTIVES

The interrogative adjective *quel* (which? what?) agrees with the noun it modifies.

|  | MASCULINE | FEMININE |
|---|---|---|
| SINGULAR | **quel** | **quelle** |
| PLURAL | **quels** | **quelles** |

Quelle heure est-il?
Quelle heure est-ce qu'il est?          *What time is it?*
Il est quelle heure?

Quelles chansons préfères-tu?
Quelles chansons est-ce que tu préfères?     *Which songs do you prefer?*
Tu préfères quelles chansons?

NOTE:

**1.** The only verb that may follow *quel* directly is *être*.

Quel est ton nom?                *What is your name?*
Quelle est ton adresse?          *What is your address?*
Quels sont tes cours favoris?    *What are your favorite classes?*

**2.** *Quel* may be preceded by a preposition.

Pour quelle raison êtes-vous ici?        *For what reason are you here?*
À quelle heure est-ce que Paul vient?    *At what time is Paul coming?*

## EXERCICE C

**You've made a new friend. Ask this friend some personal questions using *quel* + *être*.**

EXEMPLE:    nom
            **Quel est** ton nom?

**1.** adresse

_____

**2.** numéro de téléphone

_____

**3.** date de naissance

_____

**4.** sports préférés

_____

**5.** plat favori

_____

**6.** classes préférées

_____

## EXERCICE D

**Your friend's room is a mess.** *Demandez-lui ce qu'elle cherche.*

EXEMPLE:

**Quel livre cherches-tu?**

**1.**

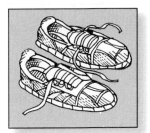

**2.**

_____

**3.**

**4.**

_____

5.

6.

_____

7.

8.

_____

## [ 3 ] INTERROGATIVE PRONOUNS

|  | PEOPLE | | THINGS | |
|---|---|---|---|---|
| SUBJECT OF A VERB | **qui?** | _who?_ | **qu'est-ce qui?** | _what?_ |
| DIRECT OBJECT OF A VERB | **qui?**<br>**qui est-ce que?** } | _whom?_ | **que?**<br>**qu'est-ce que?** } | _what?_ |

NOTE:   The _e_ of _que_ is dropped before a word beginning with a vowel; the _i_ of _qui_ is never dropped.

Qu'as-tu vu?                    _What did you see?_

Qui as-tu vu?                   _Whom did you see?_

**a.** Interrogative pronouns as subjects

_Qui? (who?)_ is used for people. _Qu'est-ce qui? (what?)_ is used for things. The verb that follows is in the third person singular.

Qui va arriver en retard?       _Who is going to arrive late?_

Qu'est-ce qui arrive?           _What is happening?_

## EXERCICE E

**M. et Mme Léger are back from vacation and they ask their children how they managed. Use** _qui_ **to write their questions based on the answers given.** _Suivez l'exemple._

EXEMPLE:     Jean a lavé la voiture.
              **Qui a lavé la voiture?**

*1.* Lucien a promené le chien.

_____

*2.* J'ai fait le lavage.

_____

*3.* Berthe et Robert ont préparé les repas.

_____

*4.* Nous avons passé l'aspirateur.

_____

*5.* Richard et Claudine ont vidé les ordures.

_____

*6.* Tout le monde a nettoyé la maison.

_____


## EXERCICE F

**M. Leduc wants to spend a relaxing day in his garden. Ask why this is impossible.** *Suivez l'exemple.*

EXEMPLE:    Un coup de tonnerre réveille M. Leduc.
            **Qu'est-ce qui réveille M. Leduc?**

*1.* Le téléphone ne cesse pas de sonner.

_____

*2.* Trois paquets arrivent.

_____

*3.* Le mauvais temps continue toute la journée.

_____

*4.* Un arbre tombe dans son jardin.

_____

*5.* Un accident de voiture dérange sa paix.

_____

*6.* Le bruit l'empêche de rester calme.

_____

## EXERCICE G

**You have been absent from school for a week. Your friends come by to visit.** *Complétez les questions que vous posez avec* **qui** *ou* **qu'est-ce qui.**

1. _____ est arrivé à Jean-François?

2. _____ a gagné le championnat de tennis?

3. _____ va aider Marie avec ses devoirs?

4. _____ se passe dans la classe de français?

5. _____ empêche Nathalie de me rendre visite?

6. _____ va me téléphoner ce soir?

7. _____ est dans cette jolie boîte?

8. _____ m'a envoyé ces cartes?

**b.** Interrogative pronouns as direct objects

*Qui* and *qui est-ce que* (whom?) are used for people. *Que* and *qu'est-ce que* (what?) are used for things.

| | |
|---|---|
| Qui aimes-tu? | |
| Qui est-ce que tu aimes? | *Whom do you love?* |
| Que fait-elle? | |
| Qu'est-ce qu'elle fait? | *What is she doing?* |
| Qu'est-ce que cet enfant raconte? | *What is this child saying?* |

NOTE:

1. After the short forms *qui* and *que* the word order is inverted; after the long form with *est-ce que,* the word order is regular.

2. *Qui* can be preceded by a preposition.

   À qui parles-tu?            *To whom do you speak?*

3. *Qu'est-ce que c'est?* means "What is it?" and is used for things.

   Qu'est-ce que c'est?          *What is it?*
   — C'est un livre.            *It's a book.*

## EXERCICE H

**Michelle is Éric's new girlfriend.** *Posez des questions sur eux.*

EXEMPLE:     Éric adore Michelle.
                   **Qui est-ce qu'Éric adore?**
                   **Qui adore-t-il?**

1. Éric accompagne Michelle au cinéma.

   _____

   _____

2. Éric ignore les autres filles.

   _____

   _____

3. Éric aide Michelle à faire ses devoirs.

   _____

   _____

4. Éric amène Michelle aux matches de foot.

   _____

   _____

5. Michelle écoute les amis d'Éric.

   _____

   _____

6. Michelle embrasse Éric tout le temps.

   _____

   _____

## EXERCICE 1

**You are going to take a trip to France.** *Exprimez les questions que vos amis vous posent en employant* **que** *et* **qu'est-ce que.**

EXEMPLE:   Je mangerai des spécialités françaises.
   **Qu'est-ce que tu mangeras?**
   **Que mangeras-tu?**

1. J'achèterai de jolis souvenirs.

   _____

   _____

2. Je verrai des monuments importants.

   _____

   _____

3. Je lirai les journaux français.

   _____

   _____

*4.* Je ferai de longues promenades en ville.

_____

_____

*5.* Je photographierai le paysage.

_____

_____

*6.* J'aimerai tout.

_____

_____

## EXERCICE J

**Votre classe va faire un pique-nique.** *Posez des questions avec* **qui** *ou* **que.**

*1.* _____ apporteras-tu?

*2.* _____ amènera-t-elle?

*3.* _____ mangerons-nous?

*4.* _____ ferons-nous s'il fait mauvais?

*5.* Avec _____ irons-nous?

*6.* _____ remercierez-vous?

*7.* _____ boirons-nous?

*8.* _____ aideras-tu?

## EXERCICE K

**Your friend is in a grumpy mood.  Ask why and what you can do.** *Complétez les questions avec* **qu'est-ce qui** *ou* **qu'est-ce que.**

*1.* _____ te dérange?

*2.* _____ tu veux faire?

*3.* _____ je peux te donner?

*4.* _____ arrive?

*5.* _____ est si terrible?

*6.* _____ tu trouves si ennuyeux?

# [ 4 ] EXCLAMATIONS

The forms of *quel* are used in exclamations to express *what a . . . !* or *what . . . !*

| | |
|---|---|
| Quel beau château! | *What a beautiful castle!* |
| Quels livres intéressants! | *What interesting books!* |
| Quelle jolie fille! | *What a pretty girl!* |
| Quelles histoires! | *What stories!* |

## EXERCICE L

**What would you say if you received the following gifts for Valentine's Day?**

EXEMPLE: livre intéressant
**Quel livre intéressant!**

*1.* belles fleurs

_____

*2.* chocolats délicieux

_____

*3.* carte magnifique

_____

*4.* splendides photos

_____

*5.* joli bracelet

_____

*6.* montre formidable

_____

## MASTERY EXERCISES

## EXERCICE M

**A little boy is lost in a department store. Based on his answers, write the questions that he was asked.** *Suivez l'exemple.*

EXEMPLE: Ma mère est Jeanne Duval.
**Qui est ta mère?**

*1.* Je suis Paul Duval.

_____

*2.* Je pleure parce que je suis perdu.

_____

*3.* Je cherche ma mère.

_____

*4.* Elle était ici.

_____

*5.* Nous sommes arrivés au magasin à deux heures.

_____

*6.* Ma mère est grande.

_____

*7.* Elle achète des vêtements.

_____

*8.* Elle porte une robe verte.

_____

*9.* Ma mère regardait les pulls.

_____

*10.* Ma tante est avec ma mère.

_____

*11.* J'ai deux dollars.

_____

*12.* Mon adresse est 57 rue Monique.

_____

*13.* Mon numéro de téléphone est 45.67.78.89.

_____

## EXERCICE N

**Ask as many questions as you can about the following situations, based on the words in bold letters.** *Suivez l'exemple.*

EXEMPLE:   Janine accompagne **Nadine** en ville. Elles décident d'aller **à une discothèque. Cette nouvelle disco** est vraiment amusante. **Les filles** rentrent très tard.

**Qui est-ce que** Janine accompagne en ville? **Où** décident-elles d'aller? **Qu'est-ce qui** est vraiment amusant? **Qui** rentre très tard?

*1.* Paco ouvre **une magnifique boîte de chocolat. Un bonbon** tombe par terre. Il appelle **son chien, Champ. Champ** trouve le bonbon délicieux.

_____

_____

_____

_____

*2.* **Le téléphone** ne marche pas. **Pierre** veut parler à son amie Leticia. Il aime beaucoup **cette fille.** Pierre décide d'aller **chez elle en vélo.**

_____

_____

_____

_____

*3.* **Georgette** accompagne son ami Mario au cinéma. **Mario** adore les films. **Ce film** est intéressant. Ils ont envie de voir **ce film.**

_____

_____

_____

_____

## EXERCICE O

**Your friend is trying to arrange a blind date for you with her cousin. She shows you his picture.** *Exprimez en français ce que vous dites.*

*1.* What a handsome boy!

_____

*2.* What is he wearing on his head? A hat?

_____

*3.* What is his name?

_____

*4.* Where does he live?

_____

*5.* Why is he happy in this picture?

_____

*6.* When does he go out?

_____

7. What does he like to do?

   _____

8. What does he do after school?

   _____

9. Who are his friends?

   _____

10. What is his phone number?

   _____

# Chapter 26
## Possession

## [ 1 ] EXPRESSING POSSESSION

**a.** The preposition *de* expresses possession and relationship in French (English *'s* or *s'*, of).

| | |
|---|---|
| les crayons de Michel | *Michel's pencils* |
| le livre du professeur | *the teacher's book* |
| le tableau de l'artiste | *the artist's painting* |
| la mère des enfants | *the children's mother* |

NOTE: *De* is repeated before each noun.

| | |
|---|---|
| le frère de Paul et de Luc | *Paul and Luc's brother* |

## EXERCICE A

**It is the end of the school year and the items in the lost and found have to be returned.**
*Déterminez le propriétaire* (owner) *de chaque objet.*

EXEMPLES: l'écharpe / Marguerite
C'est l'écharpe **de** Marguerite.

les gants / Jean
Ce sont les gants **de** Jean.

*1.* le livre / instituteur

_____

*2.* les lunettes / directeur

_____

*3.* le tee-shirt / Henri

_____

*4.* le stylo / maîtresse

_____

*5.* les bandes dessinées / Michel et Luc

_____

*6.* la brosse / Nadine

_____

*7.* la carte / professeur Lamont

_____

*8.* les cahiers / Marie et Lise

**b.** The idiom *être à* (to belong to) also expresses possession.

| | |
|---|---|
| Ces cahiers sont au garçon. | *These notebooks belong to the boy.* |
| Ce livre est à moi. | *This book belongs to me.* |
| Est-ce que ce stylo est à Éric? | *Does this pen belong to Éric?* |

NOTE: *À* is repeated before each noun.

| | |
|---|---|
| Ces cassettes sont à Marc et à Guy. | *These cassettes belong to Marc and Guy.* |

## EXERCICE B

**You are cleaning out the attic. Your mother asks to whom each of the things you find belongs.**
*En utilisant* être à, *exprimez ses questions et vos réponses.*

François
La bicyclette **est à** François?
Oui, elle **est à lui.**

EXEMPLE:

Pierre

_____

1. _____

Henri et Joseph

_____

2. _____

moi

_____

3. _____

ta sœur et toi

_____

**4.** _____

toi

_____

**5.** _____

Charline et Odette

_____

**6.** _____

ton père et moi

_____

**7.** _____

Claire

_____

**8.** _____

## [ 2 ] POSSESSIVE ADJECTIVES

| SINGULAR | | PLURAL | |
|----------|---------|--------|------|
| MASCULINE | FEMININE | | |
| **mon** | **ma** | **mes** | *my* |
| **ton** | **ta** | **tes** | *your* (familiar) |
| **son** | **sa** | **ses** | *his, her, its* |
| **notre** | **notre** | **nos** | *our* |
| **votre** | **votre** | **vos** | *your* (formal) |
| **leur** | **leur** | **leurs** | *their* |

NOTE:

1. Possessive adjectives, like other adjectives, agree with the nouns they modify. They are repeated before each noun.

   sa sœur et son frère — *his/her sister and brother*

   mes chiens et mon chat — *my dogs and my cat*

   ton livre et leurs cahiers — *your book and their notebooks*

2. The forms *mon, ton,* and *son* are used instead of *ma, ta,* and *sa* before a feminine singular noun beginning with a vowel or silent *h.*

   mon amie — *my friend*

   ton écharpe — *your scarf*

   son histoire — *his / her story*

3. With parts of the body, the possessive adjective is usually replaced by the definite article if the possessor is clear.

   Elle se lave les mains. — *She washes her hands.*

   Il a un chapeau sur la tête. — *He has a hat on his head.*

## EXERCICE C

You are in a restaurant, and the service is very slow. *Exprimez ce que vous dites au garçon* (waiter) *et ses réponses.*

EXEMPLE: sandwich
**Où est mon** sandwich?
**Ton** sandwich? Un moment.

*1.* œufs

_____

_____

*2.* salade

_____

_____

*3.* fromage

_____

_____

*4.* légumes

_____

_____

*5.* omelette

_____

_____

*6.* soupe

_____

_____

## EXERCICE D

**You and a friend are getting off a plane in Europe. The flight attendant approaches and asks if you've left something behind.** *Exprimez ses questions et vos réponses.*

EXEMPLE:

Ce sont **vos** chapeaux?
Ce ne sont pas **nos** chapeaux.

*1.* _____

_____

*2.* _____

**3.** _____

**4.** _____

**5.** _____

**6.** _____

## EXERCICE E

**Jacques is curious about his friends' families.** _Répondez à ses questions._

EXEMPLE:   Le père d'Henri est mécanicien? (ingénieur)
           Mais non. **Son** père est ingénieur.

**1.** La mère de Georgette est avocate? (docteur)

_____

**2.** Les parents de Maria sont docteurs? (professeurs)

_____

3. L'oncle de Yoko est ingénieur? (électricien)

_____

4. La cousine de Nadine est programmeuse? (secrétaire)

_____

5. Les filles de M. Dupont sont infirmières? (coiffeuses)

_____

6. Le fils de Mme Nalet est artiste? (vendeur)

_____

7. La fille cadette de Mme Lenoir est peintre? (décoratrice)

_____

8. Les grands-parents d'Yves sont professeurs? (dentistes)

_____

## EXERCICE F

**You are on a tour bus in Europe.** *Exprimez ce que les personnes suivantes ont avec elles.*

EXEMPLE:     les Dupont / enfants
                Les Dupont ont **leurs** enfants.

1. José et Richard / lunettes de soleil

_____

2. les Duchamp / crème solaire

_____

3. M. et Mme Soland / parapluie

_____

4. Nathalie et Roberto / argent

_____

5. les parents de Luc / chèques de voyage

_____

6. les Pierrot / chapeaux

_____

7. Claudine et Kadisha / appareil photo

_____

8. tous les voyageurs / guides touristiques

_____

## EXERCICE G

**You get paid to do chores in your neighborhood. Someone asks what you've done.** *Répondez-lui.*

EXEMPLE:     Tu as promené le chien des Chénier?
             Oui, j'ai promené **leur** chien.

*1.* Tu as lavé la voiture de M. Sultan?

_____

*2.* Tu as réparé la bicyclette de Juana?

_____

*3.* Tu as fait les courses des Verdon?

_____

*4.* Tu as envoyé les paquets de Paul et de Robert Picot?

_____

*5.* Tu as rangé le garage de Mlle Blanchet?

_____

*6.* Tu as nettoyé la maison de Mme Mamet?

_____

*7.* Tu as installé l'ordinateur d'Irène et de Richard?

_____

*8.* Tu as gardé les enfants des Raynaud?

_____


## EXERCICE H

**Say what the following people are wearing to Lise's party.**

EXEMPLES:     Raoul porte **son** pantalon bleu.
              Sylvie a **ses** bracelets d'argent sur **le** bras droit.

*1.* Cristina porte _____ pull rouge.

*2.* Nous portons _____ nouveaux vêtements.

*3.* Je porte _____ écharpe blanche sur _____ cou.

*4.* Marie et Louise portent _____ chapeaux verts.

5. Luca porte _____ nouvelles baskets.

6. Tu portes _____ grande chemise jaune.

7. Vous portez _____ jupe noire.

8. Lucien porte _____ chemise brune.

9. Claude a _____ mains dans les poches de _____ robe longue.

10. Henri s'est couvert _____ tête avec _____ casquette rouge.

## MASTERY EXERCISES

### EXERCICE I

**Jean and the members of his family like to share their belongings. His friend Paul is surprised.**
*Complétez leur conversation avec l'adjectif possessif correct.*

JEAN: Mes frères, mes sœurs et moi, nous partageons toutes _____ affaires.
<br>1.

PAUL: Par exemple?

JEAN: Maintenant je porte le pantalon de _____ frère Jacques et le pull de _____
<br>2.    3.

sœur Christine.

PAUL: Tu aimes porter _____ vêtements?
<br>4.

JEAN: Pourquoi pas? De cette façon, nous avons tous des vêtements très divers et _____ amis
<br>5.

pensent que nous sommes très bien vêtus.

PAUL: Quelles autres choses empruntes-tu à _____ frères et à _____ sœurs?
<br>6.    7.

JEAN: À _____ frères, j'emprunte toujours de l'équipement sportif et à _____ sœurs, des
<br>8.    9.

disques et des cassettes.

PAUL: Est-ce que tu leur prêtes _____ scooter?
<br>10.

JEAN: Bien sûr!

PAUL: _____ frères, _____ sœurs et toi, qu'est-ce que vous empruntez à _____ parents?
<br>11.    12.    13.

JEAN: _____ nouvelle voiture!
<br>14.

## EXERCICE J

**A new classmate is talking to you.** *Répondez à ses questions.*

*1.* Quel est ton nom?

_____

*2.* Tu es l'ami de qui?

_____

*3.* Ta famille habite ici maintenant?

_____

*4.* Où est votre maison?

_____

*5.* À qui est la voiture devant ta maison ?

_____

*6.* Quels sont tes sports préférés?

_____

*7.* Tu veux savoir mon numéro de téléphone?

_____

*8.* Peux-tu me présenter à tes amis?

_____

## EXERCICE K

*Écrivez une composition en français sur une camarade qui s'appelle Marie.*

*1.* My friend Marie lives with her brother and sister.

_____

*2.* Her parents stayed in France.

_____

*3.* Their jobs and their home are in Nice.

_____

*4.* Marie's sister is our teacher.

_____

*5.* Her brother is our doctor.

_____

**6.** My parents like her family very much.

_____

**7.** Marie and I share all our things.

_____

**8.** She lends me her clothes.

_____

**9.** I give her my records and my cassettes.

_____

**10.** I hope to meet her parents in their country.

_____

# Chapter 27
## Demonstrative Adjectives

Demonstrative adjectives point out the object or person referred to *(this, that, these, those)*.

| ce | before a masculine singular noun beginning with a consonant | ce garçon | this (that) boy |
|---|---|---|---|
| cet | before a masculine singular noun beginning with a vowel or silent *h* | cet avion<br>cet homme | this (that) plane<br>this (that) man |
| cette | before a feminine singular noun | cette femme | this (that) woman |
| ces | before all plural nouns | ces garçons<br>ces avions<br>ces hommes<br>ces femmes | these (those) boys<br>these (those) planes<br>these (those) men<br>these (those) women |

| | |
|---|---|
| Ce garçon est très gentil. | *This boy is very nice.* |
| Cet appartement est joli. | *This apartment is pretty.* |
| J'aime cette musique. | *I like that music.* |
| As-tu lu ces livres? | *Have you read those books?* |

NOTE:

1. Demonstrative adjectives precede and agree with the nouns they modify.

2. The demonstrative adjective is repeated before each noun.

| | |
|---|---|
| ce garçon et cette fille | *that boy and girl* |
| ces légumes et ces fruits | *these vegetables and fruits* |

3. To distinguish between *this* and *that* or between *these* and *those, -ci* and *-là* are placed, with hyphens, after the nouns being contrasted. For *this* or *these, -ci* is added; for *that* or *those, -là* is added.

| | |
|---|---|
| ce livre-ci ou ce livre-là | *this book or that book* |
| ces disques-ci et ces disques-là | *these records and those records* |

## EXERCICE A

**You are in a grocery store.** *Demandez le prix des articles suivants.*

**EXEMPLE:**

**C'est combien ce café?**

**1.**

_____

**2.**

_____

**3.**

_____

**4.**

_____

**5.**

_____

**6.**

_____

**7.**

_____

**8.**

_____

**9.**

_____

**10.**

_____

## EXERCICE B

**You are vacationing on a tropical island.** *Exprimez ce que vous dites à vos parents de regarder.*

EXEMPLE:   lac tranquille
           Regardez **ce** lac tranquille.

**1.** ciel bleu

_____

**2.** forêt magnifique

_____

**3.** herbe verte

_____

**4.** arbre gracieux

_____

**5.** hautes montagnes

_____

**6.** énorme océan

_____

**7.** jolies fleurs

_____

**8.** mer calme

_____

## EXERCICE C

**You are looking at a map, and you ask people for directions to various places.** *Exprimez vos questions.*

EXEMPLE:   tour *(f.)* (ici)
           Où est **cette tour-ci?**

*1.* musée *(m.)* (ici)

_____

*2.* avenue *(f.)* (là)

_____

*3.* parc *(m.)* (là)

_____

*4.* magasins *(m. pl.)* (ici)

_____

*5.* monument *(m.)* (là)

_____

*6.* boutiques *(f. pl.)* (ici)

_____

*7.* hôtel *(m.)* (là)

_____

*8.* cathédrale *(f.)* (là)

_____

## EXERCICE D

**You received gifts for your birthday.** *Est-ce que vous les aimez?*

EXEMPLE:     chemise / joli
             **Cette** chemise est jolie.

*1.* posters *(m. pl.)* / imaginatif

_____

*2.* pull *(m.)* / élégant

_____

*3.* montre *(f.)* / moderne

_____

*4.* cassettes *(f. pl.)* / formidable

_____

*5.* chapeau *(m.)* / beau

_____

*6.* appareil photo *(m.)* / perfectionné

_____

**7.** équipement sportif *(m.)* / pratique

_____

**8.** disques *(m. pl.)* / intéressant

_____

## M A S T E R Y   E X E R C I S E S

### EXERCICE E

**Describe the following.** *Suivez l'exemple.*

EXEMPLE:

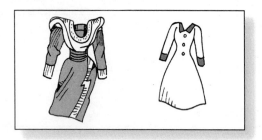

**Cette robe-ci** est élégante.
**Cette robe-là** est ordinaire.

**1.**

_____

_____

**2.**

_____

_____

**3.**

_____

_____

**4.**

_____

_____

**5.**

_____

_____

**6.**

_____

_____

**7.**

_____

_____

**8.**

_____

_____

## EXERCICE F

*Exprimez vos opinions sur les sujets suivants.*

EXEMPLE:    Kennedy: président
            **Ce** président est renommé.

*1.* Tom Cruise: acteur

_____

*2.* le français: langue

_____

*3.* *Gone With the Wind:* livre

_____

*4.* *Beverly Hills 90210:* émission

_____

*5.* le tennis et le foot: sports

_____

*6.* *Star Wars:* film

_____

**7.** *Time* et *Newsweek:* magazines

_____

**8.** Porsche: voiture

_____

## EXERCICE G

**Your parents are showing pictures they took in Europe.** *Exprimez ce qu'ils vous disent.*

**1.** These men were our guides.

_____

**2.** We took this bus that went very slowly.

_____

**3.** I admire this woman who speaks French, Italian, Spanish, and English.

_____

**4.** This mechanic repaired the bus.

_____

**5.** We saw this cathedral which is magnificent.

_____

**6.** This museum is interesting; that museum is very modern.

_____

**7.** Look at this park with these beautiful sculptures and those pretty flowers.

_____

_____

**8.** I like this castle and that church a lot.

_____

**9.** We spent four days in this city.

_____

**10.** I liked this trip.

_____

# Part four

# Word Study

QUÉBEC

SAINT-PIERRE-
ET-MIQUELON

LOUISIANE

HAÏTI    GUADELOUPE
MARTINIQUE

GUYANE

BELGIQUE

LUXEMBOURG

FRANCE    SUISSE

MONACO

CORSE

MAROC

ALGÉRIE

TUNISIE

MAURITANIE    MALI    NIGER    TCHAD

SÉNÉGAL

GUINÉE

BURKINA FASO

CÔTE-D'IVOIRE

RÉPUBLIQUE
CENTRAFRICAINE

TOGO    BÉNIN

CAMEROUN

ZAÏRE

GABON

CONGO

# Chapter 28
## Antonyms and Synonyms

## [ 1 ]  *CONTRAIRES* / ANTONYMS (OPPOSITES)

### Adjectives

| | |
|---|---|
| absent *absent* | présent *present* |
| bas *low* | haut *high* |
| beau *beautiful* | laid *ugly* |
| blanc *white* | noir *black* |
| bon *good* | mauvais *bad* |
| chaud *hot* | froid *cold* |
| cher *expensive* | bon marché *inexpensive* |
| court *short* | long *long* |
| droit *right* | gauche *left* |
| facile *easy* | difficile *difficult* |
| fort *strong* | faible *weak* |
| grand *big* | petit *little* |
| heureux *happy* | malheureux *unhappy* |
| léger *light* | lourd *heavy* |
| né *born* | mort *dead* |
| paresseux *lazy* | diligent *diligent* |
| pauvre *poor* | riche *rich* |
| plein *full* | vide *empty* |
| possible *possible* | impossible *impossible* |
| premier *first* | dernier *last* |
| utile *useful* | inutile *useless* |
| vieux *old* | { jeune *young*<br>{ neuf *(brand) new,* nouveau *new* (a different one) |
| vrai *true* | faux *false* |

### Adverbs

| | |
|---|---|
| aujourd'hui *today* | { hier *yesterday*<br>{ demain *tomorrow* |
| beaucoup *a lot, much, many* | peu *a little, few* |
| bien *well* | mal *badly* |
| enfin *finally* | d'abord *first, at first* |
| ici *here* | là *there* |
| oui *yes* | non *no* |
| plus *more* | moins *less* |
| souvent *often* | rarement *rarely* |
| vite *quickly* | lentement *slowly* |

**Nouns**

| | |
|---|---|
| l'ami *(m.) friend* | l'ennemi *(m.) enemy* |
| l'automne *(m.) autumn* | le printemps *spring* |
| le bruit *noise* | le silence *silence* |
| le commencement *beginning* | la fin *end* |
| l'été *(m.) summer* | l'hiver *(m.) winter* |
| le fils *son* | la fille *daughter* |
| le frère *brother* | la sœur *sister* |
| le garçon *boy* | la jeune fille *girl* |
| le grand-père *grandfather* | la grand-mère *grandmother* |
| la guerre *war* | la paix *peace* |
| l'homme *(m.) man* | la femme *woman* |
| le jour *day* | la nuit *night* |
| le mari *husband* | la femme *wife* |
| le matin *morning* | { le soir *evening* <br> l'après-midi *(m.) afternoon* |
| la mère *mother* | le père *father* |
| midi *noon* | minuit *midnight* |
| monsieur *sir, Mr.* | { madame *madam, Mrs.* <br> mademoiselle *Miss* |
| le neveu *nephew* | la nièce *niece* |
| le nord *north* | le sud *south* |
| l'oncle *(m.) uncle* | la tante *aunt* |
| l'ouest *(m.) west* | l'est *(m.) east* |
| le plancher *floor* | le plafond *ceiling* |
| quelque chose *something* | rien *nothing* |
| quelqu'un *someone* | personne *no one, nobody* |
| la question *question* | la réponse *answer* |
| le roi *king* | la reine *queen* |
| le soleil *sun* | la lune *moon* |
| la terre *earth, land* | { la mer *sea* <br> le ciel *heaven, sky* |
| la vie *life* | la mort *death* |
| la ville *city* | la campagne *country* |

**Prepositions**

| | |
|---|---|
| avant *before* | après *after* |
| avec *with* | sans *without* |
| devant *in front of* | derrière *behind, in back of* |
| près de *near* | loin de *far from* |
| sur *on (top of)* | sous *under* |

### Verbs

| | |
|---|---|
| accepter *to accept* | refuser *to refuse* |
| aller *to go* | venir *to come* |
| arriver *to arrive* | partir *to leave* |
| commencer *to begin* | { finir *to finish* |
| | terminer *to end* |
| demander *to ask* | répondre *to answer* |
| donner *to give* | { prendre *to take* |
| | recevoir *to receive* |
| emprunter *to borrow* | prêter *to lend* |
| fermer *to close* | ouvrir *to open* |
| jouer *to play* | travailler *to work* |
| monter *to go up* | descendre *to go down* |
| obéir *to obey* | désobéir *to disobey* |
| ôter *to remove, take off* | mettre *to put on* |
| perdre *to lose* | { trouver *to find* |
| | gagner *to win* |
| pleurer *to cry* | rire *to laugh* |
| vivre *to live* | mourir *to die* |
| voici *here is, here are* | voilà *there is, there are* |

## EXERCICE A

**Write the female counterpart of each of the following masculine terms.**

*1.* le neveu _____

*2.* le père _____

*3.* le mari _____

*4.* le fils _____

*5.* l'oncle _____

*6.* le grand-père _____

*7.* le frère _____

*8.* le garçon _____

*9.* l'homme _____

*10.* le roi _____

## EXERCICE B

**You disagree with a friend's descriptions of people and things.** *Dites le contraire de ce qu'il/elle dit.*

EXEMPLE:   Jean est grand.
           Jean est **petit.**

*1.* Lucie est diligente.

_____

*2.* Un ordinateur est inutile.

_____

*3.* M. Lenoir est vieux.

_____

*4.* Cet article est vrai.

_____

*5.* Janine est absente.

_____

*6.* Le latin est facile.

_____

*7.* Cette réponse est possible.

_____

*8.* Nos livres sont légers.

_____

*9.* Ce disque est cher.

_____

*10.* Il fait chaud.

_____

*11.* Pierre est laid.

_____

*12.* Ce sac est vide.

_____

*13.* Claude est fort.

_____

*14.* Cette soupe est bonne.

_____

*15.* Nos devoirs sont longs.

_____

## EXERCICE C

**Change this story about Mme Boyer.** *Donnez le contraire du mot en caractères gras* (boldface).

*1.* Aime-t-elle bavarder avec ses amis? **Oui.** _____

*2.* Elle parle **vite.** _____

3. Elle habite **près** de Mme Chenier. _____

4. Ces jours-ci elle téléphone **moins** à ses amies. _____

5. Elle va **rarement** au cinéma. _____

6. Elle sort **avant** midi. _____

7. Elle parle **mal** de Mme Blanchet. _____

8. Elle s'amuse **peu.** _____

9. Elle attend son amie **devant** sa maison. _____

10. Elle quitte sa maison **avec** son argent. _____

## EXERCICE D

**Jules and Jim are twins who try to be different. Each does the exact opposite of what the other does.** *Exprimez leurs actions en français. Suivez l'exemple.*

EXEMPLE:   Jules **obéit.**
              Jim **désobéit.**

1. Jules **emprunte** des disques.

   _____

2. Jules **commence** ses devoirs.

   _____

3. Jules **arrive.**

   _____

4. Jules **joue** toute la journée.

   _____

5. Jules **accepte** tout.

   _____

6. Jules **rit** souvent.

   _____

7. Jules **ôte** son chapeau.

   _____

8. Jules **monte.**

   _____

*9.* Jules **ferme** la fenêtre.

_____

*10.* Jules **perd** le match.

_____

## EXERCICE E

**Change the boldface words to make the following sentences true.** *Suivez l'exemple.*

EXEMPLE:   La neige est **noire.**
La neige est **blanche.**

*1.* On met un tapis sur **le plafond.**

_____

*2.* La nuit, on voit **le soleil** dans le ciel.

_____

*3.* Je me réveille **le soir.**

_____

*4.* Décembre est **le premier** mois de l'année.

_____

*5.* La Floride est **au nord** des États-Unis.

_____

*6.* Quand tout le monde parle, il y a **du silence.**

_____

*7.* Il est généreux. Il **prend** des cadeaux.

_____

*8.* Je déjeune **à minuit.**

_____

*9.* On met une lampe **sous** une table.

_____

*10.* Septembre marque **la fin** de l'année scolaire.

_____

*11.* Les fleurs poussent **en automne.**

_____

*12.* Quand Lucie est triste, elle **rit.**

_____

# [ 2 ] SYNONYMES / SYNONYMS

### Adjectives

| | |
|---|---|
| certain, sûr | *certain, sure* |
| heureux, content | *happy, pleased* |
| triste, malheureux | *sad, unhappy* |

### Adverbs

| | |
|---|---|
| immédiatement, tout de suite | *immediately, at once* |
| puis, ensuite, après | *then, afterwards* |
| quelquefois, parfois | *sometimes* |
| vite, rapidement | *quickly* |

### Conjunctions

| | |
|---|---|
| car, parce que | *because* |

### Nouns

| | |
|---|---|
| le château, le palais | *castle, palace* |
| le chemin, la route | *road* |
| la faute, l'erreur *(f.)* | *mistake* |
| la figure, le visage | *face* |
| l'image *(f.)*, l'illustration *(f.)* | *picture* |
| le maître, le professeur | *teacher* |
| le médecin, le docteur | *doctor* |
| le milieu, le centre | *middle* |
| le sud, le midi | *south* |
| les vêtements *(m.)*, les habits *(m.)* | *clothes* |

### Verbs

| | |
|---|---|
| finir, terminer, achever | *to finish* |
| habiter, demeurer | *to live, stay* |
| préférer, aimer mieux | *to prefer* |
| rompre, casser | *to break* |
| vouloir, désirer | *to wish, want* |

## EXERCICE F

**Change this description of Dr. Gaumont's trip to work. Give the synonym for each boldface word.**

*1.* Le **docteur** quitte sa maison pour aller travailler. _____

*2.* **Quelquefois** il arrive en retard. _____

*3.* Le docteur habite le **midi** de la France. _____

*4.* Il **habite** loin de son bureau. _____

5. Il **préfère** prendre le bus. _____

6. Aujourd'hui le bus prend **une route** étrange. _____

7. Le docteur est **certain** qu'il arrivera à l'heure. _____

8. Il est **heureux.** _____

9. En route, il **finit** un article. _____

10. Il **veut** arriver à l'heure. _____

11. Après une demi-heure, il comprend qu'il a fait une **faute.** _____

12. Regarde **sa figure.** _____

13. Il est **triste.** _____

14. Il descend vite du bus **car** il est en retard. _____

15. Il marche **vite.** _____

16. **Puis** il commence à courir. _____

17. Malheureusement, il tombe au **milieu** de la rue. _____

18. Ses **vêtements** ne sont plus propres. Quel problème! _____

## MASTERY EXERCISES

## EXERCICE G

**Each of the following items consists of a pair of related words followed by the first word of a second pair which is related in the same way.** *Complétez la deuxième paire avec le mot approprié.*

EXEMPLE:   petit / grand — bon / **mauvais**

1. court / long — droit / _____

2. médecin / docteur — illustration / _____

3. faute / erreur — professeur / _____

4. plein / vide — riche / _____

5. habiter / demeurer — rompre / _____

6. sous / sur — bas / _____

7. vrai / faux — ici / _____

**8.** nord / sud — est / _____

**9.** possible / impossible — quelque chose / _____

**10.** frère / sœur — guerre / _____

**11.** automne / printemps — hiver / _____

**12.** jour / nuit — matin / _____

**13.** accepter / refuser — donner / _____

**14.** présent / absent — blanc / _____

**15.** obéir / désobéir — demander / _____

**16.** soleil / lune — ville / _____

**17.** jeune / vieux — vivre / _____

**18.** bruit / silence — quelqu'un / _____

**19.** facile / difficile — utile / _____

**20.** premier / dernier — question / _____

## EXERCICE H

**Write the antonyms or synonyms that describe each pair you see in the illustrations below.**
*Suivez les exemples.*

EXEMPLE:

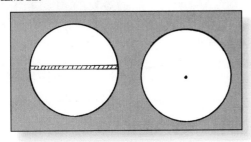

**le milieu / le centre**

**grand / petit**

**1.**

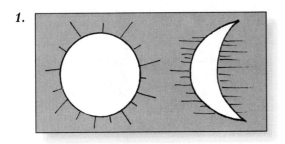

**2.**

_____ _____

**3.**

_____

**4.**

_____

**5.**

_____

**6.**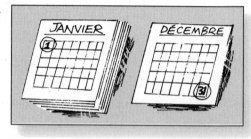

_____

**7.**

_____

**8.**

_____

**9.**

_____

**10.**

_____

**11.**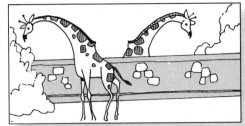

**12.**

**13.**

**14.**

**15.**

**16.**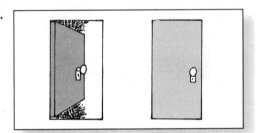

## EXERCICE I

**M. Rameau is always giving his opinion about something.** *Exprimez ce qu'il dit en employant des synonymes et des antonymes.*

1. My nephew is lazy, but my niece is diligent.

2. I want to be rich; I don't want to be poor.

3. The young doctor in this office is good; the old doctor is bad.

_____

4. Mme Aupin's son's face is sad, but her daughter's face is happy.

_____

5. The chair you want to borrow is expensive; the chair I will lend you is inexpensive.

_____

_____

6. I am pleased in the evening; I am happy in the morning.

_____

7. My friend is a poor old man who married a rich young woman.

_____

8. It is true that beginnings are difficult, but it is false that endings are always easy.

_____

_____

9. Sometimes it's hot in autumn, and sometimes it's cold in spring.

_____

_____

10. I read a lot in the summer, but very little in the winter.

_____

_____

PAYS-BAS
ANGLETERRE ALLEMAGNE
BELGIQUE
LUXEMBOURG
Brest ◆Paris Strasbourg•
AUTRICHE
Nantes FRANCE
SUISSE

# Chapter 29
## Topical Vocabulary

## [ 1 ] PERSONAL IDENTIFICATION

### a. Biographical information

**1. La nationalité / *Nationality***

| | | |
|---|---|---|
| africain *African* | canadien(ne) *Canadian* | grec(que) *Greek* |
| allemand *German* | chinois *Chinese* | haïtien(ne) *Haitian* |
| américain *American* | espagnol *Spanish* | indien(ne) *Indian* |
| anglais *English* | étranger (-ère) *foreign* | italien(ne) *Italian* |
| asiatique *Asian* | européen(ne) *European* | japonais *Japanese* |
| belge *Belgian* | français *French* | sud-américain *South American* |

**2. L'adresse *(f.)* / *Address***

| | | |
|---|---|---|
| l'avenue *(f.)* *avenue* | la place *square* | le village *village* |
| le boulevard *boulevard* | la rue *street* | la ville *city* |

**3. La famille / *Family***

| | | |
|---|---|---|
| le cousin *cousin* | la grand-mère *grandmother* | la nièce *niece* |
| la cousine *cousin* | le grand-père *grandfather* | l'oncle *uncle* |
| l'enfant *(m. or f.)* *child* | les grands-parents *grandparents* | les parents *parents* |
| la femme *wife, woman* | l'homme *man* | le père *father* |
| la fille *daughter, girl* | le mari *husband* | la personne *person* |
| le fils *son* | la mère *mother* | la sœur *sister* |
| le frère *brother* | le neveu *nephew* | la tante *aunt* |

### b. Physical characteristics

| | | |
|---|---|---|
| âgé *old* | grand *big* | mince *skinny* |
| ancien(ne) *old* | gros(se) *fat* | pauvre *poor* |
| beau (belle) *beautiful* | jeune *young* | petit *small* |
| court *short* | joli *pretty* | riche *rich* |
| faible *weak* | laid *ugly* | vieux (vieille) *old* |
| fatigué *tired* | maigre *thin* | |
| fort *strong* | malade *sick* | |

avoir... ans *to be . . . years old*

avoir les cheveux blonds *to have blond hair*

avoir les cheveux châtains *to have light brown hair*

avoir les cheveux noirs *to have black hair*

avoir les cheveux roux *to have red hair*

avoir les yeux bleus  *to have blue eyes*

avoir les yeux marron  *to have brown eyes*

avoir les yeux noirs  *to have black eyes*

avoir les yeux verts  *to have green eyes*

### c. Psychological characteristics

| | |
|---|---|
| actif (-ve) *active* | heureux (-se) *happy* |
| aimable *friendly* | honnête *honest* |
| ambitieux (-se) *ambitious* | imaginatif (-ve) *imaginative* |
| amusant *funny* | impulsif (-ve) *impulsive* |
| attentif (-ve) *attentive* | intelligent *intelligent* |
| bon(ne) *good* | intéressant *interesting* |
| consciencieux (-se) *conscientious* | intuitif (-ve) *intuitive* |
| content *happy* | malheureux (-se) *unhappy* |
| courageux (-se) *courageous* | méchant *nasty* |
| cruel(le) *cruel* | naïf (-ve) *naive* |
| curieux (-se) *curious* | paresseux (-se) *lazy* |
| drôle *funny, strange* | poli *polite* |
| dynamique *dynamic* | populaire *popular* |
| égoïste *selfish* | sérieux (-se) *serious* |
| fier (fière) *proud* | sociable *sociable* |
| franc(he) *frank* | sportif (-ve) *athletic* |
| furieux (-se) *furious* | superstitieux (-se) *superstitious* |
| généreux (-se) *generous* | sympathique *nice* |
| gentil(le) *nice* | triste *sad* |

## EXERCICE A

*Répondez aux questions que votre nouveau correspondant français vous pose dans sa première lettre.*

**1.** Quelle est ta nationalité?

_____

**2.** Comment est ta ville / ton village?

_____

**3.** Combien de personnes y a-t-il dans ta famille?

_____

**4.** Combien de frères et de sœurs as-tu?

_____

**5.** De quelle couleur sont tes yeux?

_____

**6.** De quelle couleur sont tes cheveux?

_____

**7.** Comment es-tu physiquement?

_____

**8.** Quelles sont tes bonnes qualités?

_____


## [ 2 ]   HOUSE AND HOME

### a.  La maison / *House*

l'appartement *(m.)  apartment*

l'ascenseur *(m.)  elevator*

le balcon *balcony*

la chambre (à coucher) *bedroom*

la cheminée *fireplace*

la clef *key*

le coin *corner*

le couloir *hallway*

la cour *courtyard*

la cuisine *kitchen*

la douche *shower*

l'entrée *(f.)  entrance*

l'escalier *(m.)  stairs*

l'étage *(m.)  floor, story*

la fenêtre *window*

le garage *garage*

le grenier *attic*

l'immeuble *apartment building*

le jardin *garden*

le living *living room*

le mur *wall*

la pelouse *lawn*

la penderie *closet*

la pièce *room*

le placard *cabinet*

le plafond *ceiling*

le plancher *floor*

la porte *door*

le rez-de chaussée *ground floor*

la salle à manger *dining room*

la salle de bains *bathroom*

la salle de séjour *family room*

le salon *living room*

le séjour *family room*

le sous-sol *basement*

la terrasse *terrace*

les toilettes *(f.)  toilet*

le toit *roof*

### b.  Les meubles / *Furniture*

l'armoire *(f.)  wardrobe*

le bureau *desk*

le canapé *sofa*

la chaîne stéréo *stereo*

la chaise *chair*

le congélateur *freezer*

la cuisinière *stove*

le fauteuil *armchair*

le four *oven*

la glace *mirror*

la lampe *lamp*

le lit *bed*

le magnétoscope *V.C.R.*

le meuble *piece of furniture*

le miroir *mirror*

l'ordinateur *(m.)  computer*

la pendule *clock*

le piano *piano*

le réfrigérateur *refrigerator*

le rideau *curtain*

la table *table*

la table de nuit *night table*

le tableau *picture*

le tapis *rug*

la télévision *television*

le tiroir *drawer*

## EXERCICE B

*Identifiez les parties de la maison dans l'illustration ci-dessous.*

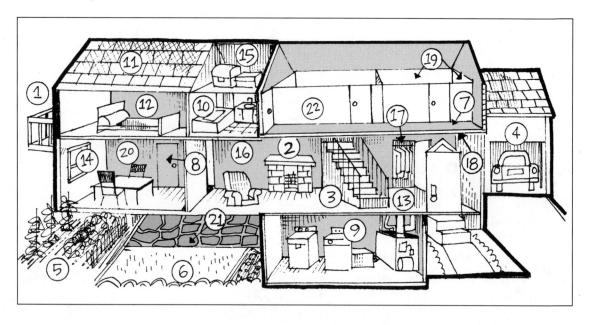

1. _____    2. _____

3. _____    4. _____

5. _____    6. _____

7. _____    8. _____

9. _____    10. _____

11. _____    12. _____

13. _____    14. _____

15. _____    16. _____

17. _____    18. _____

19. _____    20. _____

21. _____    22. _____

## EXERCICE C

**Tell what furniture or appliances you would expect to find in the following rooms.**

| la cuisine | le salon | la chambre à coucher | la salle à manger |
| --- | --- | --- | --- |
| _____ | _____ | _____ | _____ |
| _____ | _____ | _____ | _____ |

| la cuisine | le salon | la chambre à coucher | la salle à manger |
|---|---|---|---|
| _____ | _____ | _____ | _____ |
| _____ | _____ | _____ | _____ |
| _____ | _____ | _____ | _____ |
| _____ | _____ | _____ | _____ |

**c. Les travaux domestiques / *Household chores***

| | |
|---|---|
| cuisiner, faire la cuisine  *to cook* | mettre le couvert  *to set the table* |
| débarrasser la table  *to clear the table* | nettoyer la maison  *to clean the house* |
| faire la vaisselle  *to do the dishes* | passer l'aspirateur  *to vacuum* |
| faire le ménage  *to do the housework* | ranger le salon  *to tidy the living room* |
| faire les courses  *to go shopping* | vider les ordures  *to take out the garbage* |
| garder les enfants  *to watch the children* | |

## EXERCICE D

*Exprimez ce que Jacques fait pour aider sa mère.*

EXEMPLE:  **Il nettoie la maison.**

1. _____ .

2. _____ .

3. _____ .

4. _____ .

5. _____ .

6. _____ .

7. _____ .

*8.* _____ .

# [3] COMMUNITY, NEIGHBORHOOD, PHYSICAL ENVIRONMENT

### a. La ville / *The city*

l'avenue *(f.) avenue*
la banque *bank*
le bâtiment *building*
la bibliothèque *library*
la boucherie *butcher shop*
la boulangerie *bakery*
le boulevard *boulevard*
la boutique *shop*
le bureau de poste *post office*
le café *cafe*
le carrefour *intersection*
la cathédrale *cathedral*
le centre commercial *mall, shopping center*
le cinéma *movies*
l'école *(f.) school*
l'église *(f.) church*
l'épicerie *(f.) grocery store*
la fruiterie *fruit store*
la gare *station*
l'hôpital *(m.) hospital*
l'hôtel *(m.) hotel*
l'hypermarché *(m.) large supermarket*
la librairie *bookstore*
le lycée *high school*
le magasin *store*

la mairie *town hall*
la maison des jeunes et de la culture
  (M.J.C.) *youth center*
le marché *market*
la maroquinerie *leather store*
le musée *museum*
le parc *park*
la parfumerie *perfume store*
la pâtisserie *pastry shop*
la pharmacie *drugstore*
la piscine *swimming pool*
la place *square*
le pont *bridge*
la poste *post office*
le quartier *neighborhood*
le restaurant *restaurant*
la rue *street*
le stade *stadium*
la station-service *gas station*
le supermarché *supermarket*
le théâtre *theater*
le trottoir *sidewalk*
le village *village*
la ville *city*

### b. La nature / *Nature*

l'arbre *(m.) tree*
le(s) bois *(m.) woods*

la campagne *country*
le champ *field*

le ciel *sky*
le désert *desert*

l'étoile *(f.)* *star*
la feuille *leaf*
la fleur *flower*
le fleuve *river*
la forêt *forest*
l'herbe *(f.)* *grass*
la glace *ice*
l'île *(f.)* *island*

le lac *lake*
la lune *moon*
la mer *sea*
le monde *world*
la montagne *mountain*
la neige *snow*
l'océan *(m.)* *ocean*
le paysage *landscape*

la plage *beach*
la plante *plant*
la pluie *rain*
la rivière *stream*
le soleil *sun*
le temps *weather, time*
la terre *earth*
le vent *wind*

### c. Les animaux / *Animals*

l'âne *(m.)* *donkey*
l'animal *(m.)* *animal*
le chat *cat*
le cheval *horse*
le chien *dog*

le cochon *pig*
l'éléphant *(m.)* *elephant*
le lapin *(m.)* *rabbit*
le lion *lion*
le mouton *sheep*

l'oiseau *(m.)* *bird*
l'ours *(m.)* *bear*
le poisson *(m.)* *fish*
le tigre *tiger*
la vache *cow*

## EXERCICE E

**Where does one go for the following items?**

EXEMPLE:

**On va à la pâtisserie.**

*1.*

_____

*2.*

_____

**3.**

**4.**

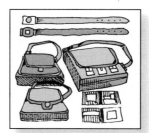

**5.**

**6.**

**7.**

**8.**

**9.**

**10.**

**11.**

_____

**12.**

_____

## EXERCICE F

**_Exprimez ce que vous voyez dans cette peinture._**

EXEMPLE:    **Il y a le soleil.**

**1.** _____

**2.** _____

**3.** _____

**4.** _____

**5.** _____

**6.** _____

**7.** _____

8. _____

9. _____

10. _____

## EXERCICE G

*Exprimez quel animal est décrit ci-dessous.*

1. _____ donne du lait.

2. _____ protège la maison.

3. _____ vole dans le ciel.

4. _____ est le roi de la jungle.

5. _____ est très grand.

6. _____ donne de la laine.

7. _____ donne du jambon et des saucisses.

8. _____ trotte dans les champs.

## [ 4 ] MEALS, FOOD, AND DRINK

### a. Les repas *(m.)* / Meals

| | | |
|---|---|---|
| l'assiette *(f.) plate* | le dîner *dinner* | la serviette *napkin* |
| la bouteille *bottle* | la fourchette *fork* | la tasse *cup* |
| le couteau *knife* | le goûter *snack* | le verre *glass* |
| la cuillère *spoon* | le petit déjeuner *breakfast* | |
| le déjeuner *lunch* | le plat *dish* | |

### b. Les aliments *(m.)* / Foods

| | |
|---|---|
| l'artichaut *(m.) artichoke* | la carotte *carrot* |
| l'asperge *(f.) asparagus* | les céréales *cereal* |
| la banane *banana* | la cerise *cherry* |
| le beurre *butter* | le chocolat *chocolate* |
| le bifteck *steak* | le cidre *cider* |
| le biscuit *cookie* | le citron *lemon* |
| le bœuf *beef* | la citronnade *lemonade* |
| les bonbons *(m.) candies* | la confiture *jelly* |
| la brioche *sweet roll* | la crème *cream* |
| le café *coffee* | le croissant *crescent roll* |

le dessert *dessert*

l'eau *(f.)* *water*

l'eau minérale *mineral water*

la fraise *strawberry*

les frites *(f.)* *french fries*

le fromage *cheese*

le fruit *fruit*

les fruits de mer *seafood*

le gâteau *cake*

le gâteau au chocolat *chocolate cake*

la glace *ice cream*

la glace à la vanille *vanilla ice cream*

le hamburger *hamburger*

les haricots verts *(m.)* *string beans*

le hors-d'œuvre *appetizer*

le jambon *ham*

le jus *juice*

le lait *milk*

la laitue *lettuce*

le légume *vegetable*

la limonade *lemon soda*

l'œuf *(m.)* *egg*

l'omelette *(f.)* *omelet*

l'orange *(f.)* *orange*

l'orangeade *(f.)* *orange soda*

le pain *bread*

le pain grillé *toast*

le pâté *meat appetizer*

la pêche *peach*

les petits pois *(m.)* *peas*

la poire *pear*

le poisson *fish*

le poivre *pepper*

la pomme *apple*

la pomme de terre *potato*

le potage *soup*

le poulet *chicken*

la prune *plum*

le rafraîchissement *refreshment*

le raisin *grape*

la salade *salad*

le sandwich *sandwich*

la saucisse *sausage*

le saucisson *hard sausage*

le sel *salt*

la soupe *soup*

le sucre *sugar*

le thé *tea*

la tomate *tomato*

le veau *veal*

la viande *meat*

le vin *wine*

## EXERCICE H

*Exprimez ce que vous mangez à chacun de ces repas.*

| le petit déjeuner | le déjeuner | le dîner |
|---|---|---|
| _____ | _____ | _____ |
| _____ | _____ | _____ |
| _____ | _____ | _____ |
| _____ | _____ | _____ |
| _____ | _____ | _____ |
| _____ | _____ | _____ |
| _____ | _____ | _____ |

## EXERCICE I

*Exprimez les objets que vous mettez sur la table à chaque repas.*

_____   _____   _____

_____   _____   _____

_____   _____   _____

## [ 5 ] HEALTH AND WELFARE

### a. Les parties du corps / *Parts of the body*

| | | |
|---|---|---|
| la bouche *mouth* | l'épaule *(f.) shoulder* | l'oreille *(f.) ear* |
| le bras *arm* | l'estomac *(m.) stomach* | l'orteil *(m.) toe* |
| les cheveux *(m.) hair* | la figure *face* | le pied *foot* |
| le cœur *heart* | la gorge *throat* | la poitrine *chest* |
| le corps *body* | la jambe *leg* | la tête *head* |
| le cou *neck* | la langue *tongue* | le ventre *stomach* |
| le coude *elbow* | la main *hand* | le visage *face* |
| la dent *tooth* | le nez *nose* | les yeux *(m.) eyes* |
| le doigt *finger* | l'œil *(m.) eye* | |
| le dos *back* | l'ongle *(m.) nail* | |

### b. Les maladies (f.) / *Illnesses*

| | |
|---|---|
| avoir mal à la gorge *to have a sore throat* | avoir mal aux dents *to have a toothache* |
| avoir mal à la tête *to have a headache* | la grippe *the flu* |
| avoir mal à l'estomac *to have a stomach ache* | la température *temperature* |
| avoir mal au pied *to have a sore foot* | une toux *a cough* |
| avoir mal au ventre *to have a stomach ache* | un rhume *a cold* |

## EXERCICE J

**Richard is a hypochondriac. Express what he imagines is wrong with him.** *Suivez l'exemple.*

EXEMPLE:

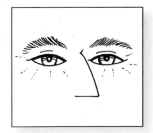

**Il a mal aux yeux.**

1.

_____

2.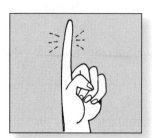

_____

3.

_____

4.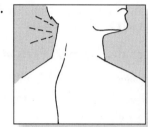

_____

5.

_____

6.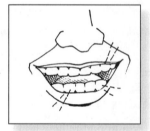

_____

7.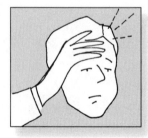

_____

8.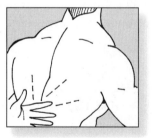

_____

## [ 6 ]  EDUCATION

### a. L'école (f.) / School

le banc  *seat, bench*

le bureau  *desk*

le cahier  *notebook*

la calculette  *calculator*

le cartable *schoolbag*
la carte *map*
la classe *class*
le classeur *loose-leaf notebook*
la cloche *bell*
la corbeille à papier *wastebasket*
la craie *chalk*
le crayon *pencil*
les devoirs *(m.) homework*
le dictionnaire *dictionary*
l'école *(f.) school*
l'élève *(m. or f.) student*
l'emploi du temps *(m.) schedule*
l'étudiant *(m.) student*
l'examen *(m.) test*
l'exemple *(m.) example*
l'exercice *(m.) exercise*
la gomme *eraser*
l'histoire *(f.) story*
l'horloge *(f.) clock*

la leçon *lesson*
la lecture *reading*
le livre *book*
le lycée *high school*
la matière *school subject*
la note *grade*
le papier *paper*
la permission *pass*
la phrase *sentence*
le pupitre *pupil's desk*
la question *question*
la règle *ruler*
la réponse *answer*
le sac à dos *backpack*
la salle de classe *classroom*
le scotch *scotch tape*
le stylo *pen*
le tableau *(chalk)board*
la trousse *pencil case*
le vocabulaire *vocabulary*

## b. Les matières *(f.) / Subjects*

l'anglais *(m.) English*
la biologie *biology*
la chimie *chemistry*
l'éducation physique *(f.) gym*
l'espagnol *(m.) Spanish*
le français *French*
la géographie *geography*
la gymnastique *gym*

l'histoire *(f.) history*
l'informatique *(f.) computer science*
le latin *Latin*
les mathématiques *(f. pl.) math*
la physique *physics*
la science *science*
la technologie *technology*

## c. Les activités scolaires *(f.) / School activities*

le cercle *club*
le cercle de maths *math club*
le cercle dramatique *drama club*
le cercle international *international club*
le cercle français *French club*
le ciné-club *film club*
le club d'échecs *chess club*
la distribution des prix *award ceremony*

l'équipe *(f.) de base-ball baseball team*
l'équipe de football *soccer team*
la fanfare *band*
les jeunesses musicales *music association*
l'orchestre *(m.) orchestra*
le prix *(m.) d'excellence prize given to best student*
le tableau *(m.) d'honneur honor roll*

## EXERCICE K

*Identifiez toutes les choses que vous voyez dans la classe de Mme Rousseau.*

1. _____
2. _____
3. _____
4. _____
5. _____
6. _____
7. _____
8. _____
9. _____
10. _____
11. _____
12. _____
13. _____
14. _____
15. _____
16. _____
17. _____
18. _____
19. _____
20. _____
21. _____

## EXERCICE L

*Identifiez les matières que vous étudiez et les activités auxquelles* (**in which**) *vous ou vos amis participez.*

| les matières | les matières | les activités |
|---|---|---|
| | | |
| | | |
| | | |
| | | |
| | | |

## [ 7 ] PROFESSIONS

| | |
|---|---|
| l'agent *(m.)* de police *police officer* | le garçon *waiter* |
| l'artiste *(m.* or *f.)* *artist* | l'infirmier (-ière) *nurse* |
| l'avocat(e) *lawyer* | l'ingénieur *(m.)* *engineer* |
| boucher (-ère) *butcher* | le médecin *doctor* |
| boulanger (-ère) *baker* | le métier *job* |
| le chef *chef* | l'ouvrier (-ière) *factory worker* |
| coiffeur (-euse) *hair stylist* | le peintre *painter* |
| le commerçant *merchant* | le président *president* |
| cuisinier (-ière) *cook* | le professeur *teacher* |
| le dentiste *dentist* | programmeur (-euse) *programmer* |
| directeur (-trice) *director, principal* | le (la) secrétaire *secretary* |
| le docteur *doctor* | la serveuse *waitress* |
| l'épicier (-ière) *grocer* | vendeur (-euse) *salesperson* |
| fermier (-ière) *farmer* | |

## EXERCICE M

*Identifiez la profession des personnes suivantes.*

EXEMPLE:   Il dessine.
**C'est un artiste.**

**1.** Il enseigne les élèves.

_____

**2.** Elle travaille dans un restaurant.

_____

**3.** Il arrête les criminels.

_____

**4.** Il prépare les repas dans un restaurant.

_____

**5.** Elle guérit les malades.

_____

**6.** Il vend de la viande.

_____

**7.** Il est expert en informatique.

_____

*8.* Il prépare des gâteaux.

_____

*9.* Elle protège les innocents au tribunal.

_____

*10.* Elle guérit un mal de dents.

_____

*11.* Il travaille dans une ferme.

_____

*12.* Elle vous coiffe les cheveux.

_____

*13.* Il aide les clients dans un magasin.

_____

# [ 8 ]  LEISURE

## a. Les loisirs (m.) / Leisure activities

| | |
|---|---|
| le bal  *ball* | le musée  *museum* |
| le ballet  *ballet* | l'opéra (m.)  *opera* |
| la campagne  *country* | le parc  *park* |
| les cartes (f.)  *cards* | le parc national  *national park* |
| le centre commercial  *mall* | le (parc) zoo(logique)  *zoo* |
| le cinéma  *movies* | la plage  *beach* |
| le concert  *concert* | la promenade  *walk* |
| la fête  *holiday, party* | la radio  *radio* |
| l'île tropicale  *tropical island* | le site pittoresque  *picturesque site* |
| le jour de congé  *day off* | la télévision  *television* |
| le jour férié  *legal holiday* | le théâtre  *theater* |
| la montagne  *mountain* | les vacances (f.)  *vacation* |

## b. Les sports (m.) / Sports

| | |
|---|---|
| le base-ball  *baseball* | la natation  *swimming* |
| le bowling  *bowling* | la pêche  *fishing* |
| le football  *soccer* | le rugby  *rugby* |
| le football américain  *football* | le stade  *stadium* |
| le golf  *golf* | le tennis  *tennis* |
| le match  *match* | le volley-ball  *volleyball* |

## EXERCICE N

**Where do these persons go to have a good time?** *Suivez l'exemple.*

EXEMPLE: Elles **vont à la montagne.**

1. Je _____ .

2. Nous _____ .

3. Ils _____ .

4. Vous _____ .

*5.*   Tu _____ .

*6.*   Il _____ .

*7.*   Elles _____ .

*8.*   Nous _____ .

*9.*   Je _____ .

**10.** Vous _____ .

## EXERCICE O

*Dites dans quel sport on utilise l'équipement suivant.*

EXEMPLE:

**le bowling**

**1.**

_____

**2.**

_____

**3.**

_____

**4.**

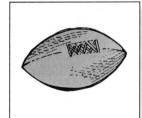

_____

6.

7.

8.

## [ 9 ] PUBLIC AND PRIVATE SERVICES

### a. Le téléphone / *Telephone*

l'annuaire *(m.) phone book*          la cabine *phone booth*          l'opératrice *(f.) operator*
l'appel *(m.) call*          le numéro *number*          le téléphone *telephone*

### b. La poste / *Post Office*

l'adresse *(f.) address*          le courrier *mail*          la lettre *letter*
la boîte aux lettres *mailbox*          l'enveloppe *(f.) envelope*          le nom *name*
la carte postale *postcard*          le facteur *mailman*          par avion *air mail*
le code postal *zip code*          le guichet *window*          le timbre *stamp*

## EXERCICE P

**Replace the pictures with the correct French words.**

Un jour, tout d'un coup, j'ai envie de parler à mon ami Georges. Je vais dans une

_____ . J'ouvre l'_____ . Je trouve son
          1.                                    2.

_____ . Malheureusement, le [image] _____ ne marche pas.
3. 4.

J'appelle l' [image] _____ . Elle dit: «Je regrette, mais la ligne est en
5.

dérangement.» Tant pis! Je vais chez moi lui écrire une [image] _____ .
6.

J'écris le [image] _____ , l' [image] _____ et
7. 8.

le [image] _____ de mon ami sur l' [image] _____ .
9. 10.

Zut! Je n'ai pas de [image] _____ . Alors je vais à la [image]
11.

_____ . Au [image] _____ , j'achète les [image]
12. 13.

_____ nécessaires et je les colle sur l' [image] _____ . Je mets
14. 15.

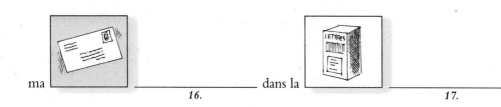

ma _____ dans la _____ . Demain le
　　　　　　　　*16.*　　　　　　　　　　　　　　*17.*

_____ la donnera à Georges.
　　*18.*

# [ 10 ] CLOTHING

### a. Les vêtements *(m.)* / *Clothing*

les bas *(m.)* *stockings*　　　　　　le maillot de bain *bathing suit*

les baskets *(f.)* *high-top sneakers*　　le manteau *coat*

la blouse *blouse*　　　　　　　　le mouchoir *handkerchief*

les bottes *(f.)* *boots*　　　　　　le pantalon *pants*

le chapeau *hat*　　　　　　　　le parapluie *umbrella*

les chaussettes *(f.)* *socks*　　　　le pardessus *overcoat*

les chaussures *(f.)* *shoes*　　　　la poche *pocket*

la chemise *shirt*　　　　　　　　le pull *pullover*

le chemisier *woman's shirt*　　　　la robe *dress*

le complet *suit*　　　　　　　　le sac *handbag*

le costume *suit*　　　　　　　　les sandales *(f.)* *sandals*

la cravate *tie*　　　　　　　　le short *shorts*

l'écharpe *(f.)* *scarf*　　　　　　les souliers *(m.)* *shoes*

les gants *(m.)* *gloves*　　　　　le tailleur *woman's suit*

les habits *(m.)* *clothing*　　　　le tee-shirt *T-shirt*

l'imperméable *(m.)* *raincoat*　　　les tennis *(f.)* *tennis sneakers*

le jean *jeans*　　　　　　　　la veste *jacket*

la jupe *skirt*

### b. Les couleurs *(f.)* / *Colors*

blanc(he) *white*　　jaune *yellow*　　rouge *red*

bleu *blue*　　　　noir *black*　　vert *green*

brun *brown*　　　orange *orange*　　violet *purple*

gris *gray*　　　　rose *pink*

## EXERCICE Q

*Vous partez en voyage.* **List the articles of clothing you are going to pack. Name their color.**

EXEMPLE:   **mes chaussettes vertes**

_____     _____

_____     _____

_____     _____

_____     _____

_____     _____

# [ 11 ] TRAVEL

l'aéroport *(m.)  airport*

l'arrêt *(m.)  stop*

l'autobus *(m.)  bus*

l'auto(mobile) *(f.)  car*

l'avion *(m.)  airplane*

le bateau  *boat*

la bicyclette  *bicycle*

le billet  *ticket*

le car  *tour bus*

le chemin  *road*

le chemin de fer  *railroad*

la gare  *train station*

le guichet  *ticket window*

l'horaire *(m.)  schedule*

le métro  *subway*

la mobylette  *moped*

la motocyclette  *motorcycle*

le moyen de transport  *means of transportation*

la porte  *gate*

la promenade  *walk*

la route  *route, road*

le scooter  *motorscooter*

la station  *station*

le taxi  *taxi*

le ticket  *ticket*

le train  *train*

le tramway  *streetcar*

le vélo  *bicycle*

la voie  *track, lane*

la voiture  *car*

le vol  *flight*

le voyage  *trip*

## EXERCICE R

*Exprimez comment les personnes suivantes vont à leur travail.*

EXEMPLE:                                  Jean **prend le tramway.**

1. Je _____.

2. Nous _____.

3. M. Dupont _____.

4. Vous _____.

5. Nadine et Raoul _____.

**6.** Tu _____ .

**7.** Marie _____ .

**8.** Les filles _____ .

**9.** M. Rameau _____ .

**10.** Mme Lefarge _____ .

## M A S T E R Y   E X E R C I S E S

## EXERCICE S

*Choisissez le mot qui n'est pas de la même classe que les autres.*

EXEMPLE:     l'immeuble, le grenier, l'escalier, la rivière
             **la rivière**

1. belge, rue, grec, chinois _____

2. neveu, sœur, fils, joli _____

3. le grenier, le balcon, le séjour, le village _____

4. la gare, la chaise, le fauteuil, le tiroir _____

5. l'épicerie, le magasin, le tapis, la banque _____

6. naïf, violet, poli, fier _____

7. le ciel, la lune, le soleil, le cochon _____

8. le cheval, le mouton, le musée, l'oiseau _____

9. le couteau, la fourchette, le pont, la cuillère _____

10. le chat, le fromage, le poisson, le jambon _____

11. les cheveux, les meubles, les orteils, les yeux _____

12. le crayon, le visage, la trousse, le stylo _____

13. le médecin, le garçon, la fille, l'avocat _____

14. la fête, le stade, le jour férié, le jour de congé _____

15. le timbre, l'enveloppe, le facteur, le tableau _____

16. le bureau, l'imperméable, le pardessus, le manteau _____

17. gris, brun, jeune, noir _____

18. le vélo, le métro, le bateau, la douche _____

## EXERCICE T

*Complétez les phrases avec les mots qui conviennent.*

1. _____ est un énorme animal gris.

2. Dans la classe de géographie on regarde _____ qui montre tous
   les pays du monde.

*3.* On va au _____ pour voir un match de football.

*4.* Après les repas on vide _____ avant de les laver.

*5.* La Seine est _____ qui traverse Paris.

*6.* _____ apporte le courrier tous les jours.

*7.* La sœur de ma mère est ma _____ .

*8.* Si j'ai envie d'emprunter des livres, je vais à _____ .

*9.* Pour chercher un numéro de téléphone, regardez dans _____ .

*10.* Pour envoyer une lettre, je vais à _____ .

*11.* Si on a mal aux dents, on va chez _____ .

*12.* On voit avec _____ .

*13.* On va à _____ si on aime nager.

*14.* Pour ouvrir la porte, il faut utiliser _____ .

*15.* Pour savoir l'heure, on regarde une _____ .

*16.* Le Concorde d'Air France est une sorte d'_____ .

*17.* Le premier repas du jour est _____ .

*18.* Le président des États-Unis habite la Maison-_____ .

*19.* On prépare les repas dans _____ .

*20.* On coupe la viande avec _____ .

## EXERCICE U

*Exprimez en français ce que Dominique dit au sujet de son voyage.*

*1.* I am going on vacation in a week with my parents, my sister, and my brother.

_____

_____

*2.* We are going by plane to a tropical island.

_____

*3.* I will put four bathing suits, seven pairs of shorts, ten shirts, and my sandals in my suitcase.

_____

_____

**4.** We are all happy because we will not cook, go shopping, or clean the house for a week.

_____

_____

**5.** The beach is beautiful, and we will go swimming every day.

_____

**6.** We will have a large room with three beds, a lamp, a television, a balcony, two chairs, a table and a refrigerator.

_____

_____

**7.** At night we will see many stars in the sky.

_____

**8.** We will eat chicken, fruits and vegetables, and many different desserts.

_____

**9.** I will write postcards to my friends and to my grandparents.

_____

**10.** We will go to the boutiques, bookstore, perfume store, and leather store to buy souvenirs.

_____

_____

# Part five
# French Civilization

QUÉBEC

SAINT-PIERRE-
ET-MIQUELON

LOUISIANE

BELGIQUE

LUXEMBOURG

FRANCE      SUISSE

MONACO

CORSE

MAROC

ALGÉRIE          TUNISIE

HAÏTI      GUADELOUPE
MARTINIQUE

MAURITANIE       MALI      NIGER      TCHAD

SÉNÉGAL

GUINÉE                                   RÉPUBLIQUE
                                          CENTRAFRICAINE
BURKINA FASO

CÔTE-D'IVOIRE

GUYANE                    TOGO    BÉNIN              ZAÏRE

CAMEROUN

GABON
CONGO

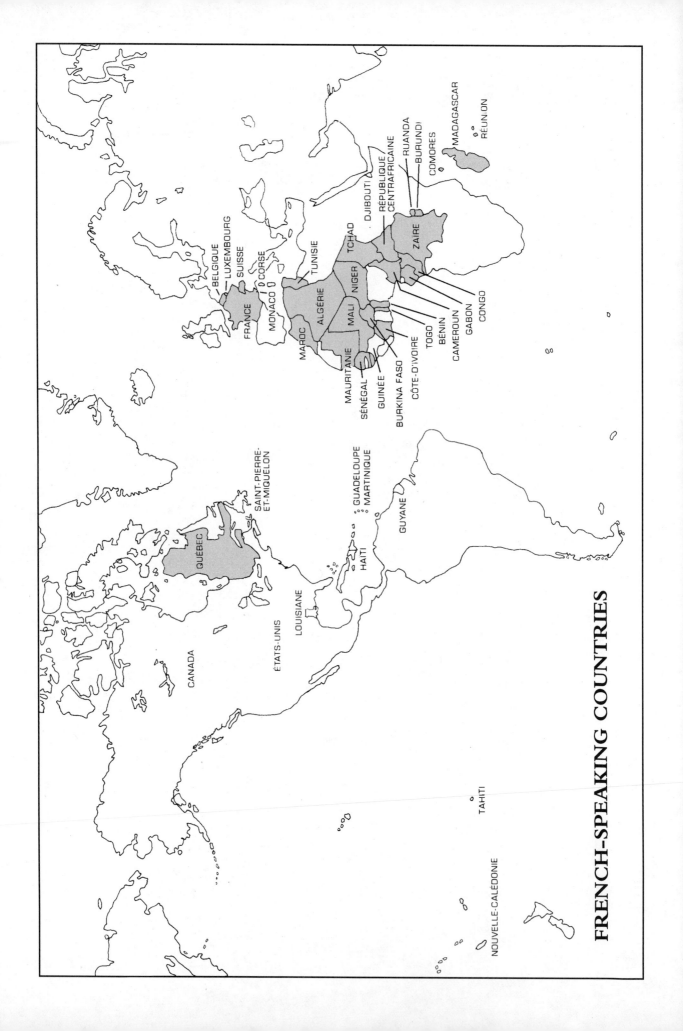

**FRENCH-SPEAKING COUNTRIES**

French is a Romance language, derived principally from the popular spoken Latin of the Romans. Over 2,000 years ago, a Roman army led by Julius Caesar invaded the country then known as Gaul, and the Gauls adopted the language of their conquerors. Their own languages, which included Celtic, and other languages such as German, have made contributions to French.

Different dialects developed in the various regions of France. The one spoken in Île-de-France, where the kings held court, became the official language of the nation.

In 1634, Cardinal Richelieu founded the French Academy (l'Académie française), whose forty members were to study, preserve, and perfect the French language.

Over two hundred million people around the world speak French. Outside of France, French is spoken in approximately forty countries of the world. (See map on facing page.). In the United States, French is still spoken in parts of Louisiana. French is also one of the official languages of the United Nations (l'Organisation des Nations Unies).

Other Romance languages are Italian, Spanish, Portuguese, and Romanian.

French has exerted a strong influence on the English language as a result of the invasion of England in 1066 by William, duke of Normandy, known as William the Conqueror (Guillaume le Conquérant). After the conquest, French became the official language of the English royal court, the educated classes, and the law courts. Thus, a vast number of French words became part of the English language. Constant cultural exchange between France and the English-speaking countries has strengthened the bond between the two languages.

Cognates are words in different languages that originate from the same source. In the case of English and French, the common root is often a Latin one. Some examples of cognates in French and English are:

| FRENCH | ENGLISH | FRENCH | ENGLISH |
|--------|---------|--------|---------|
| appeler | appeal | chien | canine |
| blanc | blank | doigt | digit |
| enfant | infant | mouton | mutton |
| état | state | pauvre | pauper |
| faim | famine | petit | petty |
| femme | feminine | pied | pedal |
| maison | mansion | sœur | sorority |

English has borrowed and incorporated a number of French words and expressions, some examples of which are listed below. In English, the accents may in some cases be omitted.

**à la carte**  term used in dining when foods are ordered individually from the menu

**blasé**  bored as a result of frequent exposure or over-indulgence; too sophisticated

**bon voyage**  have a good trip

**boulevard**  broad avenue or thoroughfare

**bourgeoisie**  the middle class of society

**camouflage**  disguise, particularly in warfare

**chaise longue**  chair with seat supporting a person's outstretched legs

**coup d'état**  sudden illegal overthrow of a government by force

**cuisine**  style and preparation of cooking

**débris**  rubbish, especially resulting from destruction

**début**  entrance into society or a career; first appearance on the stage

**demi-tasse**  small cup of black coffee

**élite**  group treated or considered as superior

**en route**  on the way

**esprit de corps**  devotion to a group

**faux pas**  social blunder

**fiancé(e)**  man or woman engaged to be married

**gourmet**  person who understands and appreciates fine food

**hors-d'œuvre**  appetizer served at the beginning of a meal

**Mardi gras**  Shrove Tuesday (last day before Lent), a day of carnival and festivity

**matinée**  daytime entertainment, especially in the afternoon

**naïve**  simple and ingenuous in manner

**née**  term applied to the maiden name of a married woman

**nom de plume**  pen name assumed by an author

**nonchalant**  appearing to be indifferent

**objet d'art**  article of artistic worth

**rendez-vous**  appointment, meeting place

**R.S.V.P. (répondez, s'il vous plaît)**  please answer

**sabotage**  malicious destruction of property

**tête-à-tête**  private conversation between two persons

Many geographical names in the United States are of French origin: Bayonne, Champlain, Detroit, Joliet, Louisiana, New Orleans, New Rochelle, St. Louis, Terre Haute, Vermont.

French has likewise borrowed many terms from the English language. For example: **club, détective, match, steak, jazz, parking, tunnel, interview, week-end.**

100

## EXERCICE A

**For each item of the first column write the letter of the matching description in the second column**

1. William the Conqueror _____
2. hors-d'œuvre _____
3. Spanish _____
4. R.S.V.P. _____
5. rendez-vous _____
6. Julius Caesar _____
7. nonchalant _____
8. Gaul _____
9. eastern Canada _____
10. faux pas _____
11. Celtic _____

*a.* appointment
*b.* Roman general
*c.* French-speaking area
*d.* former name of France
*e.* language of Gaul
*f.* duke of Normandy
*g.* Romance language
*h.* social blunder
*i.* please answer
*j.* appetizer
*k.* appearing to be indifferent

## EXERCICE B

**Give an English cognate for each French word.**

1. faim _____
2. pauvre _____
3. doigt _____
4. libre _____
5. mouton _____
6. sœur _____
7. blanc _____
8. pied _____
9. musée _____
10. petit _____
11. chien _____
12. femme _____
13. enfant _____
14. appeler _____
15. maison _____
16. main _____

## EXERCICE C

**Complete the sentences.**

1.  French is called a Romance language because it is derived chiefly from _____ ,

    the language of the _____ .

2.  Two other languages that have contributed vocabulary to French are Celtic and

    _____ .

3.  The dialect of the province of _____ became the official language of France.

4.  Other European countries besides France in which French is spoken are _____

    and _____ .

5.  A large number of French words came into the English language after the Norman invasion of

    England under the leadership of _____ .

6.  In addition to French and Spanish, _____ and _____ are
    Romance languages.

7.  Words in different languages derived from the same original source are called

    _____ .

8.  The English word *pedal* comes from the same root as the French word _____ .

9.  The French word *état* comes from the same root as the English word _____ .

10. Another name for the middle class of society is the _____ .

11. Two American cities having names of French origin are _____ and

    _____ .

12. The forty members of the _____ are entrusted with maintaining the purity of
    the French language.

13. French is still spoken in parts of the American state of _____ .

14. _____ and _____ are English terms commonly used in
    French.

## EXERCICE D

**Replace the words in italics with the appropriate French expression.**

1.  The author had chosen an original *(pen name)* _____ .

2. Mrs. Johnson, *(whose maiden name had been)* _____ Phillips, was very devoted to the Phillips family.

3. The *(style of cooking)* _____ in this restaurant is suitable for a *(person who understands fine food)* _____ .

4. During the war, military equipment was *(disguised)* _____ to prevent *(malicious destruction)* _____ by enemy agents.

5. The leaders of industry were among the social *(select group)* _____ .

6. We have *(afternoon)* _____ tickets for the *(first appearance)* _____ of the French star on the American stage.

7. Don't forget to buy an *(article of artistic value)* _____ on your trip to Paris. *(Have a good journey!)* _____ .

8. I do not want a regular dinner. I'll order *(by individual dish from the menu)* _____ and finish with a *(small cup of coffee)* _____ .

9. She is such a *(ingenuous and simple)* _____ girl; and her *(the man to whom she is engaged)* _____ always looks so *(bored with everything, as if he has seen it all)* _____ .

10. After the fire, the *(rubble)* _____ was removed.

11. The celebration of *(Shrove Tuesday)* _____ in New Orleans is a tourist attraction.

12. There is a wonderful *(group spirit)* _____ in this class.

13. *(On the way)* _____ the two friends stopped at a café to have a *(private conversation)* _____ .

14. After walking along the *(broad avenue)* _____ , she went home to relax in her *(lounge chair)* _____ .

15. Napoleon became First Consul after his celebrated *(sudden overthrow of the government)* _____ .

# Chapter 31
## Geography of France

## SIZE, POPULATION, BOUNDARIES

1 France is a country of great natural beauty and diversity. It has been called **"la belle France"** and **"la douce France."** It is located on a latitude about halfway between the equator and the North
5 Pole.

With an area of 213,000 square miles including the island of Corsica (**la Corse**), France is smaller than the state of Texas but is geographically the largest country in the European Community (**la**
10 **Communauté européenne**). It has a population of about 57,500,000 (in 1993), including Corsica.

Shaped like a hexagon, hence its nickname (**l'hexagone**), France has water on three sides: on the north, the English Channel (**la Manche**); on
15 the west, the Atlantic Ocean (**l'océan Atlantique**); on the south, the Mediterranean Sea (**la mer Méditerranée**). This geographical position gives the country an extensive coastline. The surrounding waters and the Gulf Stream make the climate
20 essentially temperate. In most of France, there is abundant rainfall.

France borders on Belgium (**la Belgique**) and Luxembourg (**le Luxembourg**) to the northeast; on Germany (**l'Allemagne**), Switzerland (**la**
25 **Suisse**), and Italy (**l'Italie**) to the east; and on Spain (**l'Espagne**) on the south.

Corsica, in the Mediterranean Sea southeast of continental France, is a mountainous island with a rugged coast. It is here, in the city of Ajaccio, that
30 Napoleon Bonaparte was born.

## PRINCIPAL MOUNTAIN RANGES

1. The Alps (**les Alpes**) form the frontier with Italy. This highest French range includes the **mont Blanc** (15,780 feet or 4,807 meters), the tallest peak in western Europe.
35 2. The Pyrenees (**les Pyrénées**) are a natural barrier separating France from Spain. This second-highest range in France has numerous steep, jagged peaks.
3. The Vosges (**les Vosges**) are located in Alsace
40 and Lorraine, near Germany. Erosion has given their summits a gently rounded shape.

4. The Jura (**le Jura**), in the east, forms the principal frontier with Switzerland. Rich in fossils, this mountain range gave its name to the Jurassic period of geologic time.
45
5. The Central Plateau (**le Massif Central**), in the south-central part of the country, comprises the oldest French mountains, formed of extinct volcanoes. The **Cévennes** are part of this range.
50

## PRINCIPAL RIVERS

1. The Seine (**la Seine**) is the most navigable and most important river. It flows through Paris and Normandy and empties into the English Channel (**la Manche**) near Le Havre.
2. The Loire (**la Loire**) is the longest river, but 55 the least navigable. It rises in the Massif Central and flows into the Atlantic at the port city of Saint-Nazaire. The Loire is famous for the magnificent châteaux along its banks.
3. The Garonne (**la Garonne**) rises in the 60 Pyrenees and flows through Bordeaux to the Atlantic, where it forms a long, wide tidal inlet named **la Gironde**.
4. The Rhone (**le Rhône**) is a swift-flowing source of waterpower exploited by many hy- 65 droelectric dams. Rising in Switzerland, it joins the Saone River (**la Saône**) at Lyon. Then it flows south and empties into the Mediterranean near Marseille, forming a large delta, **la Camargue**. 70
5. The Rhine (**le Rhin**), the river that defines part of the border between France and Germany, is Europe's main artery for navigation. The Rhine is famous for its spectacular beauty. 75

France possesses an elaborate system of canals, several of them linking the rivers. The best known is the **canal du Midi**, which connects the Mediterranean with the Garonne River and thus with the Atlantic. 80

NOTE: This book uses the French spelling of names of towns. English often has a different spelling, for instance, Lyons, Marseilles, Rheims.

## EXERCICE A

**Match the mountains and the rivers with the correct numbers on the map.**

*1.* _____ la Seine

*2.* _____ la Loire

*3.* _____ la Garonne

*4.* _____ le Rhône

*5.* _____ le Rhin

*6.* _____ les Alpes

*7.* _____ les Pyrénées

*8.* _____ les Vosges

*9.* _____ le Jura

*10.* _____ le Massif Central

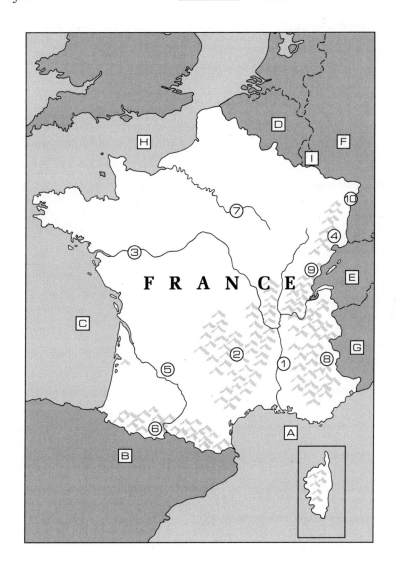

## EXERCICE B

**Match the boundaries of France with the correct letters on the map.**

*1.* _____ l'océan Atlantique

*2.* _____ la Belgique

*3.* _____ la Manche

*4.* _____ l'Allemagne

**5.** _____ l'Italie      **6.** _____ la mer Méditerranée

**7.** _____ l'Espagne      **8.** _____ la Suisse

**9.** _____ le Luxembourg

## EXERCICE C

**For each description in the first column, write the letter of the matching item in the second column.**

| | | |
|---|---|---|
| **1.** highest mountains in France | _____ | **a.** le Jura |
| **2.** French island in the Mediterranean | _____ | **b.** la Loire |
| | | **c.** le mont Blanc |
| **3.** most navigable river | _____ | **d.** Ajaccio |
| **4.** tallest peak in the Alps | _____ | **e.** la Camargue |
| | | **f.** le Massif Central |
| **5.** longest river | _____ | **g.** la Corse |
| **6.** city in which Napoleon was born | _____ | **h.** la Seine |
| | | **i.** les Alpes |
| **7.** river that rises in the Pyrenees | _____ | **j.** la Garonne |
| **8.** principal frontier between France and Switzerland | _____ | |
| **9.** delta of the Rhone | _____ | |
| **10.** oldest mountains | _____ | |

## EXERCICE D

*Complétez les phrases.*

**1.** Les montagnes qui séparent la France de l'Italie sont _____ .

**2.** Le fleuve de Paris est _____ .

**3.** En parlant de la France, on emploie souvent les adjectifs «belle» et «_____» .

**4.** _____ est une chaîne de montagnes d'origine volcanique.

**5.** Le fleuve connu pour ses beaux châteaux est _____ .

**6.** Le canal du Midi et la Garonne relient *(connect)* l'océan _____ à la

mer _____ .

**7.** Les montagnes qu'on trouve en Alsace, près de l'Allemagne, sont _____ .

**8.** La Seine se jette *(empties)* dans _____ près de la ville du Havre.

9.  Le fleuve le plus important pour la production d'énergie hydro-électrique est

    _____ .

10. Le _____ est le courant d'eau chaude qui contribue au climat
    tempéré de la France.

11. La Loire commence dans le Massif Central et se jette dans _____ .

12. Le fleuve qui passe par Bordeaux est _____ .

13. Les Pyrénées séparent la France de _____ .

14. La Saône se jette dans le Rhône dans la ville de _____ .

15. Le _____ est un fleuve qui sert de frontière entre la France et

    _____ .

# Chapter 32
## Provinces

1 Up to the French Revolution of 1789, France was divided into thirty-two provinces, each with its own customs and cultural traditions. Although these picturesque areas are no longer separate po-
5 litical divisions, they are still referred to constantly.

Each province had a regional costume that is still worn today on festive occasions. The distinctive headdress, the **coiffe,** and the wooden shoes, the **sabots,** are still seen in parts of France.

Some of the more distinctive provinces are: 10

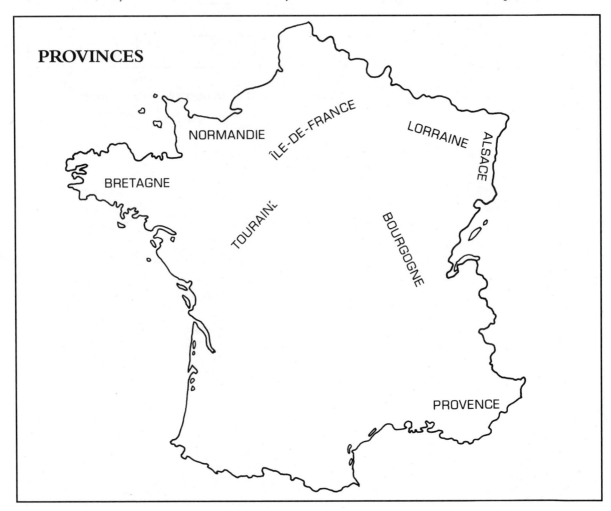

**PROVINCES**

1. **La Bretagne** (*Brittany*), the peninsula jutting out into the Atlantic in northwestern France, is known for its sturdy stock of peasants, fishermen, and sailors. Numerous fishing villages dot
15 the rugged coastline of Brittany. In addition to French, a Celtic dialect, **le breton,** is still spoken. The Bretons hold picturesque religious festivals known as "**pardons.**"
2. **La Normandie** (*Normandy*), in northwestern
20 France, bordering on the English Channel **(la Manche)**, is a region of fertile farms and

rich pastureland. The Seine flows through Normandy. In addition to producing large quantities of milk, butter, and cheese, Normandy is also an industrial center. Along the 25 coast there are several busy ports and fashionable beaches. In 1066, William the Conqueror **(Guillaume le Conquérant)** set out from here to invade England. During the Second World War, the Allies landed on the beaches of 30 Normandy to liberate France from the armed forces of Nazi Germany.

3. **L'Île-de-France,** with Paris as its capital, was the administrative heart of France, since it is there that the kings lived and held their court. The dialect spoken in Île-de-France became the official language of France.

4. **L'Alsace** and **la Lorraine,** two provinces in northeastern France, were for many years the subject of a bitter territorial dispute between France and Germany. Alsace is chiefly an agricultural area, while Lorraine, an industrial region, is valuable especially for its iron ore deposits.

5. **La Provence,** in southeastern France, borders on the Mediterranean. Here are found the best-preserved Roman monuments in France. **Provençal,** the old dialect of Provence, is still spoken by some of the inhabitants. The stretch of coast running east of Marseille to the Italian frontier — the **Riviera,** or **Côte d'Azur** — is one of the most famous resort areas of Europe.

6. **La Touraine,** in the valley of the Loire River, is often called the "Garden of France" because it produces large quantities of fruits and vegetables. Several of the famous **châteaux de la Loire** are located here: **Blois, Chambord, Chenonceaux.**

7. **La Bourgogne** *(Burgundy)* and **la Champagne** are two important grape-producing regions of France. Their wines are world famous.

## EXERCICE A

**For each description in the first column, write the letter of the matching item in the second column.**

1. region of iron-ore mines _____
2. religious festival _____
3. "garden of France" _____
4. famous wine _____
5. wooden shoe _____
6. castle near the Loire _____
7. peninsula in northwestern France _____
8. province known for its wines _____
9. capital of Île-de-France _____
10. famous resort area _____
11. where the kings had their court _____
12. landing place of Allies during Second World War _____
13. province in southeastern France _____

*a.* Paris
*b.* sabot
*c.* Riviera
*d.* Bretagne
*e.* Normandie
*f.* Lorraine
*g.* pardon
*h.* champagne
*i.* Touraine
*j.* Chenonceaux
*k.* Île de France
*l.* Bourgogne
*m.* Provence

## EXERCICE B

**Identify the provinces.**

1. Bordering on the English Channel, it is a region of fertile farms and rich pastureland: _____

2. It is known for its sturdy peasants, fishermen, and sailors: _____

*3.* Two provinces bitterly contested for years by France and Germany: _____

_____

*4.* The province of the château country: _____

*5.* It contains the best-preserved Roman monuments in France: _____

## EXERCICE C

*Complétez les phrases.*

1. Le fleuve qui traverse la Normandie est _____ .

2. On porte la coiffe sur la _____ .

3. En Provence beaucoup d'habitants parlent encore le dialecte qui s'appelle le _____ .

4. Pendant la deuxième guerre mondiale, les forces alliées ont commencé leur invasion du continent dans la province de _____ .

5. La Révolution française est un événement important de la fin du _____ siècle.

6. Avant la Révolution, la France était divisée en trente-deux _____ .

7. La Côte d'Azur est un autre nom de la _____ .

8. Beaucoup de touristes visitent les _____ de Blois et de Chambord.

9. La Touraine est dans la vallée de la _____ .

10. Les eaux de la _____ touchent la côte méridionale *(southern)* de la Provence.

11. On parle encore aujourd'hui un dialogue celtique en _____ .

12. En 1066, Guillaume le Conquérant a traversé _____ pour faire la conquête de l'Angleterre.

13. La province agricole à l'est de la France, près de l'Allemagne, est _____ .

14. La célèbre Côte d'Azur se trouve entre la ville de _____ et la frontière italienne.

15. _____ était la province des rois de France et, par conséquent, le centre administratif du pays.

# Chapter 33
# Paris

Paris (in ancient times, **Lutèce**) received its name from the **Parisii**, the Gallic tribe that founded the city over 2,000 years ago on the present **Île de la Cité**, "the cradle of Paris." The city has a population of over two million, and it forms with its suburbs a complex of about ten million inhabitants. Paris is not only the political and economic capital of France but also the center of French cultural life, and for that reason has been admiringly called **La Ville Lumière**, the city of light. For administrative purposes, the city is divided into twenty **arrondissements,** each one headed by a mayor.

The Seine River divides Paris into two parts: **la rive droite** and **la rive gauche,** the right bank and the left bank. The **rive droite** on the north is somewhat larger and includes business and commercial areas, department stores, and theaters. **Montmartre,** a colorful neighborhood long associated with artists and other free spirits, is also located on the right bank. On the left bank is the **Quartier latin,** the old student quarter. (In the Middle Ages all university students spoke Latin.) Many of the well-known institutes of higher learning are located here: **la Sorbonne, le Collège de France, l'École de Médecine, l'École Normale Supérieure.** Several bridges connect the two banks. The oldest is the **Pont-Neuf,** which was built in the sixteenth century and crosses the Seine at the **Île de la Cité.**

Paris is a city of wide boulevards, magnificent monuments, museums, churches, and parks.

## MUSEUMS

There are more than thirty museums in Paris. The following attract a great number of visitors:

1. The **musée du Louvre,** a former palace of the kings, is one of the richest art museums in the world, housing such treasures as Leonardo Da Vinci's *Joconde* (portrait of Mona Lisa) and the Greek statues known as the *Vénus de Milo* and the *Victoire de Samothrace.* A huge glass pyramid designed by the American architect I. M. Pei now serves as entrance to the Louvre.
2. The **Hôtel des Invalides,** built by Louis XIV, contains the red marble tomb of Napoleon and a military museum.
3. The **Panthéon,** in the **Quartier latin,** was originally built as a church in honor of **Sainte Geneviève,** the patron saint of Paris. It is now used as a burial place for illustrious French people: Voltaire, Rousseau, Hugo, Zola, and Marie Curie among others. Over the entrance are inscribed the words: **"Aux grands hommes la patrie reconnaissante."**
4. The **Centre national d'art et de culture Georges-Pompidou,** also known as the **Centre Beaubourg,** opened in 1977. This architecturally imaginative and modernistic museum draws more visitors each year than any other museum or monument in France. It hosts a variety of artistic, musical, and other cultural activities.
5. The **musée d'Orsay,** installed in the restored train station called the **gare d'Orsay,** contains a notable collection of late nineteenth- and early twentieth-century art, with an emphasis on Impressionist paintings.
6. The **Cité des sciences et de l'industrie** is a new museum of science and technology. In its spectacular theater, **la Géode,** three-dimensional films are shown.

## CHURCHES

1. **Notre-Dame de Paris,** on the Île de la Cité, is the majestic Gothic cathedral begun in the twelfth century.
2. The **Madeleine** is an elegant church built in the form of a Greek temple.
3. The white, mosque-like **Sacré-Cœur,** in Montmartre, overlooks the whole city.
4. The **Sainte-Chapelle,** the jewel of Gothic architecture, is famed for its beautiful stained-glass windows. It was built by Louis IX in the thirteenth century.

## PARKS

1. The **bois de Boulogne,** formerly a forest, is the city's largest park. It has quiet lakes, several restaurants, two racetracks, and even a baseball diamond; it is situated at the western end of Paris.
2. The **jardin des Tuileries,** containing numerous statues, was once the private garden of the kings of France. It is located between the Louvre and the place de la Concorde.

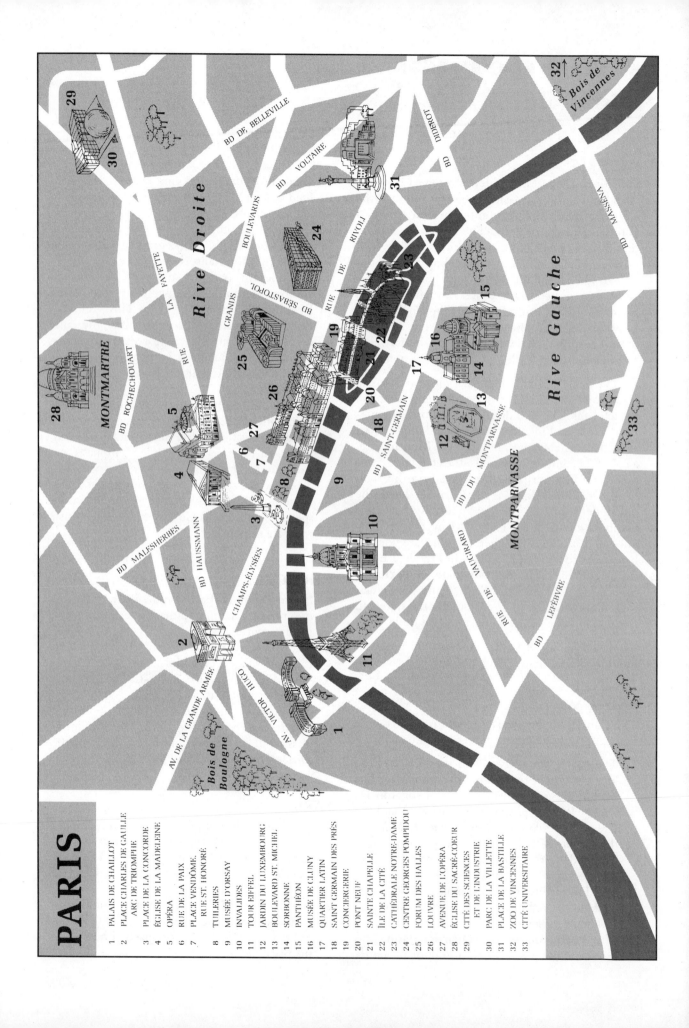

3. The **jardin du Luxembourg,** on the left bank, is a favorite meeting place for students.

## SQUARES

1. The **place de la Concorde** is the largest and most beautiful square in Paris, with its fountains, Egyptian obelisk, and statues representing important cities of France. It was originally called the **place Louis XV.** In the most violent phase of the French Revolution it was renamed the **place de la Révolution,** and a guillotine was set up where there had once been a statue of the king. More than a thousand people, including Louis XVI and Marie-Antoinette, were executed here. A few years later, in a gesture of hope by a more moderate government, it was given its present name.
2. The **place Charles de Gaulle** was formerly called the **place de l'Étoile** because twelve avenues form a star as they radiate in all directions from the **Arc de Triomphe.** Under this arch, begun by order of Napoleon to commemorate his victories, is the Tomb of the Unknown Soldier of World War I, lighted by the eternal flame.
3. The **place de l'Opéra** is named for the building that dominates the square. The **Opéra,** designed by Charles Garnier in 1875, is noted for its sculptured façade, grand marble staircase, and sumptuous foyer or gallery.
4. On the **place de la Bastille** stood the old prison that was captured and destroyed by the Parisians in 1789. On the square today is the **colonne de Juillet,** erected in memory of those killed in the revolution of 1830. Nearby is the modern **Opéra de la Bastille.**

## OTHER LANDMARKS

1. The steel **tour Eiffel** was constructed by the engineer Alexandre Gustave Eiffel for the Paris Exposition of 1889. Over 1,000 feet high, it is now used for the transmission of radio and television broadcasts. There are two restaurants on the tower.
2. The **Sorbonne,** the oldest part of the University of Paris, was founded about 1253 by Robert de Sorbon, chaplain of Louis IX.
3. The **palais de Chaillot,** across the Seine from the Eiffel Tower, houses several museums and a theater.
4. The central market **(les Halles)** was relocated to Rungis, near Orly Airport, in 1969. In its place, a large shopping center and entertainment complex called **le Forum des Halles** has been built.
5. Two celebrated palaces are in the vicinity of Paris: **Versailles,** the tremendous palace built for Louis XIV, and **Fontainebleau,** the favorite retreat of Napoleon.

## STREETS

1. The wide, tree-lined **avenue des Champs-Élysées** extends from the **place de la Concorde** to the **place Charles de Gaulle.** It is an avenue of upscale shops, boutiques, hotels, theaters, and restaurants.
2. The arcaded **rue de Rivoli** runs parallel to the Seine. Its many boutiques are popular.
3. Other streets known for their elegant boutiques are the **avenue de l'Opéra,** the **rue de la Paix,** and the **rue St-Honoré.**
4. The beautiful **grands boulevards** were built on the site of old fortifications. They are wide, tree-lined streets with many theaters, cinemas, cafés, and restaurants.
5. The **quais** are the streets that border the two banks of the Seine. They are a favorite place for Parisians to stroll and to shop for second-hand books in the bookstalls along the river.

## TRANSPORTATION

Paris enjoys a superb location for commerce. The city is the principal river port of France and the center of its highway system. All the major railroad lines pass through Paris, where there are several stations.

Two airports serve the city: **Charles de Gaulle,** the vast international airport, and **Orly** just south of Paris. Thus the city is linked to the rest of the country, the European continent, and the most distant parts of the world.

To travel within Paris itself, there are three public systems:
1. The **métro (métropolitain)** is the subway. The multiple lines extend throughout the city and intersect at many points.
2. The **R.E.R. (Réseau Express Régional)** is a network of rail lines that cross the city and its suburbs. This "super-métro" is uniquely automated.
3. Numerous bus lines serve the city and its suburbs. Taxis are generally available. There are also excursion boats **(bateaux-mouches)** that go up and down the Seine.

## EXERCICE A

**For each word in the first column, write the letter of the matching description in the second column:**

1. Orly          _____

2. Geneviève     _____

3. Versailles    _____

4. Lutèce        _____

5. Luxembourg    _____

6. quais         _____

7. Panthéon      _____

8. bois de Boulogne   _____

9. métro         _____

10. Île de la Cité   _____

a. largest park in Paris

b. ancient name of Paris

c. second airport of Paris

d. Parisian public transportation system

e. patron saint of Paris

f. palace of Louis XIV

g. handsome park

h. "cradle of Paris"

i. burial place of illustrious French people

j. streets lining the banks of the Seine

## EXERCICE B

**Read carefully the paragraph below; then answer the questions that follow.**

There we stood in what some consider the most beautiful square in the world. It certainly looked like the largest! We could not help noticing the Egyptian obelisk flanked by sparkling fountains. Gazing in one direction, we could see a magnificent arch at the end of a wide, tree-lined avenue. In the opposite direction, there was a park that looked as though it might have belonged to a king. When we reached the end of the park, we arrived in front of an imposing structure, an immense palace, now one of the richest art museums in the world.

1. What Parisian square were we in? _____

2. What is the name of the arch mentioned? _____

3. Who had it built and why? _____

4. Who is buried under this arch? _____

5. On what square is this arch located? _____

6. What was its former name, and why did the French give the square that name?

   _____

   _____

7. Which "wide, tree-lined avenue" were we looking at? _____

**8.** What park did we walk through? _____

**9.** What is the name of the art museum at the end of the park? _____

**10.** Name two art masterpieces found in this museum. _____

## EXERCICE C

**Identify the Parisian landmark being described and write its name in the blank. Choose your answers from the names below.**

| | | |
|---|---|---|
| Bastille | Madeleine | Panthéon |
| Centre Pompidou | musée d'Orsay | Sainte-Chapelle |
| Forum des Halles | Notre-Dame | Sorbonne |
| Hôtel des Invalides | Opéra | tour Eiffel |

**1.** It contains the red marble tomb of Napoléon and a military museum:

_____

**2.** A fashionable church in the style of a Greek temple: _____

**3.** The burial place for some illustrious French people: _____

**4.** The shopping center located where the central market used to be:

_____

**5.** It is noted for its sculptured façade and grand marble staircase: _____

**6.** The oldest part of the University of Paris: _____

**7.** This steel structure was built for the Paris Exposition of 1889: _____

**8.** The majestic Gothic cathedral on the Île de la Cité: _____

**9.** Modern art and culture complex: _____

**10.** Built by Louis IX, it is the jewel of Gothic architecture: _____

**11.** Art museum installed in a former railroad station: _____

**12.** Prison destroyed by Parisians on July 14, 1789: _____

## EXERCICE D

*Complétez les phrases.*

**1.** _____ divise la ville de Paris en deux parties.

**2.** Une rue célèbre de Paris est la rue de _____ .

**3.** Pour des raisons administratives, la ville de Paris est divisé en 20 _____ .

4.  Montmartre est un quartier de la _____ droite.

5.  On a guillotiné beaucoup de Français sur la place de _____ .

6.  Le plus ancien des ponts de Paris est _____ .

7.  _____ est le nom du grand aéroport international de Paris.

8.  Le palais préféré de Napoléon, pas loin de Paris, s'appelle _____ .

9.  L'église blanche, située dans le quartier de _____ et qui a la forme d'une

    mosquée, est le _____ .

10. Sur la rive gauche on trouve le vieux quartier des étudiants, le Quartier _____ .

# Chapter 34
## Other Cities

After Paris, the most populous cities in France are Lyon, Marseille, Lille, Bordeaux, Toulouse, and Nantes.

## PORTS

1. **Bordeaux,** on the Atlantic at the mouth of the Garonne, is the great wine port of France.
2. **Le Havre,** at the mouth of the Seine, is the largest seaport on the English Channel.
3. **Marseille,** on the Mediterranean near the mouth of the Rhône River, is the largest seaport of France. It is the port for extensive trade with Africa and the Orient.
4. **Nantes,** at the mouth of the Loire, is a ship-building center.
5. Other ports are

   on the Atlantic:
   **Brest, La Rochelle, Saint-Nazaire**

   on the English Channel:
   **Boulogne, Calais, Cherbourg, Dunkerque**

## INDUSTRIAL CITIES

1. **Clermont-Ferrand,** in the center of France, manufactures rubber. It is the center of the tire industry.
2. **Grenoble,** on the main road leading to the Alps, is a center for tourism and numerous industries, including the manufacture of gloves.
3. **Lille,** in northeastern France, is known for the manufacture of textiles and machinery.
4. **Lyon,** at the junction of the Rhône and Saône Rivers, is a business center and the traditional home of the silk industry.
5. **Metz** and **Nancy,** in Lorraine, are important industrial centers (iron and steel, manufacture of machinery and automobiles).
6. **Reims,** the center of the champagne industry, is the site of the beautiful Gothic cathedral where the kings of France were crowned. Other towns renowned for their Gothic cathedral are **Chartres** and **Amiens.**
7. **Rouen,** in Normandy on the Seine, is an industrial city and river port. Here Jeanne d'Arc was burned at the stake in 1431.
8. **Strasbourg,** on the Rhine River in Alsace, across from Germany, is an industrial city and an important river port. It is famous for its Gothic cathedral which contains an astronomical clock.
9. **Toulouse,** on the Garonne River where it connects with the **canal du Midi,** is a manufacturing city and an important market for the region. **Airbus-Industrie** builds its planes here.

## RESORTS

1. **Biarritz** is a noted beach resort on the Atlantic near the Spanish border.
2. **Chamonix,** located at the foot of Mont Blanc in the Alps, is a celebrated winter resort and ski center.
3. **Deauville** is a popular beach resort on the English Channel **(la Manche).**
4. **Nice,** the largest city on the French Riviera, and the neighboring town of **Cannes** are fashionable resorts, especially in winter and spring. An important international film festival is held each May in Cannes.
5. **Vichy,** a health and pleasure resort in the Massif Central, is the best known of French spas. Its mineral water is shipped all over the world. For a time during World War II, Vichy was the seat of the French government.

## HISTORICAL CITIES

1. **Avignon,** on the Rhône in Provence, is known for its **palais des Papes,** where the Popes lived in the fourteenth century. The bridge of Avignon is celebrated in the song "Sur le pont d'Avignon, l'on y danse."
2. **Arles** and **Nîmes,** in Provence, contain some of the best-preserved Roman monuments in France. The famous Roman aqueduct, the **pont du Gard,** is near Nîmes.
3. **Carcassonne,** in the south, is the best-preserved medieval fortified town in Europe, distinguished by its double ramparts and numerous towers.
4. **Lourdes,** in the Pyrenees, is the most famous shrine in France and a world-renowned Catholic pilgrimage center.
5. **Mont-Saint-Michel,** off the coast where Normandy and Brittany meet, is a medieval fortress and Benedictine abbey built on a rocky island in the English Channel.

## EXERCICE A

**For each description in the first column, write the letter of the matching name in the second column.**

1. town where Jeanne d'Arc died _____

2. large port at the mouth of the Garonne _____

3. town known for its Roman monuments _____

4. summer and winter resort on the Riviera _____

5. shipbuilding center _____

6. famous spa _____

7. Roman aqueduct _____

8. town where planes are built _____

9. center of the champagne industry _____

10. industrial town on the Rhine _____

*a.* Strasbourg

*b.* Cannes / Nice

*c.* Toulouse

*d.* Nîmes

*e.* Reims

*f.* Bordeaux

*g.* Vichy

*h.* Rouen

*i.* Nantes

*j.* pont du Gard

## EXERCICE B

**Identify the city.**

1. best-preserved medieval fortified town in Europe _____

2. seaport at the mouth of the Seine _____

3. largest city on the Riviera _____

4. a center of the glove industry, near the Alps _____

5. site of Gothic cathedral where the kings of France were crowned _____

6. ski center in the Alps at the foot of Mont Blanc _____

7. largest Mediterranean port _____

8. noted beach resort in the Atlantic near Spain _____

9. town noted for its Palace of the Popes _____

10. great wine port on the Atlantic _____

11. city where an International Film Festival is held each May _____

12. industrial city at the junction of the Rhône and Saône _____

13. fortified abbey on an island in the English Channel _____

**14.** most famous pilgrimage center in France _____

**15.** important river port in Alsace, across from Germany _____

## EXERCICE C

*Choisissez la réponse appropriée.*

**1.** Amiens et Reims sont deux villes connues pour leur (palais, cathédrale) _____ gothique.

**2.** Le grand centre de l'industrie des pneus *(tires)* est (Clermont-Ferrand, Cherbourg) _____ .

**3.** Lourdes est un grand centre religieux dans les (Alpes, Pyrénées) _____ .

**4.** (Metz, Strasbourg) _____ , en Lorraine, est le centre de la métallurgie.

**5.** (Deauville, Nantes) _____ est une plage populaire sur la Manche.

**6.** Marseille se trouve près de l'embouchure *(mouth)* (du Rhône, de la Loire) _____ .

**7.** On boit les (vins, eaux minérales) _____ de Vichy dans le monde entier.

**8.** La ville provençale d'Arles est célèbre pour ses monuments (romains, grecs) _____ .

**9.** La ville de (Boulogne, Lyon) _____ est le centre de l'industrie de la soie.

**10.** Toulouse est une ville industrielle et commerciale sur la (Seine, Garonne) _____ .

**11.** À (Lille, Dunkerque) _____ , au nord-est de la France, on fabrique des textiles et des machines.

**12.** Cherbourg et Calais sont des ports situés sur (la Manche, l'Atlantique) _____ .

**13.** Dans une célèbre chanson française, on danse sur le pont (de Lyon, d'Avignon) _____ .

**14.** Rouen, en Normandie, est une ville industrielle sur la (Loire, Seine) _____ .

**15.** Dans la cathédrale gothique de (Strasbourg, Chartres) _____ , on peut voir une célèbre horloge astronomique.

# Chapter 35
## History of France

## PREHISTORY

1 Prehistoric civilizations flourished in the land that is now France. Primitive paintings depicting animals have been found on the walls of caves at **Lascaux** and **Les Eyzies** in southwestern France.

5 These were the work of Cro-Magnon Man during the last ice age. Near **Carnac**, in Brittany, there can be seen long rows of huge, unhewn stones called **menhirs** and **dolmens**. These constructions date from about 2,000 B.C. Almost nothing is known

10 about the civilization that produced them.

In the first century B.C., France was known as Gaul (**la Gaule**). It was the land of the Celts, or Gauls (**les Gaulois**), who had a primitive civilization. The Gauls were divided into numerous tribes,

15 who often waged war on one another. Their priests, called Druids, served also as doctors and judges, and exerted social, political, and religious influence. They taught the immortality of the soul and worshipped the forces of nature, encouraging a special

20 reverence for the evergreen mistletoe (**le gui**).

## THE ROMANS

**Julius Caesar,** the Roman general, took advantage of conflicts among the Gauls to undertake the conquest of their country.

**Vercingétorix** was the courageous chieftain

25 and brilliant general who succeeded in uniting all the Gauls against Caesar in the last decisive battle of the Gallic War (52 B.C.). After his defeat, he was taken to Rome in Caesar's triumphal procession, imprisoned, and finally executed. Vercingétorix is

30 considered the first national hero of France.

The Romans gave Gaul more than 400 years of peace and prosperity. The Gauls adopted the advanced culture of the Romans, their customs, their language, and their code of justice. The Romans

35 developed agriculture and commerce. They constructed roads, aqueducts, amphitheaters, temples, and other beautiful monuments.

## THE FRANKS

The Roman Empire was vast and difficult to defend. Barbaric tribes began to invade Gaul in the

40 third century A.D. In the fifth century, a Germanic tribe called the Franks (**les Francs**) conquered the country and settled there. They gave their name to France.

**Clovis,** chief of the Franks in the fifth century, succeeded in ending Roman domination and ex- 45 tended his authority to all Gaul. He founded a dynasty and converted to Christianity, which became the official religion of the country.

## THE MIDDLE AGES

**Sainte Geneviève** is the patron saint of Paris. During the fifth century A.D., the Huns (a nomadic 50 and warlike people from north central Asia) seized control over large parts of Europe for a time. When they invaded France, the shepherd girl Geneviève gave courage to the people of Paris. The Huns never attacked the city. 55

**Charlemagne,** or Charles the Great, was one of the most powerful figures in European history. Originally king of the Franks, he was crowned in A.D. 800 as the first emperor of the vast Holy Roman Empire, consisting of most of western 60 Europe. A lover of learning, he encouraged education by founding numerous schools. As a statesman, he administered his empire with wisdom and justice. His military exploits are celebrated in the *Chanson de Roland,* the first masterpiece of French 65 literature. Unfortunately, within a generation after his death, his empire had been divided among warring princes.

Towards the end of the ninth century, the Normans (**les Normands**) invaded the country. 70 These Scandinavian pirates from the north came by sea and traveled up the rivers, looting along the way. They finally settled in the region subsequently known as Normandy.

In 1066, William the Conqueror (**Guillaume le** 75 **Conquérant**), duke of Normandy, crossed the English Channel, conquered England, and became king of that country.

**Saint Louis** (thirteenth century), or Louis IX, was considered a brave and just king, interested in 80 the welfare of all, and a friend of the poor. For religious reasons, he took an active part in the Crusades. He did much to strenghten the royal power.

## THE HUNDRED YEARS' WAR

The Hundred Years' War was a dynastic struggle
85  between the royal houses of England and France,
interrupted by several truces and lasting from 1337
to 1453. **Jeanne d'Arc,** known as "the Maid of
Orléans" **(la Pucelle d'Orléans),** is honored as a
national heroine because of the role she played in
90  that war. She was born of peasant stock in 1412, in
Domrémy, Lorraine, at a time when French for-
tunes were at their lowest. Convinced that she had
received from God the task of liberating France,
she succeeded in reuniting the scattered French
95  forces against the invading English. After winning
the battle of Orléans, she had the king crowned in
the cathedral of Reims. Later she fell into the hands
of the English, was accused of being a witch, and in
1431 was burned at the stake in Rouen. After her
100  death, the French rallied their forces and drove the
English from France.

## SIXTEENTH TO EIGHTEENTH CENTURIES

**François I<sup>er</sup>** was king of France during the first
half of the sixteenth century, the period of the
Renaissance. A brilliant administrator and patron
105  of the arts, he invited to his court Italian artists,
men of letters, and other scholars. He founded the
Collège de France, had splendid castles built along
the Loire, and encouraged exploration of the New
World.

110     **Henri IV,** the first monarch of the Bourbon
family line, was the best-loved and most democratic king of France. He is often called **"le bon roi
Henri"** because he had the welfare of his people at
heart. Born Protestant, he became Catholic to end
115  the religious wars and bring peace to France. In
1598, he issued the Edict of Nantes, granting freedom of worship to the Protestant minority. He
was a skillful statesman who established an effi-
cient and stable government, fostered commerce,
120  improved agriculture, reduced taxes, and ensured
prosperity.

     **Cardinal de Richelieu,** the talented and ener-
getic Prime Minister of Louis XIII, increased the
power and prestige of France. He made the king
125  supreme by curtailing the power of the feudal nobles. During his ministry, France became a world
power. An excellent administrator and military
strategist, he was also a patron of the arts and literature. It was he who founded the French Academy
130  **(l'Académie française)** in 1634.

**Louis XIV,** the "Sun King," ruled as an absolute monarch who could say **"L'État, c'est moi."**
His long reign of seventy-two years was marked by
the brilliance of his court and his patronage of arts
and sciences. His lavish palace at Versailles became  135
the political, social, and cultural center of the nation. Through his encouragement, art and literature reached splendid heights. But his egotism and
ambition drove him to spend money and men's
lives freely. He waged numerous wars that were  140
disastrous for France. In 1685, he revoked the
Edict of Nantes, thus destroying the religious freedom granted by Henry IV and causing many
French Protestants (called **Huguenots**) to leave the
country.  145

     **Louis XV,** who reigned from 1715 to 1774,
spent his time having fun instead of tending to af-
fairs of state. The discontent stirred up during his
reign was one of the principal causes of the French
Revolution.  150

## THE REVOLUTION OF 1789

**Louis XVI** was well-meaning but weak, and he
proved unequal to the responsibilities of a king.
The country was financially bankrupt. The queen,
**Marie-Antoinette,** was unpopular with the people. On July 14, 1789, mobs of Parisians stormed  155
the dreaded prison of the Bastille. This marked the
beginning of the French Revolution, in which the
king and queen were executed along with thousands of nobles.

     In 1789, the *Déclaration des droits de l'homme et*  160
*du citoyen* was passed, proclaiming the fundamental
rights of the individual. **La Première République,**
established in 1792 as a society based on the equality of all citizens, began with a period of crises and
violence. This was the time of **la Terreur,** master-  165
minded by **Robespierre.**

     **Napoléon Bonaparte,** who had become promi-
nent during the early years of the Revolution,
made himself First Consul by a coup d'état, and in
1804 had himself crowned Emperor. An ambitious  170
military genius and diplomat, he succeeded in con-
quering most of western Europe but was defeated
by a coalition of his enemies at Waterloo in 1815.
He died in exile on the island of St. Helena. His
tomb is in the **Hôtel des Invalides** in Paris.  175

     Although he got many people killed in war,
Napoleon established law and order and brought
about many reforms. He systematized the laws
with the **Code Napoléon** — a civil code that has

become the foundation of much modern legislation; established a central system of education; improved finances and founded the Bank of France; set up a program of public works; encouraged arts and sciences; and formed the Legion of Honor (**la Légion d'Honneur**).

## NINETEENTH AND TWENTIETH CENTURIES

**La Deuxième République** was proclaimed in 1848, and **Louis-Napoléon,** the nephew of Napoléon Bonaparte, was elected President. In 1852, he made himself emperor and set up **le Second Empire.** After the defeat of France in the Franco-Prussian War of 1870–1871, **la Troisième République** was established.

In 1914, Germany declared war on Russia and France; other nations were drawn in on both sides, and the first World War lasted till the defeat of Germany in 1918. The year 1940, when France was again invaded by Germany, saw the beginning of the German occupation. In 1944, the Allies landed on the beaches of Normandy, and France was liberated soon after. **La Quatrième République** dates from 1947.

General **Charles de Gaulle,** who headed the French Resistance movement and later the French troops, became a national hero. In 1958, he was elected to the presidency of **la Cinquième République** and held that office until 1969. Since then, there have been three other presidents: **Georges Pompidou** (1969–1974), **Valéry Giscard d'Estaing** (1974–1981), and **François Mitterrand** (1981–1995). **Jacques Chirac** was elected president in 1995.

## POLITICAL INSTITUTIONS

The constitution of the Fifth Republic guarantees public liberties and grants to all citizens who have reached the age of eighteen, regardless of origin, race, or religion, the right to vote by secret ballot.

1. *Executive power* is vested in the president of the Republic and in the cabinet of ministers led by a prime minister.

   **Le Président de la République** represents the highest authority of the nation. He is elected for seven years by direct popular vote. The president is expected to insure the stability of the nation's institutions. He appoints the prime minister based on the results of parliamentary elections, as well as the cabinet ministers proposed by the prime minister. The president may turn directly to the people by dissolving the Parliament, thus bringing about new elections, or by calling for a direct popular vote (**un référendum**) on specific issues. He is commander in chief of the armed forces and may assume exceptional powers in an emergency. His official residence is the **palais de l'Élysée,** in Paris.

   The prime minister (**le Premier Ministre**) is appointed by the president and heads the government. The prime minister and his cabinet (**le Conseil des Ministres**) formulate national policies and carry out the laws. They are responsible to the National Assembly and can be removed from office by vote of an absolute majority of that body. The cabinet ministers, who are not permitted to be members of Parliament, are free from the pressures of seeking reelection.

2. *Legislative power* is held by the Parliament (**le Parlement**) which consists of two houses:

   (a) The National Assembly (**l'Assemblée Nationale**), elected by direct popular vote for five years, is the larger and more influential of the two.

   (b) The Senate (**le Sénat**), elected indirectly for nine years by certain elected local officials, represents the departments as well as French citizens residing abroad.

   Parliament passes the laws, votes the budget, and ratifies treaties. It acts as a check on the actions of the prime minister and his cabinet and can force them to resign. War cannot be declared without the consent of Parliament.

3. *Judicial power* is held by the courts. Its independence is guaranteed by the constitution. The highest court is la **Cour de Cassation.**

   For administrative purposes, France, including Corsica, is divided into 96 **départements.** There are also four overseas departments. Each department is headed by an appointed **préfet.** In 1982, in an effort to decentralize the government, 22 **régions** were created. They are to some extent based on the old provinces and are headed by an elected regional council whose president has executive power in the region (**le préfet de région**).

   The national emblem is the tricolor flag of blue, white, and red vertical stripes. The motto (**la devise**) of the Republic is **Liberté, Égalité, Fraternité** — the slogan of the French Revolution.

*La Marseillaise,* written in 1792 by **Rouget de Lisle,** is the national anthem (**l'hymne national**).

The national holiday is **le quatorze juillet,** the anniversary of the storming of **la Bastille** by the people of Paris in 1789. The Bastille was a prison that had become a symbol of tyranny. The day is celebrated in Paris by parades, services at the Tomb of the Unknown Soldier, free performances at many theaters, fireworks, and dancing in the streets. Similar celebrations take place all over France.

## FRENCH INFLUENCE IN AMERICA

French explorers played an important part in opening up the North American continent.

**Jacques Cartier** discovered the St. Lawrence River in 1535 and took possession of Canada in the name of the king of France. Later he sailed up the river to the mountain that he named **Montréal.**

**Samuel de Champlain** founded the city of **Québec** in 1608 and discovered Lake Champlain.

Father **Jacques Marquette** explored the region of the Great Lakes and discovered the Mississippi. He and **Louis Joliet** sailed down the river in 1673.

**Robert Cavelier de La Salle** explored the Mississippi as far as the Gulf of Mexico in 1682. He took possession of the immense valley of the river, naming it "**Louisiane**" in honor of Louis XIV. In 1803, Napoleon sold the territory to the United States.

Three French nobles took an active part in the War of Independence of the American colonies.

The young **marquis de La Fayette** became a personal friend of General Washington. After the American Revolution, La Fayette returned to France to defend liberal causes in his native land. The key to the Bastille can be seen in Washington's home at Mount Vernon, Virginia. It was La Fayette who gave it to the first President of the United States.

**Le comte de Rochambeau** was head of the French army sent to defend the cause of the colonies.

**L'amiral de Grasse** commanded the French naval forces.

All three helped defeat the British at the battle of Yorktown.

## EXERCICE A

**Rewrite the following in their correct chronological order, placing the earliest figure first.**

| | | | |
|---|---|---|---|
| Charlemagne | Henri IV | Marie-Antoinette | Sainte Geneviève |
| Charles de Gaulle | Jeanne d'Arc | Napoléon Bonaparte | Saint Louis |
| Georges Pompidou | Louis XIV | Richelieu | Vercingétorix |

*1.* _____

*2.* _____

*3.* _____

*4.* _____

*5.* _____

*6.* _____

*7.* _____

*8.* _____

*9.* _____

*10.* _____

*11.* _____

*12.* _____

## EXERCICE B

**Choose the correct answer.**

*1.* The very pious French king, (Saint Louis, Charlemagne) _____ , took an active part in the Crusades.

2. Henri IV issued the Edict of (Reims, Nantes) _____ in 1598, granting freedom

   of worship to the (Catholic, Protestant) _____ minority.

3. Charlemagne means Charles the (Bold, Great) _____ . He encouraged education

   by founding numerous (schools, universities) _____ .

4. Richelieu made the (Church, king) _____ supreme by crushing the feudal nobles.

5. (Jeanne d'Arc, Vercingétorix) _____ succeeded in uniting all the Gauls in
   the last decisive battle of the Gallic War.

6. Napoleon Bonaparte was defeated in the battle of (Waterloo, Orléans) _____ .

   in 1815. He died in exile on the island of (Elba, St. Helena) _____ .

7. During the brilliant reign of (Charlemagne, Louis XIV) _____ , which

   lasted seventy-two years, art and literature flourished. His motto was "L'État, c'est (moi, grand)

   _____ ."

8. The caves of Lascaux and Les Eyzies are known for their (menhirs and dolmens, prehistoric

   paintings) _____ .

9. After winning the battle of (Carnac, Orléans) _____ , Jeanne d'Arc crowned the

   king in the cathedral of (Paris, Reims) _____ .

10. Jeanne fell into the hands of the (English, Romans) _____ and was burned at the

    stake in the city of (Rouen, Paris) _____ .

## EXERCICE C

**Identify each person.**

1. After a coup d'état, he became First Consul; he created the
   Legion of Honor.                                                   _____

2. He was crowned Emperor in 800.                                     _____

3. He revoked the Edict of Nantes; he built a splendid palace in
   Versailles.                                                        _____

4. Born to a peasant family in Domrémy in Lorraine, she is the national heroine of France.                                          _____

5. Head of the Resistance in the Second World War, he became the
   first president of the Fifth Republic.                             _____

6. The first of the Bourbon line; born Protestant, he became Catholic to bring peace to France.  _____

7. This shepherdess gave courage to the people of Paris when the Huns invaded the country.  _____

8. He crossed the English Channel to conquer England.  _____

9. She was the wife of Louis XVI.  _____

10. This French marquis became a friend of General Washington.  _____

11. Patron of the arts and literature, he founded the French Academy in 1634.  _____

12. This explorer founded the town of Québec.  _____

## EXERCICE D

**For each description in the first column, write the letter of the matching name in the second column.**

1. le bon roi  _____

2. cardinal et premier ministre  _____

3. premier héros national de la France  _____

4. Pucelle *(maid)* d'Orléans  _____

5. roi guillotiné pendant la Révolution française  _____

6. patronne *(patron saint)* de Paris  _____

7. empereur enterré *(buried)* dans les Invalides  _____

8. roi des Francs et monarque d'un vaste empire  _____

9. roi de la Renaissance  _____

10. le Roi-Soleil  _____

*a.* François I<sup>er</sup>
*b.* Napoléon Bonaparte
*c.* Louis XIV
*d.* Geneviève
*e.* Henri IV
*f.* Charlemagne
*g.* Vercingétorix
*h.* Richelieu
*i.* Louis XVI
*j.* Jeanne d'Arc

## EXERCICE E

*Choisissez la réponse correcte.*

1. Il y a aujourd'hui en France la (Quatrième, Cinquième) _____ République depuis la revolution de 1789.

2.  L'Assemblée nationale est élue *(elected)* par vote (direct, indirect) _____ .

3.  Le (Président, Premier ministre) _____ représente l'autorité suprême de la nation.

4.  L'Assemblée nationale a (plus, moins) _____ d'influence que le Sénat.

5.  Le (Président, Premier ministre) _____ est responsable devant l'Assemblée nationale.

6.  (La Fayette, Rouget de Lisle) _____ a écrit *La Marseillaise* en 1792.

7.  Le Président peut prononcer la dissolution du (Parlement, Conseil des ministres) _____ .

8.  Le Premier ministre est nommé par le (Sénat, Président) _____ .

9.  La date de la fête nationale française est le (4, 14) _____ (juillet, juin) _____ .

10.  Le (Parlement, Conseil des ministres) _____ autorise la déclaration de guerre.

11.  Les régions ont été créées en 1982 pour (centraliser, décentraliser) _____ le gouvernement.

12.  Les Français ont le droit de voter à l'âge de (18, 21) _____ ans.

## EXERCICE F

*Complétez les phrases.*

1.  Le Président de la République est élu pour _____ ans au suffrage direct.

2.  _____ a exploré le Saint-Laurent en 1535.

3.  Dans le Parlement, il y a l'Assemblée nationale et le _____ .

4.  La France est divisée en 96 _____ .

5.  Le chef du département est le _____ .

6.  Chacune des 22 _____ comptent plusieurs départements.

7.  Le _____ est le chef des armées françaises.

8.  La devise de la République est «_____ , Égalité,

_____ ».

**9.** Le drapeau tricolore français est _____ , blanc et

_____ .

**10.** Le quatorze juillet marque l'anniversaire de la prise de la _____ par le

peuple de _____ en _____ .

**11.** Le palais de _____ à Paris est la résidence officielle du Président de la
République.

**12.** Pendant la fête nationale française, on danse dans les _____ .

# Chapter 36
## Agriculture, Industry, and Commerce

## AGRICULTURE

Agriculture, industry, and commerce sustain the well-balanced economy of France. The fertile soil makes the country almost self-sufficient agriculturally. The richest farm regions are the plains and river basins. Of the countries of the European Economic Community, France is the principal agricultural producer. The French continue to develop an intensive agriculture based on modern techniques. The excellence and variety of the soil and climate have helped make France a country famous for its gastronomy.

Wheat (le blé), the principal ingredient of bread—a staple of the French diet—is an important agricultural product. An abundance of other cereals is cultivated, as well as a variety of fruits and vegetables.

Dense forests supply lumber and play an essential role in protecting the environment.

The grapes of French vineyards are used principally in the production of wines, which tend to be named after their place of origin, such as Burgundy (le bourgogne), Champagne (le champagne), and Bordeaux (le bordeaux). Cognac, a grape brandy, is distilled from wine. Drinks offered before the meal (to stimulate the appetite) are called apéritifs; those served after it are called liqueurs. Other popular beverages produced in France are mineral water from spas, such as Vichy and Vittel, and cider from Normandy.

In addition to agriculture, there is considerable cattle raising. France is noted for the excellence of its animal breeds: cows, sheep, goats, pigs, poultry, and horses. Normandy, in particular, is a rich dairy region. The French are skilled in the making of cheeses; the best known are le brie, le camembert, le chèvre, and le roquefort.

The French diet is enriched by seafood. Along the coast, and especially in Brittany, fishing is an important industry. There are many canneries in the ports.

Thanks to these riches of both land and sea, the food industries flourish in France.

## INDUSTRY

French industry is varied, ranging from the production of heavy machinery to the making of delicate precision instruments, and from the huge modern factory to the small craft shop. In general, the French are craftsmen who take pride in their work, prefer quality to quantity, and combine originality with artistic skill. To maintain its competitive position in international trade, France has intensified its scientific research and its efforts to develop commercial applications.

As a result, France remains on the leading edge of nuclear power, electrical and electronic equipment, aeronautics, aerospace, and railroad technology. The principal industrial areas are centered around Paris, Lille, Lyon, and the region of Lorraine. Metallurgy is a very important industry. France is also a major producer of industrial machinery.

The production of automobiles helps the balance of trade since a large number are exported abroad. France is the fourth-largest producer of automobiles in the world. The principal makes are Renault and Peugeot-Citroën.

The aeronautics industry produces airplanes, helicopters, and aerospace equipment. Planes manufactured by the international company Airbus-Industrie and the supersonic Franco-British Concorde fly in the entire world. The European space rocket Ariane has proven a reliable and low-cost means of launching satellites into orbit.

Shipbuilding is an important industry in ports on the Atlantic coast and the English Channel.

A flourishing chemical industry includes the processing of bauxite (an ore used in making aluminum) and potash, both found in France. The production of glass, rubber, and plastics continues to increase.

The textile industry produces cotton, silk, and synthethic fabrics. Lyon is still the center of silk production. Fashions (haute couture) famous in the whole world are created in Paris.

Porcelain and chinaware are manufactured in Sèvres, near Paris, and in Limoges in central

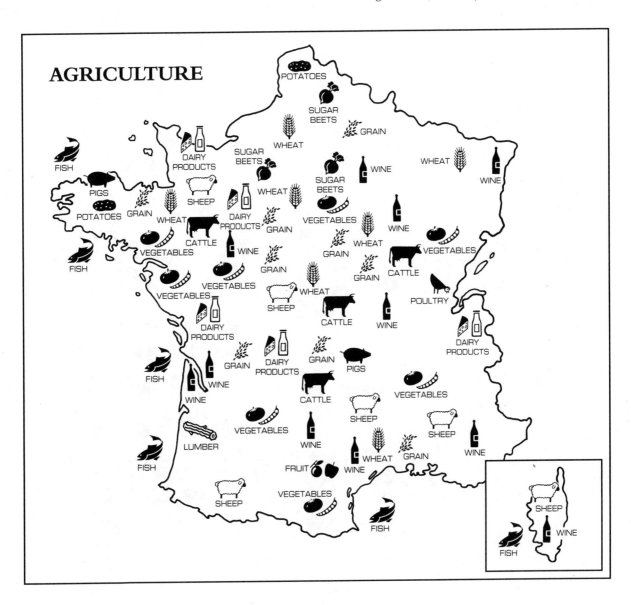

AGRICULTURE

85 France, among other places. Rugs and tapestries are created by skilled artists.

Luxury articles include gloves, leather goods, costume jewelry, watches, crystal, perfumes, and cosmetics. The fertile soil and sunny climate of the 90 French Riviera supply the enormous quantities of flowers needed at the perfume center of Grasse, near Nice. Much of the final processing of perfumes is done in Paris, the home of the cosmetics industry.

95 Because of its lack of natural energy resources, France has developed an ambitious nuclear program, which has been for years the country's principal source of energy. A limited amount of energy is also supplied by hydroelectric power produced by the fast-flowing rivers, by natural gas, solar energy, 100 and even the winds and the tides.

## COMMERCE

France exports automobiles, machinery, and chemical and pharmaceutical products. It also exports agricultural and food products as well as luxury items. France imports oil, coal, natural gas, and 105 some raw materials for its industries.

France is a member of the European Economic Community (**Communauté économique européenne**).

INDUSTRY

Economic activities are closely linked to both interior and exterior transportation systems: the road network, maritime and river navigation, and air transport.

1. The main national highways radiate out of Paris toward the frontiers. Superhighways **(auto-routes)** help the flow of traffic in many areas.

2. The **S.N.C.F. (Société nationale des chemins de fer),** an agency of the government, administers the railroad system. All the important lines form a web with Paris at its center. The network links the capital with the other important cities of France and Europe. French trains travel at great speed. The **TGV (Train à grande vitesse)** has set a world record.

3. Heavy merchandise is easily transported by river and on the excellent canal system. The main river ports are: Paris, Rouen, Strasbourg, and Lyon.

4. **Air France** is the French national airline. There are, in addition, several small private airlines.

5. Other means of communication are also the responsibility of the government. Postal, telephone, and telegraph services are administered by the state.

6. A direct link for trains and automobile traffic between France and Great Britain was established in 1994 when a tunnel, **(le chunnel)**, was opened under the English Channel **(la Manche).**

## EXERCICE A

**If a statement is true, write *true* in the space provided. If it is false, put parentheses around the incorrect word or words and write the word or words that make the statement correct.**

EXEMPLES:    Marseille is on the Mediterranean.    _____**true**_____
            (Lyon) is the capital of France.    _____**Paris**_____

1.  France is practically self-sufficient in her supply of food. _____

2.  The French forests supply fine lumber. _____

3.  Champagne is a famous cider. _____

4.  France and England are linked by a newly constructed bridge. _____

5.  The supply of French energy is insufficient for the needs of France. _____

6.  The TGV has set a world record for its punctuality. _____

7.  France has its own supply of potash and bauxite. _____

8.  Brie and camembert are delicious fish. _____

9.  France has refused to join the European Economic community.

    _____

10. Milk forms the basis of the French diet. _____

11. The quality of animal breeds in France is generally low. _____

12. The economy of France is well balanced between industry and agriculture.

    _____

13. The French are known for their elegant luxury articles. _____

14. There is little variety in the range of French industry. _____

15. Waterpower is a source of energy in France. _____

16. The French aircraft industry has produced supersonic planes. _____

17. French artisans combine originality with artistic skill. _____

18. The plains and river basins are useless for farming. _____

19. France grows many kinds of fine fruits and vegetables. _____

20. There is a flourishing chemical industry in France. _____

21. The French have to import oil to sustain their economy. _____

22. The cosmetics industry is located in Nice. _____

23. There is considerable cattle raising in France. _____

24. The French have facilities for canning the fish they catch. _____

25. The company Airbus-Industrie produces trucks and buses. _____

## EXERCICE B

**For each item in the first column, write the letter of the matching item in the second column.**

1. railroads          _____           *a.* Normandie

2. wine               _____           *b.* Côte d'Azur

                                        *c.* cognac

3. French car         _____           *d.* Renault

4. dairy products     _____           *e.* camembert

                                        *f.* Vichy

5. china              _____           *g.* S.N.C.F.

6. eau-de-vie *(brandy)*  _____       *h.* bourgogne

                                        *i.* Sèvres

7. space rocket       _____           *j.* Ariane

8. cheese             _____

9. mineral water      _____

10. flowers           _____

## EXERCICE C

*Complétez les phrases.*

1. An important grain crop in France is _____ .

2. Grasse is the center for making _____ .

3. French grapes are used mainly for producing _____ .

4. The haute couture industry is centered in the city of _____ .

5. Roquefort is a famous French _____ .

6. The city of _____ , on the Garonne, is known as a wine center.

7. Bauxite is used in the production of _____ .

8. _____ water from the spas is a popular beverage at mealtime.

9. The French international airline is _____ .

**10.** The production of silk is centered in the city of _____ .

**11.** Much French cider comes from the province of _____ .

**12.** France's principal source of energy is _____ .

**13.** The ports of the English Channel and the Atlantic coast are centers for the

_____ industry.

**14.** Beautiful chinaware is made in the town of _____ in central France.

**15.** Fishing is an important industry along the _____ , especially in the

province of _____ .

# Chapter 37
## Daily Living

### RELIGION

1  All religions are respected by the French Republic. The large majority of French people belong to the Roman Catholic faith.

### EDUCATION

Education is compulsory from the ages of six to
5  sixteen. All education, both public and private, is controlled by the national government, with similar requirements nationwide. Public education, which is free, includes elementary and secondary schools as well as a number of universities and in-
10  stitutions of higher learning. The numerous private schools are generally run by religious groups. In French education, there is stress on serious application to studies. Wednesday is a free day in the lower grades, but there are classes on Saturday
15  morning.

The five years of elementary school are followed by four years of secondary education in the **collège.** After this, students may continue their secondary education in the **lycée** or may choose a
20  program of technical courses. For more advanced work, there are numerous universities and professional schools known as **les grandes écoles.**

### LEISURE ACTIVITIES

1. Virtually all sports are practiced in France. Some of the favorite ones are: **le football** *(soccer),* **le**
25  **cyclisme** *(bicycling),* **l'alpinisme** *(mountain climbing),* **le ski, la natation** *(swimming),* **la pêche** *(fishing),* and **le tennis.** Camping and underwater sports are very popular. **Le Tour de France,** an international bicycle race which lasts for
30  several weeks each year in July, is one of the top sporting events in France.
2. The **café** plays an important role in French social life. It provides a meeting place for both serious discussion and light conversation. In cafés
35  people can also read the daily newspapers, write letters, and play cards. Most cafés have tables outside on the sidewalk as well as indoors.
3. The French enjoy the theater, the movies, opera, ballet, and concerts. National theaters
40  such as **la Comédie-Française** and **l'Opéra** are subsidized by the government. In theaters and movie-houses, it is customary to tip the usher.
4. The numerous museums and art exhibits attract large crowds. **"Son et Lumière"** shows take place at night near historic monuments.  45
The **Son** is the recorded narration, accompanied by music; the **Lumière** is the dramatic lighting effects.

### UNITS OF MEASURE

1. The metric system, based on the number 10, originated in France and is now used almost  50
universally.

The meter **(le mètre),** the unit of length, is slightly longer than the yard.

1 meter = 100 centimeters = 39.37 inches

1 kilometer **(kilomètre)** = 1,000 meters =  55
⅝ mile (approximately)

The gram **(le gramme)** is the unit of weight.

1 kilogram **(kilogramme)** = 1,000 grams = 2.2 pounds. (approximately)

The liter **(le litre),** the liquid measure, is a  60
little more than the American quart.

2. Temperature is measured on the centigrade scale: 0 (melting ice) to 100 degrees (boiling water). It is now known as the Celsius scale.
3. The monetary unit of France is the **franc.**  65
There are 100 **centimes** in a franc. The franc is abbreviated **F** or **FF** *(French franc)* to distinguish it from the Belgian franc **(FB)** and the Swiss franc **(FS).**

### CUISINE

Although the American influence has contributed  70
to the introduction of "fast-food" restaurants in France, cooking is still considered a fine art by most French people. French cuisine has achieved an international reputation. Its chefs are known particularly for their sauces, stews, and pastries. Each  75
region of France has its own delicious specialties. Some typically French foods are:

**croissant** and **brioche,** two types of flaky rolls served as part of a French breakfast

**hors-d'œuvre,** *appetizer(s)* served at the begin-  80
ning of the meal

**soupe à l'oignon,** *onion soup*

**bouillabaisse,** a stew made with a variety of fish; specialty of Provence

85 **escargots,** *snails*

**pâtés** and **foie gras,** rich and tasty dishes based on goose liver

**pot-au-feu,** a kind of stew, consisting of boiled beef and vegetables

**crêpes Suzette,** thin pancakes with a liqueur 90 sauce, served as dessert

Outside each restaurant, the menu is posted. Meals may be ordered **à la carte,** each dish individually priced, or **à prix fixe,** at one price for the complete meal. The **bistro,** a small establishment 95 that combines a simple restaurant with a bar, is very popular in France.

## EXERCICE A

**For each item in the first column, write the letter of the matching description in the second column.**

*1.* escargots _____

*2.* soupe à l'oignon _____

*3.* crêpes Suzette _____

*4.* croissant _____

*5.* gramme _____

*6.* bouillabaisse _____

*7.* pot-au-feu _____

*8.* litre _____

*9.* hors-d'œuvre _____

*10.* bistro _____

*a.* fish stew

*b.* boiled beef stew

*c.* unit of weight

*d.* snails

*e.* appetizers

*f.* pancakes with liqueur sauce

*g.* breakfast roll

*h.* simple restaurant

*i.* liquid measure

*j.* onion soup

## EXERCICE B

**Choose the correct answer.**

*1.* French education is controlled by the (municipal, national) _____ government.

*2.* There are (few, many) _____ private schools in France.

*3.* Most French people are (Catholic, Protestant) _____ .

*4.* In French schools, there are no classes on (Wednesday, Thursday) _____ .

*5.* The metric system originated in (France, Italy) _____ .

*6.* The yard is a little shorter than the (meter, liter) _____ .

*7.* A favorite sport in France is (baseball, soccer) _____ .

**8.** 1 kilometer = (⅗, ⅝) _____ mile.

**9.** Usually French people eat brioches for (dinner, breakfast) _____ .

**10.** A bistro is (a culinary specialty, a small popular restaurant) _____ .

## EXERCICE C

*Complétez les phrases.*

**1.** L'instruction en France est obligatoire pour les enfants de _____ à

_____ ans.

**2.** Les écoles secondaires sont le collège et le _____ .

**3.** L'unité monétaire de France est le _____ .

**4.** Le _____ de France, une course de bicyclettes, est un événement sportif qui crée beaucoup d'enthousiasme.

**5.** On emploie en France le thermomètre _____ , qui a une échelle de température à cent degrés.

**6.** Dans un restaurant on peut commander un repas à la _____ ou à prix

_____ .

**7.** Il y a plus de liquide dans un _____ que dans un «quart» américain.

**8.** Beaucoup de _____ ont une terrasse en plein air sur le trottoir.

**9.** Le «Son et _____ » est un spectacle nocturne, généralement historique, près d'un édifice ancien.

**10.** Il y a _____ centimètres dans un mètre et _____ mètres dans un kilomètre.

1   The literature of France is one of the great literatures of the world.

## MIDDLE AGES

The first literary works in France, the **chansons de geste,** date from the Middle Ages **(le Moyen Âge).**
5  These legendary epic poems recount the patriotic and religious exploits of the knights of feudal society. The most famous is *La Chanson de Roland,* composed at the beginning of the twelfth century by an unknown author. It deals with Charlemagne's
10  wars against the Moors of Spain.

    **François Villon,** the eloquent poet of the fifteenth century, is considered the first of the great lyric poets of France. One of his verses is often cited: **"Mais où sont les neiges d'antan?"** *("But*
15  *where are the snows of yesteryear?")*

## SIXTEENTH CENTURY

During the sixteenth century, writers turn to the classical era of ancient Greece and Rome for their inspiration. This is the period of the Renaissance.

    **François Rabelais** expresses the enthusiasm of
20  the Renaissance and the love of life. He is the author of amusing satires on the evils of society.

    **Pierre de Ronsard,** the greatest poet of the sixteenth century, finds inspiration in the poets of antiquity as he searches for new poetic styles.

25     **Michel de Montaigne,** the skeptical philosopher and moralist, recommends moderation in daily living, common sense, and a spirit of tolerance.

## SEVENTEENTH CENTURY

The seventeenth century, especially the reign of Louis XIV, is the golden age of French literature. It
30  is the period of classicism, a movement of order and discipline. The writers seek perfection in form, expression, and style.

    The two great dramatic poets are **Pierre Corneille** and **Jean Racine.** Their classical tragedies
35  for the theater are masterpieces of French drama.

    **Molière,** who is often called "the Shakespeare of France", is the greatest French writer of classical comedies. In his plays, he attacks human vices.

    **Jean de La Fontaine** is the famous writer of fables. Using the animal kingdom, he paints in verse 40
a picture of human society.

## EIGHTEENTH CENTURY

The literature of the eighteenth century, mostly in prose, sets human reason and individualism against tradition and authority. It is the period of liberal thinkers, of great philosophers who had a profound 45
influence on political thought. By stressing the need for reform and the rights of the individual, they prepared the way for the French Revolution.

    **Charles de Secondat de Montesquieu** criticized French institutions and proposed the separa- 50
tion of governmental powers. He pioneered the comparative study of social institutions, and in his classic *De l'Esprit des lois* strongly influenced the framing of the constitution of the United States.

    **Voltaire** dominates the eighteenth century. He 55
attacks social injustice and becomes the defender of humanity and liberty in all forms. His extensive work, which displays his ironic wit and skeptical philosophy, includes many genres.

    **Jean-Jacques Rousseau** is the theoretician of 60
democracy. In attacking the social order, he inspired an intellectual revolt. He defended individual liberty and upheld the sovereignty of the people.

    **Denis Diderot** directed the publication of 65
*l'Encyclopédie,* which included the ideas of all the great writers and philosophers of the period. He attacks tradition and expresses faith in the progress of humanity.

## NINETEENTH CENTURY

The first half of the nineteenth century produced 70
a reaction to classical tradition. It was the period of romanticism, which prized freedom of expression, and stemmed from the theories of Rousseau. In romantic literature, each writer expresses his own personality and individualism. The essential 75
elements are imagination, feeling, and the love of nature.

Victor Hugo, the head of the romantic school, was its greatest poet. He is also known for his plays and his novels *(Les Misérables, Notre-Dame de Paris).*

Other romantic poets are **Alphonse de Lamartine, Alfred de Vigny,** and **Alfred de Musset.**

**Honoré de Balzac** paints a picture of the customs of his time in *La Comédie humaine,* a series of twenty-four admirable novels and numerous novelettes. With Balzac, who depicts all classes of society with precision, the novel evolves from romanticism toward realism.

**Alexandre Dumas père** wrote a large number of historical novels, which became popular worldwide *(Les Trois Mousquetaires, Le Comte de Monte-Cristo).*

In the middle of the nineteenth century, there arise new movements in opposition to romanticism, which stress truth, materialism, and the reality of life. This movement of realism evolves into naturalism, which seeks to analyze and portray life and nature as they are. Writers become impersonal, intellectual, and scientific.

Famous novelists are:

**Gustave Flaubert,** whose novels are characterized by minute observation and careful documentation; he wrote *Madame Bovary;*

**Jules Verne,** author of fantastic novels of adventure; he is the creator of science fiction; he wrote *Le Tour du monde en 80 jours;*

**Alphonse Daudet,** whose sensitive novels describe life in the south of France;

**Émile Zola,** head of the naturalist school, who observed and analyzed scientifically the masses of human society;

**Guy de Maupassant,** the greatest French writer of short stories.

The poets of this time include **Lecomte de Lisle,** who defends "art for art's sake," and **Baudelaire** and **Verlaine,** who are part of the symbolist movement, which attempts to blend the arts and the functions of the senses.

## TWENTIETH CENTURY

France produced many gifted writers during the twentieth century. Several have been awarded the Nobel Prize in Literature. Following are some who have achieved world fame.

*Novelists*

**Anatole France,** novelist, satirist, and erudite philosopher;

**André Gide,** who received the Nobel Prize in 1947 for his vast and varied work and who is above all a humanist;

**Marcel Proust's** *À la recherche du temps perdu* treats unconscious memory as a work of art that is indestructible and eternal. In his work, Proust describes in great detail the beauty and happiness awakened by memory and contrasts them with the sadness and disappointments of real life.

**André Maurois,** whose extensive work includes biographies, historical studies, and essays as well as novels;

**François Mauriac,** author of novels, plays, and essays that are often influenced by his religious beliefs;

**André Malraux,** art critic and author of novels celebrating human fraternity and heroism;

**Claude Simon,** one of the authors who, in the fifties, attempted to renew the novel by changing its style and lessening its dependency on a traditional story. He was awarded the Nobel Prize in 1985.

**Marguerite Duras,** who, in addition to writing novels, has been involved in the theatre and filmmaking.

*Playwrights*

**Edmond Rostand,** dramatic author of brilliant style who wrote *Cyrano de Bergerac;*

**Paul Claudel,** powerful dramatist and mystical poet;

**Eugène Ionesco,** representative of the theater of the Absurd, who sets forth in his dramas the ridiculous tragedy of mankind;

**Samuel Beckett,** pessimistic playwright, who denounces the absurdity of the human condition.

*Philosophers*

**Henri Bergson,** a Nobel Prize winner, defines intuition as a means of attaining all knowledge.

Jean-Paul Sartre, the brilliant theoretician of atheistic existentialism, who affirms that the existence of man excludes the existence of God. He speaks of the absurdity of life and develops his theses in novels, dramas, and essays. His greatest success is in the theater.

Albert Camus, a philosopher and moralist, is the author of essays, novels, and dramas. As a representative of the "philosophy of the absurd," he writes of the mechanical character of human existence without a goal.

*Poets*

Paul Valéry creates poetry of a subtle and mysterious symbolism.

Saint-John Perse, poet and diplomat, forms exotic images and meditates on the destiny of humanity.

## EXERCICE A

*Complete the sentences.*

1. The most famous of the *chansons de geste,* _____ describes the exploits

   of _____ against the Spanish Moors.

2. The "golden age" of French literature took place during the reign of _____ .

3. In the sixteenth century, the outstanding writer of amusing satires on the evils of society was

   _____ .

4. Two great philosophers, Rousseau and _____ , had a profound influence on
   the political thought of the eigthteenth century. These liberal thinkers prepared the way for the French

   _____ .

5. Victor Hugo is known for his _____ , novels, and poetry.

6. Two novelists of the nineteenth century who received the Nobel Prize were Claude Simon and

   _____ .

## EXERCICE B

**Identify the famous writer.**

1. author of classical comedies, "the Shakespeare of France"   _____

2. the greatest writer of short stories   _____

3. the famous writer of fables   _____

4. the greatest poet of the romantic school   _____

5. the creator of science fiction   _____

6. the writer who directed the publication of *l'Encyclopédie*   _____

7. moralist and philosopher of the absurd   _____

## EXERCICE C

*Choisissez la réponse convenable.*

1. Les chansons de geste datent (de la Renaissance, du Moyen Âge) _____ .

2. Corneille et (Racine, Ronsard) _____ sont les deux grands écrivains de tragédies du 17$^e$ siècle.

3. Le (15$^e$, 16$^e$) _____ siècle est l'époque de la Renaissance.

4. *Le Comte de Monte-Cristo* et *Les Trois Mousquetaires* sont des romans historiques (de Denis Diderot, d'Alexandre Dumas père) _____ .

5. Le premier poète lyrique de France est (Michel de Montaigne, François Villon)

   _____ .

6. François Rabelais exprime l'enthousiasme de la Renaissance dans ses (satires, poèmes)

   _____ comiques.

7. La liberté d'expression, l'individualisme et l'imagination sont des éléments du (romantisme,

   classicisme) _____ .

8. Dans *La Comédie humaine* (Balzac, Montesquieu) _____ peint avec précision toutes les classes de la société du 19$^e$ siècle.

9. Deux poètes illustres du 19$^e$ siècle sont (Flaubert et Daudet, Baudelaire et Verlaine)

   _____ .

10. Philosophe et moraliste, (Camus, Claudel) _____ représente dans son œuvre la philosophie de l'absurde.

# Chapter 39
## The Arts

Throughout the centuries, the French have distinguished themselves in the arts. Many French artists and other artists working in France have achieved fame and worldwide influence.

## PAINTING

**Antoine Watteau,** the great classical painter of the eighteenth century, created beautiful pastoral scenes. His pictures reflect the elegant society of his time.

**Louis David,** head of the *neoclassical* school, was the painter of the French Revolution. He painted principally portraits and scenes from Greek and Roman history.

In the nineteenth century, Paris became the world center of painting where artists with similar tendencies grouped themselves in a variety of schools.

*Romanticism* attempted to break away from the discipline and rules of classicism. **Eugène Delacroix,** the best-known of this school, created paintings of vitality and dramatic movement.

*Realism* was the reaction against both romanticism and classicism. **Honoré Daumier,** a realist lithographer and painter, is known especially for his political and social caricatures.

Several landscape painters formed a group known as **l'École de Barbizon,** after a small village outside Paris where they liked to go. **Jean-Baptiste Corot** painted with poetic charm. **Jean-François Millet** liked to paint scenes of peasant life, and **Théodore Rousseau** painted mostly landscapes.

In the second half of the nineteenth century, *impressionism* evolved from realism. The impressionists tried to translate into painting the feelings evoked by their visual perceptions. They chose modern subjects, ignored details, and made light the essential element of their paintings.

**Édouard Manet,** one of the founders of impressionism, is famous for his dazzling texture and color.

**Edgar Degas,** an expert at expressing form and movement, painted many ballet scenes.

**Claude Monet,** the great impressionist landscape painter, often painted the same subject in varying light at different times of day.

**Auguste Renoir** was a celebrated painter of women and landscapes.

**Georges Seurat** developed *pointillism,* a technique of using many points of pure colors to create an effect of depth and light.

**Pierre Puvis de Chavannes** painted in a classical style the murals that decorate the Panthéon and the Sorbonne.

*Post-impressionism,* a modern movement at the end of the nineteenth century, was a reaction against the excesses of impressionism and realism. The modernists of this school did not hesitate to distort the appearance of nature and the human body. They are individualists who paint in their own personal styles.

**Paul Cézanne** is considered the father of modern French painting. His works, mainly landscapes and still lifes, give the impression of a third dimension.

**Paul Gauguin** is known especially for his Breton landscapes and scenes of Tahiti painted in vivid colors with moving simplicity.

**Vincent van Gogh,** from Holland, found his inspiration in Provence. His canvasses — still lifes, landscapes, portraits — are filled with brilliant colors and sunlight.

**Henri de Toulouse-Lautrec** painted music-hall and circus scenes, of which many were reproduced and distributed as posters in his time.

At the start of the twentieth century, a group of artists reacted against impressionist analyses and decided to paint as they pleased, simplifying forms and using pure strong colors. They called themselves **les Fauves** *(wild beasts).*

**Henri Matisse,** the head of *fauvism,* is considered one of the greatest painters of his time. His masterpiece of decorative art is the chapel of Vence, in southern France.

**Georges Braque** founded the school of *cubism,* which represents objects in geometric form, often

85 from different angles at the same time.

**Pablo Picasso,** the most versatile painter of the twentieth century, tried a variety of techniques, attaining a synthesis between cubism and surrealism. He had a profound influence on the evolution
90 of modern art.

*Surrealism,* in the 1920s, was opposed to every kind of convention and sought an instinctive and dreamlike expression. **André Masson** and **René Magritte** were surrealists.

95 Other important painters of the twentieth century are **Fernand Léger,** who painted monumental works inspired by modern life and machinery; and **Marc Chagall,** born in Russia, whose paintings are filled with poetic fantasy.

## SCULPTURE

100 **Jean-Antoine Houdon** (eighteenth century) produced realistic busts of several famous men: Voltaire, Rousseau, Washington, La Fayette, Franklin, Jefferson.

In the nineteenth century, **François Rude,** a
105 sculptor of the Romantic school, created the famous bas-relief *La Marseillaise* that decorates the **Arc de Triomphe** in Paris.

**Frédéric-Auguste Bartholdi** is best known as the sculptor of the Statue of Liberty *(La Liberté*
110 *éclairant le monde).*

**Auguste Rodin** is usually considered the greatest of modern sculptors. He used the human figure to express the emotions and the power of life in such works as *Le Penseur (The Thinker).*

115 In the twentieth century, **Aristide Maillol** is known particularly for his simple and graceful statues of nude women.

**Jacques Lipchitz,** who was associated with cubism in his early years, brought imaginative and
120 lyrical energy to a variety of media.

## ARCHITECTURE

In the Gallo-Roman period, remarkable structures were built: temples, arenas, amphitheaters, aqueducts. The best surviving examples are found in southern France, in Provence.

125 In the Middle Ages, the arts were mostly in the service of religion. The thick-walled *Romanesque* churches of the tenth through the mid-twelfth centuries were dark inside. Later, the French created a new style of architecture, *Gothic,* with large stained-glass windows that let in plenty of 130 light, and ornamented with sculpture, statues, and gargoyles. Outstanding examples are the cathedrals of Notre-Dame de Paris, Amiens, Chartres, and Reims.

Many splendid castles were built by the kings 135 and nobles, especially during the sixteenth and seventeenth centuries, all over France, particularly along the Loire river and around Paris.

**Jules Hardouin Mansart** (seventeenth century), the chief architect of Louis XIV, built most 140 of the palace of Versailles as well as the dome of the Invalides and the **place Vendôme** in Paris.

**Eugène Viollet-le-Duc** (nineteenth century) restored numerous historic monuments of the Middle Ages, such as Notre-Dame de Paris, the 145 cathedral of Amiens, and the Cité de Carcassonne.

**Le Corbusier** (twentieth century) exerted a wide influence through his theorical writings, his daring use of reinforced concrete, and his innovative design of urban housing developments. 150

At the present time, many important architectural projects are being built in France and especially in Paris, giving several talented architects the opportunity to impart a new look to the urban landscape. 155

## MUSIC

**Jean-Baptiste Lully,** who served at the court of Louis XIV, created the French opera. He wrote music for several comedies of Molière.

**Hector Berlioz,** the greatest composer of the Romantic school that flourished in the first half 160 of the nineteenth century, wrote beautifully orchestrated and powerful dramatic works of which *La Damnation de Faust* is now considered his masterpiece.

In the second half of the nineteenth century, 165 French music attained international prominence.

**César Franck,** an organist of great renown, wrote music that combined classical forms with romantic harmonies. As a teacher, he was very influential. 170

**Camille Saint-Saëns,** a virtuoso of the piano and organ, wrote symphonic poems *(La Danse macabre)* and operas. His masterpiece is *Samson et Dalila.*

Claude Debussy, whose career extended into the early part of the twentieth century, was influenced by the symbolists and the impressionists. His music is dreamy, delicate, and highly original. Among his principal works are: *Prélude à l'après-midi d'un faune, La Mer, Clair de lune,* and the opera *Pelléas et Mélisande.*

Maurice Ravel composed pieces for the piano and for the orchestra: *Daphnis et Chloé, Boléro, Ma mère l'Oye (Mother Goose Suite).*

Other composers of famous operas are:

Georges Bizet: *Carmen, Les Pêcheurs de perles*
Charles Gounod: *Faust, Roméo et Juliette*
Jules Massenet: *Manon, Thaïs*
Jacques Offenbach: *Les Contes d'Hoffmann*

The twentieth century has witnessed the rise of a number of talented composers, including: **Arthur Honegger, Darius Milhaud, Francis Poulenc, Georges Auric, Olivier Messiaen,** and **Pierre Boulez.**

## EXERCICE A

**Choose the suitable answer.**

1. The painter of brilliant still lifes, landscapes, and portraits who was inspired by the beauty of Provence was (Eugène Delacroix, Vincent van Gogh) _____ .

2. (Claude Monet, Antoine Watteau) _____ liked to paint the same subject at different times of the day.

3. (Henri de Toulouse-Lautrec, Paul Gauguin) _____ created posters with scenes of music-halls and circuses.

4. The great landscape painter of the Barbizon School was (Édouard Manet, Jean-Baptiste Corot) _____ .

5. Early in the twentieth century, a number of artists decided to paint as they pleased and formed the group called (the impressionists, the Fauves) _____ .

6. The best examples of structures built during the Gallo-Roman period are found in (Paris, Provence) _____ .

7. The arts of the Middle Ages were principally (romantic, religious) _____ .

8. The nineteenth-century architect who restored historic monuments such as Notre-Dame de Paris and the fortress city of Carcassonne is (Viollet-le-Duc, Aristide Maillol) _____ .

9. Stained-glass windows, sculptured facades, and gargoyles were elements of (Romanesque, Gothic) _____ architecture.

10. The sculptor of *La Marseillaise* on the *Arc de Triomphe* is (François Rude, Auguste Renoir) _____ .

## EXERCICE B

**Identify the artists.**

1. the painter of scenes of peasant life _____

2. the painter of murals for the Panthéon _____

3. the "father" of modern French painting _____

4. the painter of scenes of Tahiti _____

5. a realist painter known for his political and social caricatures _____

6. the painter of ballet scenes _____

7. the inventor of pointillism _____

8. head of the neoclassic school during the French Revolution, he painted scenes from Greek history _____

9. the most inventive painter of the twentieth century, who used many different techniques _____

10. the architect of Louis XIV _____

11. the sculptor of busts of Voltaire and Washington _____

12. a famous French architect of the twentieth century _____

13. sculptor of *Le Penseur* _____

14. the sculptor of the Statue of Liberty in New York _____

## EXERCICE C

**Complete the sentences.**

1. In the nineteenth century, the city of _____ became the international center of painting.

2. In the first half of the nineteenth century, several landscape painters formed *l'École de*

   _____ .

3. The impressionists used _____ as the principal element of their paintings.

4. The famous chapel of Vence was decorated by _____ .

5. Georges Braque started the movement called _____ , which uses geometric forms to represent objects in an abstract and analytical way.

## EXERCICE D

**Choose the suitable answer.**

*1.* While serving at the court of Louis XIV, (Lully, Berlioz) _____ created the

French opera and wrote music for (Molière's, Corneille's) _____ comedies.

*2.* (César Franck, Jules Massenet) _____ , the celebrated organist, was an influen-

tial teacher.

*3.* (Maurice Ravel, Charles Gounod) _____ , who composed the famous *Boléro,*

wrote pieces for the piano and the orchestra.

*4.* Two notable French composers of the twentieth century are Georges Auric and (Hector Berlioz,

Darius Milhaud) _____ .

*5.* The composer of *Samson et Dalila* is (Camille Saint-Saëns, Claude Debussy)

_____ .

## EXERCICE E

*Complétez les phrases.*

*1.* *Carmen* est l'œuvre de _____ .

*2.* Hector _____ était un des chefs de l'école romantique de musique.

*3.* Jacques Offenbach a composé l'opéra _____ .

*4.* _____ a écrit *Prélude à l'après-midi d'un faune* et *Clair de lune.*

*5.* Olivier _____ et Pierre _____ sont des musiciens

contemporains.

# Chapter 40
## The Sciences

1　The French have made significant contributions in many fields of science. Among French scientists, the following men and women should be mentioned:

## MATHEMATICS

René Descartes (1596–1650), philosopher and
5　mathematician, founded the scientific method, based on reasoning from the simple to the complex. Applied to philosophy, this rational method led him to prove his own existence first—**"Je pense, donc je suis"**—and then the existence of the ex-
10　terior world.

Blaise Pascal (1623–1662), mathematician, physicist, and philosopher, formulated the laws of atmospheric pressure and of hydraulics. At the age of nineteen, he invented the mechanical adding
15　machine.

Pierre-Simon de Laplace (1749–1827) made important contributions to understanding the dynamics of the solar system and to the theory of probability.

20　Henri Poincaré (1854–1912) is called the last mathematical universalist because he contributed important work to all branches of mathematics as well as the philosophy of sciences.

## PHYSICS

Charles-Augustin de Coulomb (1736–1806) stud-
25　ied the mathematical laws of electricity and magnetism. The *coulomb* is the unit of electrical charges.

André Ampère (1775–1836) developed electromagnetic theory. An *ampere* is the unit used in measuring the intensity of electrical currents.

30　Henri Becquerel (1852–1908) discovered natural radioactivity in 1896.

Pierre Curie (1859–1906) and his wife **Marie Curie** (1867–1934) discovered radium in 1899, thus effecting great changes in the fields of chem-
35　istry and physics. Their daughter and her husband, **Irène** and **Pierre Joliot-Curie,** discovered artificial radioactivity in 1934.

## CHEMISTRY

Antoine-Laurent de Lavoisier (1743–1794), one of the founders of modern chemistry, determined the composition of air and made many important
40　discoveries. One of his sayings is often quoted: **"Rien ne se perd, rien ne se crée; dans la nature tout se transforme."** *(Nothing is lost, nothing is created; in nature everything is transformed.)*

## NATURAL SCIENCE

Jean-Baptiste de Lamarck (1744–1829) devel-
45　oped a theory about the evolution of animals and plants that predates Darwin's work.

## BIOLOGY AND MEDICINE

Claude Bernard (1813–1878) is the founder of modern physiology and experimental medicine.

Louis Pasteur (1822–1895), chemist and biol-
50　ogist, is one of the great benefactors of mankind. He formulated the germ theory of infection, found a cure for rabies and anthrax, and invented the process of pasteurization. His work revolutionized medicine.
55

**L'Institut Pasteur,** founded in 1888 under his direction in Paris, remains a leading research center in the fields of biochemistry and infectious diseases.

Émile Roux (1853–1933) discovered that the
60　diphtheria bacillus produces a toxin; this was the first step in the development of effective medicines for what was once a dreaded childhood disease.

In other fields as well, French scientists have made important contributions.
65

Jean-François Champollion (1790–1832), archaeologist, succeeded in deciphering the Egyptian hieroglyphics of the Rosetta stone.

Louis-Jacques Daguerre (1789–1851), devel-
70　oped a way to record images on metal plates and deserves to be called one of the inventors of photography.

Louis Braille (1809–1852) invented a system of reading and writing for the blind.

Many French scientists have been awarded the
75　Nobel Prize for their contributions to research and science since 1911. Two Frenchmen won the Nobel Prize in Physics in 1991 and 1992, **Pierre-Gilles de Gennes** and **Georges Charpak.**

## EXERCICE A

**Choose the correct answer.**

1. (Lavoisier, Poincaré) _____ is one of the founders of modern chemistry.

2. A French scientist contributed to the discovery of a serum to cure (pneumonia, diphtheria)

   _____ .

3. (Claude Bernard, André Ampère) _____ founded modern physiology and experimental medicine.

4. Henri Becquerel won the Nobel Prize for his discovery of (photography, radioactivity).

   _____ .

5. (René Descartes, Marie Curie) _____ founded a scientific method based on reason.

6. (Laplace, Lamarck) _____ is a famous mathematician.

## EXERCICE B

*Identifiez les savants célèbres.*

1. Il a inventé un système de lecture et d'écriture pour les aveugles *(blind).*   _____

2. Ses travaux remarquables ont révolutionné la médecine.   _____

3. Il a contribué au développement de la photographie.   _____

4. Ils ont découvert le radium en 1899.   _____

5. L'unité d'intensité du courant électrique porte son nom.   _____

6. Il a écrit: «Je pense, donc je suis».   _____

## EXERCICE C

**Complete the sentences.**

1. The _____ Institute carries on the work of the famous scientist in the study of biological chemistry .

2. The archaeologist _____ deciphered the Egyptian hieroglyphics of the Rosetta stone.

**3.** The coulomb is the unit of quantity of _____ .

**4.** Blaise _____ , mathematician and philosopher, formulated the principles of hydraulics and invented the first mechanical adding machine.

**5.** One of the founders of modern chemistry, _____ , said that in nature "Rien ne se perd, rien ne se crée."

**6.** Irène _____ , who discovered artificial radioactivity with her husband, was the daughter of _____ .

# Civilization Quiz

## A. Underline the correct response.

**1.** Not a Romance language:
    *a.* French      *b.* Spanish      *c.* Latin      *d.* German

**2.** He founded the French Academy:
    *a.* Julius Caesar      *b.* Louis Pasteur      *c.* Cardinal Richelieu      *d.* Guillaume le Conquérant

**3.** To wish a good trip to a friend, you say:
    *a.* R.S.V. P.      *b.* rendez-vous      *c.* tête-à-tête      *d.* bon voyage

**4.** France is smaller than:
    *a.* Germany      *b.* Belgium      *c.* Italy      *d.* Texas

**5.** The sea bordering France on the south:
    *a.* la Manche      *b.* le Jura      *c.* la Méditerranée      *d.* l'océan Atlantique

**6.** The province where a Celtic dialect is still spoken:
    *a.* Normandie      *b.* Touraine      *c.* Alsace      *d.* Brittany

**7.** There are famous castles in:
    *a.* Bourgogne      *b.* Lorraine      *c.* Touraine      *d.* Champagne

**8.** The nickname of Paris is:
    *a.* la douce France      *b.* la belle      *c.* la ville lumière      *d.* la métropole

**9.** The cathedral of Paris is called:
    *a.* la Madeleine      *b.* Notre-Dame      *c.* Sainte-Chapelle      *d.* Sainte Geneviève

**10.** A large port in France is:
    *a.* Grenoble      *b.* Nantes      *c.* Metz      *d.* Vichy

**11.** The city of Nice is in:
    *a.* Brittany      *b.* Île-de-France      *c.* Provence      *d.* the Jura

**12.** The first national hero of France:
    *a.* Molière      *b.* Clovis      *c.* Vercingétorix      *d.* Charlemagne

**13.** She helped save France during the Hundred Years' War:
    *a.* Sainte Geneviève      *b.* Jeanne d'Arc      *c.* Marie Curie      *d.* Claude Monet

**14.** Flowers for the perfume industry are cultivated near:
    *a.* Grasse      *b.* Paris      *c.* Limoges      *d.* Lille

**15.** The metric system originated in:
    *a.* France      *b.* Algeria      *c.* Greece      *d.* Rome

**16.** The greatest writer of classical comedies:

    *a.* Jean Racine      *b.* Pierre Corneille      *c.* Molière      *d.* Voltaire

**17.** The author of *La Comédie humaine:*

    *a.* Émile Zola      *b.* Honoré de Balzac      *c.* Marcel Proust      *d.* Gustave Flaubert

**18.** He is considered the father of modern French painting:

    *a.* Georges Seurat      *b.* Claude Monet      *c.* Paul Gauguin      *d.* Paul Cézanne

**19.** The S.N.C.F. in France runs the:

    *a.* roads      *b.* subway      *c.* trains      *d.* government

**20.** The French explorer who explored the Mississippi and named Louisiana:

    *a.* La Fayette      *b.* Jacques Cartier      *c.* Champlain      *d.* Cavelier de la Salle

**21.** An agricultural product not produced in France:

    *a.* cheese      *b.* wine      *c.* dairy products      *d.* citrus fruit

## B. Choose the expression or the word that best completes the sentence.

**1.** The dialect that became French was the one spoken in _____ .

    *a.* Brittany      *b.* Belgium      *c.* Normandy      *d.* Île-de-France

**2.** William the Conqueror, duke of _____ , invaded England in 1066.

    *a.* Louisiana      *b.* Île-de-France      *c.* Normandy      *d.* Gaul

**3.** When you order one dish only in a restaurant, you order _____ .

    *a.* une demi-tasse      *b.* un nom de plume      *c.* à la carte      *d.* un apéritif

**4.** The river that flows through Paris is _____ .

    *a.* la Loire      *b.* la Seine      *c.* la Garonne      *d.* le Rhin

**5.** The river that produces a lot of hydroelectric power is _____ .

    *a.* le Rhin      *b.* le Rhône      *c.* la Loire      *d.* la Gironde

**6.** The Riviera in Provence is also called _____ .

    *a.* la Côte d'Azur      *b.* la Côte sauvage      *c.* la Côte d'Émeraude      *d.* l'Île-de-France

**7.** A region that produces great wines is _____ .

    *a.* la Normandie      *b.* la Bretagne      *c.* la Bourgogne      *d.* l'Angleterre

**8.** The richest and biggest museum in Paris is _____ .

    *a.* le Louvre      *b.* le musée d'Orsay      *c.* le Panthéon      *d.* la Géode

**9.** The subway in Paris is called _____ .

    *a.* le train      *b.* le bateau-mouche      *c.* le métro      *d.* l'autobus

**10.** Two cities that contain the best-preserved Roman monuments are Nîmes and _____ .

    *a.* Deauville        *b.* Rouen        *c.* Bordeaux        *d.* Arles

**11.** A medieval fortified town in the south of France is _____ .

    *a.* Arles        *b.* Nancy        *c.* Carcassonne        *d.* Mont-Saint-Michel

**12.** A democratic and well-loved king was _____ .

    *a.* Louis XV        *b.* Henri IV        *c.* Louis XVI        *d.* Richelieu

**13.** *"L'État, c'est moi"* was said by _____ .

    *a.* Napoléon        *b.* Louis XIV        *c.* General de Gaulle        *d.* Clovis

**14.** _____ wrote powerful dramatic works of music, including *La Damnation de Faust.*

    *a.* Hector Berlioz        *b.* César Franck        *c.* Francis Poulenc        *d.* Jacques Offenbach

**15.** _____ is one of the most illustrious composers of the early twentieth century.

    *a.* Jean-Baptiste Lully        *b.* Claude Debussy        *c.* Camille Saint-Saëns        *d.* Auguste Renoir

**16.** French bread is made mostly with _____ .

    *a.* corn        *b.* wheat        *c.* rice        *d.* potatoes

**17.** Two cheeses that are produced in France are brie and _____ .

    *a.* roquefort        *b.* champagne        *c.* Ariane        *d.* Concorde

**18.** _____ formulated the principles of hydraulics and made the first mechanical adding machine.

    *a.* Henri Poincaré        *b.* Blaise Pascal        *c.* Louis Pasteur        *d.* Auguste Rodin

**19.** The work of _____ revolutionized medicine.

    *a.* Henri Becquerel        *b.* Louis Pasteur        *c.* Louis Braille        *d.* René Descartes

**20.** Radium was discovered by _____ and his wife, Marie.

    *a.* Émile Roux        *b.* François Villon        *c.* Pierre Curie        *d.* Louis-Jacques Daguerre

**C. Choisissez l'expression ou le nom qui complète le sens de la phrase.**

**1.** L'ancien nom de la France est _____ .

    *a.* l'Île-de-France        *b.* la Suisse        *c.* la Gaule        *d.* la Louisiane

**2.** Les Cévennes font partie des montagnes qui forment _____ .

    *a.* le Jura        *b.* les Alpes        *c.* les Vosges        *d.* le Massif Central

**3.** En Provence on parle toujours un dialecte ancien, _____ .

    *a.* le breton        *b.* le latin        *c.* l'allemand        *d.* le provençal

**4.** Paris est divisé en 20 _____ .

    *a.* villages        *b.* quartiers        *c.* rives        *d.* arrondissements

5. Si vous faites du ski, vous irez peut-être à _____ .

   *a.* Reims          *b.* Chamonix          *c.* Lille          *d.* Strasbourg

6. Le Président de la République est élu pour _____ .

   *a.* cinq ans          *b.* sept ans          *c.* deux ans          *d.* quatre ans

7. «*Liberté, Égalité, Fraternité*» est _____ de la République française.

   *a.* la chanson          *b.* la devise          *c.* l'hymne national          *d.* la constitution

8. La principale ressource d'énergie de la France est _____ .

   *a.* l'énergie nucléaire          *b.* le gaz naturel          *c.* le pétrole          *d.* le vent

9. Les élèves en France vont au collège à l'âge de _____ .

   *a.* onze ans          *b.* dix-huit ans          *c.* six ans          *d.* vingt ans

10. _____ a écrit des fables qui font parler des animaux et qui ont été traduites en toutes les langues du monde.

    *a.* François Rabelais          *b.* Jean de La Fontaine          *c.* Victor Hugo          *d.* Pierre de Ronsard

11. Un grand architecte du 20$^e$ siècle est _____ .

    *a.* Viollet-le-Duc          *b.* Le Corbusier          *c.* Picasso          *d.* Matisse

12. Un des fondateurs de la chimie moderne est _____ .

    *a.* Lavoisier          *b.* Jean-Paul Sartre          *c.* Paul Claudel          *d.* Vauban

# Part six

## Comprehensive Testing:
*Speaking, Listening, Reading, Writing*

QUÉBEC

BELGIQUE

LUXEMBOURG

FRANCE          SUISSE

SAINT-PIERRE-
ET-MIQUELON

MONACO

CORSE

LOUISIANE

MAROC

ALGÉRIE          TUNISIE

MAURITANIE          MALI     NIGER     TCHAD

HAÏTI     GUADELOUPE

MARTINIQUE

SÉNÉGAL

GUINÉE

BURKINA FASO

CÔTE-D'IVOIRE

GUYANE

TOGO     BÉNIN

CAMEROUN

RÉPUBLIQUE
CENTRAFRICAINE

ZAÏRE

GABON

CONGO

# 1. SPEAKING: ORAL COMMUNICATION TASKS [20 points]

Your teacher will administer two communication tasks. Each task prescribes a simulated conversation in which the teacher assumes a specified role and you respond as yourself.

Each task requires four utterances on your part. An utterance is any spoken statement that is comprehensible and appropriate and leads to accomplishing the stated task. Assume that in each situation you are dealing with a person who speaks French.

# 2. LISTENING COMPREHENSION

## 2a Multiple Choice (English) [20 points]

Part 2a consists of ten questions. For each question, you will hear some background information in English. Then you will hear a passage in French twice, followed by a question in English. Listen carefully. After you have heard the question, read the question and the four suggested answers in your book. Choose the best suggested answer and write its number in the space provided.

*1.* What is the father doing?                                                   _____
   1 Pointing at the statue.
   2 Counting the people ahead of you in line.
   3 Paying to get in.
   4 Taking your picture.

*2.* What does your horoscope suggest?                                            _____
   1 Seek advice before making an important decision.
   2 Don't make any important decisions now.
   3 Make your important decisions today.
   4 Don't listen to others when making an important decision.

*3.* Why is your friend using her Minitel?                                        _____
   1 To get help with her homework.         2 To play a game.
   3 To buy tickets to a rock concert.       4 To meet a boy.

*4.* What is your friend explaining?                                              _____
   1 How to play a game.
   2 How to do the homework.
   3 How to improve one's memory.
   4 How to set the table.

*5.* What are you going to see?                                                   _____
   1 An art museum.                          2 A famous house.
   3 An impressive castle.                    4 An important cathedral.

*6.* What is he asking you to do?                                                 _____
   1 Go to the post office.                   2 Call the United States.
   3 Bring his car to a service station.      4 Take care of a package.

**7.** How would this card be beneficial to students?                    _____

   1  Students would get discounts for using it.

   2  Students could use it to get money.

   3  Students would need very little cash.

   4  Students could use it anywhere in the city.

**8.** What is the announcer suggesting you do for children who are sick?     _____

   1  Visit them in the hospital.

   2  Send cards to them.

   3  Volunteer to read stories to them.

   4  Contribute toys for them.

**9.** What is the employee telling you?                                 _____

   1  How to find the exit.

   2  That your luggage has been found.

   3  To go through customs with your luggage.

   4  How to leave the airport quickly.

**10.** What does the guide expect you to do?                             _____

   1  Take pictures.              2  Touch things carefully.

   3  Carry your bags with you.      4  Smoke only in designated areas.

## 2b   Multiple Choice (French) [10 points]

Part 2b consists of five questions. For each question, you will hear some background information in English. Then you will hear a passage in French twice, followed by a question in French. Listen carefully. After you have heard the question, read the question and the four suggested answers in your book. Choose the best suggested answer and write its number in the space provided.

**1.** Quand est-ce qu'on mange ce plat?                                  _____

   1  Au petit déjeuner.          2  Au déjeuner.

   3  À quatre heures.           4  Au dîner.

**2.** Pourquoi étudie-t-elle une langue étrangère?                       _____

   1  Ses parents travaillent à l'étranger.

   2  Elle est spécialiste en langues étrangères.

   3  Sa famille est étrange.

   4  Elle veut apprécier une culture différente.

**3.** Qu'est-ce qu'Armand Peugeot fabrique aussi?                        _____

   1  Des bicyclettes.          2  Des motocyclettes.

   3  Des bateaux.             4  Des avions.

**4.** Qu'est-ce que vous pouvez acheter dans ce magasin?                 _____

   1  Des chaussures.         2  Un bikini.

   3  Un chapeau.            4  Une chemise.

**5.** Que pense-t-il de l'album de Roland Castel?

1 C'est bon.

2 C'est un désastre.

3 C'est ennuyeux.

4 C'est extraordinaire.

## 2c Multiple Choice (Visual) [10 points]

For each question, you will hear some background information in English. Then you will hear a passage in French twice, followed by a question in English. Listen carefully. After you have heard the question, read the question and look at the four pictures in your book. Choose the picture that best answers the question and circle its number.

**1.** What pet is he suggesting?

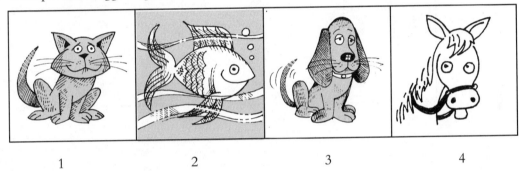

1        2        3        4

**2.** Which holiday is being celebrated?

1        2        3        4

**3.** What does your friend like to do?

1        2        3        4

**4.** Which picture most resembles Denis?

1          2          3          4

**5.** What weather should you expect?

1          2          3          4

## 3. READING COMPREHENSION

### 3a Multiple Choice (English) [10 points]

Part 3a consists of questions or incomplete statements in English, each based on a reading selection in French. Choose the expression that best answers the question or completes the statement. Base your choice on the content of the reading selection. Write the number of your answer in the space provided.

**1.** This ad offers

1 automobile protection.      2 babysitting services.
3 special flights.      4 travel insurance.

*bonne année*

Nous vous souhaitons un joyeux

*Noël*

et nous vous présentons
tous nos meilleurs vœux
de bonheur et de santé
pour la nouvelle année.

**2.** What is this person wishing you?                              _____

1  Happy Easter.                    2  A good trip.
3  Get well soon.                   4  Happy New Year.

## POUR PASSER UNE PETITE ANNONCE

Nombre de parutions souhaitées (cocher la case de votre choix)

| 1 | 2 | 3 | 4 | 5 | 6 | 7 |

Accompagner votre ordre d'insertion des renseignements suivants

Nom: _____

Adresse: _____

Tél: _____

Le prix est de 2F50 par mot avec un minimum de 50F par annonce
(le numéro de téléphone compte pour un seul mot)

Date limite de réception des annonces: mardi midi

**3.** You would fill out this coupon if you wanted to                  _____

1  place an ad.                     2  subscribe to a magazine.
3  get a free issue.                4  enter a contest.

**Carte de Groupe Sanguin et Facteur Rhésus**

Cette carte doit être fixée à votre carte d'identité.

Vous la porterez ainsi toujours sur vous.

Elle peut être précieuse en cas d'accident et vous sauver la vie.

LABORATOIRE CASTEL ET CHAVIN
23, rue Savert   07700 Bourg-en-Loing   75.64.50.72

**4.** This card

1   is for accident insurance.
2   could save your life.
3   is a national identification card.
4   should be kept in a safe place at home.

## LA TÉLÉVISION ━━━━━━━━━━ France 2

| 5.55 | 6.30 | 7.00 | 7.30 | 8.00 | 8.30 |
|------|------|------|------|------|------|
| Dessin animé | Télématin | Journal | | | |

| 8.55 | 11.30 | 11.55 | 12.00 | | 12.59 |
|------|-------|-------|-------|---|-------|
| Amour, gloire et beauté | Flash info | Pyramide | Ces années-là, animé par Laurent | | Journal, suivi de la météo |

| 14.50 | 15.30 | 17.10 | 19.15 | 20.00 | 22.00 |
|-------|-------|-------|-------|-------|-------|
| **Le Renard,** série policière | La chance aux chansons | Des chiffres et des lettres | Que le meilleur gagne! | Tirage du loto | Dernier journal |

**5.** To find out what the weather will be, watch France 2 at

1   8.55                    2   12.59
3   14.50                   4   17.10

### 3b Multiple Choice (French) [10 points]

Part 3b consists of questions or incomplete statements in French, each based on a reading selection in French. Choose the expression that best answers the question or completes the statement. Base your choice on the content of the reading selection. Write the number of your answer in the space provided.

**1.** Quel film peut-on voir à dix heures et demie?

1 Aladin.
3 Le petit Bouddha.

2 Allô maman, c'est Noël.
4 Nuits blanches à Seattle.

**2.** Où vas-tu?

1 Au cinéma.
3 A un concert.

2 Au théâtre.
4 Au musée.

### ORDINATEUR ÉDUCATIF

Pour travailler sur écran comme les grands,
cet ordinateur avec sa souris utilise
la technique de la synthèse vocale.

L'enfant apprend l'orthographe,
le vocabulaire, le calcul...

*En tout, 26 activités différentes sont possibles!*

En cas d'erreur, comme un prof, une voix de
synthèse guide le petit élève, donne des
explications simples et des encouragements.

*À partir de cinq ans, 399 F*

**3.** On donne ce cadeau à un enfant qui aime

1  les sports.

2  la musique.

3  l'informatique.

4  l'art.

---

**JEUNE FEMME** sérieuse cherche
place stable, garde bébés et enfants.
Excellentes références.

Tél: 48. 22. 34. 67

---

**4.** Que cherche cette femme?

1  Un travail.

2  Un appartement.

3  Un babysitter.

4  Un ami.

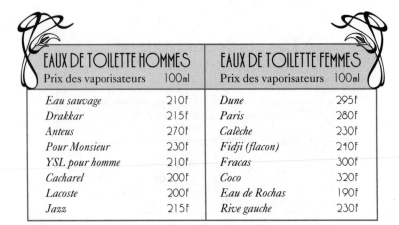

| EAUX DE TOILETTE HOMMES | | EAUX DE TOILETTE FEMMES | |
|---|---|---|---|
| Prix des vaporisateurs | 100 ml | Prix des vaporisateurs | 100 ml |
| *Eau sauvage* | 210 f | *Dune* | 295 f |
| *Drakkar* | 215 f | *Paris* | 280 f |
| *Anteus* | 270 f | *Calèche* | 230 f |
| *Pour Monsieur* | 230 f | *Fidji (flacon)* | 240 f |
| *YSL pour homme* | 210 f | *Fracas* | 300 f |
| *Cacharel* | 200 f | *Coco* | 320 f |
| *Lacoste* | 200 f | *Eau de Rochas* | 190 f |
| *Jazz* | 215 f | *Rive gauche* | 230 f |

**5.** Ce magasin vend

1  des vêtements.

2  des parfums.

3  des boissons.

4  des livres.

# 4. WRITING

## 4a Notes

Write short notes in French as directed below. Each note must consist of at least 12 words.

*1.* You were invited to a friend's party. Write him / her a note asking for information about the party.

_____

_____

_____

_____

*2.* Your friend is very shy. Write him / her a note in which you give advice on how to make friends.

_____

_____

_____

_____

*3.* Your parents are taking you on a trip. Write a note to a friend inviting him / her to go with you.

_____

_____

_____

_____

*4.* You just got a new dog. Write a note to a friend telling him / her about your pet.

_____

_____

_____

_____

**5.** You received the highest grade on your French test. Write a note to a friend explaining how you did it.

_____

_____

_____

_____

## 4b  Lists

Write lists in French as directed below. Each list must contain four items. No credit will be given for one-word items that are proper names.

**1.** Imagine that your favorite singer came to your city. Write a list of four questions you would ask him / her.

_____

_____

_____

_____

**2.** You cannot find your French text. Write a list of four places where it might be.

_____

_____

_____

_____

**3.** You are preparing breakfast for your mother to celebrate her birthday. Write a list of four things you will need to buy.

_____

_____

_____

_____

**4.** Your school is having a winter ski trip. Write a list of four reasons why your parents should let you go.

_____

_____

_____

_____

**5.** You are running for class president. Write a list of four personal qualities that make you suitable for the job.

_____

_____

_____

_____

ANGLETERRE  PAYS-BAS  BELGIQUE  ALLEMAGNE  LUXEMBOURG  AUTRICHE  FRANCE  SUISSE
Brest  Paris  Strasbourg  Nantes

## [ 1 ] VERBS WITH REGULAR FORMS

**INFINITIVE**

| parl**er** | fin**ir** | vend**re** | s'amuser |

**PAST PARTICIPLE**

| parl**é** | fin**i** | vend**u** | amusé |

**PRESENT**

| parl**e** | fin**is** | vend**s** | **m'** amuse |
| parl**es** | fin**is** | vend**s** | **t'** amuses |
| parl**e** | fin**it** | vend | **s'** amuse |
| parl**ons** | fin**issons** | vend**ons** | **nous** amusons |
| parl**ez** | fin**issez** | vend**ez** | **vous** amusez |
| parl**ent** | fin**issent** | vend**ent** | **s'** amusent |

**IMPERATIVE**

| parl**e** | fin**is** | vend**s** | amuse-**toi** |
| parl**ons** | fin**issons** | vend**ons** | amusons-**nous** |
| parl**ez** | fin**issez** | vend**ez** | amusez-**vous** |

**IMPERFECT**

| parl**ais** | finiss**ais** | vend**ais** | **m'** amusais |
| parl**ais** | finiss**ais** | vend**ais** | **t'** amusais |
| parl**ait** | finiss**ait** | vend**ait** | **s'** amusait |
| parl**ions** | finiss**ions** | vend**ions** | **nous** amusions |
| parl**iez** | finiss**iez** | vend**iez** | **vous** amusiez |
| parl**aient** | finiss**aient** | vend**aient** | **s'** amusaient |

**FUTURE**

| parler**ai** | finir**ai** | vendr**ai** | **m'** amuserai |
| parler**as** | finir**as** | vendr**as** | **t'** amuseras |
| parler**a** | finir**a** | vendr**a** | **s'** amusera |
| parler**ons** | finir**ons** | vendr**ons** | **nous** amuserons |
| parler**ez** | finir**ez** | vendr**ez** | **vous** amuserez |
| parler**ont** | finir**ont** | vendr**ont** | **s'** amuseront |

PASSÉ COMPOSÉ

| | | | |
|---|---|---|---|
| ai parlé | ai fini | ai vendu | me suis amusé(e) |
| as parlé | as fini | as vendu | t' es amusé(e) |
| a parlé | a fini | a vendu | s' est amusé(e) |
| avons parlé | avons fini | avons vendu | nous sommes amusé(e)s |
| avez parlé | avez fini | avez vendu | vous êtes amusé(e)(s) |
| ont parlé | ont fini | ont vendu | se sont amusé(e)s |

# [ 2 ] -ER VERBS WITH SPELLING CHANGES

| | -cer VERBS | -ger VERBS | -yer VERBS* | -eler / -eter VERBS | | e + CONSONANT + er VERBS | é + CONSONANT(S) + er VERBS |
|---|---|---|---|---|---|---|---|
| **INFINITIVE** | pla**cer** | man**ger** | emplo**yer** | app**eler** | j**eter** | m**e**ner | esp**é**rer |
| **PRESENT** | place | mange | **emploie** | **appelle** | **jette** | **mène** | **espère** |
| | places | manges | **emploies** | **appelles** | **jettes** | **mènes** | **espères** |
| | place | mange | **emploie** | **appelle** | **jette** | **mène** | **espère** |
| | **plaçons** | **mangeons** | employons | appelons | jetons | menons | espérons |
| | placez | mangez | employez | appelez | jetez | menez | espérez |
| | placent | mangent | **emploient** | **appellent** | **jettent** | **mènent** | **espèrent** |
| **IMPERFECT** | **plaçais** | **mangeais** | | | | | |
| | **plaçais** | **mangeais** | | | | | |
| | **plaçait** | **mangeait** | | | | | |
| | placions | mangions | | | | | |
| | placiez | mangiez | | | | | |
| | **plaçaient** | **mangeaient** | | | | | |
| **FUTURE** | | | **emploierai** | **appellerai** | **jetterai** | **mènerai** | |
| | | | **emploieras** | **appelleras** | **jetteras** | **mèneras** | |
| | | | **emploiera** | **appellera** | **jettera** | **mènera** | |
| | | | **emploierons** | **appellerons** | **jetterons** | **mènerons** | |
| | | | **emploierez** | **appellerez** | **jetterez** | **mènerez** | |
| | | | **emploieront** | **appelleront** | **jetteront** | **mèneront** | |
| **IMPERATIVE** | place | mange | **emploie** | **appelle** | **jette** | **mène** | **espère** |
| | **plaçons** | **mangeons** | employons | appelons | jetons | menons | espèrons |
| | placez | mangez | employez | appelez | jetez | menez | espérez |

*Verbs ending in –ayer, like **payer** and **balayer,** may be conjugated like **employer** or retain the y in all conjugations: je **paye** or je **paie.**

## [ 3 ] VERBS WITH IRREGULAR FORMS

NOTE:

1. Irregular forms are printed in bold type.

2. Verbs conjugated with être in compound tenses are indicated with an asterisk (*)

| INFINITIVE, PARTICIPLE | PRESENT | IMPERATIVE | IMPERFECT | FUTURE | PASSÉ COMPOSÉ |
|---|---|---|---|---|---|
| **aller*** *to go* | **vais** | va | allais | **irai** | suis allé(e) |
|  | **vas** | allons | allais | **iras** | es allé(e) |
|  | **va** | allez | allait | **ira** | est allé(e) |
| allé | allons |  | allions | **irons** | sommes allé(e)s |
|  | allez |  | alliez | **irez** | êtes allé(e)(s) |
|  | vont |  | allaient | **iront** | sont allé(e)s |

**apprendre** *to learn* (like **prendre**)

| avoir | ai | aie | avais | aurai | ai eu |
|---|---|---|---|---|---|
| *to have* | as | ayons | avais | auras | as eu |
|  | a | ayez | avait | aura | a eu |
| eu | avons |  | avions | aurons | avons eu |
|  | avez |  | aviez | aurez | avez eu |
|  | ont |  | avaient | auront | ont eu |

**comprendre** *to understand* (like **prendre**)

**découvir** *to discover* (like **ouvrir**)

**devenir*** *to become* (like **venir**)

| dire | dis | dis | disais | **dirai** | ai **dit** |
|---|---|---|---|---|---|
| *to say, tell* | dis | disons | disais | **diras** | as **dit** |
|  | **dit** | dites | disait | **dira** | a **dit** |
| **dit** | **disons** |  | disions | **dirons** | avons **dit** |
|  | **dites** |  | disiez | **direz** | avez **dit** |
|  | **disent** |  | disaient | **diront** | ont **dit** |

| **écire** | écris | écris | écrivais | écrirai | ai **écrit** |
|---|---|---|---|---|---|
| *to write* | écris | écrivons | écrivais | écriras | as **écrit** |
|  | **écrit** | écrivez | écrivait | écrira | a **écrit** |
| **écrit** | **écrivons** |  | écrivions | écrirons | avons **écrit** |
|  | **écrivez** |  | écriviez | écrirez | avez **écrit** |
|  | **écrivent** |  | écrivaient | écriront | ont **écrit** |

| INFINITIVE, PARTICIPLE | PRESENT | IMPERATIVE | IMPERFECT | FUTURE | PASSÉ COMPOSÉ |
|---|---|---|---|---|---|
| **envoyer** | **envoie** | envoie | envoyais | **enverrai** | ai envoyé |
| *to send* | **envoies** | envoyons | envoyais | **enverras** | as envoyé |
| | **envoie** | envoyez | envoyait | **enverra** | a envoyé |
| envoyé | envoyons | | envoyions | **enverrons** | avons envoyé |
| | envoyez | | envoyiez | **enverrez** | avez envoyé |
| | **envoient** | | envoyaient | **enverront** | ont envoyé |
| **être** | **suis** | **sois** | **étais** | **serai** | ai été |
| *to be* | **es** | **soyons** | **étais** | **seras** | as été |
| | **est** | **soyez** | **était** | **sera** | a été |
| été | **sommes** | | **étions** | **serons** | avons été |
| | **êtes** | | **étiez** | **serez** | avez été |
| | **sont** | | **étaient** | **seront** | ont été |
| **faire** | fais | fais | faisais | **ferai** | ai **fait** |
| *to do, make* | fais | faisons | faisais | **feras** | as **fait** |
| | **fait** | faites | faisait | **fera** | a **fait** |
| **fait** | **faisons** | | faisions | **ferons** | avons **fait** |
| | **faites** | | faisiez | **ferez** | avez **fait** |
| | **font** | | faisaient | **feront** | ont **fait** |
| **lire** | lis | lis | lisais | lirai | ai **lu** |
| *to read* | lis | lisons | lisais | liras | as **lu** |
| | **lit** | lisez | lisait | lira | a **lu** |
| **lu** | **lisons** | | lisions | lirons | avons **lu** |
| | **lisez** | | lisiez | lirez | avez **lu** |
| | **lisent** | | lisaient | liront | ont **lu** |
| **mettre** | **mets** | mets | mettais | **mettrai** | ai **mis** |
| *to put* | **mets** | mettons | mettais | **mettras** | as **mis** |
| | **met** | mettez | mettait | **mettra** | a **mis** |
| **mis** | mettons | | mettions | **mettrons** | avons **mis** |
| | mettez | | mettiez | **mettrez** | avez **mis** |
| | mettent | | mettaient | **mettront** | ont **mis** |
| **ouvrir** | **ouvre** | **ouvre** | ouvrais | ouvrirai | ai **ouvert** |
| *to open* | **ouvres** | ouvons | ouvrais | ouvriras | as **ouvert** |
| | **ouvre** | ouvrez | ouvrait | ouvrira | a **ouvert** |
| **ouvert** | **ouvrons** | | ouvrions | ouvrirons | avons **ouvert** |
| | **ouvrez** | | ouvriez | ouvrirez | avez **ouvert** |
| | **ouvrent** | | ouvraient | ouvriront | ont **ouvert** |

| INFINITIVE, PARTICIPLE | PRESENT | IMPERATIVE | IMPERFECT | FUTURE | PASSÉ COMPOSÉ |
|---|---|---|---|---|---|

**partir\*** *to leave* (like **sortir**)

**permettre** *to allow* (like **mettre**)

| INFINITIVE, PARTICIPLE | PRESENT | IMPERATIVE | IMPERFECT | FUTURE | PASSÉ COMPOSÉ |
|---|---|---|---|---|---|
| **pouvoir** *to be able* **pu** | **peux (puis)** **peux** **peut** **pouvons** **pouvez** **peuvent** | | pouvais pouvais pouvait pouvions pouviez pouvaient | **pourrai** **pourras** **pourra** pourrons pourrez pourront | ai **pu** as **pu** a **pu** avons **pu** avez **pu** ont **pu** |
| **prendre** *to take* **pris** | prends prends prend **prenons** **prenez** **prennent** | prends prenons prenez | prenais prenais prenait prenions preniez prenaient | prendrai prendras prendra prendrons prendrez prendront | ai **pris** as **pris** a **pris** avons **pris** avez **pris** ont **pris** |

**promettre** *to promise* (like **mettre**)

| INFINITIVE, PARTICIPLE | PRESENT | IMPERATIVE | IMPERFECT | FUTURE | PASSÉ COMPOSÉ |
|---|---|---|---|---|---|
| **recevoir** *to receive* **reçu** | **reçois** **reçois** **reçoit** **recevons** **recevez** **reçoivent** | reçois recevons recevez | recevais recevais recevait recevions receviez recevaient | **recevrai** **recevras** **recevra** **recevrons** **recevrez** **recevront** | ai **reçu** as **reçu** a **reçu** avons **reçu** avez **reçu** ont **reçu** |
| **savoir** *to know (how to)* **su** | **sais** **sais** **sait** **savons** **savez** **savent** | **sache** **sachons** **sachez** | savais savais savait savions saviez savaient | **saurai** **sauras** **saura** **saurons** **saurez** **sauront** | ai su as su a su avons su avez su ont su |
| **sortir\*** *to go out* **sorti** | **sors** **sors** **sort** **sortons** **sortez** **sortent** | sors sortons sortez | sortais sortais sortait sortions sortiez sortaient | sortirai sortiras sortira sortirons sortirez sortiront | suis sorti(e) es sorti(e) est sorti(e) sommes sorti(e)s êtes sorti(e)(s) sont sorti(e)s |

| INFINITIVE, PARTICIPLE | PRESENT | IMPERATIVE | IMPERFECT | FUTURE | PASSÉ COMPOSÉ |
|---|---|---|---|---|---|
| **venir*** *to come* **venu** | **viens** **viens** **vient** **venons** **venez** **viennent** | viens venons venez | venais venais venait venions veniez venaient | **viendrai** **viendras** **viendra** **viendrons** **viendrez** **viendront** | suis venu(e) es venu(e) est venu(e) sommes venu(e)s êtes venu(e)(s) sont venu(e)s |
| **voir** *to see* **vu** | vois vois voit **voyons** **voyez** **voient** | vois voyons voyez | voyais voyais voyait voyions voyiez voyaient | **verrai** **verras** **verra** **verrons** **verrez** **verront** | ai vu as vu a vu avons vu avez vu ont vu |
| **vouloir** *to want* **voulu** | **veux** **veux** **veut** voulons voulez **veulent** | **veuille** **veuillons** **veuillez** | voulais voulais voulait voulions vouliez voulaient | **voudrai** **voudras** **voudra** **voudrons** **voudrez** **voudront** | ai voulu as voulu a voulu avons voulu avez voulu ont voulu |

# [ 4 ] COMMON REFLEXIVE VERBS

**s'acheter** to buy for oneself
**s'amuser (à)** to have a good time, enjoy
**s'appeler** to be named
**se brosser** to brush oneself
**se coucher** to lie down; to go to bed
**se demander** to wonder
**se dépêcher (de)** to hurry
**se déshabiller** to undress
**s'ennuyer (à)** to get bored
**s'habiller** to dress
**se laver** to wash (oneself)

**se lever** to get up; to rise
**se maquiller** to put on makeup
**se marier avec** to get married to
**se mettre en route** to start out
**se peigner** to comb one's hair
**se préparer** to prepare oneself
**se promener** to take a walk
**se rappeler** to remember
**se raser** to shave
**se reposer** to rest
**se réveiller** to wake up

# [ 5 ] COMMON PREPOSITIONS

**a.** Simple prepositions

**à** to, at, in
**après** after
**avant** before

**avec** with
**chez** to /at, in the house (place) of (a person)
**contre** against

| | |
|---|---|
| **dans** in, into, within | **pour** for |
| **de** of, from | **sans** without |
| **depuis** since, for | **sauf** except |
| **derrière** behind | **selon** according to |
| **devant** in front of | **sous** under |
| **en** in, into, as | **sur** on |
| **entre** among, between | **vers** toward |
| **par** by, through | |

**b.** Compound prepositions

| | |
|---|---|
| **à cause de** because of, on account of | **autour de** around |
| **à côté de** next to, beside | **avant (de)** before |
| **à droite** on (to) the right | **du côté de** in the direction of, near |
| **à gauche** on (to) the left | **en face de** opposite |
| **au lieu de** instead of | **loin de** far from |
| **au milieu de** in the middle of | **près de** near |

## [ 6 ] PUNCTUATION

French punctuation, though similar to English, has the following major differences:

(a) The comma is not used before **et** or **ou** in a series.

| | |
|---|---|
| **Elle a laissé tomber le livre, le stylo et le crayon.** | *She dropped the book, the pen and the pencil.* |

(b) In numbers, French uses a comma where English uses a period and a period where English uses a comma.

| | |
|---|---|
| **7.100 (sept mille cent)** | *7,100 (seven thousand one hundred)* |
| **7,25 (sept virgule vingt-cinq)** | *7.25 (seven point two five)* |

(c) French final quotation marks, contrary to English, precede the comma or period; however, the quotation mark follows a period if the quotation mark encloses a completed statement.

| | |
|---|---|
| **Elle demande: «Est-ce que tu m'aimes?» «Oui», répond-il.** | *She asks: "Do you love me?" "Yes," he answers.* |

## [ 7 ] SYLLABICATION

French words are generally divided at the end of a line according to units of sound or syllables. A French syllable generally begins with a consonant and ends with a vowel.

(a) If a single consonant comes between two vowels, the division is made before the consonant.

ba-**la**-der   pré-**cis**   cou-**teau**

NOTE: A division cannot be made either before or after **x** or **y** when **x** or **y** come between two vowels.

**tuyau**      **exact**

**(b)** If two consonants are combined between two vowels, the division is made between the two consonants.

es-poir    al-ler    chan-ter

NOTE: If the second consonant is **r** or **l,** the division is made before the two consonants.

sa-**ble**    pro-**pre**

**(c)** If three or more consonants are combined between vowels, the division is made after the second consonant.

obs-tiné    comp-ter    ins-taller

**(d)** Two vowels may not be divided.

oa-sis    théâ-tre    es-pion

# French-English Vocabulary

The French-English vocabulary is intended to be complete for the context of this book.

Irregular plurals are given in full: **œil** *(m.)* *(pl.* **yeux***)*. Irregular feminine forms are also given in full: **beau** *(f.* **belle***)*. Regular feminine forms are indicated by showing the ending that is added to the masculine forms: **petit(e), bon(ne),** or the ending that replaces the masculine ending: **baigneur (-euse).**

An asterisk (**\***) indicates an aspirate **h: la honte, le héros.**

## ABBREVIATIONS

| *(adj.)* | adjective | *(m.)* | masculine |
| *(adv.)* | adverb | *(m./f.)* | masculine or feminine |
| *(coll.)* | colloquial | *(pl.)* | plural |
| *(inf.)* | infinitive | *(p.p.)* | past participle |
| *(f.)* | feminine | *(pron.)* | pronoun |

**à** at, to; **à bientôt** see you soon; **à cause de** because of; **à côté (de)** next (to); **à demain** see you tomorrow; **à droite (de)** to the right (of); **à gauche (de)** to the left (of); **à l'avance** in advance; **à l'heure** on time; **à partir de** from; **à peu près** about, approximately; **à pied** on foot; **à tout à l'heure** see you later; **à travers** across, through

**abord: d'abord** at first

**absence** *(f.)* absence

**absent(e)** absent

**absolument** absolutely

**absurde** absurd

**académie** *(f.)* academy

**accent** *(m.)* accent

**accepter** to accept

**accès** *(m.)* access

**accident** *(m.)* accident

**accompagner** to accompany

**accomplissement** *(m.)* accomplishment

**accusé(e)** accused

**acheter** to buy

**achever** to complete, finish

**acte** *(m.)* act

**acteur** *(m.)* actor

**actif (-ive)** active

**activement** actively

**activité** *(f.)* activity

**actrice** *(f.)* actress

**adjectif** *(m.)* adjective

**administratif (-ive)** administrative

**admiré(e)** admired

**admirer** to admire

**adolescent(e)** adolescent, teen-ager

**adorer** to adore

**adresse** *(f.)* address

**aéroport** *(m.)* airport

**affaire** *(f.)* affair; **affaires** *(f. pl.)* business; things

**affiche** *(f.)* poster

**affirmativement** affirmatively

**africain(e)** African

**Afrique** *(f.)* Africa

**âge** *(m.)* age

**âgé(e)** old

**agent de police** *(m.)* police officer

**agréable** agreeable, nice

**agricole** agricultural

**aide** *(f.)* aid, help

**aider** to help

**aimable** friendly, kind

**aimer** to like, love; **aimer mieux** to prefer

**aîné(e)** older, oldest

**air** *(m.)* air; **avoir l'air (de)** to appear, seem; **en plein air** outdoors; **prendre l'air** to get some air

**ajouter** to add

**algèbre** *(f.)* algebra

**alimentaire** food

**Allemagne** *(f.)* Germany

**allemand(e)** German

**aller** to go; **aller à la pêche** to go fishing; **aller à pied** to walk, to go on foot; **aller bien** to feel well; **aller en voiture** to go by car; **aller mal** to feel poorly

**allié(e)** allied

**allumer** to light, turn on

**alors** then, thus, so

**Alpes** *(f. pl.)* Alps

**Alsace** *(f.)* Alsace

**amaigrissant(e)** reducing

**ambitieux (-euse)** ambitious
**ambition** *(f.)* ambition
**amener** to bring; lead to
**américain(e)** American
**Amérique** *(f.)* America
**ami(e)** friend; **petit ami** boyfriend; **petite amie** girlfriend
**amitié** *(f.)* friendship
**amour** *(m.)* love
**amoureux (-euse)** in love; **tomber amoureux** to fall in love
**amusant(e)** fun, amusing
**amusement** *(m.)* fun
**amuser** to amuse; **s'amuser** to have a good time, to have fun
**an** *(m.)* year; **avoir... ans** to be ... years old
**ancien(ne)** old, ancient, former
**âne** *(m.)* donkey
**anecdote** *(f.)* anecdote, story
**anglais(e)** English
**Angleterre** *(f.)* England
**animal** *(m.) (pl. -aux)* animal
**animé(e)** animated
**année** *(f.)* year
**anniversaire** *(m.)* birthday; **bon anniversaire** happy birthday
**annonce** *(f.)* advertisement; announcement; **annonce publicitaire** advertisement; **petite annonce** classified ad
**annoncer** to announce
**annuaire** *(m.)* phone book
**anxieux (-euse)** anxious
**août** *(m.)* August
**appareil-photo** *(m.)* camera
**appartement** *(m.)* apartment
**appel** *(m.)* call
**appeler** to call; **s'appeler** to be named, call oneself
**applaudir** to applaud
**appliquer** to apply; **s'appliquer** to apply oneself

**apporter** to bring
**apprécier** to appreciate
**apprendre** *(p.p.* **appris***)* to learn; **apprendre (à)** to learn; to teach
**approprié(e)** appropriate
**après** after, afterward; **après tout** after all; **d'après** based upon
**après-midi** *(m.)* afternoon
**arbre** *(m.)* tree
**architecte** *(m. / f.)* architect
**argent** *(m.)* money; silver
**armée** *(f.)* army
**armoire** *(f.)* wardrobe
**arranger** to arrange
**arrêt** *(m.)* stop
**arrêter** to stop; to arrest; **s'arrêter (de)** to stop
**arriver** to arrive, to come; to happen
**arrondissement** *(m.)* administrative district
**artichaut** *(m.)* artichoke
**article** *(m.)* article; **articles de sport** *(m. pl.)* sporting goods
**artiste** *(m. / f.)* artist
**ascenseur** *(m.)* elevator
**asiatique** Asian
**Asie** *(f.)* Asia
**asperge** *(f.)* asparagus
**aspirateur** *(m.)* vacuum cleaner; **passer l'aspirateur** to vacuum
**assemblée** *(f.)* assembly
**assez** enough; rather; **assez (de)** enough (of)
**assiette** *(f.)* plate
**assis(e)** seated
**assister (à)** to assist; to attend
**astronaute** *(m. / f.)* astronaut
**astronomique** astronomical
**athlète** *(m. / f.)* athlete
**atmosphère** *(f.)* atmosphere
**attaché(e)** attached
**attaquer** to attack
**attendre** to wait (for)

**attentif (-ive)** attentive
**attention** *(f.)* attention; **faire attention (à)** to pay attention (to)
**attentivement** attentively
**attraction** *(f.)* attraction; **parc d'attractions** amusement park
**au** *(pl.* **aux***)* at the, to the; **au bas de** at the bottom of; **au contraire** on the contrary; **au fond (de)** in/at the bottom (of); **au haut (de)** in/at the top (of); **au lieu de** instead of; **au milieu de** in the middle of; **au moins** at least; **au rabais** at a discount; **au revoir** goodbye
**aujourd'hui** today
**aussi** also, too; as
**auteur** *(m.)* author
**auto** *(f.)* car; **en auto** by car
**autobus** *(m.)* bus
**automne** *(m.)* fall, autumn
**autoriser** to authorize
**autorité** *(f.)* authority
**autour (de)** around
**autre** other; another
**autrefois** formerly
**Autriche** *(f.)* Austria
**avance** *(f.)* advance; **à l'avance** in advance
**avancer** to advance
**avant (de)** before
**avant-hier** the day before yesterday
**avec** with
**aventure** *(f.)* adventure
**avenue** *(f.)* avenue
**aveugle** blind
**avion** *(m.)* airplane; en avion by airplane
**avocat(e)** lawyer
**avoir** to have *(pp.* **eu***)*; **avoir... ans** to be ... years old; **avoir besoin (de)** to need;

**avoir chaud** to be hot *(of persons)*; **avoir envie de** to desire, want, feel like; **avoir faim** to be hungry; **avoir froid** to be cold *(of persons)*; **avoir honte (de)** to be ashamed (of); **avoir l'air (de)** to appear, seem; **avoir l'habitude de** to be accustomed to, to be in the habit of; **avoir (de) la chance** to be lucky; **avoir le temps (de)** to have the time (to); **avoir mal à** to have an ache in; **avoir peur (de)** to be afraid (of); **avoir raison** to be right; **avoir soif** to be thirsty; **avoir sommeil** to be sleepy; **avoir tort** to be wrong

**avril** *(m.)* April

**bac, baccalauréat** *(m.)* baccalaureate examination / degree

**bagages** *(m. pl.)* luggage

**baguette** *(f.)* long French bread

**baigner** to bathe

**bain** *(m.)* bath; **maillot de bain** *(m.)* bathing suit; **salle de bains** *(f.)* bathroom

**bal** *(m.)* dance

**baladeur** *(m.)* portable cassette player, Walkman

**balcon** *(m.)* balcony

**balle** *(f.)* ball

**ballet** *(m.)* ballet

**ballon** *(m.)* balloon; ball

**banane** *(f.)* banana

**banc** *(m.)* seat, bench

**bande** *(f.)* band, strip; **bande dessinée** comic strip, comic book

**banque** *(f.)* bank

**bas(se)** low; **en bas** downstairs; **en bas (de)** at the bottom (of)

**bas** *(m.)* stocking

**base-ball** *(m.)* baseball

**basé (e)** based

**basket** *(f.)* basketball sneaker

**basket** *(m.)* basketball

**bateau** *(m.)* *(pl. -x)* boat

**bâtiment** *(m.)* building

**bâtir** to build

**bâton** *(m.)* stick, pole; **bâton de craie** stick of chalk

**bavarder** to chat

**beau, bel** *(f. belle; m. pl. beaux)* beautiful, handsome; **faire beau** to be beautiful *(weather)*; **à la belle étoile** outdoors

**beaucoup (de)** a lot (of), many, much

**beauté** *(f.)* beauty

**bébé** *(m.)* baby

**belge** Belgian

**Belgique** *(f.)* Belgium

**besoin** *(m.)* need; **avoir besoin de** to need

**beurre** *(m.)* butter

**bibliothécaire** *(m. /f.)* librarian

**bibliothèque** *(f.)* library

**bicyclette** *(f.)* bicycle; **monter à bicyclette** to go bicycle riding

**bien** well; **aller bien** to feel well; **bien sûr** of course

**bientôt** soon; **à bientôt** see you soon

**bifteck** *(m.)* steak

**bijou** *(m.)* (pl. **-x**) jewel

**billet** *(m.)* bill; ticket

**biologie** *(f.)* biology

**biscuit** *(m.)* cookie

**bise** *(f.)* *(coll.)* kiss; **(grosses) bises** lots of love *(in a letter)*

**blâmer** to blame

**blanc** *(m.)* egg white

**blanc(he)** white

**bleu(e)** blue

**blouse** *(f.)* blouse

**bœuf** *(m.)* beef

**boire** *(p.p.* **bu***)* to drink

**bois** *(m.)* wood

**boisson** *(f.)* drink

**boîte** *(f.)* box, can; **boîte aux lettres** mailbox; **boîte de conserves** can

**bol** *(m.)* bowl

**bon(ne)** good; **bon anniversaire** happy birthday; **bon marché** inexpensive; **bonne année** happy new year; **bonne chance** good luck; **de bonne heure** early

**bonbon** *(m.)* candy

**bonheur** *(m.)* happiness

**bonhomme** *(m.)* chap; **bonhomme de neige** snowman

**bonjour** hello

**bord** *(m.)* edge; **au bord de la mer** at/to the seashore

**botte** *(f.)* boot

**bouche** *(f.)* mouth

**boucher (-ère)** butcher

**boucherie** *(f.)* butcher shop

**bouger** to move

**bouillabaisse** *(f.)* fish stew

**boulanger (-ère)** baker

**boulangerie** *(f.)* bakery

**boule** *(f.)* ball; **boule de neige** snowball

**boulevard** *(m.)* boulevard

**boum** *(f.)* party

**Bourgogne** *(f.)* Burgundy

**bourse** *(f.)* scholarship

**bouteille** *(f.)* bottle

**boutique** *(f.)* boutique, store

**bowling** *(m.)* bowling

**bracelet** *(m.)* bracelet

**bras** *(m.)* arm

**brave** brave

**Brésil** *(m.)* Brazil

**Bretagne** *(f.)* Brittany

**brillant(e)** brilliant

**brioche** *(f.)* sweet roll
**brochure** *(f.)* brochure, booklet
**brosse** *(f.)* brush; **brosse à dents** toothbrush
**brosser** to brush; **se brosser** to brush one's hair
**bruit** *(m.)* noise
**brun(e)** brown, brunette
**brusque** brusque
**brusquement** brusquely
**bureau** *(m.)* *(pl. -x)* desk; office; **bureau de poste** post office
**bus** *(m.)* bus

**ça** that; **ça ne fait rien** it doesn't matter
**cabine** *(f.)* phone booth
**cadeau** *(m.)* *(pl. -x)* gift, present
**cadet(te)** younger
**cadre** *(m.)* setting; frame
**café** *(m.)* coffee; café
**cahier** *(m.)* notebook
**caissier (-ière)** cashier
**calculette** *(f.)* calculator
**calendrier** *(m.)* calendar
**calme** calm
**camarade** *(m./f.)* comrade, friend
**Cambodge** *(m.)* Cambodia
**campagne** *(f.)* country
**camper** to camp
**camping: faire du camping** to go camping
**Canada** *(m.)* Canada
**canadien(ne)** Canadian
**canapé** *(m.)* sofa
**cantine** *(f.)* cafeteria
**capitale** *(f.)* capital
**car** because
**car** *(m.)* tour bus
**caractère** *(m.)* character; **caractères gras** boldface
**Caraïbe** Caribbean
**cardinal** *(m.)* cardinal
**carnaval** *(m.)* carnival

**carotte** *(f.)* carrot
**carrefour** *(m.)* intersection
**cartable** *(m.)* school bag
**carte** *(f.)* card; map; **carte d'identité** identification card; **carte de crédit** credit card; **carte postale** postcard
**carton** *(m.)* carton
**cas** *(m.)* case; **en cas de** in case of
**case** *(f.)* box
**casquette** *(f.)* cap
**casser** to break
**casserole** *(f.)* saucepan
**cassette** *(f.)* cassette
**cathédrale** *(f.)* cathedral
**cause** *(f.)* cause; **à cause de** because of
**ce** it, he, she, they; **ce que** that which, what
**ce, cet** *(f. cette)* this, that
**céder** to yield
**cela** that
**célèbre** famous
**célébrer** to celebrate
**celtique** Celtic
**cent** one hundred
**centimètre** *(m.)* centimeter
**centraliser** to centralize
**centre** *(m.)* center; **centre commercial** shopping mall
**cercle** *(m.)* club
**céréales** *(f. pl.)* cereal
**cerise** *(f.)* cherry
**certain (e)** certain, sure
**certainement** certainly, surely
**ces** these, those
**cesser** to stop
**chacun(e)** each one
**chaîne: chaîne stéréo** *(f.)* stereo; **chaîne de montagnes** mountain range
**chaise** *(f.)* chair
**chalet** *(m.)* chalet
**chambre (à coucher)** *(f.)* bedroom
**champ** *(m.)* field

**championnat** *(m.)* championship
**chance** *(f.)* luck; **avoir (de) la chance** to be lucky; **bonne chance** good luck
**changer (de)** to change
**chanson** *(f.)* song
**chanter** to sing
**chanteur (-euse)** singer
**chapeau** *(m.)* *(pl. -x)* hat
**chapiteau** *(m.)* *(pl. -x)* circus tent
**chapitre** *(m.)* chapter
**chaque** each
**charcuterie** *(f.)* delicatessen
**charmant(e)** charming
**charme** *(m.)* charm
**chat(te)** cat
**châtain(e)** light brown (hair)
**château** *(m.)* *(pl. -x)* castle
**chaud(e)** warm, hot; **avoir chaud** to be hot *(of persons)*; **faire chaud** to be warm/hot *(weather)*
**chauffage** *(m.)* heating; **chauffage air pulsé** forced-air heating
**chauffer** to heat, warm
**chaussette** *(f.)* sock
**chaussure** *(f.)* shoe
**chef** *(m.)* chef, cook; chief, head
**chemin** *(m.)* road; **chemin de fer** *(m.)* railroad
**cheminée** *(f.)* fireplace
**chemise** *(f.)* shirt
**chemisier** *(m.)* woman's shirt
**chèque** *(m.)* check; **chèque de voyage** traveler's check
**cher (-ère)** dear; expensive
**chercher** to look for, search
**cheval** *(m.)* *(pl. -aux)* horse
**cheveu** *(m.)* *(pl. -x)* hair *(one strand)*
**chez** to/at the house/place of
**chic** stylish, fashionable
**chien(ne)** dog

**chiffre** *(m.)* number
**chimie** *(f.)* chemistry
**chimique** chemical
**chinois(e)** Chinese
**chip** *(m.)* chip
**chocolat** *(m.)* chocolate; hot chocolate; **mousse au chocolat** *(f.)* chocolate mousse
**choisir** to choose
**choix** *(m.)* choice
**chose** *(f.)* thing
**ci-dessous** below
**cidre** *(m.)* cider
**ciel** *(m.)* heaven, sky
**ciné-club** *(m.)* film club
**cinéma** *(m.)* movies; movie theater
**cinq** five
**cinquante** fifty
**cinquième** fifth
**circonstance** *(f.)* circumstance
**cirque** *(m.)* circus
**ciseaux** *(m. pl.)* scissors
**citoyen(ne)** citizen
**citron** *(m.)* lemon
**citronnade** *(f.)* lemonade
**clairement** clearly
**classe** *(f.)* class; **classe de neige** ski class; **salle de classe** *(f.)* classroom
**classeur** *(m.)* looseleaf notebook
**classique** classical
**clef** *(f.)* key
**client(e)** client, customer
**climat** *(m.)* climate
**cloche** *(f.)* bell
**clown** *(m.)* clown; **faire le clown** to clown around
**club** *(m.)* club; golf club; **ciné-club** film club
**cocher** to check
**cochon** *(m.)* pig
**code postal** *(m.)* zip code
**cœur** *(m.)* heart
**coiffe** *(f.)* headdress

**coiffer** to do the hair of
**coiffeur (-euse)** hairdresser
**coin** *(m.)* corner
**collectionner** to collect
**collège** *(m.)* secondary school
**coller** to paste
**collier** *(m.)* necklace
**colline** *(f.)* hill
**colonie** *(f.)* colony; **colonie de vacances** camp
**colonne** *(f.)* column
**combien (de)** how many, how much
**comédie** *(f.)* comedy
**comique** comical, funny
**commande** *(f.)* order
**commander** to order
**comme** as, like
**commencement** *(m.)* beginning
**commencer** to begin
**comment** how
**commerçant(e)** merchant
**commercial(e)** commercial; **centre commercial** *(m.)* (shopping) mall
**communauté** *(f.)* community
**compact** *(m.)* compact disc
**compact(e): disque compact** *(m.)* compact disc
**compagnie** *(f.)* company
**comparer** to compare
**complet (-ète)** complete
**compléter** to complete
**composer** to compose
**composition** *(f.)* composition
**comprendre** *(p.p.* **compris)** to understand
**compter** to count; to intend
**concert** *(m.)* concert
**concierge** *(m. /f.)* concierge, superintendent
**conducteur (-trice)** driver
**conduire** *(p.p.* **conduit)** to drive; **permis de conduire** *(m.)* driver's license

**confiture** *(f.)* jelly, jam
**confortable** comfortable
**congé** *(m.)* time off; **jour de congé** day off
**congélateur** *(m.)* freezer
**connaissance** *(f.)* acquaintance, knowledge; **faire la connaissance (de)** to make the acquaintance (of)
**connaître** *(p.p.* **connu)** to know, to be acquainted with
**connu(e)** known
**conquête** *(f.)* conquest
**conscience** *(f.)* conscience
**consciencieusement** conscientiously
**consciencieux (-euse)** conscientious
**conseil** *(m.)* advice; council
**conseiller** to advise
**conséquent: par conséquent** consequently
**conserves** *(f. pl.)* preserves; **boîte de conserve** can
**constitution** *(f.)* constitution
**construire** *(p.p.* **construit)** to construct, build
**consulter** to consult
**contacter** to contact
**contagieux (-euse)** contagious
**contemporain(e)** contemporary, modern
**content(e)** content, happy, glad
**continent** *(m.)* continent
**continuellement** continuously
**continuer** to continue
**contraire** *(m.)* opposite; **au contraire** on the contrary
**contre** against
**contribuer** to contribute
**convenir** to fit
**conversation** *(f.)* conversation
**copain** *(f.* **copine)** friend, pal
**copier** to copy
**corbeille** *(f.)* basket; **corbeille à papier** wastebasket

**corde** *(f.)* cord, rope; **sauter à la corde** to jump rope
**cornet** *(m.)* cone
**corps** *(m.)* body
**correct(e)** correct
**correctement** correctly
**correspondant(e)** pen pal
**correspondre** to correspond, exchange letters
**corriger** to correct
**costume** *(m.)* costume; suit
**côte** *(f.)* coast
**côté** *(m.)* side; **à côté (de)** next (to); **de côté** aside; **de l'autre côté** on the other side
**cou** *(m.)* neck
**coucher** *(m.)* setting; **coucher de soleil** sunset
**coucher** to put to bed; **se coucher** to go to bed
**coude** *(m.)* elbow
**couleur** *(f.)* color
**couloir** *(m.)* hallway
**coup** *(m.)* blow; **coup d'œil** glance; **coup de téléphone** telephone call; **coup de tonnerre** thunder clap
**couper** to cut
**cour** *(f.)* courtyard
**courage** *(m.)* courage
**courageux (-euse)** courageous
**courant** *(m.)* current
**courir** *(p.p.* **couru)** to run
**courrier** *(m.)* mail
**cours** *(m.)* course, subject
**course** *(f.)* errand; race; **faire des courses** to go shopping
**court(e)** short
**cousin(e)** cousin
**couteau** *(m.) (pl.* **-x)** knife
**coûter** to cost; **coûter cher** to be expensive
**couvert(e)** covered; **piscine couverte** indoor pool
**couvert** *(m.)* cover; **mettre le couvert** to set the table

**couverture** *(f.)* cover
**couvrir** *(p.p.* **couvert)** to couver; **se couvrir** to cover oneself
**craie** *(f.)* chalk; **bâton de craie** *(m.)* stick of chalk
**craquer** to crack
**cravate** *(f.)* tie
**crayon** *(m.)* pencil
**créer** to create
**crème** *(f.)* cream; **crème caramel** *(f.)* caramel custard dessert; **crème solaire** sun-tan lotion
**crémerie** *(f.)* dairy store
**crêpe** *(f.)* crêpe, pancake
**crier** to shout
**criminel(le)** criminal
**critique** *(m./f.)* critic; *(f.)* review
**critiquer** to criticize
**croire** to believe
**croisière** *(f.)* cruise
**croissant** *(m.)* crescent roll
**croix** *(f.)* cross
**cruel(le)** cruel
**cruellement** cruelly
**cueillir** to pick *(flowers)*
**cuiller** *(f.)* spoon
**cuir** *(m.)* leather
**cuisine** *(f.)* kitchen; cooking; **faire la cuisine** to cook
**cuisiner** to cook
**cuisinier (-ière)** cook
**cuisinière** *(f.)* stove
**culture** *(f.)* culture
**curieux (-euse)** curious
**cyclisme** *(m.)* cycling

**d'abord** first, at first
**d'accord** okay; **d'accord?** all right?
**dame** *(f.)* lady
**Danemark** *(m.)* Denmark
**dangereux (-euse)** dangerous
**dans** in, into, within

**danse** *(f.)* dance
**danser** to dance
**date** *(f.)* date; **date limite** deadline
**dater** to date
**davantage** more
**de** of, about, from; **d'abord** at first; **d'après** based upon; **de bonne heure** early; **de côté** aside; **de l'autre côté** on the other side; **de long en large** back and forth; **de nouveau** again; **de rien** you're welcome; **de temps en temps** from time to time
**débarrasser** to clear
**débat** *(m.)* debate
**debout** standing; upright
**décembre** *(m.)* December
**décentraliser** to decentralize
**décider** to decide
**déclaration** *(f.)* declaration
**déclarer** to declare
**décoiffé(e)** with mussed hair
**décorateur (-trice)** decorator
**décoration** *(f.)* decoration
**décorer** to decorate
**découvrir** *(p.p.* **découvert)** to discover
**décrire** *(p.p.* **décrit)** to describe
**dedans** inside
**défendre** to defend; to forbid
**défi** *(m.)* challenge
**degré** *(m.)* degree
**dehors** outside
**déjà** already
**déjeuner** *(m.)* lunch; **petit déjeuner** breakfast
**déjeuner** to have lunch
**délicieux (-euse)** delicious
**demain** tomorrow; **à demain** see you tomorrow
**demande** *(f.)* application
**demander** to ask (for)
**déménager** to move *(to another residence)*

**demeurer** to live, stay
**demi(e)** half
**demi-heure** *(f.)* half hour
**dent** *(f.)* tooth; **brosse à dents**
   *(f.)* toothbrush
**dentiste** *(m./f.)* dentist
**département** *(m.)* department
**dépêcher** to dispatch; **se**
   **dépêcher** to hurry
**dépenser** to spend *(money)*
**depuis** for, since
**dérangement** *(m.)* trouble
**déranger** to bother, disturb
**dernier (-ière)** last
**derrière** behind
**des** some; of the; from the;
   about the
**désastre** *(m.)* disaster
**descendre** to go down; to take
   down
**désert** *(m.)* desert
**déshabiller** to undress; **se**
   **déshabiller** to get undressed
**désirer** to desire, want
**désobéir (à)** to disobey
**dessert** *(m.)* dessert
**dessin** *(m.)* drawing, design;
   **dessin animé** cartoon
**dessiné(e)** drawn, designed;
   **bande dessinée** *(f.)* comic
   strip, comic book
**dessiner** to draw
**destination** *(f.)* destination
**détail** *(m.)* detail
**détester** to hate
**deux** two
**deuxième** second
**devant** in front (of)
**développement** *(m.)* development
**devenir** *(p.p.* **devenu)** to
   become
**devise** *(f.)* motto
**devoirs** *(m. pl.)* homework
**d'habitude** usually
**dialecte** *(m.)* dialect

**dialogue** *(m.)* dialogue
**dictionnaire** *(m.)* dictionary
**différent(e)** different
**difficile** difficult
**diligent(e)** hardworking
**dimanche** *(m.)* Sunday
**dîner** *(m.)* dinner
**dîner** to dine, have dinner
**dire** *(p.p.* **dit)** to say, tell
**directeur** *(f.* **directrice)** direc-
   tor, principal
**diriger** to direct
**discothèque** *(f.) (coll.* **disco)**
   discotheque
**discuter** *(de)* to discuss
**dispute** *(f.)* quarrel
**disque** *(m.)* record; **disque**
   **compact** compact disc, CD;
   **disque vidéo** laser disc
**dissolution** *(f.)* dissolution
**distance** *(f.)* distance
**distribution** *(f.)* distribution;
   **distribution des prix** award
   ceremony
**divan** *(m.)* sofa
**divers(e)** diverse, different
**divisé(e) (par)** divided (by)
**diviser** to divide
**dix** ten
**dix-huit** eighteen
**dix-neuf** nineteen
**dix-sept** seventeen
**docteur** *(m.)* doctor
**document** *(m.)* document
**documentaire** *(m.)* documentary
**doigt** *(m.)* finger
**dollar** *(m.)* dollar
**donc** therefore
**donné(e)** given
**donner** to give
**dormir** to sleep
**dortoir** *(m.)* dormitory
**dos** *(m.)* back; **sac à dos** *(m.)*
   backpack
**d'où** from where
**doucement** softly, gently

**douche** *(f.)* shower
**doute** *(m.)* doubt; **sans doute**
   no doubt
**doux** *(f.* **douce)** sweet, mild,
   gentle
**douzaine** *(f.)* dozen
**douze** twelve
**drame** *(m.)* drama
**drapeau** *(m.) (pl.* **-x)** flag
**droit** *(m.)* right
**droit(e)** right; **tout droit**
   straight ahead
**drôle** funny; strange
**du** some, any; of the
**dur(e)** hard
**durer** to last
**dynamique** dynamic

**eau** *(f.)* water; **eau minérale**
   mineral water
**écharpe** *(f.)* scarf
**échecs** *(m. pl.)* chess
**échelle** *(f.)* ladder, scale
**éclairer** to light
**école** *(f.)* school; **faire l'école**
   **buissonnière** to cut classes
**Écosse** *(f.)* Scotland
**écouter** to listen (to)
**écran** *(m.)* screen
**écrire** *(p.p.* **écrit)** to write;
   **machine à écrire** *(f.)* typewriter
**écriture** *(f.)* writing
**écrivain** *(m.)* writer
**édifice** *(m.)* building
**édit** *(m.)* edict
**éditeur** *(f.* **éditrice)** editor
**éditorial** *(m.)* editorial
**éducatif (-ive)** educational
**éducation physique** *(f.)* gym
**effacer** to erase
**égal(e)** *(m. pl.* **-aux)** equal
**égalité** *(f.)* equality
**église** *(f.)* church
**égoïste** selfish
**électricien(ne)** electrician

**électrique** electric
**élégant(e)** elegant
**élément** *(m.)* element
**éléphant** *(m.)* elephant
**élève** *(m./f.)* student
**élever** to bring up, raise
**élire** *(p.p.* **élu)** to elect
**elle** she, it, her
**elles** they, them
**embarrassé(e)** embarrassed
**embouchure** *(f.)* mouth *(river)*
**embrasser** to kiss
**émission** *(f.)* program
**emmener** to take away, lead away
**empêcher (de)** to prevent (from)
**empereur** *(m.)* emperor
**empire** *(m.)* empire
**emploi** *(m.)* job; **emploi du temps** schedule, program
**employé(e)** employee
**employer** to use
**emprunter (à)** to borrow (from)
**en** in; to; **en auto** by car; **en avion** by plane; **en bas** downstairs, **en bas (de)** at the bottom (of); **en cas de** in case of; **en face (de)** opposite; **en haut** upstairs; **en place** in place; **en retard** late; **en train de** in the middle of; **en ville** downtown
**en** about it/them, from it/them, of it/them; from there
**encore** still, yet, again
**encouragement** *(m.)* encouragement
**encourager** to encourage
**encre** *(f.)* ink
**endroit** *(m.)* place
**énergie** *(f.)* energy
**enfant** *(m./f.)* child
**enfin** at last, finally
**enlever** to remove, take off

**ennemi(e)** enemy
**ennui** *(m.)* boredom, problem
**ennuyer** to bore; to bother; **s'ennuyer** to become bored
**ennuyeux (-euse)** annoying, boring
**énorme** enormous
**énormément** enormously, a great deal
**enseigner** to teach
**ensemble** together
**ensuite** then
**entendre** to hear
**enterré(e)** buried
**enthousiasme** *(m.)* enthusiasm
**entier (-ière)** entire, whole
**entraîneur** *(m.)* coach
**entre** between, among
**entrée** *(f.)* entrance
**entrer** to enter, go in
**enveloppe** *(f.)* envelope
**envie** *(f.)* desire, want; **avoir envie (de)** to desire, want; to feel like
**environnement** *(m.)* environment
**envoyer** to send
**épaule** *(f.)* shoulder
**épeler** to spell
**épicerie** *(f.)* grocery store
**épicier (-ière)** grocer
**époque** *(f.)* age, era
**épouser** to marry
**équipe** *(f.)* team
**équipement** *(m.)* equipment
**erreur** *(f.)* error, mistake
**escalier** *(m.)* staircase
**escargot** *(m.)* snail
**espace** *(m.)* space
**Espagne** *(f.)* Spain
**espagnol(e)** Spanish
**espérer** to hope
**esprit** *(m.)* spirit, mind
**essai** *(m.)* essay
**essayer (de)** to try (to)
**essence** *(f.)* gasoline

**essuyer** to wipe
**est** *(m.)* east
**estimer** to hold in esteem
**estomac** *(m.)* stomach
**et** and, plus
**étage** *(m.)* floor, story
**état** *(m.)* state
**États-Unis** *(m. pl.)* United States
**été** *(m.)* summer; **en été** in the summer
**étoile** *(f.)* star; **à la belle étoile** outdoors
**étrange** strange
**étranger (-ère)** foreign
**étranger (-ère)** foreigner; **à l'étranger** abroad
**être** *(p.p.* **été)** to be; **être à** to belong to; **être en train de** to be in the process of (doing something)
**étude** *(f.)* study
**étudiant(e)** student
**étudier** to study
**européen(ne)** European
**eux** they, them
**événement** *(m.)* event
**examen** *(m.)* test
**excellent** excellent
**excitation** *(f.)* excitement
**exemple** *(m.)* example; **par exemple** for example
**exercice** *(m.)* exercise
**expérience** *(f.)* experience, experiment
**expert(e)** expert
**explication** *(f.)* explanation
**expliquer** to explain
**exploration** *(f.)* exploration
**explorer** to explore
**expression** *(f.)* expression
**exprimer** to express
**extraordinaire** extraordinary

**fable** *(f.)* fable
**fabriquer** to manufacture
**fâché(e)** angry

**facile** easy
**facilement** easily
**façon** *(f.)* fashion, way, manner;
  **de cette façon** this way
**facteur (-trice)** mail carrier
**faible** weak
**faim** *(f.)* hunger; **avoir faim**
  to be hungry
**faire** *(p.p.* **fait)** to make, do;
  **faire attention (à)** to pay
  attention (to); **faire beau** to
  be beautiful *(weather)*; **faire**
  **chaud** to be warm/hot
  *(weather)*; **faire des courses**
  to go shopping; **faire de son**
  **mieux** to do one's best; **faire**
  **du camping** to go camping;
  **faire du karaté** to do karate;
  **faire du patin à glace** to go
  ice skating; **faire du soleil**
  to be sunny; **faire du sport**
  to play sports; **faire du surf**
  to go surfing; **faire du vent**
  to be windy; **faire fortune**
  to make a fortune; **faire**
  **frais** to be cool *(weather)*;
  **faire froid** to be cold
  *(weather)*; **faire (la) connais-**
  **sance (de)** to make the
  acquaintance (of); **faire la**
  **cuisine** to cook; **faire la**
  **vaisselle** to do the dishes;
  **faire le lit** to make the bed;
  **faire le ménage** to do the
  housework; **faire mauvais**
  to be bad *(weather)*; **faire**
  **partie de** to belong to; **faire**
  **plaisir (à)** to please; **faire**
  **une promenade** to go for
  a walk; **faire un voyage** to
  take a trip
**famille** *(f.)* family; **en famille**
  with the family
**fanfare** *(f.)* band
**fatigué(e)** tired
**faute** *(f.)* mistake

**fauteuil** *(m.)* armchair
**faux (fausse)** false
**favori(te)** favorite
**félicitations** *(f.)* congratulations
**femme** *(f.)* woman, wife;
  **femme de ménage** cleaning
  woman
**fenêtre** *(f.)* window
**férié(e): jour férié** legal holiday
**ferme** *(f.)* farm
**fermer** to close
**fermier (-ière)** farmer
**fête** *(f.)* feast, holiday, party
**feu** *(m.)* fire; **feu d'artifice**
  fireworks
**feuille** *(f.)* leaf
**février** *(m.)* February
**fidèle** faithful
**fier (fière)** proud
**fièrement** proudly
**fièvre** *(f.)* fever
**figure** *(f.)* face
**fille** *(f.)* daughter, girl
**film** *(m.)* movie; **film vidéo**
  video tape
**fils** *(m.)* son; **petit-fils** *(m.)*
  grandson
**fin** *(f.)* end
**finalement** finally
**finir** to finish
**fixe** fixed
**fixé(e)** attached
**Flandre** *(f.)* Flanders
**fleur** *(f.)* flower
**fleuve** *(m.)* river
**flic** *(m.)* cop
**Floride** *(f.)* Florida
**foie gras** *(m.)* goose liver
**fois** *(f.)* time *(in a series)*; **trois**
  **fois** three times; **trois fois**
  **quatre** four times three
**fond** *(m.)* bottom; **au fond**
  **(de)** at the bottom (of)
**fondateur (-trice)** founder
**fonder** to found
**font** equals; *see* **faire**

**football** *(m.) (coll.* **foot)** soccer;
  **football américain** football
**force** *(f.)* strength; force
**forêt** *(f.)* forest
**forme** *(f.)* form
**former** to form
**formidable** great
**formulaire** *(m.)* form
**fort(e)** strong; loud *(voice)*
**fortune** *(f.)* fortune; **faire for-**
  **tune** to make a fortune
**fouetter** to whip
**four** *(m.)* oven
**fourchette** *(f.)* fork
**frais (fraîche)** fresh, cool; **faire**
  **frais** to be cool weather
**fraise** *(f.)* strawberry
**franc** *(m.)* franc
**franc(he)** frank
**français(e)** French
**France** *(f.)* France
**franchement** frankly
**frapper** to knock
**fraternité** *(f.)* fraternity, broth-
  erhood
**frère** *(m.)* brother
**frites** *(f. pl.)* french fries
**froid** *(m.)* cold; **avoir froid** to
  be cold *(of persons)*
**froid(e)** cold; **faire froid** to be
  cold *(weather)*
**fromage** *(m.)* cheese
**frontière** *(f.)* border; frontier
**fruit** *(m.)* fruit; **fruits de mer**
  *(m. pl.)* seafood
**fruiterie** *(f.)* fruit store
**furieux (-euse)** furious
**furieusement** furiously
**fusée** *(f.)* rocket

**gagner** to win; to earn
**gant** *(m.)* glove
**garage** *(m.)* garage
**garçon** *(m.)* boy; waiter
**gardé(e)** guarded
**garder** to keep; to take care of

**gare** *(f.)* train station
**gâteau** *(m.)* *(pl.* **-x**) cake; **gâteau au chocolat** chocolate cake
**gâter** to spoil
**gauche** left
**gaz** *(m.)* gas
**geler** to freeze
**général(e)** *(m. pl.* **-aux**) general
**généralement** generally
**généreux (-euse)** generous
**genre** *(m.)* type
**gens** *(m. pl.)* people
**gentil(le)** kind, nice
**gentillesse** *(f.)* kindness
**gentiment** gently
**géographie** *(f.)* geography
**geste** *(m.)* gesture
**glace** *(f.)* ice; ice cream; mirror
**gloire** *(f.)* glory
**golf** *(m.)* golf
**gomme** *(f.)* eraser
**gorge** *(f.)* throat
**gosse** *(m.)* youngster, kid
**gothique** gothic
**goûter** *(m.)* snack
**goûter** to taste
**gouvernement** *(m.)* government
**gracieux (-euse)** graceful
**gradin** *(m.)* bleachers
**grammaire** *(f.)* grammar
**gramme** *(m.)* gram
**grand** *(m.)* older (one); grown-up
**grand(e)** large, big; tall
**grandir** to grow
**grand-mère** *(f.)* grandmother
**grand-parent** *(m.)* grandparent
**grand-père** *(m.)* grandfather
**grec (grecque)** Greek
**Grèce** *(f.)* Greece
**grenier** *(m.)* attic
**grippe** *(f.)* flu
**gris(e)** gray
**gronder** to scold
**gros(se)** big; fat; **grosses bises** lots of love
**grossir** to become fat
**groupe** *(m.)* group
**guérir** to cure
**guerre** *(f.)* war
**guichet** *(m.)* ticket window
**guide** *(m.)* guide
**guillotiner** to guillotine
**guitare** *(f.)* guitar
**gymnase** *(m.)* gymnasium
**gymnastique** *(f.)* gym, gymnastics

**habiller** to dress; **s'habiller** to get dressed
**habitant(e)** inhabitant
**habiter** to live (in)
**habits** *(m. pl.)* clothes
**habitude** *(f.)* habit; **avoir l'habitude de** to be accustomed to, to be in the habit of; **d'habitude** usually
**Haïti** *(f.)* Haiti
***haïtien(ne)** Haitian
***hamburger** *(m.)* hamburger
***haricot** *(m.)* bean; **haricots verts** *(m. pl.)* green beans
***haut(e)** high; loud *(voice);* **au haut (de)** in/at the top (of); **en haut** upstairs
**herbe** *(f.)* grass
**héroïne** *(f.)* heroine
***héros** *(m.)* hero
**heure** *(f.)* hour; **une heure** one o'clock; **à l'heure** on time; **à tout à l'heure** see you later; **de bonne heure** early
**heureusement** fortunately
**heureux (-euse)** happy
**hexagone** *(m.)* hexagon
**hier** yesterday
**histoire** *(f.)* story, history
**historique** historical
**hiver** *(m.)* winter
**homme** *(m.)* man
***Hongrie** *(f.)* Hungary

**honnête** honest
**honneur** *(m.)* honor; **tableau d'honneur** *(m.)* honor roll
***honte** *(f.)* shame; **avoir honte** to be ashamed
**hôpital** *(m.)* *(pl.* **-aux**) hospital
**horaire** *(m.)* schedule
**horloge** *(f.)* clock
***hors** outside
***hors-d'œuvre** *(m.)* appetizer
**hôte** *(m.)* host
**hôtel** *(m.)* hotel
**hôtesse** *(f.)* hostess
***huit** eight
**humain(e)** human
**hydro-électrique** hydroelectric
**hymne** *(m.)* hymn
**hypermarché** *(m.)* large supermarket

**ici** here
**idée** *(f.)* idea
**identité** *(f.)* identity; **carte d'identité** *(f.)* identification card
**ignorer** to ignore
**il** he, it; **il y a** there is/are; **il n'y a pas de quoi** you're welcome
**île** *(f.)* island
**illustration** *(f.)* picture
**illustre** famous
**ils** they
**image** *(f.)* picture
**imaginatif (-ive)** imaginative
**imagination** *(f.)* imagination
**imaginer** to imagine
**immédiat** immediate
**immédiatement** immediately
**immeuble** *(m.)* apartment building
**impatience** *(f.)* impatience
**imperméable** *(m.)* raincoat
**important(e)** important
**impossible** impossible
**impressionner** to impress

**impulsif (–ive)** impulsive
**impulsivement** impulsively
**indépendant(e)** independent
**indication** *(f.)* indication
**indien(ne)** Indian
**indiqué(e)** indicated
**indiquer** to indicate
**individualisme** *(m.)* individualism
**indulgent(e)** indulgent, lenient
**industrie** *(f.)* industry
**industriel(le)** industrial
**infirmier (–ière)** nurse
**informations** *(f. pl.)* news
**informatique** *(f.)* computer science
**ingénieur** *(m.)* engineer
**injuste** unfair
**innocent(e)** innocent
**inscription** *(f.)* registration
**insecte** *(m.)* insect
**insertion** *(f.)* insertion
**inspiration** *(f.)* inspiration
**installer** to install
**instant** *(m.)* instant
**instituteur (–trice)** teacher
**instruction** *(f.)* instruction, direction
**insulte** *(f.)* insult
**intellectuel(le)** intellectual
**intelligence** *(f.)* intelligence
**intelligent(e)** intelligent
**intensité** *(f.)* intensity
**interdit(e)** forbidden, prohibited
**intéressant(e)** interesting
**intéresser** to interest
**international(e)** *(m. pl. –aux)* international
**intime** intimate
**intuitif (–ive)** intuitive
**inutile** useless
**invasion** *(f.)* invasion
**inventer** to invent
**inversion** *(f.)* inversion
**invité(e)** guest
**inviter** to invite

**irriter** to irritate
**Israël** *(m.)* Israel
**Italie** *(f.)* Italy
**italien(ne)** Italian
**itinéraire** *(m.)* itinerary

**jaloux (–ouse)** jealous
**jamais** never, ever; **jamais de la vie** out of the question; **ne… jamais** never
**jambe** *(f.)* leg
**jambon** *(m.)* ham
**janvier** *(m.)* January
**Japon** *(m.)* Japan
**japonais(e)** Japanese
**jardin** *(m.)* garden
**jardinage** *(m.)* gardening
**jardinier (–ière)** gardener
**jaune** *(m.)* yolk *(of egg)*
**jaune** yellow
**je** I
**jeter** to throw; **se jeter** to empty *(river)*
**jeu** *(m.) (pl. –x)* game; **jeu de cartes** card game
**jeudi** *(m.)* Thursday
**jeune** young
**jeunesse** *(f.)* youth; **jeunesses musicales** *(f. pl.)* musical association
**joie** *(f.)* joy
**joli(e)** pretty
**jouer** to play; **jouer à** to play *(a game / a sport)*; **jouer de** to play *(a musical instrument)*; **se jouer** to be played
**joueur (–euse)** player
**jour** *(m.)* day; **jour de congé** day off; **jour férié** legal holiday
**journal** *(m.) (pl. –aux)* newspaper; journal
**journalisme** *(m.)* journalism
**journée** *(f.)* day
**joyeux (–euse)** joyous
**juge** *(m.)* judge
**juillet** *(m.)* July

**juin** *(m.)* June
**jumeau** *(pl. –x) (f. jumelle)* twin
**jupe** *(f.)* skirt
**jus** *(m.)* juice
**jusqu'à** until
**juste** fair; right

**karaté** *(m.)* karate; **faire du karaté** to do karate
**kilo** *(m.)* kilogram
**kilogramme** *(m.)* kilogram
**kilomètre** *(m.)* kilometer

**la** the; her, it
**là** there
**lac** *(m.)* lake
**laid(e)** ugly
**laisse** *(f.)* leash
**laisser** to leave
**lait** *(m.)* milk
**laitue** *(f.)* lettuce
**lampe** *(f.)* lamp
**lancer** to throw
**langue** *(f.)* language
**lapin** *(m.)* rabbit
**latin** *(m.)* Latin
**lavage** *(m.)* wash
**laver** to wash; **laver la vaisselle** to do the dishes; **machine à laver** washing machine; **se laver** to wash oneself
**le** the; him, it
**leçon** *(f.)* lesson
**lecture** *(f.)* reading
**léger (–ère)** light *(weight)*
**légèrement** lightly
**légume** *(m.)* vegetable
**lentement** slowly
**les** the; them
**lettre** *(f.)* letter; **boîte aux lettres** *(f.)* mailbox; **en toutes lettres** in full
**leur** their; to them
**lever** to raise, lift; **se lever** to get up

**lèvre** *(f.)* lip; **rouge à lèvres** *(m.)* lipstick
**liberté** *(f.)* freedom, liberty
**librairie** *(f.)* bookstore
**libre** free
**lieu** *(m.)* place; **au lieu (de)** instead (of)
**ligne** *(f.)* line
**limite** *(f.)* limit
**limonade** *(f.)* lemon soda
**limousine** *(f.)* limousine
**lion** *(m.)* lion
**liquide** *(m.)* liquid
**lire** *(p.p.* **lu)** to read
**liste** *(f.)* list
**lit** *(m.)* bed; **faire le lit** to make the bed
**litre** *(m.)* liter
**living** *(m.)* living room
**livre** *(m.)* book
**livret** *(m.)* booklet
**location** *(f.)* rental
**loi** *(f.)* law
**loin (de)** far (from)
**Londres** *(m.)* London
**long(ue)** long; **de long en large** back and forth
**longtemps** a long time
**loterie** *(f.)* lottery
**louer** to rent
**loup** *(m.)* wolf
**lourd(e)** heavy
**loyal(e)** *(m. pl.* **-aux)** loyal
**lui** he, him, to him, her, to her
**lumière** *(f.)* light
**lundi** *(m.)* Monday
**lune** *(f.)* moon
**lunettes** *(f. pl.)* eyeglasses; **lunettes de soleil** sunglasses
**luxe** *(m.)* luxury
**luxueux (-euse)** luxurious
**lycée** *(m.)* high school
**lyrique** lyrical

**ma** my
**machine** *(f.)* machine;

**machine à écrire** typewriter; **machine à laver** washing machine
**madame** *(f.) (pl.* **mesdames)** Madam, Mrs.
**mademoiselle** *(f.) (pl.* **mesdemoiselles)** Miss
**magasin** *(m.)* store; **grand magasin** department store
**magazine** *(m.)* magazine
**magnétoscope** *(m.)* V.C.R.
**magnifique** magnificent
**mai** *(m.)* May
**maigre** thin
**maigrir** to become thin
**maillot** *(m.)* jersey; **maillot de bain** bathing suit
**main** *(f.)* hand
**maintenant** now
**maire** *(m.)* mayor
**mairie** *(f.)* town hall
**mais** but
**maison** *(f.)* house; **maison des jeunes et de la culture (M.J.C.)** youth center
**maître** master; **maître-nageur** *(m.)* lifeguard
**maîtresse** *(f.)* teacher
**mal** bad(ly); **aller mal** to feel poorly; **avoir mal à** to have an ache in
**mal** *(m.)* pain; **mal de dents** toothache
**malade** *(m./f.)* patient, sick person
**malade** sick
**maladie** *(f.)* illness, sickness
**malgré** in spite of
**malheureusement** unfortunately
**malheureux (-euse)** unhappy
**maman** *(f.)* mom
**Manche** *(f.)* English Channel
**manger** to eat
**manières** *(f. pl.)* manners
**mannequin** *(m.)* mannequin,

model
**manquer** to be missing, lack
**manteau** *(m.) (pl.* **-x)** coat
**maquiller** to apply makeup; **se maquiller** to put on one's makeup
**marchandise** *(f.)* merchandise
**marche** *(f.)* walking
**marché** *(m.)* market; **bon marché** inexpensive
**marcher** to walk; to work, function
**mardi** *(m.)* Tuesday
**marée** *(f.)* tide
**mari** *(m.)* husband
**marier** to marry; **se marier (avec)** to marry
**marmite** *(f.)* pot
**Maroc** *(m.)* Morocco
**maroquinerie** *(f.)* leather goods store
**marquer** to mark
**marron** brown
**mars** *(m.)* March
**masque** *(m.)* mask
**match** *(m.)* match, game
**matériel scolaire** *(m.)* school supplies
**mathématiques** *(f. pl.)* mathematics
**maths** *(f. pl.)* math
**matière** *(f.)* subject
**matin** *(m.)* morning
**matinée** *(f.)* morning
**mauvais(e)** bad; **faire mauvais** to be bad *(weather)*
**mauve** purple
**me** me, to me
**mécanicien(ne)** mechanic
**méchant(e)** naughty, wicked
**médecin** *(m.)* doctor
**médecine** *(f.)* medicine
**médicament** *(m.)* medicine
**Méditerranée** Mediterranean
**meilleur(e)** best
**mélanger** to mix

**membre** *(m.)* member
**même** same *(adj.)*; even *(adv.)*
**menacer** to threaten
**ménage** *(m.)* household; **faire le ménage** to do the house-work; **femme de ménage** cleaning woman
**mener** to lead
**mensonge** *(m.)* lie
**mentionner** to mention
**mer** *(f.)* sea; **au bord de la mer** to/at the seashore
**merci** thank you
**mercredi** *(m.)* Wednesday
**mère** *(f.)* mother
**méridional(e)** *(m. pl. -aux)* southern
**merveilleux (-euse)** marvelous
**mes** my
**métallurgie** *(f.)* metallurgy
**météo** *(f.)* weather report
**mètre** *(m.)* meter
**métro** *(m.)* subway
**mettre** *(p.p. mis)* to put (on); **mettre la table** to set the table; **mettre le couvert** to set the table; **se mettre à** to begin to; **se mettre en route** to start out
**meuble** *(m.)* piece of furniture; **meubles** *(m. pl.)* furniture
**Mexique** *(m.)* Mexico
**midi** *(m.)* noon; south
**mieux** better; **aimer mieux** to prefer; **faire de son mieux** to do one's best
**milieu** *(m.)* center, middle; **au milieu** in the middle
**mille** (**mil** *in dates*) (one) thou-sand
**milliard** *(m.)* billion
**million** *(m.)* million
**mince** skinny
**minéral(e)** mineral; **eau minérale** mineral water
**minimum** *(m.)* minimum

**ministre** *(m.)* minister; **premier ministre** prime minister
**minuit** *(m.)* midnight
**minute** *(f.)* minute
**miroir** *(m.)* mirror
**mobylette** *(f.)* moped
**modèle** *(m.)* model
**moderne** modern
**moi** I, me
**moins** less, minus; **au moins** at least; **moins (de)** less, fewer
**mois** *(m.)* month
**moment** *(m.)* moment
**mon** my
**monarque** *(m.)* monarch
**monde** *(m.)* world; **tout le monde** everybody; **faire le tour du monde** to go around the world
**mondial(e)** world
**monétaire** monetary
**monsieur** *(m.) (pl. messieurs)* sir, gentleman, Mr.
**montagne** *(f.)* mountain
**monter** to go up, climb; to carry up; **monter à bicyclette** to go bicycle riding
**montre** *(f.)* watch
**montrer** to show
**monument** *(m.)* monument
**morceau** *(m.) (pl. -x)* piece
**mort(e)** dead
**mosquée** *(f.)* mosque
**mot** *(m.)* word
**moteur** *(m.)* motor
**motocyclette** *(f.)* motorcycle
**mouchoir** *(m.)* handkerchief
**mourir** *(p.p. mort)* to die
**mousquetaire** *(m.)* musketeer
**mousse** *(f.)* mousse; mousse **au chocolat** chocolate mousse
**moustache** *(f.)* moustache
**mouton** *(m.)* sheep
**moyen** *(m.)* means; **moyen de transport** means of transportation

**multiplication** *(f.)* multiplication
**mur** *(m.)* wall
**musée** *(m.)* museum
**musical(e)** musical; **jeunesses musicales** *(f. pl.)* musical association
**musique** *(f.)* music; **musique rock** rock music

**nager** to swim
**naïf (-ïve)** naive
**naissance** *(f.)* birth
**naître** *(p.p. né)* to be born
**natation** *(f.)* swimming
**national(e)** *(m. pl. -aux)* national
**nationalité** *(f.)* nationality
**naturel(le)** natural
**naturellement** naturally
**nautique** nautical; **ski nautique** *(m.)* water skiing
**ne: ne... jamais** never; **ne... pas** not; **ne... personne** nobody, no one; **ne... plus** no longer, no more, anymore; **ne... rien** nothing
**né(e)** born
**nécessaire** necessary
**négatif (-ive)** negative
**négativement** negatively
**négliger** to neglect
**neige** *(f.)* snow; **bonhomme de neige** *(m.)* snowman; **boule de neige** *(f.)* snowball; **classe de neige** *(f.)* ski class
**neiger** to snow
**nerveux (-euse)** nervous
**n'est-ce pas?** isn't that so?
**nettoyage** *(m.)* cleaning
**nettoyer** to clean
**neuf (-ve)** new
**neuf** nine
**neveu** *(m.) (pl. -x)* nephew
**nez** *(m.)* nose
**nièce** *(f.)* niece
**nocturne** night
**Noël** *(m.)* Christmas

**noir** *(m.)* darkness
**noir(e)** black
**nom** *(m.)* name
**nommé(e)** named
**non** no
**nord** *(m.)* north
**Normandie** *(f.)* Normandy
**Norvège** *(f.)* Norway
**nos** our
**note** *(f.)* note, grade
**noter** to note
**notre** our
**nous** we, us, to us
**nouveau, nouvel** *(f.* **nouvelle**;
*m. pl.* **nouveaux**) new; **de
nouveau** again
**nouvelles** *(f. pl.)* news
**novembre** *(m.)* November
**nuage** *(m.)* cloud
**nucléaire** nuclear
**nuit** *(f.)* night; **table de nuit**
*(f.)* night table
**numéro** *(m.)* number; **numéro
de téléphone** telephone
number

**obéir (à)** to obey
**objet** *(m.)* object
**obligatoire** compulsory
**obliger** to oblige, compel
**observer** to observe
**occasion** *(f.)* occasion,
opportunity
**occupé(e)** busy
**océan** *(m.)* ocean
**octobre** *(m.)* October
**œil** *(m.) (pl.* **yeux**) eye; **coup
d'œil** *(m.)* glance
**œuf** *(m.)* egg
**œuvre** *(f.)* work
**officiel(le)** official
**offrir** *(p.p.* **offert**) to offer
**oignon** *(m.)* onion
**oiseau** *(m.) (pl.* **-x**) bird
**olympique** Olympic
**omelette** *(f.)* omelet

**on** one, we, you, they, people
*(in general)*
**oncle** *(m.)* uncle
**ongle** *(m.)* fingernail
**onze** eleven
**opérateur (-trice)** operator
**opinion** *(f.)* opinion
**optimiste** optimistic
**orange** *(f.)* orange
**orangeade** *(f.)* orange soda
**orchestre** *(m.)* orchestra
**ordinaire** ordinary
**ordinateur** *(m.)* computer
**ordonner** to order
**ordre** *(m.)* order
**ordures** *(f. pl.)* garbage
**oreille** *(f.)* ear
**organiser** to organize
**origine** *(f.)* origin
**orteil** *(m.)* toe
**orthographe** *(f.)* spelling
**ôter** to remove, take off
**ou** or
**où** where
**oublier** to forget
**ouest** *(m.)* west
**oui** yes
**ours** *(m.)* bear
**ouvrier (-ière)** factory worker
**ouvrir** *(p.p.* **ouvert**) to open

**page** *(f.)* page
**pain** *(m.)* bread; **pain grillé** toast
**paire** *(f.)* pair
**paix** *(f.)* peace
**palais** *(m.)* palace
**panoramique** panoramic
**pantalon** *(m.)* pants
**papier** *(m.)* paper
**paquet** *(m.)* package
**par** by, through, per; **par conséquent** consequently; **par
exemple** for example; **par
jour** per day; **par rapport à**
with regard to; **par terre** on
the ground

**paragraphe** *(m.)* paragraph
**parapluie** *(m.)* umbrella
**parc** *(m.)* park; parking; **parc
d'attractions** amusement park
**parce que** because
**pardessus** *(m.)* overcoat
**pardonner** to forgive, excuse
**parent** *(m.)* parent
**paresseux (-euse)** lazy
**parfait(e)** perfect
**parfaitement** perfectly
**parfois** sometimes
**parfum** *(m.)* perfume
**parfumer** to perfume; **se parfumer** to put perfume on
**parfumerie** *(f.)* perfume shop
**parisien(ne)** Parisian
**parler** to speak
**partager** to share, divide
**participant(e)** participant
**participer (à)** to participate (in)
**partie** *(f.)* part; **faire partie de**
to belong to
**partir** to leave, go away; **à partir de** from
**partout** everywhere
**parution** *(f.)* publication
**pas** not; **pas du tout** not at all;
**pas encore** not yet; **ne... pas**
not
**passé(e)** past; **l'année passée**
last year
**passer** to pass; to spend *(time)*;
**passer l'aspirateur** to vacuum;
**passer un examen** to take a
test; **se passer** to happen
**passionner** to interest passion-
ately, intrigue
**pâté** *(m.)* paté *(meat appetizer)*
**patience** *(f.)* patience
**patin** *(m.)* skate; **patin à glace**
ice skate, ice skating; **faire
du patin à glace** to go ice
skating
**patiner** to skate
**pâtisserie** *(f.)* pastry; pastry shop

**pâtissier (-ière)** pastry maker

**patron(ne)** boss; patron saint

**patte** *(f.)* paw

**pauvre** poor

**payer** to pay (for)

**pays** *(m.)* country

**paysage** *(m.)* countryside; landscape

**paysan(ne)** peasant

**Pays-Bas** *(m. pl.)* Netherlands, Holland

**peau** *(f.)* skin

**pêche** *(f.)* peach

**pêche** *(f.)* fishing; **aller à la pêche** to go fishing

**pêcher** to fish

**pédagogique** educational

**pédaler** to pedal

**peigne** *(m.)* comb

**peigner** to comb; **se peigner** to comb one's hair

**peindre** *(p.p.* **peint)** to paint

**peintre** *(m.)* painter

**pelouse** *(f.)* lawn

**pendant** during; **pendant que** while

**penderie** *(f.)* closet

**pendule** *(f.)* clock

**penser** to think; to intend

**perdre** to lose; **perdre son temps** to waste one's time

**père** *(m.)* father

**perfectionné(e)** perfected, improved

**perfectionner** to improve

**perle** *(f.)* pearl

**permettre** *(p.p.* **permis)** to allow, permit

**permis** *(m.)* permit; **permis de conduire** driver's license

**permission** *(f.)* pass; permission

**personne** *(f.)* person

**personne** nobody, no one; **ne... personne** nobody, no one; **personne ne** no one, nobody

**personnel(le)** personal

**peser** to weigh

**petit(e)** little, small; short; **petit ami** *(m.)* boyfriend; **petite amie** *(f.)* girlfriend; **petit déjeuner** *(m.)* breakfast; **petits pois** *(m. pl.)* peas

**petite-fille** *(f.)* granddaughter

**petit-fils** *(m.)* grandson

**pétrole** *(m.)* oil

**peu (de)** little, few; **à peu près** about, approximately; **un peu** a little

**peuple** *(m.)* people *(of a nation)*

**peur** *(f.)* fear; **avoir peur de** to be afraid of

**peut** *(inf.* **pouvoir)** can

**peut-être** perhaps, maybe

**pharmacie** *(f.)* pharmacy, drugstore

**philosophe** *(m. / f.)* philosopher

**philosophie** *(f.)* philosophy

**photo** *(f.)* photo, picture; **prendre une photo** to take a picture

**photographie** *(f.)* photography

**photographier** to photograph

**phrase** *(f.)* phrase, sentence

**physique** *(f.)* physics

**physique** physical; **éducation physique** *(f.)* gym

**physiquement** physically

**piano** *(m.)* piano

**pièce** *(f.)* play

**pied** *(m.)* foot; **aller à pied** to walk, go on foot

**piscine** *(f.)* swimming pool; **piscine couverte** indoor pool

**pittoresque** picturesque

**placard** *(m.)* cabinet, cupboard

**place** *(f.)* seat, place, square; **en place** in place

**placer** to place, set

**plafond** *(m.)* ceiling

**plage** *(f.)* beach

**plaisir** *(m.)* pleasure;

**faire plaisir (à)** to please

**plancher** *(m.)* floor

**plante** *(f.)* plant; **plante verte** potted plant

**plastique** *(m.)* plastic

**plat** *(m.)* dish

**plein(e)** full; **en plein air** outdoors

**pleurer** to cry

**pleuvoir** *(p.p.* **plu)** to rain

**plonger** to plunge, dive

**pluie** *(f.)* rain

**plus (de)** more; **plus tard** later; **ne... plus** no longer, no more, anymore

**plusieurs** several

**pneu** *(m.)* tire

**poche** *(f.)* pocket

**poème** *(m.)* poem

**poésie** *(f.)* poetry

**point** *(m.)* point; period; **point de vue** point of view

**poire** *(f.)* pear

**poisson** *(m.)* fish

**poissonnerie** *(f.)* fish store

**poitrine** *(f.)* chest

**poivre** *(m.)* pepper

**poli(e)** polite

**policier (-ière)** police

**poliment** politely

**pomme** *(f.)* apple

**pomme de terre** *(f.)* potato

**pont** *(m.)* bridge

**populaire** popular

**port** *(m.)* port

**porte** *(f.)* door, gate

**portefeuille** *(m.)* wallet

**porter** to carry; to wear

**poser** to place; to ask *(questions)*

**position** *(f.)* position

**posséder** to possess, own

**possible** possible

**possiblement** possibly

**postal(e)** postal; **carte postale** *(f.)* postcard; **code postal** *(m.)* zip code

**poste** *(f.)* post office; **bureau de poste** *(m.)* post office
**poster** *(m.)* poster
**potage** *(m.)* soup
**pot-au-feu** *(m.)* beef stew
**poule** *(f.)* chicken
**poulet** *(m.)* chicken
**poupée** *(f.)* doll
**pour** for, in order to
**pourquoi** why
**pousser** to push; to grow; **pousser un soupir de soulagement** to breathe a sigh of relief
**pouvoir** *(p.p. **pu**)* to be able to, can
**pratique** practical
**pratiquer** to practice
**précieux (-euse)** precious, important
**précis(e)** precise; **à deux heures précises** at two o'clock exactly
**précision** *(f.)* precision
**préférer** to prefer
**premier (-ière)** first; **premier ministre** *(m.)* prime minister
**prendre** *(p.p. **pris**)* to take; **prendre soin** to take care
**préparatifs** *(m. pl.)* preparations
**préparer** to prepare; **se préparer** to prepare oneself
**près (de)** near; **à peu près** about, approximately
**présent(e)** present
**présenter** to introduce; to offer
**président(e)** president
**pressé(e)** in a hurry
**prêt(e)** ready
**prétendre** to claim
**prêter** to lend
**prince** *(m.)* prince
**princesse** *(f.)* princess
**principal(e)** *(m. pl. **-aux**)* principal, main
**printemps** *(m.)* spring

**prise** *(f.)* taking
**privé(e)** private
**prix** *(m.)* prize; price
**probable** probable
**probablement** probably
**problème** *(m.)* problem
**prochain(e)** next
**proche** nearby
**proclamer** to proclaim
**production** *(f.)* production
**produit** *(m.)* product
**professeur** *(m.)* *(coll. **prof**)* teacher
**profession** *(f.)* profession
**profiterole** *(f.)* cream puff with chocolate sauce
**programme** *(m.)* program
**programmeur (-euse)** programmer
**progrès** *(m.)* progress
**projet** *(m.)* project
**promenade** *(f.)* walk; **faire une promenade** to go for a walk
**promener** to walk; **se promener** to take a walk
**prononcer** to pronounce; to declare
**propriétaire** *(m. / f.)* owner
**protéger** to protect
**provençal(e)** *(m. pl. **-aux**)* Provençal, from Provence
**province** *(f.)* province
**prudemment** prudently
**prudence** *(f.)* prudence, wisdom
**prune** *(f.)* plum
**public** *(m.)* public, audience
**publicité** *(f.)* publicity
**publier** to publish
**puis** then
**puisque** since
**pull** *(m.)* pullover sweater
**punir** to punish
**pupitre** *(m.)* pupil's desk
**pyjama** *(m.)* pyjama
**Pyrénées** *(f. pl.)* Pyrenees

**quai** *(m.)* quay
**qualité** *(f.)* quality
**quand** when
**quarante** forty
**quart** *(m.)* quarter
**quartier** *(m.)* neighborhood
**quatorze** fourteen
**quatre** four
**quatre-vingt-dix** ninety
**quatre-vingts** eighty
**quatrième** fourth
**que** that, whom, which; what; than; **ce que** that which, what; **qu'est-ce que** what
**quel(le)** what, which; what a
**quelque** some; **quelques** *(m. / f. pl.)* a few, some
**quelque chose** something
**quelquefois** sometimes
**quelqu'un** someone
**querelle** *(f.)* quarrel
**qu'est-ce que** what
**question** *(f.)* question
**qui** who, whom, which, that
**quinze** fifteen
**quitter** to leave
**quoi** what; **(il n'y a) pas de quoi** you're welcome

**rabais** *(m.)* discount; **au rabais** at a discount
**raconter** to tell; to describe
**radio** *(f.)* radio
**radium** *(m.)* radium
**rafraîchissement** *(m.)* refreshment
**ragoût** *(m.)* stew
**raisin** *(m.)* grape
**raison** *(f.)* reason; **avoir raison** to be right
**ramasser** to pick up
**ramener** to bring back
**rang** *(m.)* row
**ranger** to put away; to put in order, tidy
**rapide** rapid, fast

**rapidement** quickly, rapidly

**rappeler** to recall; **se rappeler** to remember

**rapport** (*m.*) report; **par rapport** à with regard to

**raquette** (*f.*) racket

**rarement** rarely

**raser** to shave; **se raser** to shave (oneself)

**rasoir** (*m.*) razor

**rassuré(e)** reassured

**rassurer** to reassure

**réception** (*f.*) receipt

**recette** (*f.*) recipe

**recevoir** (*p.p.* **reçu**) to receive

**recherche** (*f.*) search

**recommander** to recommend

**récompense** (*f.*) reward

**refaire** to redo

**refermer** to close again

**réfléchir** to reflect, think

**réfrigérateur** (*m.*) refrigerator

**refuser (de)** to refuse (to)

**regarder** to look at, watch

**régime** (*m.*) diet

**région** (*f.*) region

**règle** (*f.*) ruler

**règlement** (*m.*) rules

**régler** to set

**regret** (*m.*) regret, sorrow

**regretter (de)** to regret (to)

**régulièrement** regularly

**reine** (*f.*) queen

**relier** to connect

**religieux (-euse)** religious

**remarquable** remarkable

**remercier** to thank

**remettre** (*p.p.* **remis**) to put back; to deliver

**remplacer** to replace

**remplir** to fill

**rencontrer** to meet

**rendre** to give back, return; **rendre visite (à)** to visit

**renommé(e)** renowned

**renoncer (à)** to give up, renounce

**renseignements** (*m. pl.*) information

**rentrée** (*f.*) return; **rentrée scolaire** return to school

**rentrer** to return

**renvoyer** to send back; to fire

**réparer** to repair

**repas** (*m.*) meal

**répéter** to repeat

**répondre (à)** to answer

**réponse** (*f.*) answer

**reposer** to rest; **se reposer** to rest, relax

**représenter** to represent

**république** (*f.*) republic

**résidence** (*f.*) residence, home

**résoudre** to solve, resolve

**respect** (*m.*) respect

**respecter** to respect

**responsabilité** (*f.*) responsibility

**responsable** responsible

**ressembler (à)** to resemble; **se ressembler** to look alike

**restaurant** (*m.*) restaurant

**rester** to remain, stay

**résultat** (*m.*) result

**retard** (*m.*) lateness; **en retard** late

**retourner** to return

**retraite** (*f.*) retirement; retreat

**réussir (à)** to succeed (in)

**réveil** (*m.*) alarm clock

**réveiller** to awaken; **se réveiller** to wake up

**revenir** (*p.p.* **revenu**) to come back

**rêver (de)** to dream (of)

**revoir** (*p.p.* **revu**) to see again; **au revoir** good-bye

**révolutionner** to revolutionize

**revue** (*f.*) magazine

**rez-de-chaussée** (*m.*) ground floor

**Rhin** (*m.*) Rhine

**Rhône** (*m.*) Rhone

**rhume** (*m.*) cold

**riche** rich

**rideau** (*m.*) (*pl.* **-x**) curtain

**rien** nothing; **de rien** you're welcome; **ne... rien** nothing; **rien ne** nothing

**rire** to laugh

**rive** (*f.*) bank

**rivière** (*f.*) stream

**robe** (*f.*) dress

**roi** (*m.*) king

**rôle** (*m.*) role

**romain(e)** Roman

**roman** (*m.*) novel; **roman policier** detective story

**romantique** romantic

**rompre** to break

**ronde** (*f.*) round; ring-around-a-rosy

**rose** pink

**rôtir** to roast

**roue** (*f.*) wheel

**rouge** red

**rouge à lèvres** (*m.*) lipstick

**rougir** to blush

**rouler** to roll along

**Roumanie** (*f.*) Romania

**route** (*f.*) road, route; **en route** on the way; **se mettre en route** to start out

**roux (rousse)** red (hair)

**rue** (*f.*) street

**rugby** (*m.*) rugby

**russe** (*m.*) Russian

**sa** his, her

**sable** (*m.*) sand

**sac** (*m.*) bag, sack, pocketbook; **sac à dos** backpack

**sage** wise; well-behaved

**saisir** to seize, grab

**saison** (*f.*) season

**salade** (*f.*) salad

**sale** dirty

**salle** (*f.*) room; **salle à manger** dining room; **salle de bains** bathroom; **salle de classe** classroom; **salle de séjour** living room

**salon** (*m.*) living room; lounge

**salut** hi

**samedi** (*m.*) Saturday

**sandale** (*f.*) sandal

**sandwich** (*m.*) sandwich

**sanguin(e)** blood (*adj.*)

**sans** without; **sans doute** no doubt

**santé** (*f.*) health

**satire** (*f.*) satire

**saucisse** (*f.*) sausage

**saucisson** (*m.*) dry sausage

**sauter** to jump; **sauter à la corde** to jump rope

**sauvage** savage

**sauver** to save

**savoir** (*p.p.* **su**) to know (how to)

**savon** (*m.*) soap

**science** (*f.*) science

**science-fiction** (*f.*) science fiction

**scientifique** scientific

**scolaire** school (*adj.*); **matériel scolaire** (*m.*) school supplies; **rentrée scolaire** (*f.*) return to school

**scooter** (*m.*) (motor) scooter

**Scotch** (*m.*) Scotch tape

**se** (to) himself, (to) herself, (to) oneself, (to) themselves

**second(e)** second

**secondaire** secondary

**secret (-ète)** secret

**secrétaire** secretary

**secrètement** secretly

**Seine** (*f.*) Seine

**seize** sixteen

**séjour** (*m.*) stay; family room; **salle de séjour** (*f.*) family room

**sel** (*m.*) salt

**selon** according to

**semaine** (*f.*) week

**semestre** (*m.*) semester

**semi-valide** semi-ambulatory

**séparer** to separate

**sept** seven

**septembre** (*m.*) September

**série** (*f.*) series

**sérieusement** seriously

**sérieux (-euse)** serious

**serveur** (*m.*) waiter

**service** (*m.*) service

**serviette** (*f.*) briefcase; napkin

**servir (de)** to serve (as)

**ses** his, her

**seul(e)** only, single, alone

**seulement** only

**short** (*m.*) shorts

**si** if; yes; so

**siècle** (*m.*) century

**silence** (*m.*) silence

**s'il te plaît** please

**s'il vous plaît** please

**simple** simple

**sincère** sincere

**sincèrement** sincerely

**site** (*m.*) site

**situation** (*f.*) situation

**situé(e)** situated

**six** six

**sixième** sixth

**ski** (*m.*) ski; **ski nautique** water skiing; **faire du ski** to go skiing

**skier** to ski

**sociable** sociable

**social(e)** (*m. pl.* **-aux**) social

**société** (*f.*) company; society

**soda** (*m.*) soda

**sœur** (*f.*) sister

**soie** (*f.*) silk

**soif** (*f.*) thirst; **avoir soif** to be thirsty

**soin** (*m.*) care; **prendre soin (de)** to take care (of)

**soir** (*m.*) evening

**soirée** (*f.*) evening

**soixante** sixty

**soixante-dix** seventy

**solaire** solar, sun

**soleil** (*m.*) sun; **coucher de soleil** (*m.*) sunset; **lunettes de soleil** (*f. pl.*) sunglasses; **faire du soleil** to be sunny

**solide** solid

**somme** (*f.*) sum

**sommeil** (*m.*) sleep; **avoir sommeil** to be sleepy

**son** (*m.*) sound

**son** his, her, its

**songer (à)** to think (of)

**sonner** to ring

**sorte** (*f.*) sort, type

**sortir** to go out

**souhaiter** to wish

**soulagement** (*m.*) relief

**soulier** (*m.*) shoe

**soupe** (*f.*) soup

**soupir** (*m.*) sigh; **pousser un soupir de soulagement** to breathe a sigh of relief

**souris** (*f.*) mouse

**sous** under

**sous-sol** (*m.*) basement

**souvenir** (*m.*) souvenir

**souvent** often

**spécial(e)** (*m. pl.* **-aux**) special

**spécialiste** (*m./f.*) specialist

**spécialité** (*f.*) specialty

**spectacle** (*m.*) show

**splendide** splendid

**sport** (*m.*) sport; **voiture de sport** sports car; **faire du sport** to play sports

**sportif (-ve)** sports, sporty; athletic

**stable** stable

**stade** (*m.*) stadium

**station-service** (*f.*) service station

**store** (*m.*) shade, blind

**studieux (-euse)** studious

**stylo** (*m.*) pen

**succès** (*m.*) success

**sucre** (*m.*) sugar

**sud** (*m.*) south

**sud-américain(e)** South American
**Suède** (f.) Sweden
**suffrage** (m.) vote
**suggérer** to suggest
**suggestion** (f.) suggestion
**suisse** Swiss
**Suisse** (f.) Switzerland
**suivant(e)** following
**suivre** (p.p. **suivi**) to follow
**sujet** (m.) subject; **au sujet de** about
**super** super
**supermarché** (m.) supermarket
**superstitieux (-euse)** superstitious
**supplément** (m.) supplement
**suprême** supreme
**sur** on, upon
**sûr(e)** sure; **bien sûr** of course
**surf** (m.) surf; **faire du surf** to go surfing
**surprise** (f.) surprise
**surtout** especially
**survêtement** (m.) warm-up suit
**sympathique** likable, nice
**synthèse** (f.) synthesis
**système** (m.) system

**ta** your
**table** (f.) table; **table de nuit** night table; **mettre la table** to set the table
**tableau** (m.) (pl. **-x**) chalkboard; painting; **tableau d'honneur** honor roll
**tailleur** (m.) woman's suit
**talent** (m.) talent
**tant** so much/many; **tant pis** too bad
**tante** (f.) aunt
**tapis** (m.) rug
**tard** late; **plus tard** later
**tarif** (m.) rate
**tarte** (f.) pie
**tasse** (f.) cup

**taxi** (m.) taxi
**te** you, to you
**technique** (f.) technique
**technologie** (f.) technology
**tee-shirt** (m.) T-shirt
**tel(le)** such
**téléphone** (m.) telephone; **au téléphone** on the telephone; **coup de téléphone** (m.) telephone call; **numéro de téléphone** (m.) telephone number
**téléphoner** to phone
**télévision** (f.) television
**tellement** so
**température** (f.) temperature
**tempéré(e)** temperate
**temps** (m.) time; weather; **emploi du temps** schedule, program; **de temps en temps** from time to time; **perdre son temps** to waste one's time; **tout le temps** all the time
**tennis** (m.) tennis
**tennis** (f.) tennis sneaker
**tente** (f.) tent
**terminer** to end
**terrasse** (f.) terrace
**terre** (f.) earth, land; **par terre** on the ground
**terrible** terrible
**tes** your
**tête** (f.) head
**texte** (m.) text
**textile** (m.) textile
**thé** (m.) tea
**théâtre** (m.) theater
**thermomètre** (m.) thermometer
**thon** (m.) tuna
**ticket** (m.) ticket
**tigre** (m.) tiger
**timbre** (m.) stamp
**timide** shy
**tirage** (m.) drawing
**tiroir** (m.) drawer
**toi** you
**toilettes** (f. pl.) toilet

**toit** (m.) roof
**tomate** (f.) tomato
**tomber** to fall; **tomber amoureux** to fall in love
**ton** your
**tondre** to mow
**tonnerre** (m.) thunder; **coup de tonnerre** (m.) thunder clap
**tort** (m.) error; **avoir tort** to be wrong
**tôt** early; soon
**toucher** to touch; **toucher un chèque** to cash a check
**toujours** always, still
**tour** (m.) tour; **faire le tour du monde** to go around the world
**tour** (f.) tower
**touriste** (m./f.) tourist
**touristique** tourist
**tourner** to turn
**tout** (adv.) quite, entirely; **à tout à l'heure** see you later; **tout à coup** suddenly; **tout à fait** entirely; **tout d'un coup** suddenly; **tout de suite** immediately; **tout droit** straight ahead
**tout** (pron.) everything; **après tout** after all
**tout(e)** (m. pl. **tous**) all; every; **tous les jours** every day; **tout le monde** everybody; **tout le temps** all the time
**toux** (f.) cough
**traduit(e)** translated
**tragédie** (f.) tragedy
**trahir** to betray
**train** (m.) train; **être en train de** to be in the process of (doing something)
**traiter** to treat
**tramway** (m.) streetcar
**tranquille** tranquil, calm
**tranquillement** calmly
**transformer** to transform
**transport** (m.) transportation;

**moyen de transport** *(m.)* means of transportation

**travail** *(m.)* *(pl.* **-aux***)* work; **travaux ménagers** housework

**travailler** to work

**travers: à travers** across, through

**traverser** to cross

**treize** thirteen

**trente** thirty

**très** very

**tribunal** *(m.)* court of justice

**tricolore** three-colored

**triste** sad

**tristement** sadly

**trois** three

**trop (de)** too; too many, too much

**tropical(e)** tropical

**trottoir** *(m.)* sidewalk

**trousse** *(f.)* pencil case

**trouver** to find; **se trouver** to be (found)

**tu** you *(fam.)*

**typique** typical

**un(e)** a, an, one

**unité** *(f.)* unit

**université** *(f.)* university

**urgent(e)** urgent

**usé(e)** worn

**utile** useful

**utiliser** to use

**va** *(inf.* **aller***)*

**vacances** *(f. pl.)* vacation; **colonie de vacances** *(f.)* camp

**vache** *(f.)* cow

**vaisselle** *(f.)* dishes; **faire / laver la vaisselle** to do the dishes

**Valentin** *(m.)* Valentine

**valide** healthy, ambulatory

**valise** *(f.)* suitcase

**vallée** *(f.)* valley

**vanille** *(f.)* vanilla

**vaporisateur** *(m.)* atomizer

**vase** *(m.)* vase

**vaste** vast

**veau** *(m.)* veal

**vélo** *(m.)* bicycle

**vendeur (-euse)** salesperson

**vendre** to sell

**vendredi** *(m.)* Friday

**venir** *(p.p.* **venu***)* to come

**vent** *(m.)* wind; **faire du vent** to be windy

**ventre** *(m.)* stomach

**verbe** *(m.)* verb

**verité** *(f.)* truth

**verre** *(m.)* glass

**vers** towards

**vert(e)** green; **haricots verts** *(m. pl.)* green beans; **plante verte** potted plant

**veste** *(f.)* jacket

**vêtements** *(m. pl.)* clothes; **vêtements sport** sport clothes

**vêtu(e)** dressed

**viande** *(f.)* meat

**victime** *(f.)* victim

**vide** empty

**vider** to empty

**vie** *(f.)* life

**vieux, vieil** *(f.* **vieille***)* old

**vif (vive)** lively

**villa** *(f.)* villa, house

**village** *(m.)* village

**ville** *(f.)* city; **en ville** downtown

**vin** *(m.)* wine

**vingt** twenty

**violent(e)** violent

**violet(te)** purple

**violon** *(m.)* violin

**virgule** *(f.)* comma; (decimal) point

**visage** *(m.)* face

**visite** *(f.)* visit

**visiter** to visit

**vitamine** *(f.)* vitamin

**vite** rapidly, quickly

**vivre** *(p.p.* **vécu***)* to live

**vocabulaire** *(m.)* vocabulary

**vocal(e)** *(m. pl.* **-aux***)* vocal

**vœu** *(m.)* *(pl.* **vœux***)* vow, wish

**voici** here!, here is/are

**voie** *(f.)* track

**voilà** there!, there is/are

**voir** *(p.p.* **vu***)* to see

**voisin(e)** neighbor

**voiture** *(f.)* car; **voiture de sport** sports car; **aller en voiture** to go by car

**voix** *(f.)* voice; **à haute voix / à voix haute** out loud; **à voix basse** in a low voice

**vol** *(m.)* flight

**volaille** *(f.)* poultry

**volcanique** volcanic

**voler** to fly

**voleur** *(m.)* robber

**volley-ball** *(m.)* volleyball

**vos** your

**vote** *(m.)* vote

**voter** to vote

**votre** your

**vouloir** *(p.p.* **voulu***)* to want

**vous** you, to you

**voyage** *(m.)* trip, voyage; **chèque de voyage** *(m.)* traveler's check; **faire un voyage** to take a trip

**voyager** to travel

**vrai(e)** true

**vraiment** truly, really

**vue** *(f.)* view

**week-end** *(m.)* weekend

**y** to it / them, in it / them, on it / them; there; **il y a** there is

**yeux** *(m. pl)* eyes

**yogourt** *(m.)* yogurt

**zéro** *(m.)* zero

**zoo** *(m.)* zoo

# English-French Vocabulary

The English–French vocabulary includes all the words that occur in the English to French translation exercises.

## ABBREVIATIONS

| | | | |
|---|---|---|---|
| *(adj.)* | adjective | *(m.)* | masculine |
| *(adv.)* | adverb | *(pl.)* | plural |
| *(f.)* | feminine | *(pron.)* | pronoun |
| *(inf.)* | infinitive | | |

**able: be able** pouvoir

**accept** accepter

**active** actif (–ive)

**actress** actrice *(f.)*

**add** ajouter

**address** adresse *(f.)*

**admire** admirer

**adore** adorer

**advance** avance *(f.);*
  **in advance** à l'avance

**advertisement** annonce *(f.)*

**afraid: be afraid** avoir peur

**after** après

**afternoon** après-midi *(m.)*

**afterwards** après

**again** encore une fois

**age** âge *(m.)*

**airplane** avion *(m.)*

**all** tout(e) *(m. pl.* tous); **all the
  time** tout le temps

**almost** presque

**alone** seul(e)

**along: come along** venir

**also** aussi

**always** toujours

**A.M.** du matin

**ambitious** ambitieux (–euse)

**American** américain(e)

**amusing** amusant(e)

**and** et

**angry** fâché(e)

**animal** animal *(m.) (pl.* -aux)

**another** un(e) autre

**answer** répondre (à); réponse *(f.)*

**any** de

**anymore: not . . . anymore**
  ne... plus

**anything: not . . . anything**
  ne... rien

**apartment** appartement (m.)

**apple** pomme *(f.);* **apple pie**
  tarte aux pommes *(f.)*

**April** avril *(m.)*

**arm** bras *(m.)*

**around** autour (de)

**arrange** arranger

**arrive** arriver

**article** article *(m.)*

**ask (for)** demander

**at** à; **at home** à la maison

**attention** attention *(f.);* **pay
  attention** faire attention

**attentively** attentivement

**August** août *(m.)*

**aunt** tante *(f.)*

**autumn** automne *(m.)*

**avenue** avenue *(f.)*

**back** dos *(m.)*

**backpack** sac à dos *(m.)*

**bad** mauvais(e)

**bag** sac *(m.)*

**baker** boulanger (-ère);
  pâtissier (-ière)

**bakery** boulangerie *(f.)*, pâtisserie *(f.)*

**balcony** balcon *(m.)*

**ballet** ballet *(m.)*

**bank** banque *(f.); (river)* rive *(f.)*

**baseball** base-ball *(m.)*

**basement** sous-sol *(m.)*

**basketball** basket(ball) *(m.)*

**bathing suit** maillot de bain *(m.)*

**bathroom** salle de bains *(f.)*

**be** être; **be . . . years old**
  avoir... ans

**beach** plage *(f.)*

**beautiful** beau, bel *(f.* belle; *m.
  pl.* beaux)

**because** car, parce que

**become** devenir; **become fat**
  grossir

**bed** lit *(m.);* **go to bed** se
  coucher

**bedroom** chambre
  (à coucher) *(f.)*

**before** avant (de)

**beginning** commencement
  *(m.)*

**behind** derrière

**bell** cloche *(f.)*

**between** entre

**bicycle** bicyclette *(f.)*, vélo
  *(m.)*

**big** grand(e)

**bird** oiseau *(m.) (pl.* -x)

**black** noir(e)
**blond** blond(e)
**blue** bleu(e)
**blush** rougir
**board** tableau *(m.) (pl. -x)*
**boat** bateau *(m.) (pl. -x)*
**book** livre *(m.)*
**bookstore** librairie *(f.)*
**boot** botte *(f.)*
**bore** ennuyer
**bored: get bored** s'ennuyer
**borrow** emprunter
**bother** ennuyer, gêner
**bottle** bouteille *(f.)*
**bouillabaisse** bouillabaisse *(f.)*
  *(fish stew)*
**boutique** boutique *(f.)*
**box** boîte *(f.)*
**boy** garçon *(m.)*
**bread** pain *(m.)*
**break** rompre, casser
**breakfast** petit déjeuner *(m.)*
**bring** apporter
**brother** frère *(m.)*
**brush** brosser; **brush one's hair**
  se brosser les cheveux
**build** bâtir
**bus** bus *(m.),* autobus *(m.)*
**but** mais
**butcher** boucher (-ère);
  **butcher shop** boucherie *(f.)*
**butter** beurre *(m.)*
**buy** acheter
**by** par; **by bus** en bus

**cake** gâteau *(m.) (pl. -x)*
**calendar** calendrier *(m.)*
**call** appeler; téléphoner (à)
**camp** camper
**can** pouvoir
**Canada** Canada *(m.)*
**Canadian** canadien(ne)
**candy** bonbon *(m.)*
**car** voiture *(f.)*
**card** carte *(f.); postcard* carte
  postale *(f.)*

**cassette** cassette *(f.)*
**castle** château *(m.) (pl. -x)*
**cat** chat *(m.)*
**cathedral** cathédrale *(f.)*
**ceiling** plafond *(m.)*
**celebration** fête *(f.)*
**certain** certain(e), sûr(e)
**chair** chaise *(f.)*
**chalk** craie *(f.)*
**change** changer; **change one's
  mind** changer d'avis
**charming** charmant(e)
**chat** bavarder
**cheap** bon marché
**cheese** fromage *(m.)*
**chef** chef *(m.)*
**chicken** poulet *(m.)*
**child** enfant *(m. /f.)*
**China** Chine *(f.)*
**chocolate** chocolat *(m.);*
  **chocolate mousse** mousse
  au chocolat *(f.);* **chocolate
  cake** gâteau au chocolat *(m.)*
**choose** choisir
**church** église *(f.)*
**cider** cidre *(m.)*
**city** ville *(f.)*
**class** classe *(f.)*
**clean** nettoyer
**clock** horloge *(f.)*
**close** fermer
**closed** fermé(e)
**closet** penderie *(f.)*
**clothes** vêtements *(m. pl.)*
**clothing** vêtements *(m. pl.),*
  habits *(m. pl.)*
**cold** froid; **be cold** *(person)*
  avoir froid; **be cold** *(weather)*
  faire froid
**come** venir; **come along** venir
**comfortable** confortable
**compact disc** disque compact
  *(m.);* compact *(m.)*
**concert** concert *(m.);* **rock
  concert** concert de rock
**cook** cuisiner, faire la cuisine

**cookie** biscuit *(m.)*
**correct** correct(e)
**country** campagne *(f.);* pays *(m.)*
**courageous** courageux (-euse)
**courageously** courageusement
**course** cours *(m.);* **of course**
  bien sûr
**cousin** cousin(e)
**cow** vache *(f.)*
**criticize** critiquer
**cross** croix *(f.)*
**cruel** cruel(le)
**cry** pleurer
**cup** tasse *(f.)*
**cure** guérir

**dance** danser
**daughter** fille *(f.)*
**day** jour *(m.);* journée *(f.)*
**December** décembre *(m.)*
**decide** décider (de)
**defend** défendre
**delicious** délicieux (-ieuse)
**department** département *(m.)*
**descend** descendre
**desk** bureau *(m.) (pl. -x);*
  *(pupil's)* pupitre *(m.)*
**dessert** dessert *(m.)*
**dictionary** dictionnaire *(m.)*
**die** mourir
**different** différent(e)
**difficult** difficile
**diligent** diligent(e)
**dining room** salle à manger *(f.)*
**dinner** dîner *(m.);* **eat dinner**
  dîner
**discotheque** discothèque *(f.)*
**disobey** désobéir
**dive** plonger
**do** faire
**doctor** docteur *(m.),* médecin
  *(m.)*
**dog** chien *(m.)*
**dollar** dollar *(m.)*
**donkey** âne *(m.)*
**door** porte *(f.)*

**down: go down** descendre
**downtown** en ville
**dozen** douzaine *(f.)*
**dress** habiller; **dress (oneself)**
  s'habiller
**dress** robe *(f.)*
**during** pendant

**each** chaque
**ear** oreille *(f.)*
**easy** facile
**eat** manger; **eat dinner** dîner
**eclair** éclair *(m.)*
**egg** œuf *(m.)*
**eight** huit
**eighteen** dix-huit
**eighty** quatre-vingts
**eleven** onze
**empty** vider
**encourage** encourager
**end** fin *(f.)*
**ending** fin *(f.)*
**enemy** ennemi *(m.)*
**England** Angleterre *(f.)*
**English** anglais *(m.)*
**enter** entrer
**entire** entier (–ière)
**entrance** entrée *(f.)*
**equals** font
**eraser** gomme *(f.)*; brosse *(f.)*
**Europe** Europe *(f.)*
**evening** soir *(m.)*
**ever** jamais
**every** chaque; tout (tous,
  toute, toutes); **every day**
  tous les jours
**everybody** tout le monde *(m.)*
**everyone** tout le monde *(m.)*
**everything** tout *(m.)*
**excellent** excellent(e)
**exchange** échanger; **exchange
  letters** correspondre
**excursion** excursion *(f.)*
**expensive** cher (chère)
**explain** expliquer
**eye** œil *(m.) (pl.* yeux)

**face** figure *(f.),* visage *(m.)*
**false** faux (fausse)
**family** famille *(f.)*
**famous** célèbre
**far** loin (de)
**farmer** fermier (–ière)
**fast** vite, rapidement
**fat** gros(se); **become fat** grossir
**favorite** favori(te), préféré(e)
**fear** peur (f.); **be afraid**
  avoir peur
**February** février *(m.)*
**field** champ *(m.)*
**fifteen** quinze
**fifty** cinquante
**fill** remplir
**film** film *(m.)*
**find** trouver
**finger** doigt *(m.)*
**finish** finir, achever, terminer
**fire** feu *(m.)*
**fireplace** cheminée *(f.)*
**first** premier (–ière)
**fish** poisson *(m.)*
**fish** pêcher, aller à la pêche
**five** cinq
**flight** vol *(m.)*
**floor** plancher *(m.)*
**flower** fleur *(f.)*
**food** nourriture *(f.),* aliments
  *(m. pl.)*
**foot** pied *(m.)*
**football** football américain *(m.)*
**for** pour
**forget** oublier
**fortunately** heureusement
**forty** quarante
**four** quatre
**fourteen** quatorze
**France** France *(f.)*
**frank** franc(he)
**French** français(e)
**Friday** vendredi *(m.)*
**friend** ami(e), copain *(m.),*
  copine *(f.),* camarade *(m./f.)*
**friendly** amical(e) *(m. pl.* -aux),

aimable
**from** de; **from the** du, de la,
  de l', des
**front: in front of** devant
**fruit** fruit *(m.);* **fruit store**
  fruiterie *(f.)*
**full** plein(e)
**fun: have fun** s'amuser
**funny** drôle, comique,
  amusant(e)

**gain** gagner; **gain weight**
  grossir
**game** match *(m.)*
**garage** garage
**garbage** ordures *(f. pl.)*
**garden** jardin *(m.)*
**gas(oline)** essence *(f.)*
**gas station** station-service *(f.)*
**generally** généralement,
  d'habitude
**generous** généreux (–euse)
**gently** doucement
**get: get bored** s'ennuyer; **get
  dressed** s'habiller; **get up**
  se lever
**gift** cadeau *(m.) (pl.* -x)
**girl** fille *(f.)*
**girlfriend** petite amie *(f.)*
**give** donner
**glass** verre *(m.)*
**glasses** lunettes *(f. pl.)*
**go** aller; **go back home**
  rentrer; **go down** descendre;
  **go out** sortir
**golf** golf *(m.)*
**good** bon(ne); **have a good
  time** s'amuser
**good-bye** au revoir
**grandfather** grand-père *(m.)*
**grandmother** grand-mère *(f.)*
**grandparents** grands-parents
  *(m. pl.)*
**great** formidable, super
**grow** grandir
**guard** garder

**guide** guide *(m.)*
**guitar** guitare *(f.)*

**hair** cheveux *(m. pl.)*
**half** demi(e)
**hallway** couloir *(m.)*
**ham** jambon *(m.)*
**handsome** beau, bel
    *(f.* belle; *m. pl.* beaux)
**happy** content(e), heureux
    (-euse)
**hat** chapeau *(m.) (pl.* -x)
**have** avoir
**he** il, lui
**head** tête *(f.)*
**hear** entendre
**heavy** lourd(e)
**help** aider
**her** la, lui; son, sa, ses
**here** ici; **here is** voici; **here are**
    voici
**high** haut(e)
**his** son, sa, ses
**history** histoire *(f.)*
**Holland** Pays-Bas *(m. pl.)*
**home** maison *(f.);* **(at) home**
    à la maison; **at the home**
    **of** chez
**homework** devoirs *(m. pl.);* **do**
    **homework** faire les devoirs
**honest** honnête
**hope** espérer
**horse** cheval *(m.) (pl.* -aux)
**hot** chaud(e); **be hot** *(person)*
    avoir chaud; **be hot** *(weather)*
    faire chaud
**hotel** hôtel *(m.)*
**hour** heure *(f.)*
**house** maison *(f.)*
**how** comment; **how**
    **much/many** combien (de)
**huge** énorme
**hundred** cent
**hurry (up)** se dépêcher

**I** je, moi

**ice cream** glace *(f.)*
**ice skating** patin à glace *(m.);*
    **go ice skating** faire du
    patin à glace
**idea** idée *(f.)*
**ideal** idéal(e)
**if** si
**imaginative** imaginatif (-ive)
**immediately** immédiatement,
    tout de suite
**impossible** impossible
**in** dans, en, à
**inexpensive** bon marché
**instead (of)** au lieu (de)
**intelligent** intelligent(e)
**intend** compter
**interesting** intéressant(e)
**invitation** invitation *(f.)*
**island** île *(f.)*
**it** il, elle; le, la
**Italian** italien *(m.)*
**Italy** Italie *(f.)*

**jacket** veste *(f.)*
**January** janvier *(m.)*
**job** emploi *(m.)*
**July** juillet *(m.)*
**June** juin *(m.)*

**keep** garder
**key** clef *(f.)*
**kind** gentil(le), aimable
**king** roi *(m.)*
**kitchen** cuisine *(f.)*
**knife** couteau *(m.) (pl.* -x)
**know** connaître, savoir

**lake** lac *(m.)*
**lamp** lampe *(f.)*
**large** grand(e)
**last** dernier (-ière); **last night**
    hier soir
**late** tard
**later** plus tard
**lawn** pelouse *(f.)*
**lawyer** avocat(e)

**lazy** paresseux (-euse)
**lead** mener
**leaf** feuille *(f.)*
**least: at least** au moins
**leather store**
    maroquinerie *(f.)*
**leave** partir
**left** gauche
**lemonade** citronnade *(f.)*
**lend** prêter
**lesson** leçon *(f.)*
**letter** lettre *(f.)*
**library** bibliothèque *(f.)*
**life** vie *(f.)*
**light** léger (-ère)
**like** aimer
**lion** lion *(m.)*
**listen (to)** écouter
**little** petit(e) *(adj.);* peu *(adv.)*
**live** habiter, demeurer, vivre
**living room** salon *(m.)*
**long** long(ue); **a long time**
    longtemps
**longer: no longer** ne... plus
**look** regarder
**loose-leaf binder** classeur *(m.)*
**lose** perdre
**lot: a lot** beaucoup; **lots of**
    beaucoup de
**loud** fort(e); **louder** plus fort
**love** aimer
**loyal** fidèle
**lunch** déjeuner *(m.)*

**magazine** magazine *(m.),*
    revue *(f.)*
**magnificent** magnifique
**make** faire
**makeup** maquillage *(m.);* **put**
    **makeup on** se maquiller
**mall** centre commercial *(m.)*
**man** homme *(m.)*
**many** beaucoup (de);
    **how many** combien (de)
**map** carte *(f.)*
**March** mars *(m.)*

**marry** épouser, se marier avec

**matter: it doesn't matter** ça ne fait rien

**May** mai *(m.)*

**me** me; moi

**meal** repas *(m.)*

**meat** viande *(f.)*

**mechanic** mécanicien(ne)

**meet** rencontrer, faire la connaissance de

**metro** métro *(m.)*

**Mexico** Méxique *(m.)*

**middle** milieu *(m.)*, centre *(m.)*

**midnight** minuit *(m.)*

**million** million *(m.)*

**mind** esprit *(m.)*; **change one's mind** changer d'avis

**minus** moins

**mistake** faute *(f.)*, erreur *(f.)*

**modern** moderne

**Monday** lundi *(m.)*

**money** argent *(m.)*

**month** mois *(m.)*

**moon** lune *(f.)*

**moped** mobylette *(f.)*

**more** plus

**morning** matin *(m.)*

**mother** mère *(f.)*

**motorcycle** motocyclette *(f.)*

**motor scooter** scooter *(m.)*

**mountain** montagne *(f.)*

**move** déménager

**movie** film *(m.)*; **movies** cinéma *(m.)*

**much** beaucoup; **how much** combien (de)

**multiplied** by fois

**museum** musée *(m.)*

**my** mon, ma, mes

**name** nom *(m.)*

**naturally** naturellement

**near** près (de)

**neck** cou *(m.)*

**need** besoin *(m.)*

**need** avoir besoin de

**neighborhood** quartier *(m.)*

**nephew** neveu *(m.)* *(pl. -x)*

**never** ne... jamais, jamais

**new** nouveau, nouvel *(f.* nouvelle; *m. pl.* nouveaux)

**newspaper** journal *(m.)* *(pl. -aux)*

**next** prochain(e)

**nice** sympathique, agréable, gentil(le); **be nice** *(weather)* faire beau

**niece** nièce *(f.)*

**night** nuit *(f.)*, soir *(m.)*; **night table** table de nuit *(f.)*

**nine** neuf

**nineteen** dix-neuf

**ninety** quatre-vingt-dix

**ninth** neuvième

**no** non; **no longer** ne... plus; **no one** ne... personne, personne, personne ne...

**nobody** ne... personne, personne, personne ne...

**noise** bruit *(m.)*

**noon** midi *(m.)*

**no one** ne... personne, personne, personne ne...

**nose** nez *(m.)*

**not** ne... pas

**notebook** cahier *(m.)*

**nothing** rien

**November** novembre *(m.)*

**now** maintenant

**number** numéro *(m.)*; **telephone number** numéro de téléphone

**nut** noix *(f.)*

**obey** obéir

**o'clock** heure *(f.)*

**October** octobre *(m.)*

**of** de (du, des); **of course** bien sûr

**office** bureau *(m.)* *(pl. -x)*

**often** souvent

**old** vieux, vieil *(f.* vieille); **be ... years old** avoir... ans

**on** sur, de; **on Mondays** le lundi; **on time** à l'heure

**once** une fois

**one** un(e); **the one who** celui / lui qui

**only** seul(e) *(adj.)*; seulement *(adv.)*

**open** ouvrir; **open up** s'ouvrir

**operator** opérateur (-trice)

**opportunity** occasion *(f.)*

**organize** organiser

**our** notre, nos

**out: go out** sortir

**over there** là-bas

**package** paquet *(m.)*

**painting** tableau *(m.)* *(pl. -x)*

**pair** paire *(f.)*

**palace** palais *(m.)*

**pants** pantalon *(m.)*

**paper** papier *(m.)*

**parent** parent *(m.)*

**park** parc *(m.)*

**party** fête *(f.)*, boum *(f.)*

**passport** passeport *(m.)*

**pastry** pâtisserie *(f.)*; **pastry shop** pâtisserie *(f.)*

**pay** (for) payer; **pay attention** faire attention

**peace** paix *(f.)*

**pen** stylo *(m.)*; **pen pal** correspondant(e)

**pencil** crayon *(m.)*; **pencil case** trousse *(f.)*

**people** gens *(m. pl.)*

**perform** jouer

**perfume store** parfumerie *(f.)*

**phone** téléphone *(m.)*; **phone book** annuaire *(m.)*; **phone booth** cabine *(f.)* **phone number** numéro de téléphone *(m.)*

**photo** photo *(f.)*

**picture** image *(f.)*, illustration

(f.), photo (f.)

**pie** tarte (f.)

**plane** avion (m.)

**play** jouer; **play** (an instrument) jouer de; **play** (a sport) jouer à, faire de

**please** s'il te plaît, s'il vous plaît

**pleased** content(e), heureux (-euse)

**pleasure** plaisir (m.)

**plus** et; plus

**P.M.** de l'après-midi, du soir

**police** police (f.); **police officer** agent de police (m.)

**pool** piscine (f.)

**poor** pauvre

**post office** poste (f.), bureau de poste (m.) (pl. -x)

**postcard** carte postale (f.)

**poster** poster (m.), affiche (f.)

**potato** pomme de terre (f.)

**prefer** préférer, aimer mieux

**prepare** préparer

**present** cadeau (m.) (pl. -x)

**present** présent(e)

**president** président (m.)

**pretty** joli(e)

**price** prix (m.)

**principal** principal(e) (m. pl. -aux)

**problem** problème (m.)

**programmer** programmeur (-euse)

**protect** protéger

**proudly** fièrement

**prudent** prudent(e)

**punish** punir

**put (on)** mettre

**quarter** quart (m.)

**question** question (f.); **out of the question** pas question

**quickly** vite, rapidement

**rain** pluie (f.)

**rain** pleuvoir

**read** lire

**reasonable** raisonnable

**receive** recevoir

**recipe** recette (f.)

**record** disque (m.)

**red** rouge

**refrigerator** réfrigérateur (m.)

**refuse** refuser

**remain** rester

**repair** réparer

**repeat** répéter

**respond** répondre

**responsible** responsable

**restaurant** restaurant (m.)

**return** (home) rentrer; **return** (an item) rendre, retourner

**rich** riche

**right** correct(e)

**river** fleuve (m.)

**road** route (f.), chemin (m.)

**roof** toit (m.)

**room** chambre (f.)

**route** route (f.), chemin (m.)

**sad** triste

**salad** salade (f.)

**same** même

**sandal** sandale (f.)

**Saturday** samedi (m.)

**say** dire

**school** école (f.)

**sculpture** sculpture (f.)

**sea** mer (f.)

**see** voir

**seize** saisir

**selfish** égoïste

**sell** vendre

**send** envoyer

**sentence** phrase (f.)

**September** septembre (m.)

**set: set the table** mettre le couvert

**seven** sept

**seventeen** dix-sept

**seventy** soixante-dix

**shade** store (m.)

**share** partager

**she** elle

**shirt** (men's) chemise (f.), (women's) chemisier (m.)

**shop** faire les courses

**short** court(e)

**shorts** short (m.)

**show** montrer

**shy** timide

**sick** malade

**sing** chanter

**sister** sœur (f.)

**six** six

**sixteen** seize

**sixty** soixante

**skate** patin; patiner; **go ice skating** faire du patin à glace

**ski** ski (m.); **ski instructor** moniteur de ski (m.)

**skiing: go skiing** faire du ski

**skirt** jupe (f.)

**sky** ciel (m.)

**sleep** sommeil (m.)

**sleep** dormir

**sleepy: be sleepy** avoir sommeil

**slowly** lentement

**small** petit(e)

**sneaker** basket (f.); tennis (f.)

**snow** neiger

**so** donc; si

**soccer** football (m.)

**sock** chaussette (f.)

**soft** doux (douce)

**some** du, de la, de l', des, en

**sometimes** quelquefois, parfois

**son** fils (m.)

**song** chanson (f.)

**soup** soupe (f.)

**south** sud (m.), midi (m.)

**souvenir** souvenir (m.)

**Spanish** espagnol(e)

**speak** parler

**spend** dépenser (money); passer (time)

**sport** sport (m.)

**spring** printemps *(m.)*
**stamp** timbre *(m.)*
**star** étoile *(f.)*
**start** commencer (à); **start out** se mettre en route
**station** gare *(f.)*
**stay** rester
**stereo** chaîne stéréo *(f.)*
**store** magasin *(m.)*
**story** histoire *(f.)*
**street** rue *(f.)*
**strict** sévère
**strong** fort(e)
**student** élève *(m./f.)*, étudiant(e)
**study** étudier
**subway** métro *(m.)*
**succeed** réussir
**success** succès *(m.)*
**sugar** sucre *(m.)*
**suitcase** valise *(f.)*
**summer** été *(m.)*
**sun** soleil *(m.)*; **be sunny** *(weather)* faire du soleil
**superstitious** superstitieux (-ieuse)
**sure** certain(e), sûr(e)
**sweater** pull *(m.)*
**swim** nager
**swimming** nage *(f.)*, natation *(f.)*; **swimming pool** piscine *(f.)*; **go swimming** aller nager
**swimsuit** maillot de bain *(m.)*

**table** table *(f.)*; **set the table** mettre le couvert
**take** prendre; apporter; **take a trip** faire un voyage; **take a walk** faire une promenade, se promener; **take care of** garder
**tall** grand(e)
**taste** goûter
**taxi** taxi *(m.)*
**teacher** professeur *(m.)*, maître *(m.)*
**telephone** téléphone *(m.)*;

**on the telephone** au téléphone; **telephone book** annuaire *(m.)*; **telephone booth** cabine *(f.)*
**television** télévision *(f.)*
**tell** dire
**ten** dix
**tennis** tennis *(m.)*
**terrace** terrasse *(f.)*
**than** que
**thank you** merci
**that** que; qui *(pron.)*; ce, cet, cette *(adj.)*
**the** le, la, l', les
**theater** théâtre *(m.)*
**their** leur, leurs
**them** eux, elles, les
**then** puis, alors, ensuite
**there** là; y; **over there** là-bas; **there is/are** il y a; voilà
**these** ces; **these are** ce sont
**they** ils, elles
**thing** chose *(f.)*
**think** penser
**thirst** soif *(f.)*
**thirsty: be thirsty** avoir soif
**thirteen** treize
**thirty** trente
**this** ce, cet, cette *(adj.)*; **this is** c'est
**those** ces
**thousand** mille, mil *(in dates)*
**three** trois
**Thursday** jeudi *(m.)*
**tidy** ranger
**tie** cravate *(f.)*
**till** jusqu'à
**time** temps *(m.)*; **all the time** tout le temps; **from time to time** de temps en temps; **have a good time** s'amuser; **a long time** longtemps; **on time** à l'heure
**to** à; **in order to** pour
**today** aujourd'hui
**together** ensemble

**toilet** toilettes *(f. pl.)*
**tomorrow** demain
**too** aussi
**tooth** dent *(f.)*
**tourist** touriste *(m./f.)*
**toward(s)** vers
**tower** tour *(f.)*
**town** ville *(f.)*
**toy** jouet *(m.)*
**train** train *(m.)*; **by train** en train; **train station** gare *(f.)*
**travel** voyager
**tree** arbre *(m.)*
**trip** voyage *(m.)*; **take a trip** faire un voyage
**tropical** tropical(e) *(m. pl. -aux)*
**true** vrai(e)
**truly** vraiment
**truth** vérité *(f.)*
**try** essayer (de)
**Tuesday** mardi *(m.)*
**twelfth** douzième
**twelve** douze
**twenty** vingt
**two** deux

**United States** États-Unis *(m. pl.)*
**umbrella** parapluie *(m.)*
**under** sous
**undress** se déshabiller
**unhappy** triste, malheureux (-euse)
**university** université *(f.)*
**upstairs** en haut; **go upstairs** monter
**us** nous
**useful** utile
**useless** inutile
**usually** généralement, d'habitude

**vacation** vacances *(f. pl.)*; **go on vacation** aller en vacances
**vacuum** aspirateur *(m.)*
**vacuum** passer l'aspirateur

**vegetable** légume *(m.)*
**very** très
**visit** visiter
**volleyball** volley-ball *(m.)*

**wait (for)** attendre
**waitress** serveuse *(f.)*
**wake** réveiller; **wake (oneself)** se réveiller
**walk** marcher; promener; **go for a walk** se promener; **take a walk** se promener
**Walkman** baladeur *(m.)*
**wall** mur *(m.)*
**want** désirer, vouloir
**war** guerre *(f.)*
**wash** laver; **wash (oneself)** se laver
**wastebasket** corbeille à papier *(f.)*
**watch** montre *(f.)*
**watch** regarder
**water** eau *(f.);* **mineral water** eau minérale
**we** nous
**weak** faible
**wear** porter

**weather** temps *(m.);* **bad weather** mauvais temps
**Wednesday** mercredi *(m.)*
**week** semaine *(f.)*
**weekend** fin de semaine *(f.),* week-end *(m.)*
**well** bien
**weight** poids *(m.);* **gain weight** grossir
**west** ouest *(m.)*
**what** que, qu'est-ce que, quoi; quel(le); ce que
**when** quand
**where** où
**white** blanc(he)
**who** qui
**whole** entier (-ière); tout(e)
**whom** qui
**why** pourquoi
**wife** femme *(f.)*
**win** gagner
**wind** vent *(m.)*
**windy: be windy** faire du vent
**wine** vin *(m.)*
**winter** hiver *(m.);* **winter sports** sports d'hiver *(m. pl.)*
**wise** sage

**with** avec
**without** sans
**woman** femme *(f.)*
**wonderful** merveilleux (-euse), formidable
**word** mot *(m.)*
**work** travailler; marcher *(machines);* travail *(m.)*
**world** monde *(m.)*
**write** écrire

**year** an *(m.);* **be . . . years old** avoir... ans
**yes** oui
**yesterday** hier
**yet** encore; **not yet** pas encore
**yogurt** yogourt *(m.)*
**you** tu, toi, vous
**young** jeune; **young people** jeunes gens *(m. pl.)*
**younger** cadet(te)
**your** ton, ta, tes, votre, vos

**zip code** code postal *(m.)*
**zoo** zoo *(m.),* parc zoologique *(m.)*

# Index

NOTE: For specific verb conjugations, see the Appendix.